SOCIOLOGY

GCSE

Pauline Wilson and Allan Kidd

Collins Educational
An imprint of HarperCollins*Publishers*

Published by Collins Educational
An imprint of HarperCollins*Publishers* Ltd
77–85 Fulham Palace Road
London W6 8JB

First published 1998,
10 9 8
ISBN 0003224449

British Library Cataloguing in Publication Data
A catalogue record for this book is available from the British Library.

Commissioned by Emma Dunlop
Project management by Patricia Briggs
Edited by Brigitte Lee and Jack Messenger
Cover design by Patricia Briggs
Cover photograph courtesy of Getty Images
Text design and layout by Patricia Briggs
Illustrations by Gay Gallsworthy
Cartoons by Martin Shovel
Production by Emma Lloyd-Jones
Printed and bound by Imago, Thailand.

Contents

Acknowledgements

The publishers would like to thank the following for permission to reproduce photographs, pictures and artwork in this book.

Age Concern, p. 95; All Sport, p. 46/Karen Smith, p. 46/John Gichigi; Amnesty International, p. 268; BBC, p. 298; Barnardos, p. 95; The Big Issue, p. 111; Body Positive, p. 95; The Body Shop International plc, p. 31; Patricia Briggs, pp. 56, 64, 123, 134, 159; Camera Press Ltd, p. 143/Vince Streano; Channel 4, p. 298; Child Poverty Action Group, p. 94; Child Poverty Action Group, p. 95; Colorific!, p. 126/Gerald Davis, p. 126/Jim Pickerell, p. 200/John Moss, p. 233/Tim Graham, p. 255/Dennis Brack; The Conservative Party, p. 266; Corbis-Bettmann/UPI, pp. 128, 327; Mary Evans Picture Library, pp. 358, 53, 133, 155, 348; Famous, pp. 20, 28, p. 31/Desmond Clarke, p. 31/Simon Guy, p. 237/Fred Duval (×2); Charlotte Fawley, p. 337; Format, p. 40/Ulrike Preuss, p. 73/Sharon Baseley, p. 92, Paula Solloway, p. 97/Brenda Prince (×2), p. 107/Brenda Prince, p. 211/Sheila Gray, p. 253/Melanie Friend, p. 270/Brenda Prince, p. 349/Mo Wilson; Gay Gallsworthy, pp. 77 (×2), 79, 152 (×4), 181 (×4), 195 (×3), 206 (×3); Getty Images, p. 198; The Ronald Grant Archive (×3), p. 306; Rachel Haggaty, p. 30; HarperCollins, p. 26; The Labour Party, p. 266; The Liberal Democrats, p. 266/Dr. Nicholas Posner; London Docklands Development Corporation, p. 358; LWT, p. 297; Magnum, Photos p. 42/Ian Berry, p. 45/Peter Marlow, p. 320/Gideon Mendel, p. 320/Chris Steele-Perkins, p. 320/Paul Fusco, p. 323/Chris Steele-Perkins, p. 323/Paul Fusco; Matrix, p. 255/Alex Quesada; Metropolitan Police Service, pp. 61 (×3), 233; Midland Bank, p. 199; News Corporation Ltd, p. 292; PA News, p. 22/Peter Jordan, p. 28/Tim Ockenden, p. 73, Sean Dempsey, p. 73, Fiona Hanson, p. 91, Stefan Rousseau, p. 118/Tim Ockenden, p. 118/Barry Bachelor, p. 219/Sean Dempsey, p. 254, p. 270, p. 321/Barry Bachelor; Photofusion, p. 19/Mark Campbell, p. 113/George Montgomery, p. 160/Crispin Hughes, p. 167/Steve Eason, p. 170/Debbie Humphrey, p. 176/Julia Martin, p. 213/Steve Eason, p. 231/Mark Campbell, p. 294/Crispin Hughes, p. 320/Bob Watkins; Pictor International Ltd, pp. 200, 287; Popperfoto, p. 329, p. 329/G. Reed Schumann/Reuters, p. 253/Edide Mulholland-Daily; Renault, p. 175; Rex Features, p. 21/Paul Brown; RoSPA, p. 256; The Samaritans, p. 95; Martin Shovel, pp. 18, 23, 31, 41, 53, 87, 149, 168, 178, 193, 214, 234 (×2), 247, 274, 333; Still Pictures, p. 118/David Hoffman, p. 237/Mike Shroder, p. 255/Jorgen Schytte, p. 256/Jorgen Schytte, p. 285/Nigel Dickinson; Tony Stone Images, p. 28/Oliver Benn, p. 201/Peter Cade; Telegraph Colour Library, p. 123/J.L. Banus-March, p. 199/J. Kugler, p. 200/Benelux Press, p. 200/J.T. Turner, p. 205/J. Thorogood; Topham Picturepoint, p. 134, p. 254, p. 256; Universal Pictorial Press, p. 262; The Walking Camera, p. 317; John Walmsley, pp. 154, 156; Woman's Own, p. 225;

Every effort has been made to contact copyright holders, but if any have been inadvertently overlooked, the publishers will be pleased to make the necessary arrangements at the first opportunity.

Authors' acknowledgements

We would like to thank our colleagues at OSFC for their support, encouragement and practical help with the book. Sincere thanks also to Emma Dunlop for having faith in us, Patricia Briggs for good humouredly keeping us on track throughout the past year, Pat McNeill and Tony Breslin for pointing us in the right direction with their detailed comments on each chapter, and Brigitte Lee and Jack Messenger for expert editing and proofreading. Special mention from Pauline to Jeremy, Mum, Dad, Heather, Pat, Kit and Jo. Special mention from Allan to Mum, Dad and long-suffering friends.

CHAPTER 1

How to Use this Textbook

This book is designed to provide a student-centred and active introduction to sociology at GCSE level.

1. **The text will provide you with the knowledge and understanding needed to meet the requirements of all the major GCSE syllabuses in sociology as well as related areas, such as modern studies and social science.**
2. **Working through the activities in each chapter will develop your critical and evaluative skills, and provide you with the opportunity to undertake your own research.**
3. **The 'Check your understanding' feature, and the examination questions at the end of each chapter, will allow you to test and assess your understanding as you go along.**

In this way, this book will provide you with all you need to enjoy, and be successful in, your sociology.

HOW TO GET THE MOST FROM THIS BOOK

The chapters in this book have been ordered carefully to enable you to make links between the different topic areas in sociology. Chapter 2, The Sociological Approach, for example, provides much of the underpinning knowledge for later chapters. Key terms – such as 'socialization' – are introduced in this chapter, before being developed further in the context of later chapters.

Similarly, in Chapter 3, Stratification and Differentiation, terms such as 'social class', 'gender', 'ethnicity' and 'age' are introduced, described and explained. Their importance is then further developed in later chapters, as these factors influence other aspects of social life, such as educational achievement or employment opportunities.

Thus it is important to realize that the subject of sociology should be seen as a whole rather than as a group of unconnected topic areas. To reinforce this idea further, cross-references have been included for particular terms or concepts where appropriate.

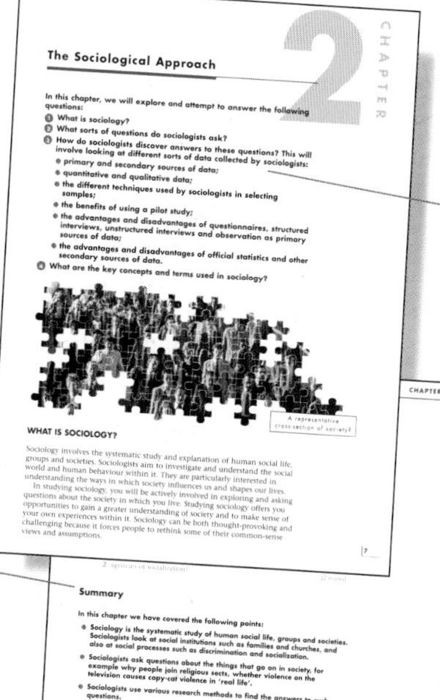

2 CHAPTER

The Sociological Approach

In this chapter, we will explore and attempt to answer the following questions:

1. What is sociology?
2. What sorts of questions do sociologists ask?
3. How do sociologists discover answers to these questions? This will involve looking at different sorts of data collected by sociologists:
   - primary and secondary sources of data;
   - quantitative and qualitative data;
   - the different techniques used by sociologists in selecting samples;
   - the benefits of using a pilot study;
   - the advantages and disadvantages of questionnaires, structured interviews, unstructured interviews and observation as primary sources of data;
   - the advantages and disadvantages of official statistics and other secondary sources of data.
4. What are the key concepts and terms used in sociology?

A representative cross-section of society?

WHAT IS SOCIOLOGY?

Sociology involves the systematic study and explanation of human social life, groups and societies. Sociologists aim to investigate and understand the social world and human behaviour within it. They are particularly interested in understanding the ways in which society influences us and shapes our lives.

In studying sociology, you will be actively involved in exploring and asking questions about the society in which you live. Studying sociology offers you opportunities to gain a greater understanding of society and to make sense of your own experiences within it. Sociology can be both thought-provoking and challenging because it forces people to rethink some of their common-sense views and assumptions.

7

CHAPTER 2

Summary

In this chapter we have covered the following points:

- Sociology is the systematic study of human social life, groups and societies. Sociologists look at social institutions such as families and churches, and also at social processes such as discrimination and socialization.
- Sociologists ask questions about the things that go on in society, for example why people join religious sects, whether violence on the television causes copy-cat violence in 'real life'.
- Sociologists use various research methods to find the answers to such questions.
- Sources are either primary or secondary. Primary sources are based on research conducted at first hand, for example through questionnaires, interviews and participant observation. Secondary sources consist of data that has already been collated, for example official statistics, media reports, letters and diaries.
- Data is either quantitative or qualitative. Quantitative data is presented in numerical form, for example 97 per cent of people watch television. Qualitative data is presented in words and deals with preferences and feelings, which cannot always be put into figures.
- When conducting research, sociologists normally begin by selecting a sample, or subgroup of the population. Samples are selected either randomly or non-randomly.
- It is a good idea to use a pilot study to trial the chosen research method. This ensures that the method works and that it is cost-effective.
- Questionnaires are a popular way of conducting social research. Questions can be open-ended or closed. An advantage of questionnaires is that they can be a cost-effective way of reaching a large sample. A disadvantage is that they can have a low response rate.
- Interviews can be either structured or unstructured. Interviews are usually conducted face-to-face, so one problem to look out for is interview bias.

35

TEXT FEATURES

Chapter outlines and summaries

Each chapter in this book begins with an outline of the key questions and issues to be examined in a topic area (1), enabling you to see what areas you will be covering and in what order you can expect to find them in the text. The chapter outline can also be used later as a revision aid, as you should be able to identify the knowledge and ideas to answer the questions in the outline. Each chapter then closes with a summary (2), which identifies the main learning points you should have covered. Both of these features serve as valuable points of reference for revision.

Activities

In each chapter you will find a range of activities that are designed to give you the opportunity to get more involved with the topic you are covering. There are two types of activity: discussion activities and written activities.

Discussion activities

Discussion activities (3) are designed to stimulate discussion and debate on sociological issues. They may be used as the basis for a whole-class discussion or small-group discussion. You may be asked to note down the main points of your discussion or to feed your ideas back to the rest of the class. In this way, you will deepen your understanding of a topic and develop your critical and evaluative skills. It is important to understand that there may be no 'right' answer to a discussion activity. Everyone's views should be considered equally, which can lead to lively and interesting debates.

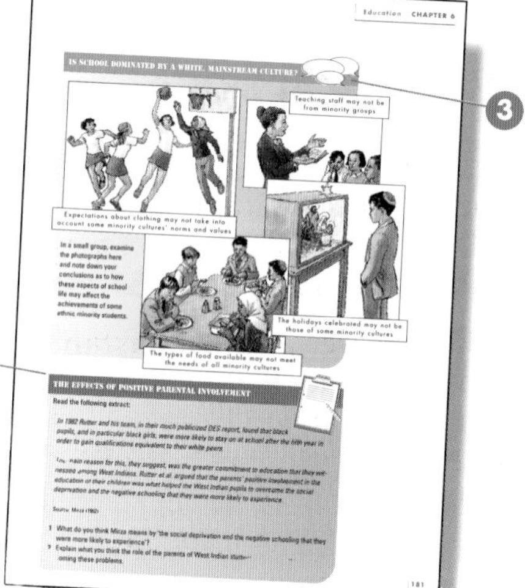

Written activities

Written activities (4) may present you with some statistical data or an extract from an article and you will be asked to answer questions based on this. This will allow you to develop your ability to interpret and make sense of information, and then to respond to it using your own ideas. In some cases, you may also be asked to produce a summary of a key idea or issue.

Research activities

You will find at least one research activity (5) in each chapter. These provide you with the opportunity to explore more fully a particular aspect of the topic you are covering, in many cases using the methods of research available for coursework. These activities are a useful introduction to the skills needed in coursework and you will find it helpful to refer to the section on the research process (pp. 367–8) when doing them.

Check your understanding and examination questions

These activities are designed to allow you to check that you have understood the topic you have been studying. Check your understanding questions (6) appear throughout each chapter at points where major areas of knowledge have been covered. Sample examination questions (7) appear at the end of each chapter and have been selected from different examining boards. These allow you to check your understanding under exam conditions.

Key terms

All major sociological concepts or key terms (8) are emboldened in the text where they first appear, and are explained or defined there too. In addition, all these key terms appear in the index to the book, where the page reference that will lead to the definition or explanation is also emboldened.

SOCIOLOGICAL SKILLS

This book is designed to help you develop the skills needed to be a good sociologist. Most examination boards assess students with reference to a range of skills. These can be summarized as follows:

- **Knowledge and Understanding** – Put simply: can you demonstrate that you know and understand the subject matter that you have been studying?
- **Interpretation and Application** – Here, you will be expected to demonstrate that you are able to interpret and make sense of sociological knowledge and information that is presented to you, for example in the form of a statistical table. The ability to apply knowledge and information correctly in response to a set question is also important.
- **Evaluation** – You should be able to weigh up, assess and criticize different ideas, arguments and information, and to reach conclusions as a result.

A good sociologist does not simply memorize facts, but develops a combination of all the skills outlined here.

STUDY SKILLS

The sociological skills outlined above are an important part of all the major GCSE sociology syllabuses, but, in addition, you should seek to develop a range of other skills to maximize your success. These can be termed 'study skills'.

Time management

Have you ever felt that you have too much to do and too little time in which to do it? This is a common problem for people who are studying. One way to help ease this situation is to examine your time management: in other words, try to make better use of the time you have available.

The first step is to identify how much time you have available for study in a given week and establish when exactly this is. You will need to consider all your other commitments and then, in theory, the time left over can be used as study time.

The next step is to prioritize the tasks you have to complete – perhaps according to when they have to be done by.

Once you have done this you can produce a study plan for the week. This identifies what you will do and when you will do it. All you then have to do is stick to your plan!

Time	Monday	Tuesday	Wednesday	Thursday	Friday	Saturday	Sunday
9 am							
10 am							
11 am							
12 noon							
6 pm							
evening							

An example of how you might organize a weekly study plan

Note-taking

In order to develop your sociological knowledge and understanding further, it is often a good idea to read around a subject. You might look at other books or articles related to a particular topic you are studying. This can be especially useful when doing coursework.

As a result of your reading, you may wish to make some notes for later use. While everyone may have their own approach to taking notes, it is useful to examine some suggestions for effective note-taking.

Notes should be as clear as possible

How schools affect educational achievement

Teachers:

1 may **label** students – on the basis of social class background, behaviour, etc.;

2 may develop **self-fulfilling prophecy** – based on labels – may lead student to believe teacher's opinion of them;

3 may influence decisions about **setting and streaming** – bottom sets may receive less help and encouragement;

4 may treat **male and female** students differently – in different subject areas – may explain differences in subject choices at A level and at degree levels.

- Do not simply produce a slightly shortened version of the material you are taking notes on.
- Do skim read the information to get a general understanding first.
- Do use headings and sub-headings to identify key areas.
- Do use numbers or letters to identify key points.
- Do use underlining or indentation to help make notes clearer.
- Do use abbreviations if you prefer – for example, '+' for 'and'.

Understanding statistical information

You will come across many examples of statistical tables and charts in this book and throughout your study of sociology. It is important for you to be able to interpret these tables accurately.

The following example is taken from Chapter 11 (see p. 334). With any table, there are a number of features that need to be examined.

1 *Heading* – What is the general subject being referred to? (Here, it is church membership in the United Kingdom.)

2 *Relationships in the table* – What is being referred to in particular and what is it being related to? (Here, the table refers to church membership for a range of religions over time.)

3 *Timescale* – Are there any dates shown? (Here, we are looking at church membership between 1970 and 1995.)

4 *What units of measurement are used?* – Are the figures shown actual numbers or percentages; shown in thousands, millions, or numbers per thousand of the population? (Here, the unit of measurement is millions.)

5 *What is the source of the statistics?* – Can this be relied upon? Is it likely to be biased and inaccurate in any way? (Here, the table is from *Social Trends*, which is a major source of government statistics published annually.)

6 *Date* – When were the statistics produced? Are they out of date? (Here, the statistics are from 1997.)

Table 11.2 Church membership in the UK

	Membership (millions)	
	1970	1995
Trinitarian churches		
Roman Catholic	2.7	2.0
Anglican	3.0	1.7
Presbyterian	1.8	1.1
Methodist	0.7	0.4
Baptist	0.3	0.2
Other Free Churches	0.5	0.7
Orthodox	0.2	0.3
Total	**9.2**	**6.4**
Non-Trinitarian churches		
Mormons	0.1	0.2
Jehovah's Witnesses	0.1	0.1
Other Non-Trinitarian	0.1	0.3
Total	**0.3**	**0.6**
Other religions		
Muslims	0.1	0.6
Sikhs	0.1	0.4
Hindus	0.1	0.1
Jews	0.1	0.1
Others	0.0	0.1
Total	**0.4**	**1.3**

Source: *Social Trends* (1997)

Identifying trends

In many cases, you will be asked to identify trends in the statistics. This refers to how a pattern has changed over time. In the case of this table, we could look at a number of general trends, for example, changes in membership for all Trinitarian Churches or for other religions. We could also look at specific trends, for example, changes in membership for Roman Catholics or Hindus. We could also compare trends for different religions; for example, membership for Anglicans has gone down, but membership for Sikhs has gone up.

Statistics may also come in a variety of other forms, such as bar charts (where columns are used to represent trends), or graphs (where the rise and fall of a line is used to represent a trend). Pie charts can also be used to represent statistics in the form of percentages in a highly visual way.

The main thing to remember about statistics is not to be afraid of them. Consider them carefully, using the advice given and look for the general trends first of all.

Other suggestions

As part of your studies, you may also wish to carry out some independent learning in your own time and without the help of a teacher. Here are two ideas for activities you could work on.

1 *Glossary*

Create a glossary of key terms, concepts and explanations using the format shown below:

WORD	DEFINITION	TOPIC AREAS
Socialization	The process by which people learn the culture and way of life of their society.	• Family • Media • Religion • Education

Some terms may relate to a range of topic areas, while others may be specific to only one. Your glossary could be used as a revision aid if you keep separate lists for each topic area you study. You might also like to add to your glossary after reading around the subject.

2 *Cuttings*

Develop a book or file of cuttings from a variety of sources, such as newspaper articles, magazines, leaflets, etc. Collect cuttings relevant to each topic area you study. As you enter each cutting into your book or file, include a brief explanation of its relevance.

This will ensure you build up a bank of up-to-date examples which could be linked to examination questions or coursework. It will also help you to interpret contemporary issues in society more easily.

CHAPTER 2

The Sociological Approach

In this chapter, we will explore and attempt to answer the following questions:

1. **What is sociology?**
2. **What sorts of questions do sociologists ask?**
3. **How do sociologists discover answers to these questions? This will involve looking at different sorts of data collected by sociologists:**
   - **primary and secondary sources of data;**
   - **quantitative and qualitative data;**
   - **the different techniques used by sociologists in selecting samples;**
   - **the benefits of using a pilot study;**
   - **the advantages and disadvantages of questionnaires, structured interviews, unstructured interviews and observation as primary sources of data;**
   - **the advantages and disadvantages of official statistics and other secondary sources of data.**
4. **What are the key concepts and terms used in sociology?**

A representative cross-section of society?

WHAT IS SOCIOLOGY?

Sociology involves the systematic study and explanation of human social life, groups and societies. Sociologists aim to investigate and understand the social world and human behaviour within it. They are particularly interested in understanding the ways in which society influences us and shapes our lives.

In studying sociology, you will be actively involved in exploring and asking questions about the society in which you live. Studying sociology offers you opportunities to gain a greater understanding of society and to make sense of your own experiences within it. Sociology can be both thought-provoking and challenging because it forces people to rethink some of their common-sense views and assumptions.

In studying contemporary British society, we will examine the main social institutions and groups such as families, schools and the workplace. Other areas of interest include crime and deviance, politics, wealth and poverty. Social processes such as socialization, discrimination and social change will also be investigated. We will explore ranking within society and the impact of social class, gender, ethnicity and age on the opportunities open to individuals and groups.

Table 2.1 gives some examples of the sociological themes of social groups, processes and stratification.

Table 2.1 Social groups, social processes and stratification

Social groups	Social processes	Social stratification
		Ranking according to:
Families	Discrimination	Age
Pressure groups	Peer pressure	Gender
Peer groups	Socialization	Ethnicity
	Labelling	Social class
	Social change	Wealth
		Power
		Status

WHAT SORTS OF QUESTIONS DO SOCIOLOGISTS ASK?

Sociologists ask important questions covering a huge range of topics. Here are some examples:

- Who does the housework when men become unemployed?
- What are the causes of hooliganism among English fans at football matches in Europe?
- What are teenage girls' future ideas about work and marriage?
- Why would anyone join a religious sect?
- Why do British migrants move to Spain's Costa del Sol?
- How can we make sense of the world of teenage drug dealers?
- How do first-time mothers experience childbirth?

HOW DO SOCIOLOGISTS DISCOVER ANSWERS TO THESE QUESTIONS?

In trying to answer such questions, sociologists have developed a tool kit of **research techniques** – methods of collecting data, such as questionnaires, interviews and observation. In addition to collecting their own data, sociologists may also make use of existing sources of data such as official statistics or newspaper reports.

Primary and secondary sources of data

Primary data is actually generated and collected by the sociologist doing research, for example by using techniques such as questionnaires or interviews. Secondary data already exists and has previously been generated or collected by other people.

Sources of primary data include:

- questionnaires;
- structured interviews;
- unstructured interviews;
- participant observation.

Sources of secondary data include:

- official statistics;
- media reports;
- letters;
- diaries.

Quantitative and qualitative data

Data used by sociologists may be quantitative or qualitative. Quantitative data is presented in numerical form. Official statistics on crime rates, for example, are sources of quantitative secondary data which have been compiled by the Home Office. Sociologists generate quantitative primary data in their own research using standardized, large-scale methods such as questionnaires.

Qualitative data is presented as words. Media reports, letters and diaries are sources of qualitative secondary data. Sociologists generate qualitative primary data, consisting of verbatim or word-for-word accounts from the people under study, using less standardized methods such as participant observation and unstructured interviews.

In doing sociological research, sociologists can select one or more methods from a range of research techniques in order to collect primary data. They may also make use of varied sources of secondary data in their research. A **research design** is a particular combination of techniques and sources. It is possible to combine techniques and sources in a wide variety of ways. Eileen Barker (1984), for example, wanted to find out what sort of people joined the Unification Church, known as the Moonies, and why they joined. She combined participant observation, questionnaires and in-depth interviews in her study because she believed that no one method would suffice.

Finding out through social surveys

A social survey involves collecting information from a large number of people, usually through questionnaires or structured interviews.

There are two main types of survey which sociologists use. **Cross-sectional surveys** take a cross-section of the population and question them on the relevant issues only once. This is a one-off, quick method but only gives us a 'snapshot' view – it only tells us about people at one particular point in time. **Longitudinal studies** are studies of the same group of people conducted over time. A longitudinal study allows us to examine social change over time, for example changes in the lives, experiences, behaviour and attitudes of individuals.

J. W. B. Douglas, for example, began research in 1945 to study the effectiveness of services offered to pregnant women. He obtained information from every woman in Britain who had given birth during the first week in March 1946. The study followed the children from birth, so they and their parents were interviewed many times after 1946. In *The Home and the School* (1964)

Douglas followed the children through their primary school years until they sat the 11+ examination in 1957. In *All Our Future* (Douglas, Ross and Simpson, 1968) he followed their subsequent educational progress through secondary school until they reached the age of 16 in 1962.

HOW DO SOCIOLOGISTS DECIDE WHO TO QUESTION?

Before beginning a survey the researcher must identify the **population**, i.e. the group under study. The population may, for example, be students, the unemployed, pensioners or house husbands, depending on the aims of the study.

In practice, it may be too expensive or time consuming for the sociologist to question all the members of a population. If this is the case, **a sample** or subgroup of the population will be selected for questioning. In selecting the sample, **a sampling frame**, which is a complete list of all members of the population, is required. Examples of sampling frames are the electoral roll, a college register or a doctor's list.

Many researchers are interested in making **generalizations** about the group under study. Generalizations are general statements and conclusions that apply not only to the sample but to the population as a whole. If the researcher is to generalize, then it is essential that the sample is **representative** or typical of the population.

There are a number of **sampling techniques** used by sociologists in order to obtain a sample. These sampling techniques fall into two categories.

Random sampling:

- simple;
- stratified;
- cluster.

Non-random sampling:

- systematic;
- snowball;
- quota.

A **random sample** is one in which each member of the sampling frame has an equal chance of being selected. If the sample is selected randomly, it is likely that it will mirror the population, therefore general conclusions can be made.

Random sampling

Simple random sampling

The most straightforward way of selecting a simple random sample is by drawing names from a hat. This, however, is only practical for small populations! For larger populations, researchers use a computer to select their sample randomly. The potential problem with simple random sampling, however, is that, by chance, the random sample may not be representative of the population.

Stratified random sampling

Imagine that a sociologist is interested in researching the attitudes of members of a group involved in environmental issues. She does not have sufficient time or money to interview the full population, so she will have to interview a sample of members. She has a list of members, has advance knowledge of their age and gender, and wants the sample to reflect the age and gender characteristics of the population.

To achieve this, stratified random sampling can be used. This involves dividing the population into strata or sub-populations, in this case according to age and gender. The population might be divided into the following strata:

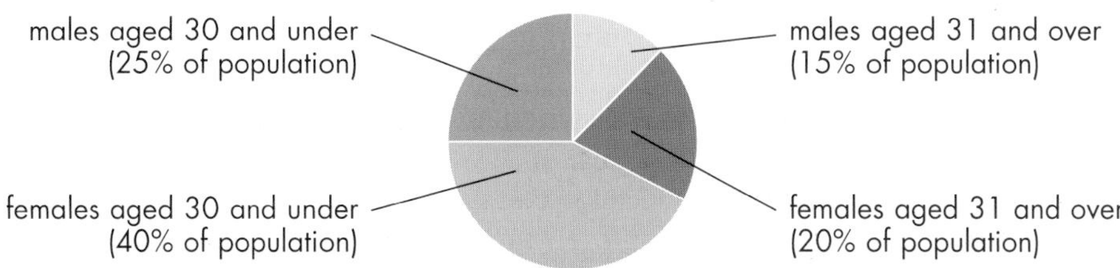

A sample is then drawn randomly from each stratum or group in proportion to their numbers in the population as a whole. The sociologist would, for example, select 15 per cent of her sample from males aged 31 and over. It's a bit like sorting the names into a number of hats and then drawing them out randomly.

Cluster sampling

If, for example, the survey population is spread out across the country, it would prove relatively expensive and time consuming to interview a randomly selected sample. Instead of going all over the country to get information from the sample, the researcher could use cluster sampling. This involves selecting certain areas at random, e.g. London and Manchester, and then selecting a sample of people from these areas. The sample will therefore be located in clusters around a geographical area so it is easier to collect the data.

Non-random sampling

Systematic sampling

Systematic sampling involves taking every *n*th name from the sampling frame, e.g. systematically taking every tenth name from the electoral register. Imagine that the population consists of 1,000 people and a sample size of 100 is required. Using systematic sampling, the researcher would select a number at random between 1 and 10. If this turned out to be 5, then the 5th, 15th, 25th name – and so on up to the 995th name – would be selected from the sampling frame. This would give the required sample size.

Snowball sampling

A sociologist may be interested in studying a population for which there is no sampling frame, for example people who fraudulently claim DSS benefits while working in paid employment. Without a sampling frame the researcher would not be able to select a random or systematic sample. Using the snowball sampling technique, the researcher would begin by making contact with one member of the population, gradually gaining his or her confidence until that person is willing to divulge the names of others who might co-operate. In such a way, the researcher would obtain a sample, although it is unlikely to be a representative one.

Quota sampling

This is a technique favoured by market research companies which employ and train paid workers to interview people on the street. Each interviewer is told to interview an exact number (or quota) of people from categories or groups such as females, pensioners or teenagers, in proportion to their numbers in the population as a whole.

This method is not random and it depends on the interviewer's ability to 'spot' the right type of person to fill their quota. One problem with quota sampling is that the interviewer may, in practice, make a mistake. Another problem is that the interviewer may, at the end of a long hard day, 'fiddle' the quota.

Quota sampling will only work well when the researcher knows a lot about the population under study.

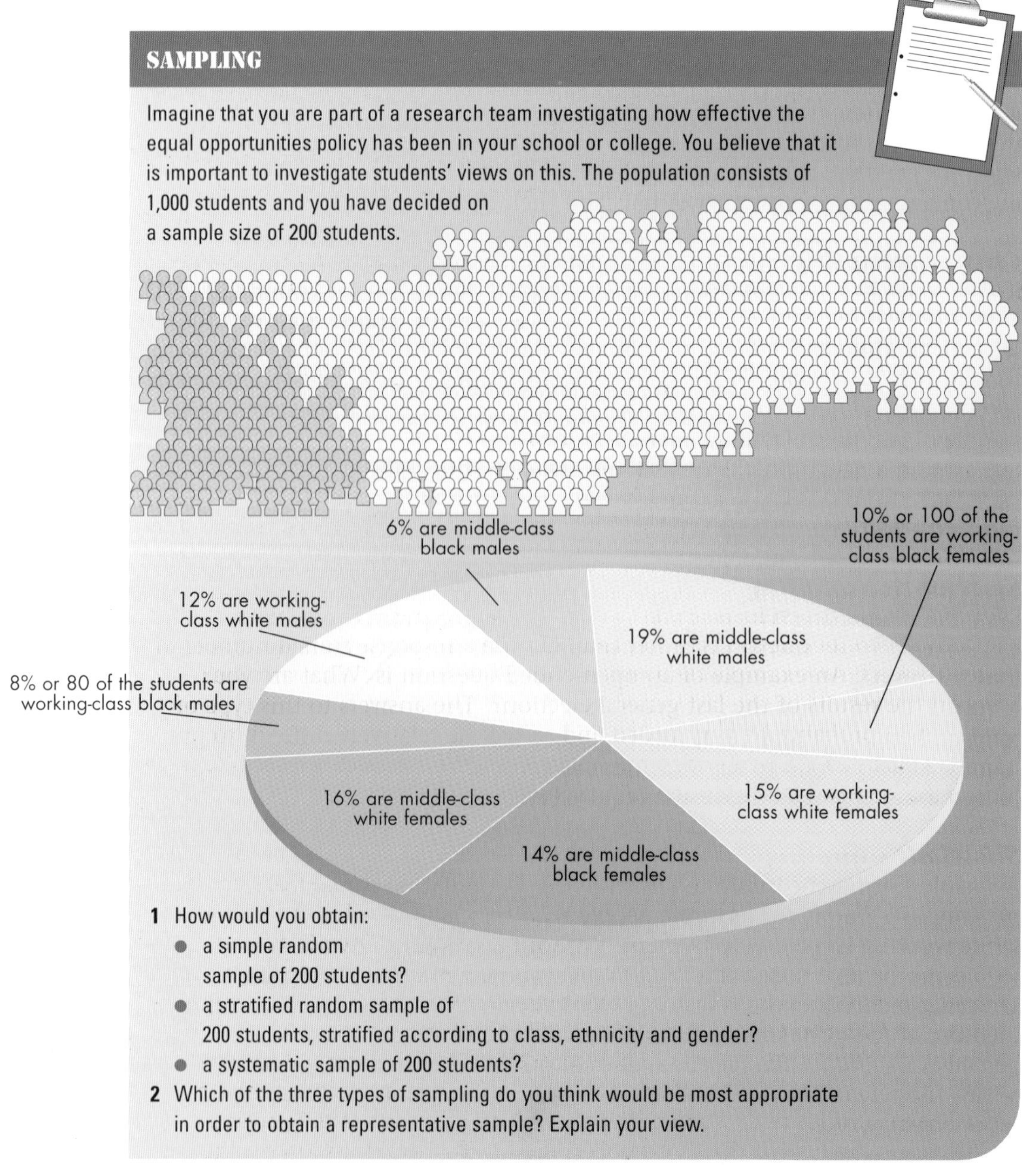

SAMPLING

Imagine that you are part of a research team investigating how effective the equal opportunities policy has been in your school or college. You believe that it is important to investigate students' views on this. The population consists of 1,000 students and you have decided on a sample size of 200 students.

1 How would you obtain:
- a simple random sample of 200 students?
- a stratified random sample of 200 students, stratified according to class, ethnicity and gender?
- a systematic sample of 200 students?

2 Which of the three types of sampling do you think would be most appropriate in order to obtain a representative sample? Explain your view.

CHECK YOUR UNDERSTANDING

1 What is a representative sample? (2 marks)
2 Identify and explain two reasons why researchers might find it difficult to obtain a representative sample. (4 marks)
3 Identify one type of random sample and one type of non-random sample used by researchers. Outline briefly in each case how the sample is constructed. (4 marks)

Asking questions through questionnaires

Social surveys are often carried out by means of questionnaires. A questionnaire consists of a list of pre-set, standardized questions to which the respondent (the person from whom information is sought) supplies the answers. There are three main ways of delivering questionnaires:

1 Postal questionnaires: the questionnaire is posted to the respondent, who completes it and sends it back to the researcher.
2 Formal or structured interviews: the interviewer reads the standard questions from the pre-set list or schedule and the respondent gives his or her answers there and then. This is a formal face-to-face, question and answer session.
3 A third possibility is that the researcher hands the questionnaire to the respondent and returns to collect the completed questionnaire at a later date.

There are two types of questions that may be used in a questionnaire. Fixed-choice or **closed questions** require the respondent to choose between a number of given answers to such questions as, for example, 'Did you vote in the last general election?' Frequently, the respondent will merely be required to tick the appropriate box in response to a given question. The answers to closed questions will be relatively easy to add up and present in statistical form, e.g. in a study on voting behaviour, it might be found that 72 per cent of respondents voted in the last general election. Answers may, however, lack depth and questions will not allow the respondent to develop an answer fully. The respondent would not, for example, have the opportunity to explain fully why they did not vote. Closed questions, therefore, would not be suitable if the researcher wanted in-depth accounts.

Open-ended questions allow the respondent to put forward his or her own answers to set questions rather than choose a response from a number of pre-set answers. An example of an open-ended question is 'What are your views on the results of the last general election?' The answers to this type of question will probably be very varied and so will be relatively difficult to put into statistical form. Open-ended questions, therefore, would not be suitable if the researcher was only interested in gaining quantitative data.

The pilot study

Once the researcher has selected the sample, he or she must then design the questionnaire. In doing so, sociologists use a pilot study, which is a small-scale trial run before the main research; it is a feasibility study. The pilot study allows the researcher to check whether the chosen method of gathering data is appropriate. The researcher will be particularly keen to check the wording of questions in order to ensure that they are clear and straightforward.

A pilot study helps to overcome potential problems that may otherwise occur in the main study. The pilot study may save time, money and effort in the long run. This is illustrated by the work of Schofield (1965), who conducted research with the Central Council for Health Education on the

USING QUESTIONNAIRES

Questionnaire

1 How long have you been employed in your current job?

- less than one year
- between one and five years
- between six and ten years
- over ten years

2 Have you been promoted while employed in your current job?

yes no

3 Do you feel that your job affects your family life outside work?

yes no don't know

4 If yes, please give some examples of how your job affects your family life.

5 Do you feel that your job affects your leisure activities outside work?

yes no don't know

6 If yes, please give some examples of how your job affects your leisure activities.

Here is an example of part of a questionnaire on 'work, leisure and family life' which combines open-ended and closed questions.

1 State which questions are open-ended and which are closed.
2 Write a paragraph explaining why the answers to the open-ended questions will be more difficult and time consuming for the researcher to make use of.

sexual attitudes and behaviour of young people aged fifteen to nineteen. After a series of pilot interviews, the research team met with a group of young people who were encouraged to criticize the questions they had been asked. This helped the research team to frame their questions in a way which would be meaningful to the young people.

This is an extract from Schofield's research report:

Boy: *'Nearly everything you've said we don't use the same word for.'*

Boy: (about having the interview in a church hall) *'You couldn't say anything there.'*

Boy: *'You want to get us where we're not interested in anything'* (i.e. not in a youth club where they could be doing something else).

Source: Schofield (1965) pp. 263–4

GETTING IT RIGHT

In the light of the remarks made during Schofield's pilot study, make a note of three pieces of advice for the researchers.

QUESTIONNAIRE DESIGN

It is both difficult and time consuming to devise a good questionnaire. Read through the following pilot study questionnaire, which was designed to examine whether domestic tasks are divided equally between partners with children.

1 Identify the problems with the introduction and rewrite it in a more appropriate way.
2 Identify the questions which are clear and straightforward.
3 Identify the questions which are poorly worded and rewrite them in a more appropriate way.

Questionnaire

Dear Sir/Madam

This is a feminist study of changing conjugal roles. Please help me by answering the following questions.

1 AGE

2 Are you: ☐ married ☐ cohabiting?

3 GENDER ☐ Male ☐ Female

4 How many children do you have? ☐ 0 ☐ 1–3 ☐ 3–4 ☐ 4 or more

5 OCCUPATION (please state)

6 Who mainly carries out the following tasks:

	Mainly you	*Mainly partner*	*Mainly shared*	*Other*
Washing up				
Cooking				
Shopping				
Dusting				
Hoovering				
DIY				
Gardening				
Looking after sick children				

7 How much housework does your partner do each week?

☐ none ☐ not much ☐ not enough ☐ a bit ☐ quite a bit
☐ average ☐ quite a lot ☐ a lot ☐ too much

8 Do you think that most married women definitely do more housework and childcare than their husbands?

☐ Yes ☐ No ☐ Unsure

9 Explain in detail your views on this topic.

Thank you

CHECK YOUR UNDERSTANDING

Identify two advantages a researcher may gain by doing a pilot study. (2 marks)

RESEARCHING THE COSTA DEL SOL

Karen O'Reilly (1996) conducted sociological research into the lifestyles and experiences of British migrants to Spain's Costa del Sol. Between June 1993 and September 1994 she lived there with her family. She used a combination of research methods including a questionnaire survey:

> *'I decided to conduct a survey of the British migrants in order to obtain statistical data to add to my more general findings on migration ... With respect to my own research, data is available on Britons living or owning property in Spain, but the figures are wildly inaccurate. Additionally, there is no data on the large group of migrants who regularly go back and forth from Britain to Spain ... I realized the only way to get figures was to do a survey of my own.'*

The major problem O'Reilly faced, however, concerned the response rate – the number of replies received as a proportion of the total number of questionnaires distributed. She states that the response rate to the questionnaire survey was so low as to make it useless: 'They responded kindly and enthusiastically on the surface but then omitted to return forms to me or to explain why.'

Source: O'Reilly (1996)

1 Why did O'Reilly decide to use a questionnaire survey?
2 Why could she not rely on secondary sources of data?
3 What serious problem did she face with her questionnaire?

What are the advantages of questionnaires?

Questionnaires provide a relatively cheap, quick and efficient way of obtaining large amounts of information from large numbers of people. This is particularly so with the **postal questionnaire**, which has no geographical restrictions and can be mailed anywhere. Schofield (1965) conducted research into the sexual attitudes and behaviour of young people aged fifteen to nineteen. He states that a 1 per cent sample of this age group would consist of 35,000 young people. It would have been far too expensive to interview such a large sample in person, but a postal questionnaire was more feasible.

Another advantage of questionnaires is that they provide quantitative data; that is, data which is in statistical form, e.g. 50 per cent of respondents support the present government; 50 per cent of respondents belong to a trade union. This is particularly true for closed questions.

With statistical data, it is possible to measure the strength of a connection between different factors, for example between support for the present government, occupation, and trade union membership. Comparisons between respondents can be made and any differences can be highlighted – it might be found, for example, that members of trade unions are more likely to vote Labour than non-unionized people.

As the questions it asks are standardized, a questionnaire can be replicated easily to check for reliability. This means that a second sociologist can repeat the questionnaire to check that the results are consistent. If the results are consistent then they can be seen as **reliable** or accurate.

With postal questionnaires the researcher is not present with the respondent, so people may be more likely to answer personal or embarrassing questions, for example about their sexual activity.

What are the disadvantages of questionnaires?

Postal questionnaires have particular problems of their own. The response rate is usually low; those who choose to reply may not be representative or typical of the population under study. If this is the case, it will be impossible to generalize accurately or draw general conclusions from the sample of respondents to the population as a whole.

Postal questionnaires generally consist of at least some closed questions. With closed questions, it is difficult for respondents to develop and elaborate their answers in much depth. This means that the results may not be **valid**, in that they do not give a true picture of the respondent's point of view.

If the interviewer is not present, questions may be misunderstood or misinterpreted by the respondent. Schofield (1965) quotes research during which written questionnaires were given to girls. One of the questions asked 'Are you a virgin?' One girl wrote 'Not yet'.

We can never really be sure that the right person actually completed the posted questionnaire. The completed questionnaire may be the result of a group effort or it may be treated as a joke. Postal questionnaires are also inappropriate for certain populations, for example in a study focusing on homeless or illiterate people.

Asking questions through structured interviews

Structured interviews are questionnaires that are delivered face to face. As such, they have problems which arise from the interaction between interviewer and interviewee.

The questionnaire may not be filled in by the right person, or the questions may not be understood

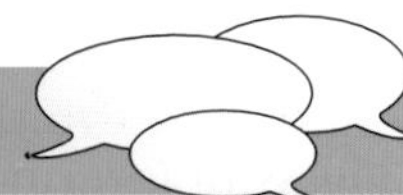

PROBLEMS WITH STRUCTURED INTERVIEWS

The problems illustrated in the cartoon above might apply to postal questionnaires! Which other problems would apply if the questionnaire were delivered face to face as a structured interview?

What are the disadvantages of structured interviews?

Interview bias: in an interview, interviewees may give answers which they think are socially acceptable or which show them in a positive light. In this way, they might not reveal their true thoughts or behaviour so the results may be invalid.

In an interview, the age, gender, ethnicity or appearance of the interviewer may influence the respondent. The respondent may also lie or try to shock the researcher.

Postal questionnaires and structured interviews are both based on a pre-set list of standardized questions. The wording, order and focus of the questions are predetermined by the researcher. This assumes that the researcher knows, in advance, what all of the relevant questions are. Critics argue that these techniques impose the researcher's prior assumptions about the situation being researched. In this sense, questionnaires and structured interviews close off rather than open up new and interesting issues and areas. They can be seen as invalid because they do not provide a true picture of what is being studied.

ADVANTAGES OF THE STRUCTURED INTERVIEW

We have focused on the disadvantages of the structured interview. What are the advantages of this research technique? Make a note of three advantages.

CHECK YOUR UNDERSTANDING

1 The way people behave and think in Britain today is often studied by social surveys. To what extent are the results of surveys likely to be valid? (8 marks)

2 State two advantages and two disadvantages of postal questionnaires. (4 marks)

Asking questions through unstructured or in-depth interviews

In an unstructured interview, instead of following a rigidly structured and standardized list of questions, the interviewer will have an idea of the areas to be covered. An in-depth interview is more like an informal, guided conversation and no two interviews will be exactly alike. The interviewer can rephrase questions, clarify them, probe and ask extra questions.

What are the advantages of unstructured interviews?

Informal interviews have a higher response rate than postal questionnaires. Interviewees have the opportunity to talk at length using their own words and ideas. They can develop their answers, giving a more in-depth account. Informal interviews may also allow the interviewer to compare what he or she observes with what the interviewee says, and thus check the validity of replies.

In an informal interview, questions can also be rephrased and any misunderstandings clarified. The method allows more complex issues to be examined.

What are the disadvantages of unstructured interviews?

Successful informal interviewing needs a skilled and trained interviewer in order, for example, to keep the conversation going and to encourage people to open up. Unstructured interviews may also be affected by interview bias. The interviewee may give a socially desirable response to please the interviewer or may not be totally frank with the interviewer. There is also potential for interviewer bias, where the interviewer may lead or influence the interviewee. If this happens, the results will be invalid.

Informal interviews are relatively time consuming and expensive and therefore fewer can be undertaken, making for smaller samples. With no standardized schedule of questions to follow, it is difficult to replicate the interview in order to check for reliability.

RESEARCHING YOUTH SUBCULTURES

In his postgraduate research on acid house subculture, Andrew Hill decided to use unstructured interviews with individuals who were involved in the subculture, as he wanted to gain an understanding of their experiences. Unstructured interviews would give the interviewees the opportunity to talk freely about what *they* saw as important. This technique would also allow Hill to respond flexibly to what interviewees told him.

- Explain briefly why unstructured interviews would allow Hill to respond more flexibly than structured interviews.

RESEARCHING GIRLS

Sue Sharpe (1994) used questionnaires followed up by in-depth interviews in her studies of fourteen- and fifteen-year-old girls' ideas about education, work and marriage. In-depth interviews allowed the girls to contribute as individuals and provided Sharpe with rich and detailed data. In the course of one interview, 'Catherine' said:

When my brother was doing his GCSEs it was 'Terence can't wash the dishes, his GCSEs are important.' So I had to wash the dishes and all that. Now he's doing his A levels and I'm doing my GCSEs and now they say 'Oh, Terence has so much A level coursework to do,' they don't say the same things about me doing my GCSEs. That's not fair, I think that's a bit sexist. Well, my mum expects me to cook and do the ironing and wash dishes, despite what homework I get. They automatically assume I can do it, they don't bother asking me if I've got homework that night.

Source: Sharpe (1994) p. 107

1. In two or three paragraphs explain why, compared with written questionnaires, in-depth interviews allow the interviewees to put forward their own ideas in their own words. Illustrate your answer with examples.
2. Write a paragraph explaining why it would not be easy to replicate an in-depth informal interview in order to double check the findings.
3. Discuss how far it is possible to reach general conclusions about all girls' experiences on the basis of the evidence collected by Sharpe.

CHECK YOUR UNDERSTANDING

1. Identify one research topic for which a researcher might decide to use interviews as a research method. (1 mark)
2. Explain fully why interviews would be a good method to use in this situation. (3 marks)
3. State one advantage and one disadvantage of unstructured interviews. (2 marks)

Finding out through observing

We have seen that much sociological research involves asking questions, either formally or informally. Sociologists may also conduct research using **observation**, which involves watching and listening to the group under study and recording what is observed. There are two types of observation: participant observation (either overt or covert) and non-participant observation.

In a participant observation (PO) study, the researcher joins a group and participates in its activities as a full member on a daily basis in order to study it. The researcher has to decide whether to carry out the study **overtly** or **covertly**.

Overt PO involves the researcher 'coming clean', so that the group is aware of his or her research activities. The potential problem with overt participant observation, however, is that the researcher's presence may affect the behaviour of the group under study. This is known as the 'observer effect'.

RESEARCHING COCAINE KIDS

Williams (1989) used PO to study teenage members of a cocaine ring in New York. He describes his study of cocaine dealers as follows:

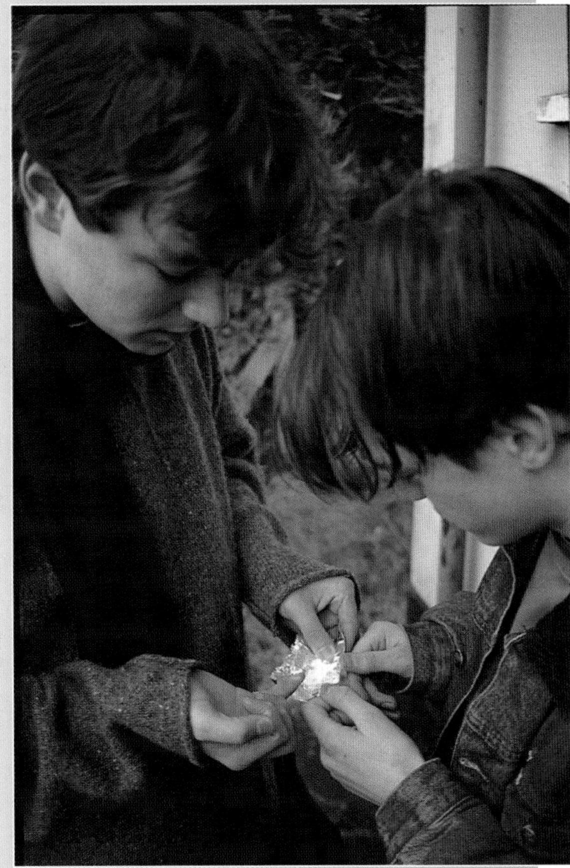

> *It focuses on the lives of eight young cocaine dealers in New York City. From 1982 to 1986, I spent some two hours a day, three days a week, hanging out with these kids in cocaine bars, after-hours spots, discos, restaurants, crack houses, on street corners, in their homes and at family gatherings and parties.*

He continues:

> *This is a book about kids, cocaine and crack. But it is also a book about work and money, love and deceit, hope and ambition. It describes – as much as possible in their own words – the world of teenage members of a cocaine ring: the way they do business, their neighbourhood, their families, their highs and lows.*

Williams aimed to provide a rounded and dynamic portrait of the kids, their work and their world. In so doing, he needed to build up a close relationship with the kids, which was necessarily a slow process. He points out that, although he became close to the kids, 'some important distances could not be breached: for one thing, they were teenagers; for another, while cocaine use is a routine part of their daily lives, I never consumed any drug stronger than alcohol, and did not participate in any way in the preparation, transport or sale of drugs.'

Source: Williams (1989) pp. ix, 1, 4

The class should divide into small groups to discuss the following questions:

1. Terry Williams was much older than the cocaine kids he studied. Why does this make overt participant observation a more realistic approach for him?
2. Why do you think he didn't participate fully in all of the group's activities?
3. If he had not been an overt participant observer, what might have been the effect of his refusal to become involved in selling drugs?

Covert PO involves the researcher joining a group without the group's knowledge of his or her research activities. One problem with covert participant observation is that it is considered unethical or dishonest to deceive people.

RESEARCHING FOOTBALL HOOLIGANS ABROAD

British hooligans running riot in 1996 in Trafalgar Square

Read through the following extracts and, dividing into small groups, discuss the questions that follow.

The bulk of Hooligans Abroad *is devoted to three 'participant observation' studies carried out by John Williams. He is young enough and sufficiently 'street wise' and interested in football to pass himself off as an 'ordinary' English football fan.*

Source: Williams, Dunning and Murphy (1989) p. xiii

1 What role did the researcher adopt?
2 Why was this role quite easy for him to adopt?
3 Which social groups might find this role less easy to adopt?

Each of the three studies reported in this book was based on the 'covert' form of participant observation. For the Aston Villa–Bayern Munich match, one of us travelled to Holland as an 'ordinary' Villa supporter, remaining inconspicuous by wearing, in common with large numbers of the fans themselves, an Aston Villa football shirt on the trip … On each occasion, his task was not only to observe the behaviour of the fans who seem to be most regularly involved in disorder but also to experience events which they themselves experienced.

Source: Williams, Dunning and Murphy (1989) p. xix

4 How did the researcher blend in with the supporters?
5 Why was it important that the researcher used covert rather than overt participant observation?

What are the advantages of participant observation?

PO allows the researcher to study a group in its natural surroundings during daily life, so it is a lot less artificial than other methods. The researcher can see things from the group's point of view and so can discover more and obtain a deeper understanding of the group, its behaviour and activities, at first hand. This allows the researcher to obtain a more valid or true picture of the group.

Some groups, such as violent football supporters and users of illegal drugs, may not agree to be interviewed, so PO may be the only method available.

What are the disadvantages of participant observation?

It may often be difficult to gain entry to the group under study. It may also be hard to gain acceptance and trust. The researcher may find it difficult to take notes and record data; often, he or she will have to rely on memory. This is particularly true for covert PO, where the group is not aware of the true identity of the researcher. Terry Williams (1989), for example, reveals that although the kids fully accepted him and his work, their customers were not necessarily informed of his role. Producing a pad or tape recorder would, he argues, definitely have aroused suspicion.

There is a danger that a researcher may become too involved with a group and its activities. Such over-involvement may invalidate the findings and results of the research if they are biased or one-sided.

With overt PO, the very presence of the researcher may influence the group and its activities and so the group may act differently. This is called the observer effect: if it occurs, then the validity of the results will be affected. PO can also be time consuming and therefore expensive. Some researchers have spent over two years on a study, so by the time the results are published, they may be out of date!

It would be very difficult to repeat a PO study exactly because each one is unique. A second sociologist would find it difficult, therefore, to check the reliability of the results of the first sociologist's work.

Over-involvement may lead to bias

A GLASGOW GANG

In order to obtain information about a delinquent Glasgow gang, James Patrick (1973), a young teacher in an approved school, used covert participant observation. He adopted the role of gang member and, with the help of Tim, who was at the approved school, spent many hours with the gang over a number of weekends.

1 Why do you think Patrick chose this method of research?
2 What problems do you think he might have faced?

STUDYING ONE GROUP

A PO study is unique and usually focuses on a small number of people or a single group.

- How far can we draw general conclusions about all such groups on the basis of a study of one group?

Advantages and disadvantages of non-participant observation

With non-participant observation the researcher is like a 'fly on the wall', observing but not participating in the group's activities. The researcher is consequently less likely to be drawn into the group's activities. As a result, the researcher may be more objective and less influenced by feelings about the group than the participant observer. On the other hand, it is more difficult for the researcher to see the world through the eyes of group members. The researcher is less likely to understand things in the same way as group members.

CHECK YOUR UNDERSTANDING

Identify and explain two advantages of using covert PO to study sexism within the classroom. (4 marks)

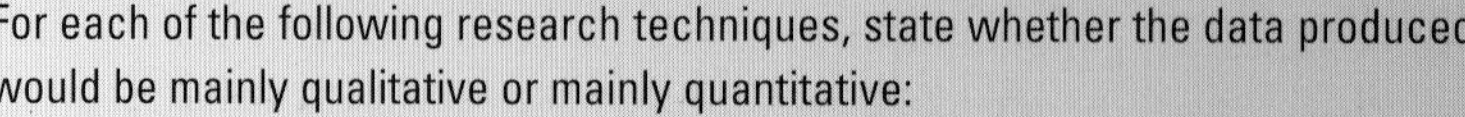

LOOKING AT DATA

For each of the following research techniques, state whether the data produced would be mainly qualitative or mainly quantitative:

- structured interview;
- unstructured interview;
- questionnaire;
- participant observation.

Sources of secondary data

So far, sources of primary data, such as questionnaires, interviews and observation, have been examined. Secondary data is information which has been collected by other people or organizations such as government agencies and which is available to the sociologist second hand. Secondary data can be either quantitative or qualitative.

Quantitative data is presented in statistical form, for example as percentages. When data is presented in words rather than numbers, it is known as qualitative data. Examples of quantitative secondary data include official statistics such as:

- birth rates;
- marriage rates;
- death rates;
- suicide rates;
- unemployment rates;
- crime rates.

Examples of qualitative secondary data include:

- newspaper reports;
- diaries;
- letters;
- autobiographies;
- novels.

Quantitative secondary data

Official statistics, compiled by government agencies, are an important source of quantitative secondary data. The census, for example, is a useful source of statistical information. It is conducted every ten years, involves sending a questionnaire to every household in the country and collects information on the full population. The 1991 census had a response rate of 97.8 per cent, but the response rate was lower among particular groups, e.g. men aged 20–34 in city districts.

Up-to-date official statistics can be found in *Social Trends*, published every year by the Office for National Statistics. It contains a wide range of statistical data, for example on birth, marriage, divorce and death rates, education, crime and employment.

What are the advantages of official statistics?

Official statistics are cheap, readily available and cover many aspects of social life. They may be the only source of data on a topic – on the suicide rate 100 years ago, for instance. They allow sociologists to do 'before and after' studies. For example, researchers could study the effects of the Divorce Law Reform Act (1969) by examining the official statistics on divorce before and after the Act.

Official statistics may be used as part of a research design which combines primary and secondary sources. If the researcher were investigating educational achievement and gender, for example, then official statistics on gender, subject choice and examination results would provide useful quantitative secondary data. In addition, qualitative primary data could be generated through participant observation and unstructured interviews in order to understand social processes in the school and classroom.

What are the disadvantages of official statistics?

Many sociologists are wary of official statistics and tend to handle them with caution. Such statistics are collected not by sociologists but by officials, so the definitions used may not be acceptable to sociologists. Statistics on the divorce rate, for example, obviously provide us with useful information on the number of divorces recorded each year. Such data, however, tells us nothing about the important question of the strength of marriage in society because divorce statistics exclude 'empty shell' marriages and separations.

It is not possible for the sociologist to check the validity of the statistics. The number of births recorded is likely to be valid, but the number of unemployed recorded will depend on how officials define unemployment, e.g. people on training schemes and married women may be excluded. Crime statistics, for example, may be invalid or incomplete: some crimes may not be detected or, if detected, may not be reported. Domestic violence, rape and vandalism, for instance, are likely to be under-recorded.

In addition, official statistics on unemployment or divorce, for example, can tell us nothing about what it means to the individual to be unemployed or divorced.

Qualitative secondary data

We have seen that official statistics are an important secondary source of quantitative information. Qualitative secondary data is also often useful and includes historical documents (such as diaries and letters), media reports (such as newspaper articles and television documentaries), biographies, autobiographies and novels.

WILD SWANS

The book *Wild Swans* is an account of the family history of Jung Chang, who was born in China in 1952. The author describes her own life and the lives of her grandmother and mother. In the following extract, she gives an account of the practice of binding the feet of female children:

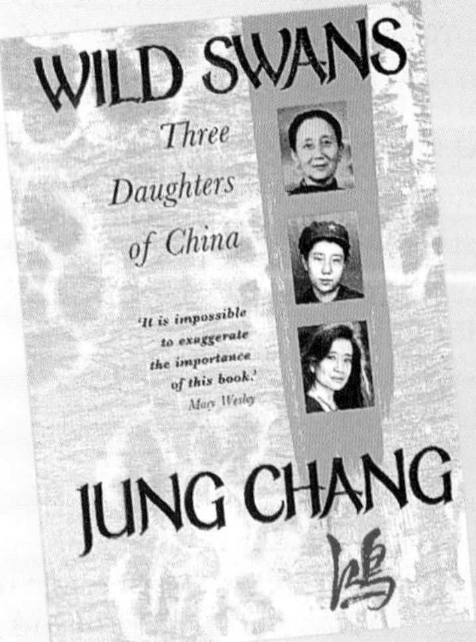

My grandmother was a beauty ... her greatest assets were her bound feet.... My grandmother's feet had been bound when she was two years old. Her mother, who herself had bound feet, first wound a piece of white cloth about twenty feet long round her feet, bending all the toes except the big toe inward and under the sole. Then she placed a large stone on top to crush the arch.... The process lasted several years. Even after the bones had been broken, the feet had to be bound day and night in thick cloth because the moment they were released they would try to recover.

Source: Chang (1993) pp. 30–1

Chang explains that in China around 1910, it was essential for a female to have bound feet in order to have a good marriage. If a newly married woman had normal-size feet, this would bring shame on her husband's household.

How might qualitative secondary data such as this be useful as part of the research design of a sociologist who was studying

- the changing role of women over time in China?
- differences between countries and cultures in the role of women?

QUALITATIVE SECONDARY DATA

Make a list of the advantages and disadvantages of qualitative secondary data such as novels, letters and media reports.

CHECK YOUR UNDERSTANDING

1 Identify two types of secondary sources that sociologists might use. In each case, explain what the researcher might gain by using them. (4 marks)

2 Many sociologists use official statistics. Why should they be careful when using them in their research? (8 marks)

RESEARCH DESIGNS

Imagine that you have been given a large grant to fund your research into one of the following topics:

- sexism within the classroom.
- Irish immigrants' experience of racism.
- girls' ideas about work and marriage.

Choose one of these topics and create a research design outlining how you will combine the available research techniques and sources of secondary data. In order to produce a focused study, you could begin by stating two research questions that you want to investigate.

WHAT ARE THE KEY CONCEPTS AND TERMS USED IN SOCIOLOGY?

In trying to explain human social life, sociologists have built up a body of concepts (or key ideas) and terms (a specialized vocabulary). Central to the study of sociology are concepts such as culture, subculture, values, norms, status, roles and socialization, which are explained below.

Culture

The term 'culture' refers to the whole way of life of a particular society. It includes the values, norms, customs, beliefs, knowledge, skills and language of a society. Sociologists recognize that culture is not fixed and uniform around the world but varies according to time and place. This can be illustrated with reference to food and diet, as the following examples show.

- Meat such as roast lamb is eaten without a second thought by many people in Britain, but roast horse or dog are not. Whole roasted guinea pig is enjoyed as a traditional delicacy in Ecuador, while guinea pigs are often kept as family pets in Britain.
- Traditionally, the Apache of North America would eat neither reptiles nor any other creatures that ate reptiles, as they were considered a cultural taboo. This meant, in practice, that they would not eat fish, snakes or frogs.

BEHAVIOUR AND BELIEFS

There are lots of other examples which show that behaviour and beliefs vary from society to society, for instance with regard to diet, dress and religion. Identify three other examples to show that behaviour and beliefs vary from culture to culture.

Subculture

Sociologists appreciate that within any one society there may be a variety of subcultures or social groups which differ from the dominant culture in terms of language, dress, norms and values. Youth subcultures, for example, have a distinct set of values within the dominant culture. Youth subcultures such as hippies, mods and punks have their own particular style of dress and music which mark them off from others.

FAIRGROUND PEOPLE

Read through the extract below, which describes the lifestyle of fairground people in Britain today, then answer the questions that follow.

Subcultures

Showpeople are Britain's last lost tribe. They don't reside in our road, they don't drink in our local, and their children don't go to school with our children. They don't even tap into our gas and electricity grids. They have their own language and their own culture. There are an estimated 21,000 of them, married almost exclusively to each other.... Showpeople are nomadic, moving from town to town as we surrender the streets to them.

No people are less integrated* or assimilated** than showpeople. And there is no way of becoming a showman, any more than there is of becoming black. Michael's eldest son is courting – as showpeople still call it – a girl from a travelling family. 'It's very awkward to go out with someone not in the business. It's very hard for them to fit in. People have married out of the business and it hasn't worked out, only because the boy or girl can't adapt to it.' he says.

Source: Dea Birkett, 'The show on the road', *The Guardian*, 14 December 1996

* 'integrated' – fitting in
** 'assimilated' – absorbed into the wider society

1 Identify four ways in which the fairground people's lifestyle differs from yours.
2 Explain, in each case, how it differs.

Values

Values provide general guidelines for conduct. A value is a belief that something is desirable and worth striving for. Privacy and respect for human life, for example, are highly valued by most people in Britain.

Values vary cross-culturally, which means that they vary from culture to culture. Different societies may value different things. In Western societies, for example, material possessions are often highly valued and considered worth striving for by most people. The Cheyenne of North America, on the other hand, valued the giving away of possessions. The Apache gave away the property of deceased relatives rather than inherit it. They believed that keeping the property might have encouraged inheriting relatives to feel glad when a person died.

VALUES

Consider the following:

- buying more and more consumer goods;
- honesty and truth;
- respect for human life;
- respect for elders;
- privacy;
- educational success;
- 'getting on' in life;
- helping the poor.

1 Which of these values do you think most people in Britain today would share?
2 Which of these values do you support? Explain how you support each value in practice.

Norms

Whereas values provide general guidelines for conduct, norms are more specific to particular situations. Norms define appropriate and acceptable behaviour in the classroom and in the cinema, for instance. To return to the privacy example: privacy is the value, while the related norms would be that we do not open other people's letters or listen to their telephone conversations.

Norms provide order in society and allow it to function smoothly and without chaos. They are enforced by positive and negative sanctions, rather like a system of rewards and punishments. Positive sanctions reward people for conforming to the norms and negative sanctions punish those who deviate from the norms. Among the Maya civilization of Mexico and Central America, for example, the punishment for adultery was death. Among the Apache of North America, people who broke the rules were banished from the tribe. Examples such as these show that, as part of culture, norms vary from one society to another. People learn the norms and values of their society during the process of growing up.

Status

Status refers to the amount of prestige or social standing that a person has in a particular social position. Important sources of status are jobs, families and gender. Occupational status positions include teacher, judge and bus driver; family status positions include mother and daughter; gender status position is related to being a man or a woman.

The status of women has varied historically and from culture to culture. Among the native North American people, for example, different groups viewed women differently and this can be seen in the penalties imposed for killing a woman. Among some groups, the penalty for killing a woman was only half that given for killing a man. Among other groups, however, the penalty was twice that given for killing a man because a woman's death was seen as the loss of a long line of potential offspring.

Achieved status

Status can be **ascribed** or **achieved**. Ascribed status refers to status which is fixed at birth, such as gender and hereditary title.

Achieved status refers to status which is earned on the basis of personal achievement, merit or action. A person's occupation is usually the result of individual ability and effort; promotion at work, for example, is generally achieved. Ascribed status is fixed, whereas achieved status requires some degree of definite action on the part of the individual. Marital status, for example, is achieved in so far as a person has a choice and makes the decision to get married.

Ascribed status

In a society based on ascribed status, there will be little opportunity for movement up or down between status groups. In an achievement-based society, however, such opportunities do exist and people will be able to take advantage of them.

Role

A role defines the expected and acceptable behaviour of those people who occupy a particular status. The role of 'teacher', for example, defines how a teacher is expected to behave during the working day. An individual does not perform his or her role in isolation, but in relation to other people in their roles. A teacher, for example, performs a role in relation to students and to colleagues, a doctor in relation to patients and a shop assistant in relation to customers.

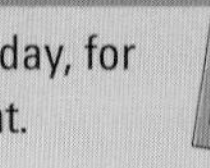

DIFFERENT ROLES

In everyday life, we have different roles at different times. During any one day, for example, a person might be a student, boyfriend, son, customer and patient.

1 Identify three roles which you play.
2 For each role, identify and explain two associated norms.

In practice, our roles do not necessarily fall neatly into separate categories and so it is possible to experience **role conflict**. This occurs when the demands of one of our roles conflict with those of another. As a student, for example, we are expected to spend a considerable amount of time studying, but this may come into conflict with our role as boyfriend, best friend or part-time employee.

STATUS

Look at the following photographs. For each one, decide whether the individual's status is ascribed or achieved. Explain why.

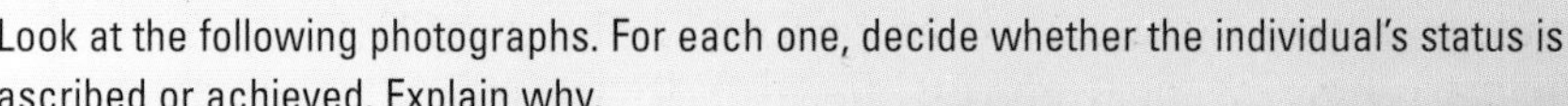

ROLE CONFLICT

Look at the following cartoon to explain what is meant by role conflict. Identify a situation in which you have experienced role conflict and explain what the source of the conflict was.

CHECK YOUR UNDERSTANDING

1 Explain fully, with examples, the following terms:
 (a) culture (4 marks)
 (b) subculture (4 marks)
 (c) values and norms (4 marks)
 (d) status and role (4 marks)

2 Explain, using examples, the difference between ascribed and achieved status. (4 marks)

Roles vary cross-culturally and this can be seen in the expectations that different cultures have concerning the social roles of women and men.

CROSS-CULTURAL DIFFERENCES

Read through the newspaper extract below, which describes aspects of the lives of women and men in Saudi Arabia. Identify three points from the information in the extract to support the view that norms vary cross culturally.

Saudi Arabia has some of the harshest codes governing social behaviour in the world – codes which foreigners must obey. Outside the compound, single men and women are forbidden to mix at the workplace or even take taxis together.

Even the local McDonald's is segregated between the sexes.... Women are forbidden to drive and must not be seen in the company of a man who is not a close relative – husband, brother or father. 'I couldn't go anywhere without being chaperoned by a man,' said Anne Froelich, whose husband got a job at a Saudi university.

Source: Kathy Evans, 'Expatriate games', *The Guardian*, 28 December 1996

Socialization

We have seen that culture, values and norms are not fixed but vary from one society to another. Sociologists, therefore, point out that culture is learnt. How does this learning process actually take place?

By **socialization**, sociologists mean the process by which the individual learns the culture and appropriate behaviour of his or her society. Socialization prepares the individual from birth for the role which he or she will play in society. A baby will gradually learn the behaviour considered appropriate for its society and also for its gender.

The extract on the left illustrates the idea that culture, and therefore socialization, varies from one group to another. It describes an aspect of the socialization of boys of the Hidatsa native people of North America.

Widespread was the practice of boys being taught how to hunt and trap by their fathers, older relatives or a trusted family friend; their roles as hunters were thus conditioned from an early age. Typical are the experiences of the Hidatsa men, Wolf Chief and Goodbird ... Wolf Chief told of his early use of the bow and arrow: 'I began using a bow, I think, when I was four years of age ... I very often went out to hunt birds for so my father bade me do'. Armed with blunt arrows and snares, the Hidatsa boys learned skills they would need as hunters and warriors.

Source: Taylor (1996) p. 87

Sociologists distinguish between **primary** and **secondary** socialization. Primary socialization refers to early childhood learning during which we acquire the basic behaviour patterns, language and skills that we will need in later life. The **agencies** of primary socialization are usually families and parents who ensure that this learning takes place. Secondary socialization takes place during later childhood and continues into adulthood, during which we learn society's norms and values. The agencies of secondary socialization include the peer group, the school, the workplace, religion and the media.

WOLF CHILDREN

Case studies of children who have not been socialized can be used to illustrate that socialization is a learning process. The following extract is from a case study of two girls thought by some to have been reared by wolves in India, and discovered in a wolf's lair in the Bengali jungle in 1920.

1 Identify four examples of behaviour that the children may have learned from the wolves.
2 Identify four examples of human behaviour that they have not learned.
3 Note down three points from the case study of the 'wolf children' to support the view that human behaviour is linked to the process of socialization rather than instinct.

Their bodies were encrusted with dirt and mud, smelt strongly of the wolves' den and appeared from their scratching to be full of fleas and other parasites.... The children reacted violently to being touched or to any contact with water. What dirt could be removed revealed a large number of small scars and scratches all over their bodies, and on their elbows, knees and the heels of their hands, heavy callouses – presumably from going on all fours.

All attempts to make them eat, however, failed until one afternoon they were taken out into the courtyard at the time when the orphanage dogs were being fed.... Showing no fear ... the girl ... lowered her face to the dog bowl, seized her food and bolted it with compulsive shakes of her upper body, keeping her head close to the ground. She secured a large bone and carried it off in her mouth to a corner of the yard away from the others, where she soon settled down, holding it under her hands as if they were paws, and began to gnaw at it, occasionally rubbing it along the ground to help separate the meat from the bone.

They slept little, either by day or at night, though they would lie down for an hour or two at about midday and were often caught dozing while sitting in a corner.... When they did sleep, it was usually lying one on top of the other, like puppies in a litter.... They were noisy sleepers, snoring, grunting, grinding their teeth and at times giving little cries, but they slept lightly and the least sound awoke them....

After midnight, the children never slept and were constantly on the move, prowling around, pacing to and fro, whether in their cage, the outhouse or in the yard where they were taken for exercise. Sometimes they howled.... They always howled at night, never during the day, and to begin with the noise alarmed everyone at the orphanage.

Source: Maclean (1979) pp. 69–70, 79

How do the agencies of socialization operate?

Families

Families are important in the process of primary or early socialization of children. Through interaction within their families, children are helped to acquire language and other essential skills. Families are expected to teach children the norms and values of the wider society and, in so doing, may exert a powerful influence on attitudes and behaviour.

Norms regarding how control over children's behaviour is exercised have varied from culture to culture and over time. The Cheyenne of North America, for example, controlled a baby's crying by hanging the cradle from a tree, well away from the camp.

Peer groups

Peer groups are groups of people who share a similar social status and position in society, such as people of similar age, outlook or occupational status. They can exert considerable pressure on their members to conform to the group's norms and values, for example within a school or workplace. Members of a group may feel the need to prove that they are accepted by other group members. In this way, such groups can be very powerful in ensuring conformity. Failure to conform may involve the risk of rejection by the group.

James Patrick (1973), in his covert PO study of a Glasgow gang, had to learn their norms and values in order to fit in and be accepted. He felt at times that some gang members viewed him with suspicion and hostility because of his behaviour; for example, unlike them, he made every effort to avoid involvement in violence.

Schools

Schools are important in the process of secondary socialization. During the years of compulsory schooling, pupils are expected to learn how to interact in groups larger than the family. They learn important new skills. They learn also that they are expected to conform to rules and regulations – regarding punctuality and dress, for example.

Some pupils, however, will resist the rules and oppose the authority of teachers. Paul Willis's (1977) study of a group of 12 working-class boys, 'the lads', in a secondary school in the Midlands, showed that not all pupils are prepared to conform to the school's rules. 'The lads' developed their own informal counter-school culture based on opposition to the school. They would reject anyone who 'grassed' or who conformed.

Workplaces

On starting a new job, it is necessary to learn the culture of the workplace – the particular office, factory or hospital, for example. Newly appointed employees will learn the formal and informal rules regarding dress, punctuality and safety. They will learn tips informally from work mates and colleagues on such things as how much work is expected and which of the bosses to avoid.

Religions

Religions provide guidelines for behaviour and sanctions when those guidelines are broken. Christianity, for example, provides the ten commandments as a guide to how followers should behave. Muslims are expected to put into practice the five pillars of Islam, including the alms tax (giving a proportion of one's wealth to the poor) and fasting during daylight in the month of Ramadan.

Mass media

The mass media, which include television, radio and newspapers, are a powerful source of information and knowledge. The media have a role in gender socialization. Research, for example, has focused on the way in which males and females are represented in children's educational programmes such as *Sesame Street*. Dohrmann (1975) found that the male child was much more likely to be shown as heroic, whereas the female child was more likely to be shown as helpless and passive. It is possible that such messages affect attitudes and behaviour, particularly when reinforced within families and schools.

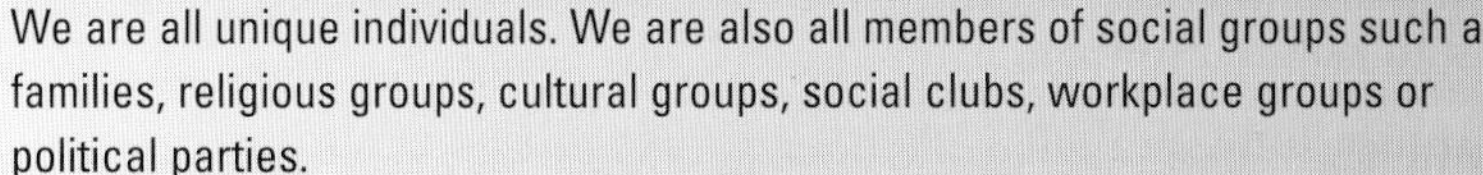

GROUP MEMBERS

We are all unique individuals. We are also all members of social groups such as families, religious groups, cultural groups, social clubs, workplace groups or political parties.

1 Identify two groups of which you are a member and, for each, explain briefly how the group has influenced your behaviour or the way you see yourself.
2 Do you think that human behaviour and beliefs are learned or instinctive?

CHECK YOUR UNDERSTANDING

What do sociologists mean by the terms:

1 socialization? (2 marks)
2 agencies of socialization? (2 marks)

SUMMARY

In this chapter we have covered the following points:

- **Sociology is the systematic study of human social life, groups and societies. Sociologists look at social institutions such as families and churches, and also at social processes such as discrimination and socialization.**
- **Sociologists ask questions about the things that go on in society, for example why people join religious sects, whether violence on the television causes copy-cat violence in 'real life'.**
- **Sociologists use various research methods to find the answers to such questions.**
- **Sources are either primary or secondary. Primary sources are based on research conducted at first hand, for example through questionnaires, interviews and participant observation. Secondary sources consist of data that has already been collated, for example official statistics, media reports, letters and diaries.**
- **Data is either quantitative or qualitative. Quantitative data is presented in numerical form, for example 97 per cent of people watch television. Qualitative data is presented in words and deals with preferences and feelings, which cannot always be put into figures.**
- **When conducting research, sociologists normally begin by selecting a sample, or subgroup of the population. Samples are selected either randomly or non-randomly.**
- **It is a good idea to use a pilot study to trial the chosen research method. This ensures that the method works and that it is cost-effective.**
- **Questionnaires are a popular way of conducting social research. Questions can be open-ended or closed. An advantage of questionnaires is that they can be a cost-effective way of reaching a large sample. A disadvantage is that they can have a low response rate.**
- **Interviews can be either structured or unstructured. Interviews are usually conducted face-to-face, so one problem to look out for is interview bias.**

- **Sociologists can also observe social groups to obtain information. Observation can be done either through participation (overt or covert) or through non-participation. Again, there are advantages and disadvantages to either method.**
- **In trying to explain human social life, sociologists have built up a vocabulary of key terms. You should be familiar with the following concepts: culture and subculture; values and norms; status and roles; socialization and the main agencies of socialization.**

EXAMINATION QUESTION 1

Read **Item A**. Then answer **all** parts of the question that follow.

Item A

The researchers carried out an investigation into the extent of poverty. It was based on whether or not individuals had a range of articles or possessions and, if they did not have them, whether this was because they could not afford them or by choice. They interviewed 91 people between November 1989 and May 1990. They used a 'quota sample', selecting possible interviewees to obtain the groups they were looking for. All the interviews with the Asian families were conducted in their mother tongue of Urdu or Pakistani by Asian researchers. The interviews were lengthy and were tape-recorded. The interview schedule was piloted in two areas similar to those in which the final study was conducted.

Adapted from R. Cohen, J. Coxley, G. Craig and A. Sadiq-Sangstar, *Hardship Britain: Being Poor in the 1990s*.

(a) With reference to **Item A**, identify the kind of sample used by the researchers. Indicate why they used this technique. (2 marks)

(b) With reference to **Item A**, what were the two ways in which the researchers attempted to make the Asian families feel comfortable and able to communicate easily? (2 marks)

(c) Suggest **one** reason why the researchers piloted their interview schedule. Why might they have used areas similar to those in the final study? (2 marks)

(d) (i) Suggest **one** reason why it might be better to use a relative rather than an absolute definition of poverty in this kind of study. (1 mark)

(ii) Identify and explain **one** advantage to the researchers of tape-recording the interviews. (3 marks)

(e) What advantages might face-to-face interviews have over postal questionnaires in this type of study? (8 marks)

Source: SEG GCSE Sociology, Summer 1997
Higher Tier Paper 2, Section C, Question 1, p. 3

EXAMINATION QUESTION 2

Study **Item A**. Then answer **all** parts of the question that follow.

Item A

Serious crimes recorded by the police in 1992 (England & Wales and Northern Ireland)

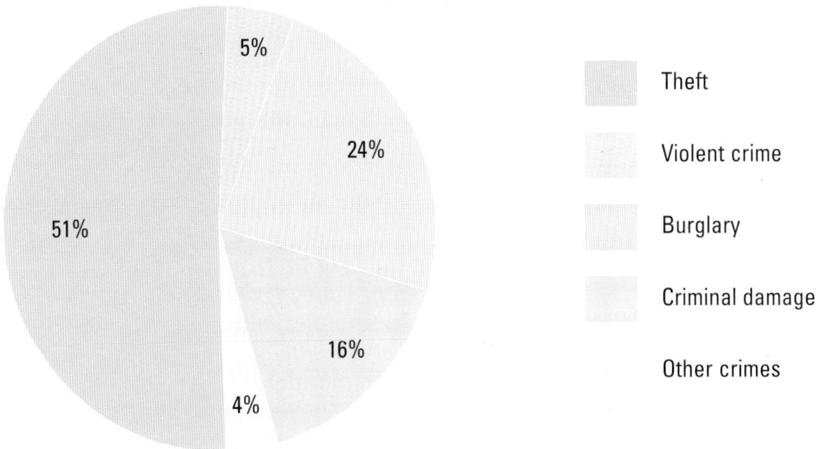

Source: *Social Trends* (1994)

(a) According to the information in **Item A**,

(i) what percentage of serious crime was recorded as
(1) violent crime;
(2) theft? (2 marks)

(ii) which serious crime made up 24 per cent of all crimes recorded? (1 mark)

(iii) in what year were these crimes recorded by the police? (1 mark)

(b) Give your answers as **Yes** or **No** to the following questions.

(i) Is it possible to tell from the pie chart how many offences of criminal damage were **actually** committed? (1 mark)

(ii) Is it possible to tell from the pie chart what type of crime was most commonly committed? (1 mark)

(c) Imagine you wish to do some research into criminal activities amongst 14- to 16-year-olds.

(i) Suggest **two** examples of information which you might want to find about this topic. In **each** case give a reason why. (4 marks)

(ii) Suggest **two** examples of secondary sources which you could use. Briefly explain why you might choose them. (4 marks)

(iii) Identify **two** suitable primary methods of research. In each case, explain why the method would be appropriate. (6 marks)

Source: SEG GCSE Sociology, Summer 1996
Foundation Tier, Paper 1, Section A, Question 1, pp. 2–3

BIBLIOGRAPHY

Barker, E. (1984) *The Making of a Moonie: Choice or Brainwashing?* Blackwell Publishers.

Billington, R., Strawbridge, S., Greensides, L. and Fitzsimons, A. (1991) *Culture and Society*, Macmillan.

Chang, J. (1993) *Wild Swans*, HarperCollins*Publishers*.

Cochran, W. G. (1977) *Sampling Techniques*, John Wiley and Sons.

Coleman, D. and Salt, J. (eds) (1996) *Ethnicity in the 1991 Census*, HMSO.

Denzin, N. K. and Lincoln, Y. S. (eds) (1994) *Handbook of Qualitative Research*, Sage.

Dohrmann, R. (1975) 'A gender profile of children's educational TV', *Journal of Communication*, No. 25, pp. 56–65.

Douglas, J. W. B. (1964) *The Home and the School*, Macgibbon & Kee.

Douglas, J. W. B., Ross, J. M. and Simpson, H. R. (1968) *All Our Future*, Peter Davies.

Maclean, C. (1979) *The Wolf Children: Fact or Fantasy?* Penguin Books.

O'Reilly, K. (1996) 'Using surveys and quantitative data in field research', *Sociology Review*, Volume 5, No. 3.

Patrick, J. (1973) *A Glasgow Gang Observed*, Eyre Methuen.

Schofield, M. (1965) *The Sexual Behaviour of Young People*, Longman.

Sharpe, S. (1994) *Just Like A Girl: From the Seventies to the Nineties*, Penguin Books.

Singh, J. A. L. and Zingg, R. M. (1966) *Wolf-Children and Feral Man*, Archon Books.

Taylor, C. F. (1996) *Native American Life*, Salamander Books.

Williams, J., Dunning, E. and Murphy, P. (1989) *Hooligans Abroad*, Routledge.

Williams, T. M. (1989) *The Cocaine Kids*, Addison-Wesley.

Willis, P. (1977) *Learning to Labour: How Working-Class Kids Get Working-Class Jobs*, Saxon House.

CHAPTER 3

Stratification and Differentiation

In this chapter, we will explore and attempt to answer the following questions:

1. **What are stratification and differentiation?**
2. **What types of stratification are there?**
   - **Caste**
   - **Apartheid**
   - **Feudalism**
3. **How is modern Britain stratified?**
4. **How important are:**
   - **gender**
   - **ethnicity**
   - **age**

   as forms of differentiation?
5. **Social class as a form of stratification.**
   - **How have sociologists tried to describe social class?**
   - **How can we measure social class?**
   - **What is the importance of social class?**
   - **What changes have taken place in the class structure of modern Britain?**
6. **What is the importance of wealth and income?**
7. **How socially mobile is modern Britain?**

WHAT ARE STRATIFICATION AND DIFFERENTIATION?

These terms are used by sociologists to describe the ways in which individuals in a society are divided up into various social groups.

- **Stratification** refers to the division of a society into hierarchically ordered layers – or strata – with the most privileged at the top and the least favoured at the bottom. The different layers tend to have unequally distributed levels of power, wealth and prestige.
- The term **power** refers to the ability of individuals to achieve their goals in society. Those at the top of the strata are likely to have the most power.
- **Wealth** refers to the possessions held by an individual. Those at the top of the strata are likely to have more wealth than those lower down.
- **Prestige** refers to the honour given to a particular job or role in society. This honour is often rewarded through high levels of pay. Those in the top strata tend to have roles that are high in prestige.

Different societies use various principles for deciding who will be placed where in the hierarchy. Once placed in the hierarchy, individuals may find it difficult to change or improve their position, although this will depend on the type of society in which they live.

Differentiation is a broader term that refers to social characteristics that make an individual or group separate and distinct from another, such as type of occupation, income, gender or ethnic background. Within each layer of a stratification system individuals may still be differentiated, for example by gender.

The forms of stratification and differentiation in a society are important to individuals in social groups as they can affect people's **life chances**. This term refers to a person's opportunities for success or failure in all aspects of life – health, education, employment and so on – as measured by what is considered desirable or undesirable. For example, in terms of health, women may have better life chances than men as they tend to live longer.

Two social groups with very different life chances

LIFE CHANCES

Life chances are measured in terms of such factors as health, education, income, leisure and housing.

1 For each of these factors, identify what might be the minimum desirable level; for example, under health, you might consider access to a general practitioner as the minimum desirable level.

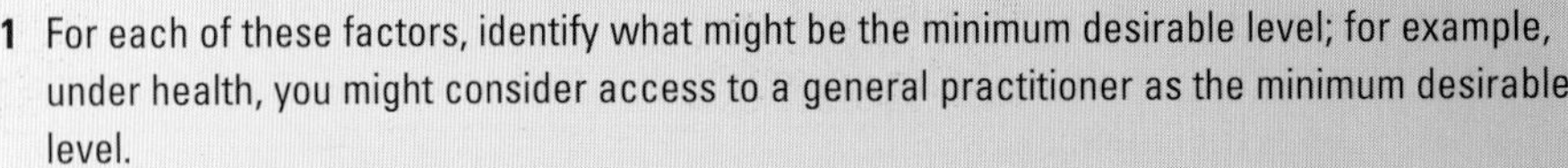

2 For each of these factors, compare the life chances of the social groups shown in the photos.

It is clear, then, that the study of stratification and differentiation is fundamental to our understanding of the divisions that exist in contemporary society.

WHAT TYPES OF STRATIFICATION ARE THERE?

The principles used to stratify people change over time and can vary between societies. For example, slavery was, historically, a common form of stratification, and the major division between people was whether or not they were free.

The social characteristics of age, gender, ethnic origin and social class have also been used as ways to rank people according to their access to wealth, power and prestige.

STRATIFYING BRITAIN

In a small group, complete the following tasks:

1 Make a list of criteria that could be used to stratify or divide people up in Britain.
2 Rank your list in order of what you think are the most to least important criteria. Be prepared to explain your decisions.

Some systems of stratification are based on the idea of ascription, that is, that your position in society is ascribed to you at birth. Other systems are based on the idea that individuals can achieve their position in society, for example through hard work, education, marriage or a windfall such as a National Lottery win. In some cases, an individual's position may result from a mix of ascription and achievement.

A stratification system can also be analysed according to how **open** or **closed** it is. These terms refer to how easy it is for an individual to move up, or down, in the strata of that society.

In an open society, people can move between the layers. This will be easier in some societies than others depending on the degree of openness. In closed societies, this movement is unlikely. This movement between layers is known as **social mobility**.

Societies based on ascription will be closed and have relatively little or no mobility, while those in which social position can be achieved are said to be more open, with higher levels of mobility.

Social characteristics and position can be ascribed at birth

CASE STUDIES: SYSTEMS OF STRATIFICATION

The caste system

Figure 3.1 The caste system
(Traditionally found in India)

BRAHMIN	priests/teachers	higher status
KSHATRYAS	soldiers/landlords	
VAISHYAS	merchants/traders	lower status
SHUDRAS	servants/manual workers	
DALITS ('untouchables')	do the worst jobs in society	social outcasts

The caste system illustrated in Figure 3.1 is based on ascription – a person is born into a particular caste. The system is closed, with little or no social mobility, and contact between members of different castes is frowned upon. The caste system was founded on Hinduism and the belief in reincarnation – that is, that individuals are reborn into a new life after death. A person's position in the caste system depends on their conduct in their previous life – the worse their conduct then, the lower their caste in this life. A person's caste position is effectively God-given, and there is little a person can do about it except to try to live a good life in the hope of being reborn into a higher caste.

Apartheid

This stratification system used to operate in South Africa. Under apartheid, ethnic background was used as the basis for stratifying people. Every aspect of society – including access to health, education, housing and employment – was segregated according to whether a person was black or white. Vigorous opposition to apartheid within South Africa was led by individuals such as Nelson Mandela and Archbishop Desmond Tutu, while many thousands of people in countries around the world also strongly opposed the apartheid system.

This system had similarities with the caste system in that a person's position in society was ascribed at birth. Black people were denied the educational and employment opportunities available to white people and their life chances were consequently much worse, with little or no possibility of moving from one layer of society to another.

An example of how apartheid in South Africa divided people up

Feudalism

King

Nobility

Knights

Peasants (serfs)

The feudal system

This system operated, for example, in medieval Europe, Russia and Japan in the early twentieth century.

In this system, stratification was based on four layers in society called estates. All subjects swore allegiance to the king, whose authority was seen as God-given. Nobles were rewarded by the king with land. Some of this land was, in turn, given by the nobles to knights who swore allegiance to them. At the bottom of the system, peasants, or serfs, were given the use of small pieces of land in exchange for some of their produce and for military service.

A person's position in society was ascribed and there was little or no chance of moving up to the next estate. As with the caste system and apartheid, marriage between members of different estates was unthinkable.

HOW IS MODERN BRITAIN STRATIFIED?

In most modern industrial societies **social class** is the major form of division between individuals and groups.

Social class is based on **economic factors**, such as occupation and income, and not on religious teaching or ethnic background. Although people might be divided into different social class groups, this stratification system is said to be open in the sense that class position can be achieved, social mobility is possible and intermarriage is acceptable between members of different classes.

However, it is important to note that sociologists are increasingly examining the importance of other forms of differentiation in British society based on **gender**, **ethnic background** and **age**. For example, within a particular social class, men and women may have very different experiences or life chances. Some sociologists argue that women from lower and higher social classes have more in common with one another than they do with men from their own social class. In other words, gender is a more important division in society than social class.

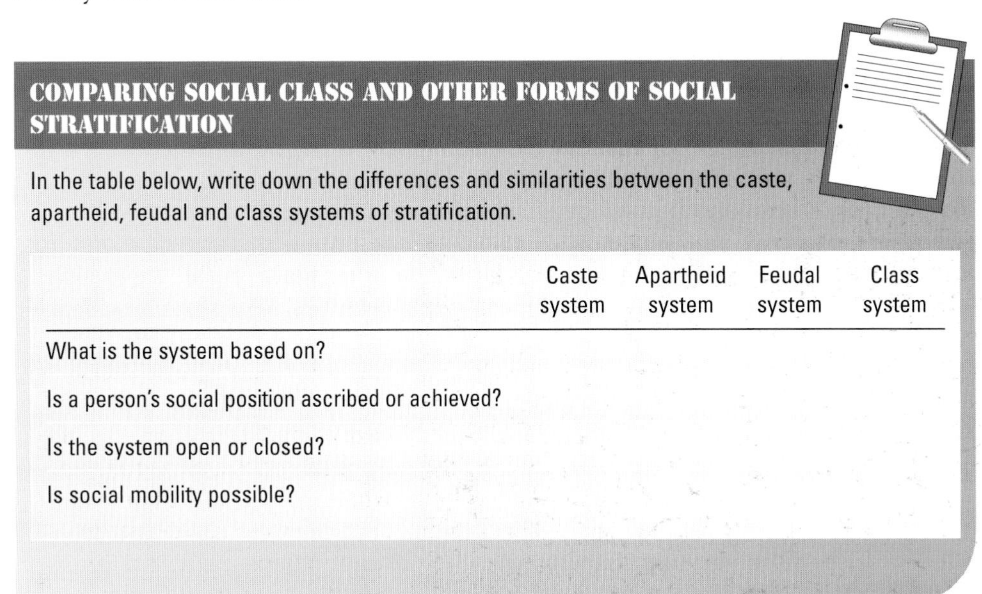

COMPARING SOCIAL CLASS AND OTHER FORMS OF SOCIAL STRATIFICATION

In the table below, write down the differences and similarities between the caste, apartheid, feudal and class systems of stratification.

	Caste system	Apartheid system	Feudal system	Class system
What is the system based on?				
Is a person's social position ascribed or achieved?				
Is the system open or closed?				
Is social mobility possible?				

CHECK YOUR UNDERSTANDING

1 Identify and explain one form of social stratification other than social class. (4 marks)
2 Identify and explain two differences between class and feudalism. (4 marks)
3 Identify two other sources of differentiation in modern Britain other than class. (2 marks)

HOW IMPORTANT IS GENDER AS A FORM OF DIFFERENTIATION?

For some sociologists, the divisions in society between men and women are seen as being more important than social class as a form of difference.

Feminist researchers, in particular, are interested in examining the position and role of women in society in relation to men. From the feminist point of view, society is seen as **patriarchal**. This refers to the idea that males are the leaders of society and exercise control in a range of areas, for example within the family or at work. As such, they may experience better life chances than women.

This situation is often thought to be based on the idea that males are somehow naturally superior to females. Feminists question this assumption and seek to attribute the source of differences between men and women to the influence of the socialization process.

What is the difference between sex and gender?

The term **sex** is used to describe the **natural** or **biological** differences between males and females, such as differences in genitalia and reproductive roles. These characteristics are ascribed at birth and are usually permanent.

Gender refers to the cultural differences between men and women that are usually learned through the process of socialization. This leads to individuals displaying the appropriate masculine or feminine behaviour for their sex. For example, a masculine gender role (the expected behaviour for a man), learned through socialization, might be that of 'breadwinner' in a family. A feminine gender role might be that of 'homemaker'.

As these differences are learned through the process of socialization into the culture of a society, they can be said to be **socially constructed** rather than naturally occurring.

The nature/nurture debate

Some researchers argue that **nature** (sex difference) is the main influence on the roles played by men and women in society. The role of women as homemakers, for example, is seen as a natural extension of their biological role in giving birth. For others, **nurture** (influence of society) is thought to be the main factor, with women seen, instead, as being socialized into the homemaker role.

ARE DIFFERENCES BETWEEN MEN AND WOMEN 'NATURAL'?

In a small group,

1 Make a list of ways in which men and women can be seen as different.
2 Discuss whether or not these differences are natural or a result of the influence of society.
3 Are any of the differences a mixture of both?

Ann Oakley (1972) suggests that although a person's sex may be identified through biological evidence, it cannot be assumed that they will display behaviour appropriate to their masculine or feminine gender roles. Males and females may behave in ways usually associated with the opposite gender.

Equally, as a result of advances in technology, it is now possible for individuals to take on the biological characteristics of the opposite sex. In this way, it can be seen that sex is usually, but not always, constant, while gender varies culturally and historically.

How might gender vary between cultures?

It is argued that different cultures define gender differently – in other words, there is cultural variation in gender roles.

In 1935, the anthropologist Margaret Mead studied three tribes in New Guinea:

(a) The Arapesh – in which the ideal for adults of both sexes was to be gentle, caring and passive and to share in the care and upbringing of children. In other words, both sexes behaved in ways that we might define as feminine.

(b) The Mundugumor – in which adults were assertive, aggressive and hated childbirth and child rearing. Here, both sexes behaved in what we might consider a masculine way.

(c) The Tchambuli – among whom the women were assertive, practical and managing. The men, on the other hand, were interested in art, gossip and jewellery. In this case, the gender roles we might expect were reversed.

Although the truth of Margaret Mead's findings has been called into question in recent years, her examples suggest that, although biological differences might remain the same, gender roles differ in different societies and are therefore not natural.

CULTURAL DIFFERENCES IN GENDER ROLES

Examine the photograph and the extract below.

There have been some symbolic successes for women in Britain which the optimist might interpret as the beginning of further changes to come. In the armed forces, for example, 1995 saw the first female bomber pilot to be declared combat ready. Flight Lieutenant Jo Salter, a pilot with the RAF, flies Tornado bombers and serves with 617 squadron – the legendary Dambusters. Her combat-ready status means that she may be sent into action in war – thus overturning a policy that has hitherto prevented women in the forces from engaging in active combat. The RAF started training female air-crew in 1989 for transport aircraft duties. Since 1991, though, the training has opened up to combat training as well. In 1995, there were 28 female pilots in training and 9 female pilots actually on duty with squadrons.

Source: adapted from Denscombe (1996)

Women in Israel have been in combat troops for many years

1. What cultural difference in gender roles is being described?
2. Explain what the extract tells us about how gender roles have changed over time.

How have gender divisions in Britain changed?

If gender divisions are socially constructed, then we should expect them to alter over time to reflect changes in how society sees the role of men and women and the socialization process. In other words, gender varies historically.

Clearly, many changes have already taken place, for example in education and employment. These have been supported by legal changes, such as the Sex Discrimination Act in 1975, which made it unlawful for an employer to discriminate against women, or men, on the grounds of sex or marriage. The **Equal Opportunities Commission** was also set up at this time to ensure that this Act and others are properly enforced in order to challenge **sexism**. This term refers to discrimination against a person or group because of their biological sex. Historically, most sexism has been directed at women, but the term can equally be applied to men.

Table 3.1 Some key changes in women's employment status, 1972–95

1972	First woman judge to sit at the Old Bailey: Rose Heilbron QC
1973	First woman on London Stock Exchange: Susan Shaw
1979	First woman Prime Minister: Margaret Thatcher
1979	First woman president of British Medical Association: Josephine Barnes
1983	First woman Lord Mayor of London: Dame Mary Donaldson
1984	First woman General Secretary of a large trade union: Brenda Dean, SOGAT
1984	First woman Law Commissioner: Brenda Hoggett
1992	First woman Speaker of the House of Commons: Betty Boothroyd
1992	First woman Director of the Crown Prosecution Service: Barbara Mills
1993	First woman Civil Service Commissioner: Ann Bowtell
1993	First woman Head of MI5: Stella Rimmington
1995	First woman member of Bank of England's Court of Directors: Frances Heaton
1995	First woman Chief Constable: Pauline Clare, Lancashire Constabulary
1995	First woman Executive Director under 30 of a top company: Lisa Gordon, Chrysalis

Source: Equal Opportunities Commission, in Donnellan (1996)

Some aspects of sport have changed

THE CHANGING FACE OF SPORT

Examine the following extract and answer the questions:

1 Identify in which sports sexism has only recently been successfully challenged.
2 Outline how ideas to do with (a) biological differences and (b) gender socialization might be used to explain the continued existence of this discrimination.

Sporting chances

1976: Then...

Twenty years ago, girls were not allowed to play rugby or football at school and women were not even allowed to play in official darts games.

1996: Now...

In 1995, for the first time, a girl – Sophie Cox, age 11 – played Rugby League for her team at Wembley, and women competed equally with men for a place in the darts World Championships.

Sport is one of the areas in which long, hard battles have been fought for greater equality between the sexes. Many schools now offer the full range of sports to girls and boys. Women now compete in almost all sports and take part increasingly in traditional men's sports such as rugby and cricket. However, outside the education system, many sporting activities are still open to young people of one sex only, and there are still male domains which women have not entered, such as the pavilion at Lords' Cricket Ground.

Source: adapted from Equal Opportunities Commission, in Donnellan (1996)

Some researchers argue that the types of changes examined so far have clearly affected the values and aspirations of younger women in society.

According to the Fawcett Society (1996), 'the 7.5 million young women between 18 and 34 in the UK are the first generation to have benefited entirely from the battles of the women's rights movements of the 1970s ... they want to work, to be economically independent, to choose when and whether to have a family, and expect to be able to continue their careers.' In this way, it is suggested, young women today are less likely to be socialized to accept the traditional gender roles of the past.

Indeed, there are some who now believe that it is young men who are becoming increasingly likely to find that their traditional gender roles are being challenged and that they face sexism.

A CRISIS IN MASCULINITY?

1 According to the extract, what changes have taken place in male and female gender characteristics?
2 What might the effect of this change be on men?
3 Identify two arguments for and two against the idea that it is now men who are the victims of sexism and negative stereotyping.

'There is a genuine crisis among young males. Twenty years ago, psychological research indicated that male characteristics, such as decisiveness and rational thinking, were perceived by both men and women to be more valuable than female characteristics such as tearfulness and emotional subjectivity. Nowadays, the situation is reversed, men are seen as violent and insensitive, women as thoughtful and in touch with their feelings.

Feminists rightly opposed negative stereotyping of women. They did not want girls to be told that they were good for little more than looking pretty and raising babies. Why should young men who have been told that their sex is inferior not be equally diminished by the experience?

Source: adapted from an article by David Thomas, quoted in Donnellan (1994)

Look carefully: who is treating whom in a sexist way?

How can gender affect life chances?

We can assess the influence of gender as a form of division in society by examining its influence on the life chances of men and women in a range of areas.

Figure 3.2 The influence of gender

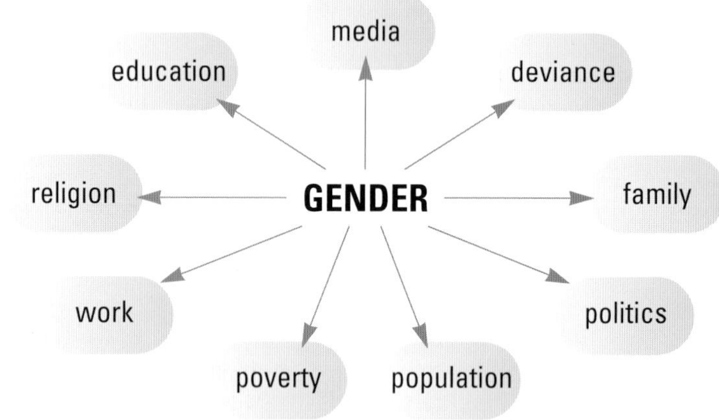

In order to explore further the influence of gender in these areas, refer to the relevant chapters in this book.

It is important to realize that gender is not an isolated influence. It may combine with social class, ethnic background and age to create further sources of difference. For example, while two women may face discrimination on the basis of their gender, if one is black, this may lead to a different form of discrimination for her.

CHECK YOUR UNDERSTANDING

1. Identify and explain two ways in which gender differences in society have changed. (4 marks)
2. Identify two ways in which gender could affect an individual's life chances. (2 marks)

HOW IMPORTANT IS ETHNICITY AS A FORM OF DIFFERENTIATION?

As we have seen in the case of apartheid in South Africa, ethnic background can be used as the main basis for stratification in a society. However, some sociologists argue that in any society, ethnicity will form a major area of division affecting an individual's life chances significantly.

The term **ethnicity** describes a characteristic of social groups who have a sense of shared identity based on cultural, religious or traditional influences. Such social groups are described as **ethnic groups**, for example Indians, African Asians, Greek Cypriots.

The term **ethnic minority** is used to describe groups of people who are from a different ethnic group to the general population – who, in turn, may be described as the **ethnic majority**. The label 'ethnic minority' is often used in Britain to refer only to a limited number of ethnic groups, such as people whose family origin is India, Pakistan, Bangladesh, the Caribbean or Africa. However, it is important to remember that Britain has always been home to a wide range of ethnic groups, including those of Irish, Chinese, Greek, Italian and Polish origin.

A BRIEF HISTORY OF ETHNIC MINORITIES IN BRITAIN

Read the following extract.

Britain has for centuries been home to people from many parts of the world. Romans, Angles, Saxons and Normans came as invaders and conquerors. Others came as traders or to find work. Jewish and Irish people – and many others – came to escape from war, famine or religious hatred in their own countries. There were also those who had no choice – Africans brought to Britain by force as slaves or servants. People from countries such as India, Pakistan, Bangladesh and the West Indies were invited here after the Second World War because there were not enough people to do all the jobs.

There have always been people with roots in other parts of the world. In 1764, there were about 20,000 black people in London. When Jewish people first came to Britain more than 1,000 years ago, they had to obey all sorts of special rules. They were treated cruelly, called names and often attacked. When black and Asian people arrived in the 1940s, they faced similar experiences to Jewish people centuries before.

Source: adapted from Commission for Racial Equality and BBC, 'No room for racism' (1994), in Donnellan (1995a)

1 Identify reasons why people have come to Britain in the past.
2 Using the extract, write a short paragraph explaining how ethnic minority communities, and some of the problems they face, are not 'new' to Britain.

The level of **discrimination** is one of the main reasons why ethnicity is seen as a key source of inequality and division in society.

The term **racism** (or **racial discrimination**) can be used here. This refers to the way in which people are treated less favourably or in an openly hostile manner as a result of their ethnic origin. Racism can take the form of **individual racism**, for example using abusive language or behaviour, and **institutional racism**, with discrimination existing in the laws and policies of a society, such as being denied access to jobs, housing, education and other services.

The term **race** refers to the idea that human beings could be divided up into different 'racial groups' as a result of physical characteristics. Some 'races' were thought to be more advanced than others and this has been used to justify the oppression of one group by another, for example the colonization of parts of Africa and Asia in the nineteenth century by Europeans.

These ideas about 'races' have now been shown to have no scientific basis. In this way, the idea of racial differences can be seen to have been **socially constructed**, in much the same way as gender differences. However, ideas about 'races' are still used by some to justify their discrimination against ethnic minorities.

RACIST VIOLENCE

In a small group, read the following extracts and note down answers to the questions that follow.

Reported incidents of racial violence have increased sharply in the past year and doubled in the last five years, a new survey of police forces in England and Wales shows. In some regions, the number of reported incidents, including assaults, threats and vandalism, has risen by up to twentyfold.

The Home Office says the number of reported incidents may have risen during the past five years because of the increased confidence and awareness among ethnic minority groups, who are now more willing to contact the police. Yesterday's figures, however, still only give a snapshot of the true scale of racist abuse in Britain – there could be as many as 130,000 incidents every year.

Source: adapted from Donnellan (1995a) and an article by Jason Bennetto, *The Independent*, March 1994

Asif is an Asian shopkeeper on a large housing estate in Derby, highlighted by the police as a problem area. His family have been terrorized by a teenage gang hurling bricks and bottles at his property and screaming racist abuse. 'The strain on my wife and three children is tremendous,' he said. 'They can't even walk alone around here in case they are picked on.'

During the latest incident, Asif was comforting his frightened, 11-year-old asthmatic son when a brick hit the window. 'I could have been killed' he says, as he draws back the curtain to show the shattered glass. However, having recognized some of the youths earlier that day, Asif provided names and descriptions and six members of the gang were arrested.

For the police, catching members of the gang has proved difficult, as WPC Kim Davidson explains. 'People won't give us their name or come to court. They will tell you what they've seen off the record but daren't make statements. They are simply too scared.'

Source: adapted from Donnellan (1995a) and an article by Patrick Weir, *The Guardian*, July 1994

1 Give reasons why the statistics on the numbers of racist attacks might be an underestimate.
2 Make a list of the effects these incidents could have on a family.

DISCRIMINATION IN LANGUAGE

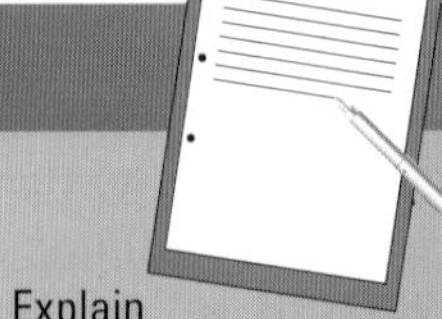

Read the extract and answer the questions that follow:

Discrimination is reinforced by our language. We can choose to dehumanize and focus attention on one aspect of an individual by using terms such as 'blacks'. However, we could choose to recognize that people are people first of all by saying 'black people'. Black people are saying that care should be taken to choose terms that value rather than devalue them as individuals.

The term 'black' includes people from a wide range of communities with huge cultural, social, linguistic and religious differences. Nevertheless, it is a convenient way of emphasizing black people's shared experience as identifiable targets and victims of racism.

So next time how about:	instead of:
black person	coloured
mixed race	half-caste
black people	blacks

Language perpetuates stereotypes ... stereotypes perpetuate racism ... Mind your language!

Source: adapted from Donnellan (1995a) and SCADU, 'They all look the same to me – combating racism through language', February 1994

1 Explain why choice of language is important.
2 Why is the term 'black' used to describe people from a wide range of communities?
3 Explain how use of language could lead to discrimination against two other groups of people in society.

Some racism can be related to a lack of knowledge of the facts about ethnic minority groups and a range of issues, such as population levels and employment.

The **Commission for Racial Equality (CRE)** was set up in 1976 as a result of the Race Relations Act. Its role is to work towards the elimination of racial discrimination through promoting equal opportunities and ensuring that relevant legislation is adhered to in practice.

HOW IS THE POSITION OF ETHNIC MINORITIES IN BRITAIN CHANGING?

Some researchers argue that there is much evidence to suggest that ethnicity is becoming less important as a form of stratification in Britain, and black people are gaining more influence in society.

For example, in politics, the numbers of non-white Members of Parliament (MPs) and local councillors are increasing, although they are still massively under-represented. Black people also have a higher profile in the media, arts, sport and trade unions. Indeed, a recent report in *The Guardian* (1995) suggested that people felt, overall, that things had improved, with racism seen as less blatant than it used to be.

However, others argue that in some of the most vital areas – such as employment, treatment by the criminal justice system, education and racist violence – little has really changed. Even in areas where progress appears to have been made, for example in the media, critics express doubts:

WITHOUT PREJUDICE

These things are as easy to repeat as they are untrue. Next time you hear the things they say, remember the facts we give you here.

THEY SAY...
They're still flooding in when the country's crowded with millions of them.

FACT
Immigration is strictly controlled and relatively few people are allowed to settle. More people leave Britain to live abroad than come to live here. Of those who come to live in Britain, 61 per cent are white. Only 1 in 20 people living in Britain – that's 5 per cent of the population – is black or Asian.

THEY SAY...
They should learn to be British like us.

FACT
Nearly half the black and Asian people living here were born in Britain. People abroad are quite clear who they see as British. For them the British person they know is now as likely to be Linford Christie winning a gold medal in the Olympics as it is to be John Major or Tony Blair.

THEY SAY...
They're taking our jobs.

FACT
Black, Asian or Irish people are more likely to be unemployed than the average. Far from taking our jobs, such workers are often doing jobs others have chosen not to do, perhaps because they are too dirty, too hard or the wages are too low.

Source: Commission for Racial Equality and BBC, 'No room for racism' (1994), in Donnellan (1995a)

The Commission for Racial Equality tries to promote the facts

There are now more black people in front of the camera than ever before. But on the executive floors – where real decisions are made about scheduling, programme style and tone – there are virtually no black faces. Minorities, it seems, are welcome as long as they don't expect to have any influence. This is a picture that would be recognizable in virtually every walk of life in Britain.

Source: Trevor Phillips, in a speech to the Runnymede Trust, September 1994, quoted in Gary Younge, 'Where are we now?', *The Guardian*, Black in Britain series, 20 March 1995

From this point of view, changes have been made, but not in terms of access to power and influence in society.

A SIGN OF PROGRESS?

Read the extract and answer the questions that follow.

Naomi Campbell apart, black models are rare in British advertising. But that may be about to change.

Black sportsmen, musicians and celebrities have been used within mainstream advertising, but the use of anonymous black models in both fashion and advertising is still rare.

In the UK, the representation of black beauty in advertising fashion or in magazines is significantly lower than in the US. The most common explanation for the infrequent use of black models in fashion is that they are bad for business. The argument goes that because black families have lower household incomes than their white counterparts, it does not make financial sense to promote products using black models – as though black models could not appeal to every other ethnic group in the population.

Current statistics suggest that there is every reason to feature more black models within advertising and fashion as a result of the gradual establishment of a black middle class.

Source: adapted from Harriet Quick, 'Undercover girls', *The Guardian*, Black in Britain series, 22 March 1995

Modelling opportunities for black people may be improving

1 In which areas of advertising are black models unlikely to be used?
2 According to the extract, why are black models less likely to be used than white models?
3 What criticism can be made of this argument?
4 Why might we expect to see more black models in the future?

A. Sivanandan, a director of the Institute for Race Relations, has suggested that there has been an improvement in the situation of some black people in Britain, who now form what has been termed a black middle class. They may be in professional and managerial occupations but are likely to have had very different social circumstances to their white counterparts and are as likely to experience racism as other black people in Britain. Nevertheless, changes such as this have made black communities in Britain more diverse and stratified, experiencing different lifestyles and life chances.

In order more fully to assess the influence of ethnicity as a form of stratification, you should refer to other relevant chapters in this book. It is also important to remember that ethnicity can combine with gender, age and social class to create further sources of difference among individuals. For example, the experiences of young, black, unemployed males will be different to those of female black professionals.

CHECK YOUR UNDERSTANDING

1 Identify two ways in which racism could take place in modern Britain. (2 marks)
2 Identify and explain two ways in which the position of ethnic minority groups may have changed in contemporary British society. (4 marks)

HOW IMPORTANT IS AGE AS A FORM OF DIFFERENTIATION?

What is 'age'? We can answer this question in a number of different ways:

1 We can see an individual's age as being determined by how long they have been alive. Thus, someone born in 1930 would be 67 years old in 1997. This is known as a person's **chronological** age and it may be used to indicate what kinds of activities an individual can become involved in. For example, someone with a chronological age of 16 would not be allowed to buy an alcoholic drink in British society. However, the chronological age for drinking may be different depending on the society in which you live.

2 Age can also be seen in **biological** terms. Here, a person's age may be related to the physical changes taking place in their bodies. For example, early in a human's life, the process of puberty takes place, while greying hair and wrinkles usually indicate a person is in the later stages of life. Biological changes are usually linked to a person's chronological age.

3 Sociologists are particularly interested in the way age can be seen in **social** terms. People will be treated differently, and be associated with certain expectations, according to their age. For example, a person of 72 would not be expected to play with children's toys on their own. Equally, a person of 14 is not expected to have the ability to make an informed decision and vote in a general election.

Age can determine what you are expected to do by other people

In this way, age can be seen as being **socially constructed** as expectations of different age groups will vary between cultures and at different times in history.

We can examine how historical and cultural attitudes and expectations related to age can affect individuals and their life chances by looking at three broad groups: childhood, youth and old age.

Childhood

Some researchers argue that in the past, childhood was very different to that experienced in modern Britain. For example, Ariès (1962) suggests that in medieval times children were seen as small adults and fully participated in the adult worlds of work and leisure. In the nineteenth century, child labour was the norm in the working classes – children were considered as particularly suitable for certain kinds of work such as chimney sweeping. In contemporary Britain, child labour is not only considered unacceptable but it is illegal.

Changes have taken place in laws relating to children, such as their legal rights, sexual

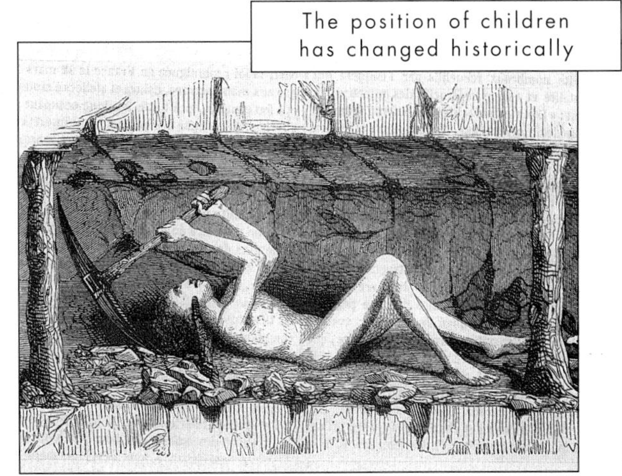
The position of children has changed historically

behaviour and employment opportunities, as well as in education with the gradual introduction of compulsory schooling. In this way, the position and status of children in Britain can be seen to have changed **historically**, with children in contemporary society clearly having a different status to adults.

DIFFERENT ATTITUDES TO CHILDREN AND ADULTS

In a small group, discuss the different attitudes and expectations associated with children and adults in modern Britain in terms of the law, food habits, clothing styles and television preferences.

To what extent, and in which circumstances, is it possible for children and adults to go against expectations in each of these areas?

In most Western societies, childhood is seen as a separate stage to adulthood, and children are regarded as dependent and vulnerable. Children are legally protected from exploitation in the workplace. However, in some other cultures, the division between childhood and adulthood is less marked, with children often being expected to fend for themselves or to play an adult role at work. In this way, childhood can be seen to vary culturally.

CHILD LABOUR

Read the following extract and answer the questions that follow.

> *The exploitation of children as a source of cheap labour has emerged as a growing concern. The International Labour Organization (ILO) estimates that, worldwide, the number of children involved in full-time jobs is 120 million. If part-time labour is included the figure for child workers rises to double that amount – around 250 million. The ILO report concludes that the use of child labour is most concentrated in developing countries, such as parts of Africa, Indonesia and Latin America.*
>
> *A large proportion, says the report, work in dangerous industries like mining, agriculture and glass factories, where they work long hours and are exposed to disease. Very young children are working in firework and match factories across the Indian subcontinent. An increasing number of children are involved in the sex trade – as many as 1 million in Asia alone.*
>
> Source: Denscombe (1997)

1. According to the extract, where does most child labour take place?
2. Identify three types of jobs children are doing.
3. In what ways might working long hours, in poor conditions, for low pay affect children's life chances?

Youth

This is seen as a period of transition between childhood and adulthood. In contemporary Britain, youth is recognized as an important stage of development in which individuals begin to leave the dependent and powerless world of the child and enter the world of the adult.

Key changes during youth:

- may leave education and enter employment
- may become independent of family
- may become involved in adult activities, such as drinking, driving a car, sex
- increased status in society

However, it is difficult to decide chronologically when youth begins and ends. For example, some researchers suggest that children in Britain are growing up more quickly in terms of their attitudes and expectations in a range of areas of life, for example having bank accounts, attitudes to fashion, sexual behaviour, and so on. Thus, is a 13-year-old a child or a youth?

Equally, young people may continue to be partially dependent on their parents or guardians into their twenties, for example university students or those living at home because of a lack of work. In this sense, we may not consider them to be independent adults. The transition to adulthood is therefore not clear or precise in modern Britain.

However, in some other cultures (especially those where adults and children lead very similar lives in terms of work, leisure, and so on) the transition from childhood to adulthood is more clearly marked, with no period of 'youth'. Here, greater significance may be placed on the biological process of puberty as a sign of adulthood and the transition from childhood status is easier to complete. Individuals may undergo a **rite of passage** (a social event or ceremony) to indicate their new status.

RITES OF PASSAGE

Read the following extract.

In a small group, discuss whether or not there are any rites of passage in modern Britain to mark the transition between:

- childhood and adulthood;
- adulthood and the onset of old age.

Make a note of your responses.

The Chisunga initiation ceremony of the Bemba people of Zambia

According to a study by Richards in 1982, this ceremony secures the transition from a calm but unproductive girlhood to a potentially dangerous but fertile womanhood. The ceremony takes place after a girl has had her first period and after this event has itself been marked by a separate puberty rite. The puberty rite may involve ceremonial washing of the girl and isolation indoors before her return to the community.

The girl then waits until it is convenient for her Chisunga ceremony to begin. This ceremony is composed of many individual rituals, including the physical testing of the girl through various ordeals, her social isolation as a form of ritual separation and the singing of ritual songs. The ceremony lasts for over a month and ends with the girl's change of status being marked by the end of her social isolation.

The girl is bathed, dressed in new clothes, brought out of the hut and placed on a new mat outside its door. The girl sits in silence in front of the villagers, who throw small presents onto the mat. At the end of the ceremony, girls are considered ready for marriage, and often a marriage ceremony immediately follows.

Source: Pilcher (1995)

Youth subcultures

An important aspect of youth in some modern industrial societies is the growth of **youth subcultures** (see p. 28). This has been linked to the growing affluence of young people, with manufacturers increasingly targeting products such as music and fashion at the 'youth market'.

The growth of the mass media has also been seen as important in the rapid transmission of new ideas and trends to young people. Coupled with this, the amount of leisure time available to young people has increased since children became freed from paid employment, thus giving time for them to become interested in music, fashion, and so on.

These changes have given rise to a huge range of different youth subcultures, some of which reflect specific gender, ethnic, and social class differences.

THE YOUTH MARKET

Read the following extract and answer the questions.

Manufacturers have sought to target young consumers

Alcopops

*Hooper's Hooch was launched in 1995. It has paved the way for about 90 brands of alcopop drinks on the market with estimated UK sales for 1997 of $200 million. The vast majority of alcopop sales – 70 per cent – are in pubs. Alcopop is marketed at the young, inexperienced drinker and is regarded as 'effectively a mechanism for getting alcohol into the bloodstream without having to upset unsophisticated taste buds with all those nasty warm beers and strong-smelling whiskies' (*The Guardian*, 12 September 1996).*

The cider market has been hit hard by the success of alcopops. Cider manufacturers have spent large sums of money in recent years trying to give cider a new image to appeal to a younger clientele. Young women, in particular, have been targeted. Alcopops have proved to be much more appealing to this group since the launch of Hooch and other alcopop brands. Not surprisingly, cider manufacturers are quickly shifting their output from cider to new brands of alcopop.

Source: Denscombe (1997)

1. What were the estimated sales of alcopops in 1997?
2. At which group are alcopops marketed?
3. Why are alcopops thought to appeal to this group in particular?
4. Which youth group has now been targeted by cider manufacturers?
5. Explain why cider manufacturers have done this.
6. To what extent would you agree that young people are exploited by advertisers and manufacturers? Explain your answer.

The 'problem' of youth

Other researchers, such as Ian Taylor (1996), have suggested that young people are now being blamed for many of society's problems, such as increasing violence, crime, drug use and lack of morality. In effect, youth is seen as a **problem**.

As a result, governments have reacted in a variety of ways, for example excluding troublesome young people from schools, introducing 'boot camps' for young offenders and criticizing young single parents. Taylor argues that rather than young people being the problem, they are the ones facing the problems, for example: high unemployment; homelessness; increased stress and anxiety as a result of pressures to succeed educationally; often being the victims of crime themselves; and increased peer-group pressures arising from media advertising.

From this point of view, youth can be seen as an age where individuals may encounter significant social and personal problems.

Old age

Many of the aspects of old age that we take for granted in contemporary Britain, such as retirement and pensions, are in fact relatively recent developments. Before the introduction of state-run old age pensions in 1908, older people stopped working once they were physically unable to continue rather than at a specified age. Retirement has only really been accepted as the norm in Britain since the middle of the twentieth century. Thus the position of older people in society has changed **historically**.

WHEN DOES OLD AGE BEGIN?

Read the following extract and answer the questions.

You're as old as you feel

There is no fixed point at which old age begins. Are you old when your hair turns grey and you start to get wrinkles? This is a gradual process and does not happen at the same time for all people.

Or are you old when you retire from work? Again, this is not a foolproof test because, in Western societies, people are retiring earlier and earlier. Even being a grandparent is not a sure sign: it is quite possible to have grandchildren in your early 40s and some people do not have children at all.

Age Concern publishes a leaflet for the elderly about 'ageism' – prejudice against old people – called *How to Avoid Becoming an Old Codger*. 'Unfortunately, it's not that easy,' it begins. 'That's because you don't choose when you become an old codger. It's up to other people.' Old age, like beauty, is in the eye of the beholder.

Source: article in *The Guardian*, 1994, from Donnellan (1995b)

1 Explain why retirement and being a grandparent are not necessarily good indicators of old age.
2 Explain what is meant by the idea that it is up to other people to decide when you are old.
3 What does this information suggest about how our ideas about old age might change in the future?

The status of older people can also be viewed in terms of **cultural** differences. In modern Britain, getting older is often seen as something to be avoided. Indeed, some people turn to plastic surgery as a means of combating the ageing process. However, in certain other cultures, old age is viewed as something to look forward to, with older people receiving high status in a society.

OLD AGE AND CULTURAL DIFFERENCES

Read the following extract and answer the questions.

For the Sherbro people of Sierra Leone, incoherent or incomprehensible speech by an aged person is viewed as a positive sign. Their incoherence indicates their close communication with ancestors, who are regarded as important in deciding an individual's destiny.

Similarly, for the Venda-speaking people of Southern Africa, old age is regarded as a 'pleasure'. Signs of old age, such as greying hair or the birth of a grandchild, are welcomed as indications of a person's approaching contact with the 'real' world of the spirits. In cultures where the afterlife is given great significance, old people's closeness to death enhances rather than reduces their status.

Source: adapted from Pilcher (1995)

1 According to the extract, why are older people in some cultures given high status?
2 How might a culture such as that of modern Britain explain the incoherent or incomprehensible speech of an older person?
3 Identify some examples to show how older people in Britain may have both high and low status in society.

Ageism

This term can be used to describe discrimination against people because of their age. It is usually applied to problems faced by older people.

Older people may find it more difficult to gain employment or may find themselves living in poverty as a result of low state pensions. Equally, they may face discrimination and stereotyping based on people's ideas about their mental or physical capabilities.

GREY POWER

In a small group, read the article and then answer the questions.

The first mass leisure class in history is on its way, according to a recent study. It will be made up of people aged between 50 and 75 who have more free time and money, and higher expectations, than their predecessors. Thus, the 'Third Agers' of tomorrow, now in their forties, will represent a decisive break with the past.

The rise of a relatively affluent and leisured Third Age, combined with changes in population that are producing fewer young people, will gradually shift the cultural centre of gravity away from youth to age, the study says.

Among the implications are a rise in grey power. This has already happened in the US, where groups such as the American Association of Retired People have 37 million members and represent a powerful lobby – and important new markets for leisure and education.

Source: adapted from an article in *The Independent*, April 1994, in Donnellan (1995b)

1 What changes does the article suggest will take place in the older population in the future?
2 Note down some ideas for the markets that might be opened up for this new class of older people.

It is important to recognize that within the ranks of older people, there are a wide range of experiences. Some older people may live in poverty while others may enjoy an affluent and high-status position in society. For example, many world statesmen and women are over 65 years of age, as are many of the wealthiest company directors.

Indeed, some researchers have suggested that as the population of older people continues to grow, they will increasingly become a powerful political and consumer force.

Clearly, then, age can be seen as a source of difference between individuals and groups in a society. Within each age range, too, further differences can be found based on historical and cultural factors.

In order more fully to assess the importance of age as a form of stratification, refer to the other chapters in this book. It is important to note here, also, that age may be linked to other forms of division, such as gender or ethnicity, to create further difference in society. For example, the life chances of older women may be different to those of older men.

CHECK YOUR UNDERSTANDING

1. Identify and explain two ways in which differences based on age could affect an individual's status in society. (4 marks)
2. Explain three ways in which ideas about age vary culturally. (6 marks)

HOW HAVE SOCIOLOGISTS TRIED TO DESCRIBE SOCIAL CLASS?

Different sociologists have differing views on social class. All agree that it is an important aspect of society, but there is disagreement about the definition and origins of class.

Three broad views can be identified.

1 The functionalist viewpoint

Functionalists see society as working in a harmonious way, with each institution having a function to perform. From this point of view, a system of ranking people in a hierarchy through stratification is also thought to perform a function for society.

Thus, having a hierarchy of social classes:

(a) identifies which are the most important or highly thought-of roles in a society – these are placed at the top of the hierarchy;
(b) allows society to reward those performing the roles seen as most important through pay and prestige;
(c) gives an incentive to individuals to strive to achieve their best in order to move up the hierarchy and receive greater economic rewards (such as more pay), and increased prestige.

In this way, functionalists argue that a social class system, which is open and allows mobility between classes, will ensure that the most talented individuals are given the opportunity to reach the top to perform the roles most vital for society.

2 The Marxist viewpoint

Karl Marx (see p. 254) believed that in a **capitalist** society (as most modern industrial countries are thought to be) people were divided into two social classes. Membership of these classes was determined by economic factors – which, for Marx, meant the ownership or non-ownership of **property**. Marx saw ownership as the most important division in society.

The **bourgeoisie** are the ruling class; they are the owners of wealth and property, for example in the form of factories, businesses or land.

The **proletariat** are the subordinate or working class. They are the non-owners of property so they have to sell their labour in order to survive. Marx saw a hierarchy between these two classes, with the proletariat being 'ruled' by the bourgeoisie.

These two classes have conflicting interests; for example, the bourgeoisie aim for ever-increasing profits while the proletariat want higher wages. The bourgeoisie are seen as trying to exploit the proletariat and this situation leads to **class conflict**.

Marx believed that the bourgeoisie would decline in size and get richer, while the proletariat would grow in size and become increasingly poor. Eventually, the proletariat would reach a point where they would **rebel** or revolt in anger, leading to a **revolution**. The result of this would be that the social class system would disappear and people would live in a more equal society.

Marx's predictions about revolution have not occurred in Britain, partly as a result of increased standards of living and the welfare state preventing the proletariat reaching the necessary levels of poverty.

Also, critics argue that social class in modern society is more complex than Marx predicted; for example, the development of a large middle class and opportunities for social mobility challenge his ideas of only two, relatively closed, classes.

However, modern Marxists still see the enormous differences in wealth and power (the ability of individuals to achieve their aims) between business owners and workers as the key division in contemporary society affecting life chances.

3 The Weberian viewpoint

Max Weber (see p. 254) agreed with Marx in so far as they both saw class as being based on economic factors such as income and wealth and that classes were in conflict with each other.

However, Weber also stressed the importance of **status** (that is, prestige or social standing) and **power**. Thus, from this viewpoint, a person's status might be different to their class (or economic) position. For example:

- An individual may be wealthy but lack status, such as a National Lottery winner.
- An individual may be poor but have high status, such as a religious leader or a nurse.
- Some individuals may be powerful but not very wealthy, such as some politicians.

For Weber these three factors – economic position, status and power – had to be taken into consideration before a person's social class position could be decided.

Weber's ideas allow us to explain why a teacher may be in a higher class position than a used car salesman, even though the salesman may earn a higher income. This is because the teacher's role has a higher status in society.

Weberian sociologists also argue that *within* each class there are further divisions based on status and power, for example between skilled and unskilled workers. In this way, rather than having just two divisions as Marx suggested, the stratification system is divided into an almost endless number of layers.

If we add to this picture status and power divisions based on gender and ethnic background, then from this viewpoint it is clear that stratification is a highly complex issue.

People with similar incomes and power may still face status differences based on gender and ethnic background

WEALTH, STATUS AND POWER

Identify one other example of (a) an individual who may be wealthy but lack status; (b) an individual who may be relatively poor but have high status in society.

COMPARING MARX AND WEBER

1 Using the following table, compare Marx's and Weber's ideas about social class.

	Marx	Weber
Number of social classes		
Social class based on:		
• economic factors (income, wealth, ownership or non-ownership of property)		
• status		
• power		

2 Examine the following list of roles and individuals and place them in order using (a) Marx's ideas, (b) Weber's ideas about social class.

- Small business owner
- Pop star
- Nurse
- Rupert Murdoch (owner of News International and Sky TV)

Explain the reasons for your choices.

CHECK YOUR UNDERSTANDING

1 Identify and explain two differences between Marx's and Weber's views on the nature of social class. (4 marks)

2 Explain what the terms 'status' and 'power' mean. (4 marks)

HOW CAN WE MEASURE SOCIAL CLASS?

Information on social class is used by a range of different people, for example governments, market researchers and sociologists. In order for comparisons to be made between different social classes and for conclusions to be drawn, a common agreement is needed as to how to determine an individual's social class.

INDICATORS OF SOCIAL CLASS

In a small group, discuss the list of suggested indicators for determining a person's social class.

- income
- wealth
- area lived in
- educational qualifications
- car
- type of housing
- occupation
- political party supported
- accent
- clothing
- leisure activities

Note down your answers to the following tasks.

1 Rank the indicators in order of most to least useful.
2 Identify possible problems in using each indicator.
3 Explain how some indicators could be linked together.

Social class is usually measured by occupation as this may be related to income, status, lifestyle, educational background and life chances, such as health. Occupation can, in some cases, be linked to style of dress and speech.

THE INFLUENCE OF OCCUPATION

Examine figure 3.3 showing the influence of occupation.

Draw similar diagrams to show how two very different occupations could affect an individual's lifestyle and future plans.

Figure 3.3 The influence of occupation

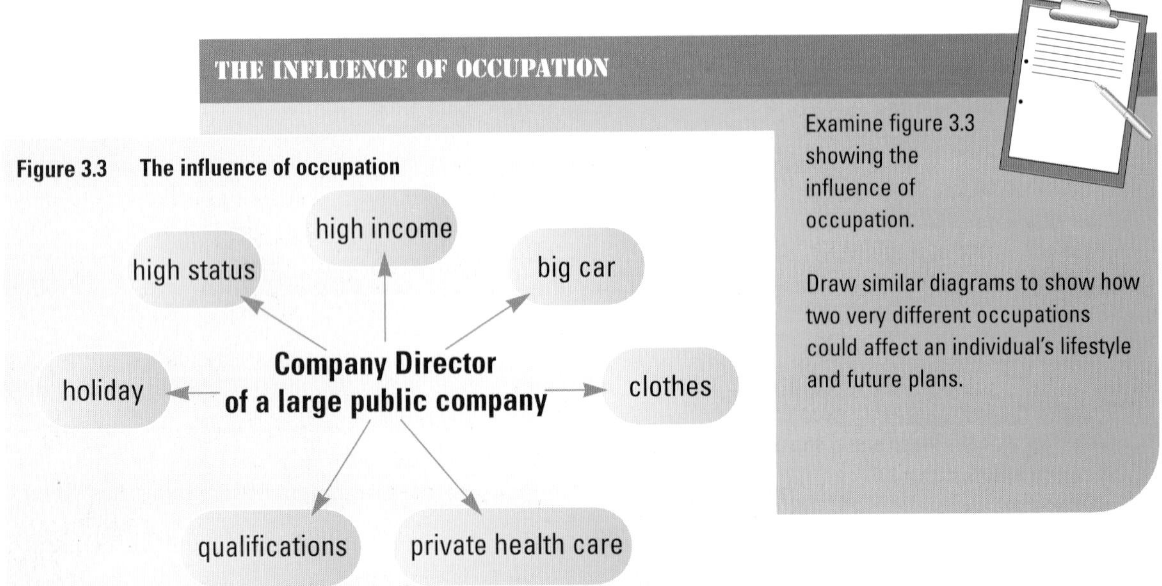

Occupational scales

Occupational scales are used to rank occupations and relate them to a social class, which may be given a name or a number.

A distinction is often made between **manual** and **non-manual** work in these classification scales. Manual work refers to occupations that involve a fair amount of physical effort such as labouring or road building. This type of work is usually seen as working class. Non-manual work does not involve as much physical effort and is usually seen as middle class.

The term **blue collar** is sometimes used to describe manual work and **white collar** to describe non-manual work. These terms refer to traditional ideas on work clothing – (blue) overalls for manual work and (white) shirt and tie or blouse for non-manual work.

A range of scales can be used, each involving a different approach to linking occupations to social classes. For example, the **Registrar General's Scale** uses the status associated with an occupation to rank it. The **Standard Occupational Classification**, on the other hand, groups occupations together according to similarity of qualifications and training needed, as well as the skills and experience required to perform them.

EXAMINING OCCUPATIONAL SCALES

Examine the two tables below and answer the questions that follow.

Table 3.2 The Registrar General's Scale

Middle class	
class	I: Professional and managerial, e.g. architects, doctors, solicitors II: Intermediate, e.g. teachers, nurses, pilots, farmers III (non-manual): Skilled occupations non-manual, e.g. clerical workers, secretaries, shop assistants
Working class	
class	III (manual): Skilled occupations manual, e.g. bus drivers, electricians, cooks IV: Semi-skilled occupations, e.g. bartenders, postal workers V: Unskilled occupations, e.g. road sweepers, labourers, refuse collectors

Table 3.3 The Standard Occupational Classification

Class 1: Managers and Administrators
Managers and administrators in government and large companies

Class 2: Professional
Teachers, solicitors, architects, social workers, librarians

Class 3: Associate Professional and Technical
Computer programmers, nurses, journalists, surveyors

Class 4: Clerical and Secretarial
Clerical workers, secretaries, typists, receptionists

Class 5: Craft and Related
Bricklayers, electricians, car mechanics, bakers

Class 6: Personal and Protective Services
Traffic wardens, police officers (sergeant and below), hairdressers, waiters/waitresses

Class 7: Sales
Sales reps, supermarket checkout operators

Class 8: Plant and Machine Operatives
Assembly line workers, bus conductors, lorry/taxi/bus drivers

Class 9: Other Occupations
Coal miners, refuse collectors, cleaners, postal workers

1. Identify differences between the scales in the placement of particular occupations.
2. Identify any social groups that have been left out of the scales.
3. Explain whether or not the scales are based on either Marx's or Weber's ideas.

What problems are there in using occupation to measure social class?

Although occupation is the most usual way of measuring social class, it is not without its difficulties.

- Very rich people who do not work are not included. For example, where would the Royal family be placed? Where would Lords and Ladies who inherit their wealth and power (hereditary nobles) be placed? What about National Lottery winners who give up their jobs?
- Classifications based on occupation ignore groups who are unemployed or not in paid employment, for example housewives can be seen as having an occupation but they do not appear in these scales.
- The scales are not detailed enough. The same job title may mean different things in different circumstances, for example the title 'farmer' can hide very big differences in income, status and qualification levels depending on the size and type of farm involved. The same may be true of doctors and teachers.

Two individuals in the same profession may occupy different class positions

- The scales are usually based on the idea of an individual being seen as the 'head' of a household – traditionally assumed to be the male. Thus a woman's class is judged in terms of her partner's job, even though she may be in a different class based on her own occupation.
- The scales therefore ignore relationships where both partners work (dual-worker families). In these relationships incomes may be combined, enabling the couple to live a better lifestyle than that associated with the head of the household's occupation.

Should the social class position of women be measured separately to that of men?

As the position and role of women in society changes, some sociologists argue that existing social class scales are outdated and do not accurately measure women's social class position. In particular, existing scales:

- focus mainly on men's occupations;
- assume the male is head of the household;
- ignore changes in family/household arrangements such as increases in female-headed single-parent families;
- ignore differences in status attached to male and female versions of the same job; for example, clerical work for men may be seen as a career route to management, whereas this may not be true for female clerical workers.

Two general solutions have been suggested:

1. Class position should still be based on the idea of the household, but the woman's occupational position should also be taken into account in determining the position of the household.
2. Women should be located in the class system as separate individuals based on their employment position. Thus, people would be placed in class scales as individuals and not as households.

MEASURING WOMEN'S SOCIAL CLASS

In a small group, examine the following occupational scale developed to measure women's class position, based on wage levels, fringe benefits and qualifications.

Table 3.4 Surrey Group Classification (preliminary)

Full-time scale

1 Professional
Schoolteachers, managers of nurses, social workers, professional workers
2 Technical and Supervisory
Supervisors and managers of clerks, office workers or typists, police officers, nurses
3 Clerical Workers, etc.
Clerks, cashiers, typists, secretaries, sales managers (large firms)
4 Service and Productive Workers
Assemblers, barmaids, canteen assistants, shop assistants
5 Manual Workers in Manufacturing

Source: adapted from Abbott and Sapsford (1987)

1. In what ways is this scale different to the Registrar General's Scale and the Standard Occupational Classification?
2. Note down advantages and disadvantages of the two solutions suggested to the problem of measuring women's social class.

CHECK YOUR UNDERSTANDING

1 Identify two reasons why an individual's social class is usually based on the work they do. (2 marks)
2 Identify and explain two problems related to determining an individual's social class in this way. (4 marks)
3 Explain two reasons why some sociologists suggest that women's social class should be measured separately to that of men. (4 marks)

WHAT IS THE IMPORTANCE OF SOCIAL CLASS?

For many people in Britain, social class is seen as being of less importance than it used to be. Greater equality is said to exist in all aspects of people's lives, from education to health care, and individuals no longer see themselves as part of a distinctive social class. In effect, Britain is seen as a 'classless' society.

However, others argue that if we examine the influence of social class on people's life chances, it becomes clear that class is still of importance in contemporary Britain.

Consider the following examples:

- **Income** – the incomes of people in higher social classes increase more rapidly than those in lower classes. For example, between April 1993 and April 1994, the top 10 per cent of earners saw their pay increase by 3.4 per cent, while the bottom 10 per cent averaged an increase of only 1.1 per cent.
- **Life expectancy** – in 1996, a person born into the professional class was expected to live seven years longer than someone born into an unskilled manual background.
- **Accidents** – children born into professional backgrounds were four times less likely to suffer accidental death than those from unskilled manual backgrounds, according to figures in 1996.
- **Infant mortality** – babies whose fathers are in semi-skilled or unskilled manual occupations have a higher mortality rate than those from higher social classes.
- **Health** – in 1995, men from unskilled manual backgrounds were three times more likely to smoke than those from professional backgrounds.
- **Education** – the higher a child's social class background, the more chance he or she has of achieving high educational qualifications. For example, in 1990, 81 per cent of university students came from middle-class backgrounds.
- **Leisure** – people from professional and intermediate backgrounds are more likely to take holidays than those from lower social class backgrounds.
- **Housing** – in 1993, 90 per cent of professionals were homeowners compared to 42 per cent of unskilled manual workers.

CHECK YOUR UNDERSTANDING

1 Explain the term 'life chances'. (3 marks)
2 Identify two ways in which social class might affect an individual's life chances. (2 marks)
3 Identify and explain two reasons why a middle-class child's life chances might be better than those of a working-class child. (4 marks)

CLASS AND LIFE CHANCES

Look again at the examples given on p. 66 of the different ways in which class can affect life chances.

1 For each aspect shown, state how you would explain the differences.

2 Do some research into two other areas in which social class can affect life chances. In order to access this information, you could: use your local library; use statistical sources (such as *Social Trends*); contact the appropriate government department; or contact relevant voluntary organizations.

WHAT CHANGES ARE TAKING PLACE IN THE SOCIAL CLASS STRUCTURE OF MODERN BRITAIN?

We have examined some of the ways in which social class can be influential in people's lives, but it is important to remember that class is not fixed and unchanging.

Over the past 40 years, the class structure in Britain has changed. The divisions between classes have altered and continue to alter, as do the characteristics of the members of these classes.

Before we examine these changes in detail, we need to look at the **background** to these changes; that is, we need to identify the changes in British society that will help us to understand the changing class structure.

How has society changed?

- Britain has become a more **affluent** society, with increased home ownership, for example, and a growth in the ownership of consumer goods such as video recorders, televisions and so on.
- Other sociologists point out the increasing division between those who earn a wage or salary and those who rely on the benefits system. This is related to increases in unemployment.
- Greater opportunities in **education** have given those from working-class backgrounds the possibility of entering professional jobs and moving up the class scale. This was less likely in the past.
- The **occupational structure** has changed, with a movement from manual to white-collar work and a growth in professional and managerial jobs. There has also been an increase in the number of working women, particularly in part-time jobs.

The class structure in the 1950s

The class structure in the 1950s was more clearly defined.

- The working class: consisting of skilled and unskilled manual workers who were, in general, relatively badly paid.
- The middle class: consisting of those in non-manual work, for example clerical, management and professional, who were relatively well paid and had greater job security.

GROWING AFFLUENCE?

Read the following extract and examine the bar chart.

Figure 3.4 Percentage of households with new technology, by social class, 1996–7

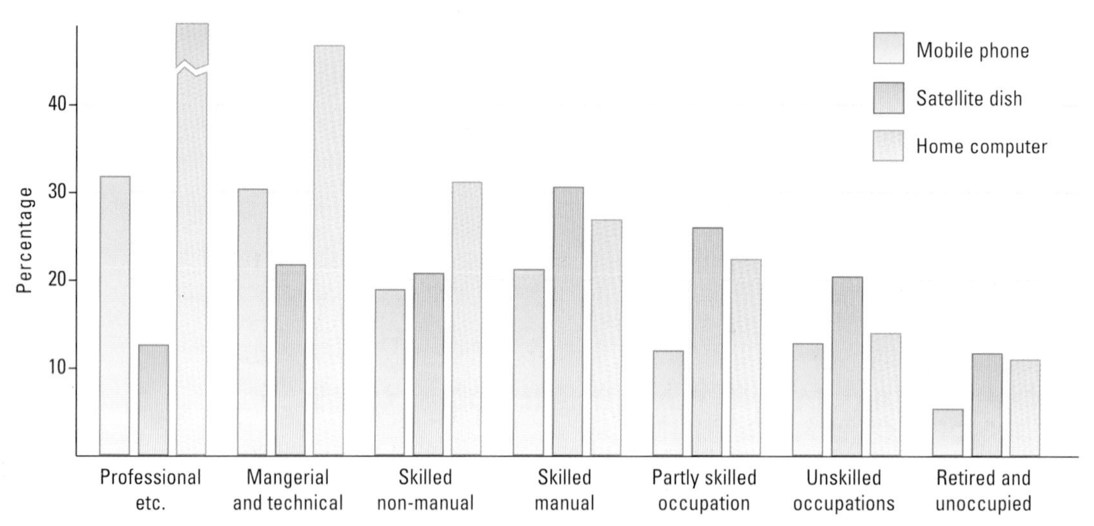

Source: adapted from an article by James Meikle, *The Guardian*, 31 October 1997

Computers and mobile phones are becoming essentials rather than luxuries, a government statistician said yesterday. More than a quarter of households have a computer, nearly one in six has a mobile phone, and about one in five has a television satellite dish, according to official figures on domestic life.

But the survey by the Office for National Statistics also confirms how the nation is divided over its ownership of new technology.

Two-thirds of professional households have a computer compared with fewer than one in ten homes headed by a retired or unemployed person. Four in ten homes led by 30- to 50-year-olds have one; less than 4 per cent headed by over-75s do. Nearly one in three homes in London and the south-east is wired up; fewer than one in five is in the north-east. Professionals are nearly three times as likely to have mobile phones as the partly skilled. Nearly four in ten of the very highest earners have them.

But satellite dishes are far more likely to be fixed to the side of homes of skilled manual workers (30 per cent) than those of the professional classes (just under 14 per cent).

Source: adapted from an article by James Meikle, *The Guardian*, 31 October 1997

Using the article and bar chart:

1 Identify the trends in ownership of new technology according to social class.
2 Identify how age and region of the country in which a person lives can affect ownership of new technology.
3 Explain whether this information supports the idea that Britain is an increasingly affluent, or an increasingly divided, society.

- The upper class: the rich – living off investments and inheritance rather than working, or the owners and directors of large companies.

The contemporary class structure

Some sociologists argue that the clear divisions of the past between classes have now become increasingly blurred. Differences in income, affluence and specific areas such as leisure interests have all **narrowed**.

Who are the contemporary working class?

Here we can examine two general views.

1. Some sociologists argue that a process of **embourgeoisement** has taken place. This word derives from the idea of the bourgeoisie and simply means to become middle class. Thus the term 'embourgeoisement' describes a process whereby the better-off or more affluent sections of the working class are actually becoming middle class in terms of their values, expectations, behaviour, lifestyles and possession of consumer goods.
2. Other sociologists argue that the working class is increasingly divided into two groups:
   - The '**traditional**' working class may be more likely to live in the north of England and Scotland and to live in council houses, inner-city areas or industrial towns. Communities may be close-knit and hold traditional values, for example a belief in the importance of trade unions. Work may be mainly manual (for example in declining areas such as shipbuilding and heavy industry) and, consequently, unemployment may be more of a threat.
   - The '**new**' working class may live in the south of England and be more likely to be homeowners, living in the suburbs. This group of workers may be more affluent and more likely to be in secure jobs, for example in the newer industries of advanced technology and other light industry. Their values may be less traditional and they may aspire to become middle class.

Who are the contemporary middle class?

It is possible to identify two groups here – those in clerical (white-collar) work and those in the professions.

Clerical workers

Some Marxist sociologists argue that a process of **proletarianization** of clerical workers has occurred. This means that clerical workers have joined the working class in that their work has become more routine and less skilled – in this respect, it is argued, they are similar to factory workers. Their income and status have declined and there are fewer opportunities for promotion. The growing areas of telephone sales and telephone banking might fall into this category.

Other sociologists, however, deny that this process has occurred. They point out that clerical workers enjoy better working conditions and greater fringe benefits than manual workers. Although promotion opportunities may have declined, they still exist. Also – importantly – clerical workers often see themselves as middle class.

The professions

This is seen as a growing group made up of 'traditional' professions – for example doctors and solicitors – which have more status and a higher income, and 'new' professions, often found in the public sector, such as teachers and social workers. These professions are seen as having less status and lower pay than traditional professions.

A new class structure?

For some sociologists, the changes we have examined mean that Britain's class structure is now increasingly **fragmented**. In other words, there are divisions both **between** and **within** social classes.

Figure 3.5 Possible changes in the class structure

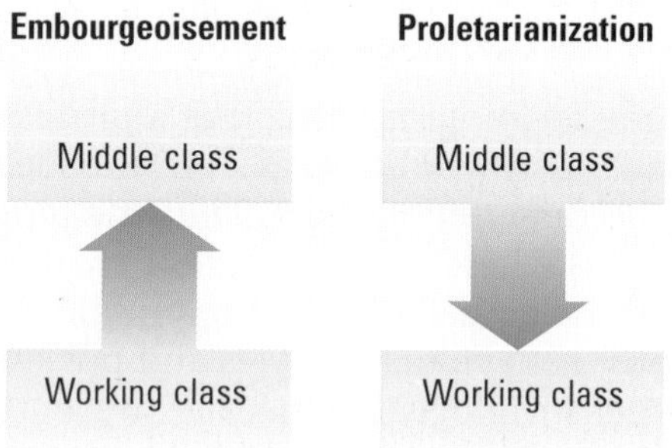

Embourgeoisement	Proletarianization
Middle class	Middle class
↑	↓
Working class	Working class

The clear division that used to exist between a working class of manual workers and a middle class of white-collar workers and professionals may no longer be appropriate to contemporary Britain. Instead, a class structure that includes at least six categories is seen as better representing the current situation. Figure 3.6 provides an outline of these categories.

We have examined some of the changes in the working and middle classes, but it is important, also, to recognize the changes that have taken place at the top and bottom of the class structure.

What is the underclass?

This is a term that has been used to describe groups at the bottom of the class structure, whose access to good life chances are significantly worse than the rest of society.

Figure 3.6 The contemporary class structure

The underclass	– unemployed and poor
Traditional working class	
New or affluent working class	
Clerical workers	– those seeing themselves as working class – those seeing themselves as middle class
Professional and managerial	– see themselves as middle class
The rich or upper class	– the landowners – the entrepreneurial rich – the self-made rich

For some sociologists, this group is seen as being the most disadvantaged part of the working class; for others, it is seen as a separate class in itself.

Members of the underclass are said to include: the unemployed; young single parents; the homeless; disadvantaged members of ethnic minority groups; and elderly people living in poverty.

The underclass has been associated with a rise in violent crime, increases in the numbers of births outside of marriage, and a general decline in moral standards. In other words, its members have been blamed for many issues seen as problems in contemporary society.

The American writer, Charles Murray, produced a series of articles on the underclass in the 1980s and 1990s. He suggests that:

> *'the growth of the underclass is profoundly important for the future of society ... the physical separation of the classes will become more extreme, shops and other businesses in working-class areas will become vacated, resulting in widespread squatting and arson in these areas. The middle classes will begin to move to gated communities, that is, residential areas surrounded by barriers to prevent unauthorized access.'*
>
> Source: adapted from Lawson and Garrod (1996)

ARE THE HOMELESS PART OF AN UNDERCLASS?

In a small group, read the following extracts and answer the questions.

Homelessness – from Crisis (formerly Crisis at Christmas), December 1992

Q *Why can't homeless people help themselves?*

A *Many do, but many can't. Without a permanent address, they are denied the opportunity to live a normal life. They can't get work and without work they can't save the money to secure the permanent home they need.*

Q *Who are the homeless?*

A *Homelessness doesn't discriminate. Debts, redundancy, relationship breakdown, eviction or simple bad luck can happen to anyone. These factors can easily lead to homelessness and a life of misery and despair. People with a history of mental health problems and physical abuse are also particularly vulnerable to homelessness.*

Homelessness in England – The facts from Shelter, April–December 1992

Local authority figures show only part of the problem: official statistics exclude many young single people and couples without children. Shelter estimates that between two and three million people in Britain are without safe, secure accommodation which they can call home.

People on low incomes, unable to buy their own home, rely on rented housing. According to a national report, commissioned by the Association of District Councils in 1991, only 26 per cent of new households in London can afford to buy their own home. Despite an ever-increasing need, there are fewer and fewer rented homes available.

Shelter estimates that there are as many as 2,000–3,000 people sleeping rough in London and up to 5,000 people in the rest of England. Recent research suggests that the average age of death of people sleeping rough is only 47 years, compared with an average life expectancy of 73 for men and 79 for women.

Source: both extracts taken from Donnellan (1993)

1. What explanations are given by Crisis and Shelter as to why people become homeless?
2. Using evidence from the extracts, explain how being homeless could affect an individual's life chances.
3. Should homeless individuals be blamed for being in their situation? Explain your answer.

However, not all sociologists accept the idea that individuals in an underclass can be blamed for these problems. They argue instead that high levels of unemployment and social inequalities in income, housing and education are the true cause.

Who are the rich, or upper class?

Here we can identify three general groups. (Note that groups 2 and 3 may to some extent overlap.)

1 The landowners and aristocracy – these are the traditional members of the upper class whose wealth and income may be acquired through inheritance of land and property. The Royal family and individual landowners such as the Duke of Westminster fall into this category.
2 The entrepreneurial rich – these are the owners of companies, industry and commerce. Wealth may be self-made during an individual's lifetime but is mostly inherited through families who have traditionally been associated with an industry or business, for example the Guinness family (brewing) or the Sainsbury family (retailing).
3 The self-made rich – these are individuals whose wealth and income may result from a specific talent they have, a bright idea that was successful, or even through pure chance. Entertainers, pop stars, sports stars, National Lottery winners and individuals such as Bill Gates, the founder of Microsoft, fall into this category.

How is the upper class changing?

Historically, the rich, or upper class, have been made up of landowners and aristocrats whose wealth was inherited. However, this seems to be changing slowly.

According to a yearly survey by *The Sunday Times*, in 1996 only 15 per cent of the richest 500 in Britain were from these backgrounds, while those whose fortunes were based on industry had risen from 7.5 per cent in 1989 to 20 per cent in 1996.

In other words, it is argued, the upper class is increasingly likely to be made up of the self-made and entrepreneurial rich.

A NEW 'SUPER CLASS'?

Britain has a new upper class – the 'super class', an elite of highly paid top professionals and managers who dominate business, the City (London's financial centre) and the private sector professions. Pay can range from £190,000 to £1 million per year, compared to £75,000 for other professional groups.

Living in London and the south-east, the super class is increasingly separated from the rest of society by wealth, education, values, residence and lifestyle. Servants, second homes, the best of private education, health and leisure, and exotic foreign holidays – these are the dominant themes in the life of the super class.

Source: adapted from Andrew Adonis and Stephen Pollard, 'Class: the curse of Blair's new Britain', in *The Observer*, 21 September 1997

Read the extract on the left and answer the questions.

1 What type of occupations do members of the super class have?
2 How does the pay of members of this class compare to that of other classes?
3 Give three examples of how this affects their life chances.

WHO ARE THE RICH?

Consider the following case studies.

David Sainsbury and family

age: 55

estimated fortune: £2,520 million

source of income: retailing

details: runs J. Sainsbury retail business, receives share of profits and salary of £389,000, gives generously to charities

Source: adapted from 'Britain's Richest 500' supplement, compiled by Philip Beresford and Stephen Boyd, *The Sunday Times*, 14 April 1996

The Duke of Westminster

age: 44

estimated fortune: £1,650 million

source of income: landowner

details: owns 300 acres of Mayfair in London, large areas in Vancouver and North America. Runs property company – Grosvenor Estates (with assets of £637 million in 1994)

David Bowie

David Bowie has overtaken Sir Paul McCartney as Britain's richest pop star, according to a survey of pop wealth in *Business Age* magazine, with the highest-placed star from the 1990s being Noel Gallagher (at number 32 with £30 million).

The youngest person in the top 50 is 20-year-old Baby Spice, who is joint 42nd with the other Spice Girls on £14.5 million each.

British stars look like paupers compared to those from the US. The magazine estimates Michael Jackson and Bruce Springsteen are worth $1 billion each.

The Top Ten

1	David Bowie	£550 million
2	Sir Paul McCartney	£520 million
3	Tom Jones	£275 million
4	Phil Collins	£220 million
5	Elton John	£200 million
6	Mick Jagger	£135 million
7	Eric Clapton	£120 million
8	George Harrison	£105 million
9	Sting	£97 million
10	Keith Richards	£96 million

Source: adapted from an article by Alex Bellos, *The Guardian*, 29 October 1997

1. From the examples given in the three case studies above, note down who is the richest.
2. Identify the sources of their fortunes for each of the three men.
3. In which category of the rich would you place each of the three? Explain your answers.

CHECK YOUR UNDERSTANDING

1 What is meant by the terms 'embourgeoisement' and 'proletarianization'? (4 marks)

2 Identify and explain one way in which the class structure in Britain has changed since the 1950s. (6 marks)

WHAT IS THE IMPORTANCE OF WEALTH?

The term **wealth** refers to marketable, income-generating assets, which simply means things that can be bought and sold. This includes ownership of goods that are kept for their own value and can easily be sold rather than goods that are used by an individual. For example, a home that you own and live in may not be regarded as wealth, but a second home would be.

There are a number of types of wealth, including ownership of stocks and shares, land, property, companies, works of art, jewellery, and so on. As we have seen, an individual's ownership of these types of possessions is an important indicator of their social class position. For example, members of the upper class may own companies or land. In this way, an individual's wealth can be linked to the amount of **power**, **prestige** and **status** they possess. However, we should realize that great wealth does not always lead to a higher disposable income.

An important point to note about wealth is that it is often passed down from one generation to another through **inheritance** – the Royal family, for example, has inherited much of its wealth. In this way, power, prestige and status can also be inherited.

How is wealth distributed in Britain?

We can examine changes in the distribution of wealth in Britain by dividing the population into different groups and looking at the percentage of all wealth owned by them.

THE DISTRIBUTION OF WEALTH

Examine Table 3.5 and answer the questions that follow.

Table 3.5 Distribution of marketable wealth in the UK, 1976-93

Marketable wealth	1976	1981	1986	1991	1993
			Percentages		
Percentage of wealth owned by:					
most wealthy 1%	21	18	18	17	17
most wealthy 5%	38	36	36	35	36
most wealthy 10%	50	50	50	47	48
most wealthy 25%	71	73	73	71	72
most wealthy 50%	92	92	90	92	93
Total marketable wealth (£ billion)	**280**	**565**	**955**	**1,711**	**1,746**

Source: *Social Trends* (1997)

1 What percentage of the total wealth in the UK did the wealthiest 1 per cent own in 1993?

2 What percentage of the wealth in the UK did the wealthiest 50 per cent of the population own in 1993?

3 Which group has seen the biggest decrease in its share of wealth since 1976?

4 What percentage of the wealth in the UK did the poorest 50 per cent of the population own in 1993?

5 Has there been any significant redistribution of wealth in the UK from the wealthiest 50 per cent to the poorest 50 per cent since 1976?

Some sociologists are reluctant to take the official figures on the distribution of wealth at face value, arguing that they understate the true proportion of the rich's wealth. The rich are able to employ tax advisers, who can juggle figures to help them appear less wealthy so that they do not have to pay out so much in tax on income generated from their wealth. It has been suggested that the richest 10 per cent of the population own about 70 per cent of wealth.

WHAT IS THE IMPORTANCE OF INCOME?

Income refers to the flow of money that households receive from various sources, for example from employment in the form of salaries and wages, from occupational pensions, investments, gifts, state benefits and rent from property.

There are two types of income – **original** income and **disposable** income.

- Original income is the total income that a household receives before that income is taxed and before state benefits, such as retirement pension, are paid.
- Disposable income is the total income that a household receives after income tax, national insurance contributions and state benefits are paid.

Income is an important factor in determining life chances, for example whether or not private education or health care can be afforded. Equally, access to a large income can allow individuals to increase their wealth, for example through the purchase of property. As with wealth, changes in the distribution of income can be analysed in order to examine changes in the levels of inequality in society. Indeed, Richard Wilkinson (1996) has argued that countries with a wide gap between the high-paid and low-paid are more likely to suffer from social disorder, high crime and murder rates, and lower life expectancy.

How is income distributed in Britain?

The distribution of income can be examined first of all by adding up the income received by everyone. Those with the highest income are placed at one end of the scale, and those with the lowest are placed at the other end. They are then divided into five equal groups, with the richest fifth at one end and the poorest fifth at the other end. Each fifth therefore equals 20 per cent of all households.

Some sociologists argue that figures on income do not really give the full picture. This is because they do not take into account 'perks of the job' or fringe benefits. The higher up the occupational scale you are, the more 'perks' there are; for example, a manager may get a company car, help with fees for a private school for his or her children, membership of a private health scheme or help with a mortgage. In this way, they are able to spend more of their disposable income on other things.

Table 3.6 A league table of pay in Great Britain, April 1995

Occupation	Average gross weekly earnings (£)
Treasurers and company financial managers	797
Medical practitioners	764
Solicitors	585
Software engineers	493
Police officers (sergeant and below)	439
Sales reps	356
Nurses	329
Laboratory technicians	296
Goods drivers	276
Telephone operators	243
Receptionists	188
Petrol pump attendants	152

Source: Central Statistical Office, *New Earnings Survey* (1995)

INCOME DISTRIBUTION

Examine Figure 3.7 and answer the questions.

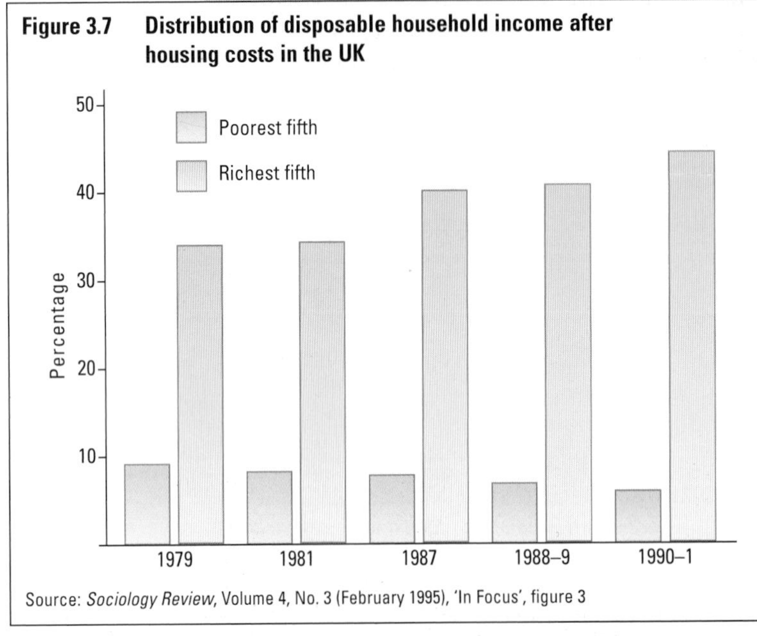

Figure 3.7 Distribution of disposable household income after housing costs in the UK

Source: *Sociology Review*, Volume 4, No. 3 (February 1995), 'In Focus', figure 3

1 What is the trend in the percentage of disposable income for the richest fifth of households?
2 What is the trend in the percentage of disposable income for the poorest fifth of households?
3 What conclusions can you reach about trends in the distribution of income in Britain?

INCOME INEQUALITIES

Read the extract and answer the questions that follow.

Britain is a far more unequal society than 20 years ago, according to a report by the Institute of Fiscal Studies. The report, *Inequality in the UK*, reveals that incomes of the bottom 5 per cent of earners hardly changed between 1983 and 1993, while, by contrast, the incomes of the top 5 per cent of earners rose nearly 50 per cent.

If income were translated into height terms, nearly 60 per cent of people would be at or below an average height of 5ft 9in, with a handful of tallest entrepreneurs standing nearly twice the height of Nelson's Column. One estimate puts the height of John Paul Getty, one of the world's richest men, at more than 10 miles.

'The increase in inequality is probably the biggest social change in the last 20 years,' said Paul Johnson, an author of the report. 'With no apparent change of higher social security benefits, higher taxes or better earnings prospects for the low paid, this change – and all its consequences – is here to stay.'

Source: adapted from an article by Kamal Ahmed, *The Guardian*

1 What differences were there in the changes in income for the top 5 per cent and bottom 5 per cent of earners?
2 Explain what Paul Johnson might mean by the 'consequences' of these changes.

CHECK YOUR UNDERSTANDING

1 What is the difference between wealth and income? (4 marks)
2 Explain how wealth and income can be linked to power in society. (4 marks)
3 Give two examples of the ways in which wealth can affect a person's life chances. (2 marks)

HOW SOCIALLY MOBILE IS MODERN BRITAIN?

As we saw on page 41, social mobility refers to the movement of people up and down the social scale between social classes. It is measured using occupational scales and can be an important indicator of how far a society is open and **meritocratic** (where class position is achieved by effort and talent).

There are two types of social mobility:

1 Intra-generational mobility – this term refers to the movement of an individual over his or her lifetime, for example as a result of changing career or promotion.
2 Inter-generational mobility – this refers to movement between generations, that is, movement from one class to another between parents and children. Thus, an individual's occupation would be compared to that of his or her father.

TYPES OF SOCIAL MOBILITY

Examine the two sets of illustrations below and, for each one, identify:

(**a**) what type of mobility is being shown;
(**b**) whether or not mobility has occurred.

1st job

2nd job

3rd job

Grandfather

Father

Daughter

RESEARCHING SOCIAL MOBILITY

Your brief is to conduct some research on intra-generational and inter-generational mobility.

(a) Intra-generational mobility. Here you should interview an older relative or friend about the different occupations they have had in their lifetime.

(b) Inter-generational mobility. Here you will need to interview an individual about their family's occupations. As mobility is usually based on the father's occupation, you will need to find out in particular about the occupations held by their father, grandfather, great-grandfather and so on, as far back as they can go.

Once you have completed your interviews, you will need to use an occupational scale in order to see if the individual and the family have been socially mobile. You should also make a note of any problems you identify or encounter while undertaking this research.

The **extent** of social mobility can be described in three ways:

1 **Long range** – a movement of two or more occupational groups as classified by, for example, the Registrar General's Scale.
2 **Short range** – a movement of only one occupational group.
3 **Self-recruitment** – this refers to a situation in which children are in the same occupational group as their parents, for example when the son is a doctor and the mother a solicitor. In this instance, no mobility has taken place.

It is also important to distinguish between **sponsored** mobility, that is, mobility as a result of help from friends, through inheritance or through a privileged education, and **contest** mobility, where mobility is achieved as a result of one's own merit and ability. A high level of contest mobility would indicate a more meritocratic society. Indeed, evidence suggests that contest mobility is increasing.

What problems are there in trying to measure social mobility?

- As we mentioned previously, most mobility studies use occupation as a measure of social class position. Earlier we noted that there are problems in using occupation to measure social class. These difficulties may thus affect the accuracy of mobility studies.
- Over time the status of many jobs has changed, for example in the nineteenth century, a clerk had high status compared with today. Also, new types of jobs may emerge and others may disappear altogether. So, when making comparisons over time – especially with inter-generational mobility – the changing nature and status of jobs needs to be taken into account and can lead to difficulties in making accurate comparisons.
- Problems arise because we have to decide upon the point in an individual's career from which we are going to measure mobility. For example, if the daughter of a rich stockbroker takes her first job as a cashier for 18 months while waiting for a suitable opening in the London Stock Exchange, do we measure her mobility from her first job or from her second?

PROBLEMS IN MEASURING SOCIAL MOBILITY

In a small group, discuss:

(a) the changes that have taken place in the status of certain jobs;
(b) any occupations that have only come into existence recently.

As a result of your discussion identify:

1. Two jobs whose status has changed over time.
2. Two jobs that no longer exist.
3. Two jobs that have recently come into existence.

At what point do we start measuring mobility?

What are the trends in social mobility in modern Britain?

Inter-generational mobility

Since the 1950s, the pattern of mobility has shown a general **upward** movement. More people from working-class backgrounds are entering professional and managerial jobs than before. However, this does not necessarily mean that society has become more open, that is, based on achievement.

The explanation lies elsewhere. The changes in the occupational structure that we discussed earlier have led to there being **more room at the top** rather than working-class people necessarily being mobile as a result of their own merits.

Indeed, the **relative** chances of children from other backgrounds entering professional jobs compared to those from professional backgrounds has changed very little. A working-class child's chances of entering a professional or managerial job are half those of a child from the intermediate class and a quarter of those of a child from the professional class.

Intra-generational mobility

Here, trends suggest that it is increasingly difficult for individuals to work their way up to the top of an occupation. Instead, the emphasis on qualifications has led graduates to be recruited into positions that lead to the top jobs rather than working their way up in a company.

Thus, working-class people with good qualifications have the possibility to enter top jobs, but it is more difficult for those entering at lower levels with fewer qualifications.

What other influences on mobility are there?

Apart from changes in the occupational structure and the need for educational qualifications, sociologists have identified a number of other factors that may lead to mobility.

- **Changes in fertility rates** for the middle class have led to fewer middle-class children being available to fill the growing number of non-manual jobs. This gap has been filled by the children of the working class.
- **Marriage** is a route to mobility, especially for women, who may then take on the class position of their husbands. However, most people will marry someone from a similar background to themselves.
- **Social background** can be seen as highly influential. For example, children from middle-class or privileged backgrounds may have a greater expectation of success, receive more encouragement, and enjoy certain advantages, perhaps based on educational opportunities or family contacts.
- **Windfalls**, such as a Lottery win or an inheritance, can also lead to mobility in terms of lifestyle, although an individual may choose to remain in his or her present occupation.

ARE LOTTERY WINNERS MOBILE?

In a small group, discuss the problems in measuring the mobility of Lottery winners. Consider, for example, the following points:

- If they remain in employment, will they have been mobile?
- If they stop working, how will we measure their mobility?

What barriers are there to mobility?

In an open society, the social background of individuals should make no difference to their chances of mobility. However, as we have seen, **social class background** and low levels of educational qualifications can reduce people's chances of mobility.

Gender and **ethnic background** can also influence opportunities. For example, although women may achieve better qualifications than men, they may be less likely to move upwards through employment than men as a result of taking time out to bring up children.

Equally, women and people from ethnic minority backgrounds may face **discrimination**, for example in job interviews, and so may not have the same chances of employment or promotion.

WOMEN AND SOCIAL MOBILITY

In a small group, read the following extract and note down answers to the questions.

1. Why might the fact that a married woman is not in employment make it difficult to measure her social mobility?
2. Why might measuring a married woman's mobility based on her part-time work not be a good idea?
3. How might a woman's childcare responsibilities affect her chances of being mobile?
4. How might women's concentration in a narrow range of occupations affect their chances of mobility?
5. Identify arguments for and against the idea that single women will have more chance of being socially mobile than married women.

'There are some serious problems in measuring women's social mobility. Not all married women are in employment, and even where they are this may be part-time, low-status work, taken to fit in with having a family, which would be a poor indicator of their lifestyle.

Also, because married women typically move in and out of the labour market as the demands of their families change, they tend not to have a career in the sense in which at least some men have one.

Furthermore, women tend to be concentrated in a narrow range of occupations, mainly routine non-manual and unskilled manual work, and are under-represented in high-status occupations and skilled manual work.'

Source: Abbott and Sapsford (1987)

CHECK YOUR UNDERSTANDING

1. Explain the difference between inter-generational mobility and intra-generational mobility. (4 marks)
2. Explain why sociologists wish to study social mobility. (3 marks)
3. Identify and explain two problems faced when trying to measure social mobility. (4 marks)
4. Identify two factors that might prevent an individual being socially mobile. (2 marks)
5. 'Everyone has the opportunity to reach the top in contemporary Britain.' To what extent do you agree or disagree with this viewpoint? Explain your answer fully. (8 marks)

SUMMARY

In this chapter we have covered the following points:

- **Stratification is the division of society into layers, with the most privileged at the top and the least favoured at the bottom. Different societies use different criteria for deciding who will be placed where in the hierarchy.**
- **Differentiation refers to those things that make an individual or group separate and distinct from another: for example age, gender or ethnic background.**
- **Different forms of stratification have existed in different cultures and at particular periods in history. These include apartheid, the caste system and feudalism.**
- **In modern Britain, social class is the major form of division between both individuals and groups. Social class is based largely on economic factors, such as occupation and income.**

- **Gender, ethnic background and age are also important factors in stratification in modern Britain.**
  - **Some sociologists, especially feminists, have argued that gender is a more important division than social class because whatever their social class position, women have more in common with each other than they do with men from their own social class.**
  - **Many sociologists argue that life chances are also influenced by ethnic background, with those from ethnic minorities still experiencing individual and institutional racism and unequal access to power and influence in society.**
  - **Age is another source of difference between individuals and groups in society. Within each age range, further differences can be identified based on historical and cultural factors.**

  It is important to note that each form of division – gender, ethnicity, age – can be linked to others forms to create further, more complex differences in society. For example the life chances of older women may be different from those of older men.

- **Social class has been defined in various ways by different groups of sociologists.**
  - **Functionalists argue that an open social class system that allows mobility between classes, ensures that the most talented individuals are given opportunities to reach the top and to perform the roles most vital for society.**
  - **Modern Marxists argue that the different access to wealth and power given to business owners and to workers is the key division in society which affects life chances.**
  - **Weber and his followers see that class is not only based on economic factors but also on status and power, so, for example, an individual may be powerful but not very wealthy, for example, some politicians. Weberians look at status and power divisions that are based on gender and ethnic background as well as on economic wealth.**
- **There are a number of ways of measuring social class, the most popular of which are occupational scales such as the Registrar General's scale.**
- **Some sociologists argue that class divisions are becoming less important and that Britain is a 'classless' society. However statistics on such factors as life expectancy, education or housing, for instance, indicate that social class still has a huge effect on life chances.**
- **Social class is not fixed. Over the past 40 years huge changes have taken place in the class structure of modern Britain. The once-clear division between working class and middle class is becoming blurred and more fragmented. Some sociologists argue that a new, highly disadvantaged class which they call the underclass has appeared, consisting of the unemployed, single parents, the homeless and elderly people living in poverty. At the other end of the spectrum, the upper class is increasingly likely to be made up of the self-made and entrepreneurial rich rather than traditional landowners and aristocrats.**
- **Sociologists are interested in how socially mobile modern Britain is. Since the 1950s the pattern of mobility has shown a general upward movement with more people from working-class backgrounds entering professional and managerial jobs . However, this does not necessarily mean that Britain is a more open or meritocratic society: changes in the occupational structure mean that there is `more room at the top'. We must also remember that age, gender and ethnic background all influence social mobility.**

EXAMINATION QUESTION 1

Study **Items A** and **B**. Then answer **all** parts of the questions that follow.

Item A Distribution of shareholders in Great Britain (Buying a share means that you own part of a company.)

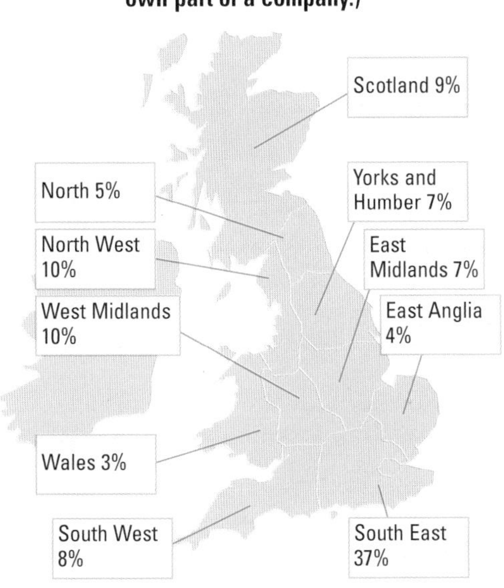

Source: adapted from *Education Guardian*, September 1993

Item B Ownership of shares: in percentages

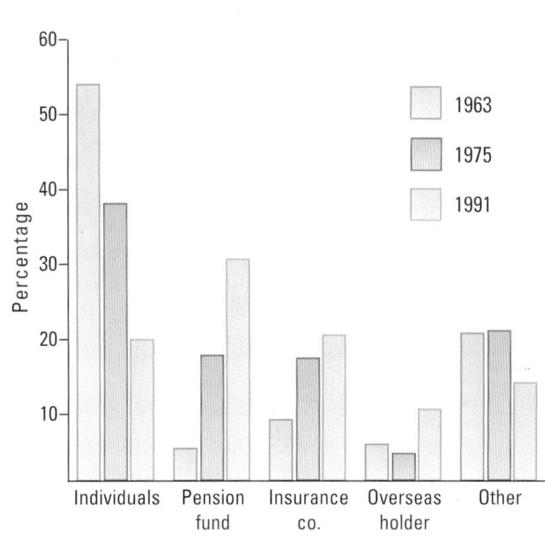

Source: adapted from *Education Guardian*, September 1993

(a) According to the information in **Item A**:

(i) in which region did the highest percentage of shareholders live? (1 mark)

(ii) in which region did 5% of the nation's shareholders live? (1 mark)

(b) According to the information in **Item B**:

(i) how has the percentage of shares owned by individuals changed between 1963 and 1991? (1 mark)

(ii) what percentage of shares was owned by pension funds in 1991? (1 mark)

(c) Give **two** ways in which the social class structure of Britain has changed in the last forty years. (2 marks)

(d) **(i)** What is meant by the term 'occupational status'? (1 mark)

(ii) Explain **one** way in which occupational status can affect an individual's life chances. (3 marks)

(e) **(i)** Identify **one** factor, other than occupational status, which affects an individual's life chances. (1 mark)

(ii) Explain how this factor is linked to inequality in Britain. (3 marks)

Source: SEG GCSE Sociology, Summer 1996
Higher Tier Paper 2, Question 5

EXAMINATION QUESTION 2

(a) Using examples, show the difference between the terms 'caste' and 'class'. (4 marks)

(b) Why might it be difficult to decide to which social class a person belongs? (6 marks)

(c) Describe some of the ways in which Britain's social class structure has changed (6 marks)

(d) How might an individual's social class position affect his/her life chances? (9 marks)

Source: NEAB GCSE Sociology, June 1996
Tier P, Section B, Question B4

BIBLIOGRAPHY

Abbott, Pamela and Sapsford, Roger (1987) *Women and Social Class*, Tavistock Publications.

Ariès (1962) *Centuries of Childhood*, Jonathan Cape.

Denscombe, Martyn (1996) *Sociology Update*, Olympus Books.

Denscombe, Martyn (1997) *Sociology Update*, Olympus Books.

Donnellan, Craig (ed.) (1993) 'No place like home', *Issues for the 90s* series, Independence Publishing.

Donnellan, Craig (ed.) (1994) 'Gender and prejudice', *Issues for the 90s* series, Volume 18, Independence Publishing.

Donnellan, Craig (ed.) (1995a) 'Racial discrimination', *Issues for the 90s* series, Volume 6, Independence Publishing.

Donnellan, Craig (ed.) (1995b) 'Our ageing generation', *Issues for the 90s* series, Independence Publishing.

Donnellan, Craig (ed.) (1996) 'Men, women and equality', *Issues for the 90s* series, Volume 18, Independence Publishing.

Lawson, T. and Garrod, J. (1996) *The Complete A–Z Sociology Handbook*, Hodder and Stoughton.

Oakley, A. (1972) *Sex, Gender and Society*, Temple Smith.

Pilcher, J. (1995) 'Growing up and growing older', *Sociology Review*, Volume 5, No. 1 (September), Philip Allan.

Social Trends (1997) Office for National Statistics and HMSO.

Taylor, I. (1996) *Sociology Updates Conference Notes* (November), Sociology Updates, Manchester.

Wilkinson, R. (1996) *Unhealthy Societies: The Afflictions of Inequality*, Routledge.

CHAPTER 4

Poverty and the Welfare State

In this chapter, we will explore and attempt to answer the following questions:

1. **What is the welfare state?**
2. **What services does the welfare state provide?**
3. **How successful have these services been?**
4. **What is the role of voluntary organizations in providing welfare services?**
5. **What is poverty?**
6. **How do we measure poverty?**
7. **Who are the poor?**
8. **What are the sociological explanations of poverty?**
9. **Can poverty and inequality be eliminated?**

WELFARE

Welfare issues provoke much heated debate among sociologists, politicians and the media because they involve important questions about how our society tackles inequality and poverty. Questions include:

- Should we take greater responsibility for our own and our families' welfare, health and well-being, or should we expect the state to provide for us?
- Is private health insurance the way forward, or should the state provide free health care for all?
- Do heavy smokers deserve less speedy treatment than non-smokers within the National Health Service?
- Is it realistic to expect the state to provide for our well-being and financial security when we reach pension age?
- Is it true that generous welfare state provisions discourage the unemployed from genuinely looking for jobs?
- Are the poor to blame for their predicament?
- Is welfare spending a waste of money?
- Should welfare services be built up or slimmed down?

Some of these questions have generated a wide range of responses.

Types of welfare provision

Welfare services in Britain today are provided:

- informally through families, friends and neighbours;
- privately through profit-making businesses;
- through 'occupational welfare' such as company pension schemes, sick pay schemes, maternity leave and other arrangements;
- via the voluntary (non-statutory) sector;
- formally through the state sector.

The **informal sector** is an important source of welfare provision. Our families, relatives and friends may help us out in all sorts of ways, for example by providing financial help or by looking after us when we are ill. In practice, the responsibility for providing this help and care often falls on women. Many women provide care informally in their local community, for instance by looking after their children for a few hours during school holidays or by keeping an eye on an elderly neighbour or relative.

Within the **private sector**, people operate businesses that may fill gaps in state sector provision, for example registered child minding, and residential rest and nursing homes. In education, private and independent schools compete with state provision. Companies operate pension schemes or sick pay schemes, and some may help with loans, housing or by offering to pay private health insurance subscriptions for their employees.

Within the **voluntary sector**, voluntary (non-statutory) agencies provide welfare services. Body Positive, for example, provides support for people who are living with HIV/AIDS.

Within the **state sector**, local authorities may provide services such as pre-school nursery places and play schemes for young children during school holidays. They also provide public housing and social services such as child protection teams of social workers. Nationally, the welfare state provides a range of health and welfare services, including the National Health Service (NHS) and social security benefits.

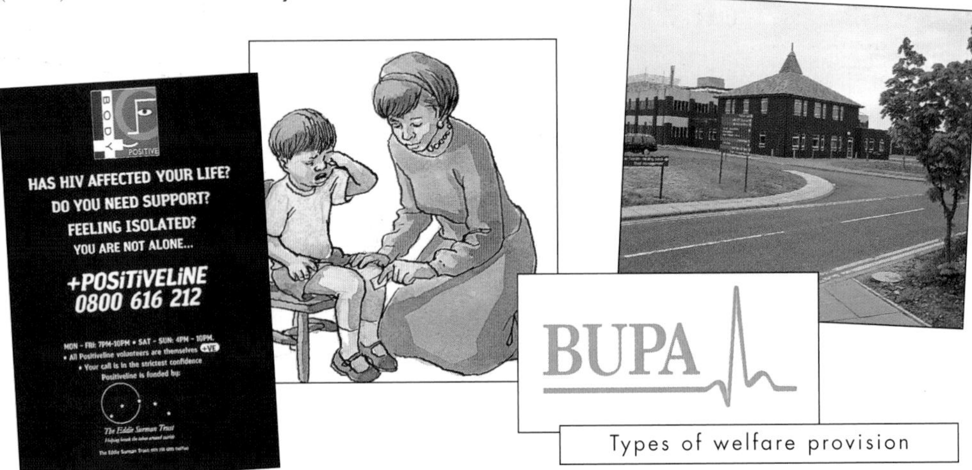

Types of welfare provision

Since the 1970s, there has been vigorous debate among sociologists, politicans and policy makers on the role of the state in welfare provision. This debate has centred on:

- who should provide welfare services and what the balance should be between the state, private, voluntary and informal sectors as providers. For example, should families be expected to provide more welfare support for family members and the state less?
- whether benefits and services should be provided to everyone or targeted only at those in need. For example, eye and dental check-ups used to be available to all without charge. Today, only people on low incomes are entitled to free check-ups.
- what level of services and benefits should be provided. Towards the end of 1997, the government's decision to cut benefit payments to lone parents received an angry response. Fears over government plans to reform disability benefits resulted in protestors handcuffing themselves to railings in Downing Street.

WHAT IS THE WELFARE STATE?

The term welfare state describes a system in which the state takes responsibility for protecting the health and welfare of its citizens, and for meeting social needs. The state does this through its provision of services and benefits, which ensure that people are looked after and their well-being taken care of.

In Britain, the welfare state was established as a safety net to protect the most vulnerable members of society and to guarantee them an adequate level of income, health care, education and housing.

Origins and development of the British welfare state

The origins of the British welfare state can be traced back to the reforms of the Liberal government between 1906 and 1919. Free school meals were introduced in 1906, for example, while old age pensions were introduced in 1909.

It was not until the 1940s, however, that the welfare state was firmly established. Its foundations were laid by the Beveridge Report (1942), which identified the **five giant evils** – Want, Disease, Ignorance, Squalor and Idleness – that the state was to combat. The Beveridge plan envisaged a cradle-to-grave provision of benefits, including unemployment and sickness benefits. Particular groups such as the elderly, widows and orphans were to be provided for. The idea was that in return for insurance contributions paid while in work, people would be entitled to draw out benefits when they were unable to work.

The welfare state as a safety net

In 1945, after a landslide general election victory, the Labour Party formed the post-war government (1945–50, 1950–1). Its aims were:

- To remove want and poverty, and to redistribute income more equally via social security. In July 1948, a social security system came into operation that was designed to protect and help people who needed support, for example because of unemployment, ill health or retirement.
- To tackle disease by providing free health care to all. The NHS came into operation in July 1948.
- To tackle ignorance by providing free secondary education to all children. Butler's Education Act (1944) had introduced a system of free secondary state education and in 1947 the school leaving age was raised to 15.
- To remove squalor by getting rid of poor housing and replacing it with adequate state and private provision.
- To tackle idleness and unemployment through job creation.

> **The great day has arrived. You wanted the State to assume greater responsibility for individual citizens. You wanted social security. From today you have it.**
>
> Source: *Daily Mirror*, 5 July 1948, quoted in Fraser (1984)

What services are provided by the welfare state today?

Today, the welfare state provides services in relation to education, training, health, housing and social security. It also provides personal social services, such as meals-on-wheels, home helps and funding of day centres.

The **National Health Service** (NHS) provides us with general practitioners (GPs), health centres, hospitals, opticians, dentists, the ambulance service, the immunization service and pre- and post-natal clinics.

National benefits are the responsibility of central government. They include national insurance benefits and social security benefits.

National insurance benefits

National insurance (NI) benefits are contributory benefits, which means that, in order to qualify for them, the recipient has to have paid sufficient contributions into the national insurance scheme.

People in paid employment pay part of their weekly or monthly salary into the NI scheme. This payment is deducted automatically. NI contributions are also paid by the self-employed. People who are not working can choose to make voluntary contributions. If a person who has paid sufficient NI contributions becomes unemployed, he or she can claim NI benefits. Currently, these benefits include the retirement pension and the contribution-based Jobseeker's Allowance.

- The **retirement pension** is paid weekly to people who have reached state pension age (65 for men and 60 for women). Many people retire before this, either voluntarily or otherwise.
- Contribution-based **Jobseeker's Allowance** is paid for up to six months to jobseekers over 18 who are unemployed, actively seeking work, and capable of and available for work.

Social security benefits

Social security benefits are paid by the Department of Social Security (the DSS) and are mainly for people who do not qualify for NI benefits because they have not paid sufficient NI contributions.

Social security benefits are provided selectively on the basis of a **means test**. Whether or not claimants qualify for means-tested benefits, and how much they receive, depends on factors such as their income and savings. The range of social security benefits has changed as governments introduce new ones and phase out old ones. The current range of benefits includes the following:

- **Income support** is paid to people aged 16 or over who do not have enough money to live on because their income is below a certain level. It is designed for people who are not required to be available for work, for example people aged over 60, lone parents, people who are sick, disabled or looking after a person who has a disability.
- **Family credit** is paid to working people who are responsible for a child or children. To receive family credit, the recipient must work for 16 hours or more per week on a low wage.
- The **Social Fund** is designed to help people with expenses that are difficult to pay for out of their weekly income. Examples include: a cold weather payment, maternity payment, funeral payment, and community care grant. The Social Fund may also provide budgeting loans or crisis loans.

Most benefits are **selective**, which means that they are targeted at those in greatest financial need on the basis of a means test. Child benefit is different in that it is a **universal** rather than a selective benefit, available to anyone who is responsible for a child. It is paid monthly for each child until he or she leaves full-time education, regardless of parental income. Child benefit is non-contributory (that is, recipients do not have to pay contributions) and is not means tested.

THE DEBATE SURROUNDING CHILD BENEFIT

Some people are critical of universal benefits. In a small group, discuss the pros and cons of universal child benefit for children, families and for society.

Note down two reasons for (a) maintaining this benefit for all; (b) paying it only to families on low incomes.

Local benefits differ from national benefits in that they are the responsibility of the local authority (LA), for example Lambeth, Teesside or Oldham.

- **Housing benefit** and **council tax benefit** are for people on a low income who pay rent and council tax regardless of whether or not they are employed. They are non-contributory benefits but they are means tested.
- The **local education authority** provides free school and college places. It may provide means-tested help with children's clothing and grants for those in school beyond the age of 16. Free school meals are provided on a means-tested basis.
- The local **social services** provide residential services and personal social services such as home helps. It also employs teams of social workers, for example in child protection.

The LA also has **public health** responsibilities, for example it is responsible for refuse disposal, monitoring pollution levels, the control of infectious diseases and monitoring standards in catering outlets such as cafés and restaurants. The LA also has a role in local planning issues, for example it has the power to order the compulsory purchase of slum property.

CHECK YOUR UNDERSTANDING

1. State three examples of services provided by the welfare state. (3 marks)
2. Explain what is meant by a means-tested benefit. (2 marks)
3. Briefly explain the difference between selective and universal welfare benefits. (2 marks)
4. Identify and explain one reason why a government might decide against using universal welfare benefits to reduce poverty. (2 marks)

HOW SUCCESSFUL HAS THE WELFARE STATE BEEN?

As we noted earlier, sociologists and politicians disagree on issues relating to the welfare state. Some believe that the welfare state has been reasonably successful as a safety net, while others argue that it has been far from successful in tackling poverty and inequality. A third view is that the welfare state is wasteful and should be slimmed down. Let's examine these views in more detail.

The welfare state as a success story

This view focuses on the role of the welfare state in dealing with the basic problems of poverty and inequality in society. The welfare state is seen as playing a crucial part in providing equal educational opportunities for all, a more equal distribution of wealth and income, and a fairer society.

WELFARE-TO-WORK

Gordon Brown, Labour MP and Chancellor of the Exchequer, is optimistic about the potential of the welfare state to tackle the problems of unemployment, low skills and low wages. Read through this extract and then answer the questions.

> **No one in our society today should be excluded from the opportunity to work. So in modernizing the welfare state, it is necessary to open up work opportunities to those denied them. The Labour government's welfare-to-work programme is designed to help those out of work to realize their potential through fulfilling employment. It will put the young unemployed, the long-term unemployed and single parents back to work.**
>
> **The introduction of a minimum wage will improve the incentive to work. Our modernization of the welfare state will create work, make sure that work always pays, and provide opportunities for life-long learning. These measures will help to tackle inequality and poverty at source.**
>
> Source: adapted from an essay by Gordon Brown in *The Guardian*, 2 August 1997

1 Which three groups are to be placed in work under Labour's welfare-to-work proposals?
2 How will the government encourage people to take up jobs?

Optimistic views focus on the positive achievements of the welfare state. Supporters suggest that it has effectively tackled the five giant evils, arguing that:

- The welfare state has removed absolute poverty. It supports those who, through no fault of their own, cannot work and who would otherwise be forced to beg or to rely on charity. State pensions, for instance, provide those of us who have reached pension age with sufficient money to enable us to live in financial security.
- Through the NHS, we all have access to medical treatment. As a result, there are fewer diseases, longer life expectancy and lower rates of infant deaths (see pp. 350–2).
- Equality of educational opportunity is provided via free state education available to those aged 16 and under. Since 1979, there have been improvements in terms of formal qualifications, staying-on rates and access to higher education.
- Slum housing has been demolished. Homeless people in priority need have access to temporary accommodation.
- People have been given the means to train or retrain for jobs.

Maths and sciences strong as grades rise

Source: *The Times*, 22 August 1996

Many sub-standard blocks of flats have been demolished

The welfare state as failing

This view focuses on the failings or shortcomings of the welfare state. Critics voice the following concerns:

- The welfare state provides neither sufficient money nor support services to those in need, for example people with disabilities and those who are sick, unemployed or elderly. The policy of 'care in the community' is a case in point. It involves people with special needs – for instance, the elderly, people with physical disabilities or mental health problems – being looked after in the community rather than in residential homes or hospitals. The idea is that such people gain more from living in the community rather than being shut away in institutions. However, critics suggest that the motivation behind 'care in the community' is financial – an exercise in cutting costs – because it has resulted in vulnerable people leaving institutional care without the support of alternative care structures.
- The introduction of charges (based on a means test) for eye and dental checks is criticized. Such charges reflect the move away from the principle of universal provision to the principle of selective provision.
- NHS hospital waiting lists are a major problem, and in November 1997 they reached record length. The following extract illustrates the point:

Hospital waiting lists over the year ending June 1997 increased by nearly 13 per cent, according to official statistics. This was one of the steepest rises since the NHS was set up. Nearly 1.2 million people are waiting to be admitted for treatment in NHS hospitals in England. The present Labour government blamed the rise on under-spending by former Conservative governments. Sandy Macara, chair of the British Medical Association, said the figures were no surprise and 'grim news for patients, for doctors and for all those who work in the NHS'.

Source: adapted from an article by Chris Mihill, *The Guardian*, 22 August 1997, p. 3

Homelessness is a growing social problem

- Equality of educational outcome is a myth. Despite reforms, middle-class children tend to leave school with better qualifications than working-class children. State schools are under-resourced. Smith et al. (1997) quote figures that suggested that in the mid-1990s, 23 per cent of secondary schools and 13 per cent of primary schools suffered from a shortage of books which negatively affected the standards of lessons. They argue that educational opportunities and results have become more unequal in social terms during the 1980s and 1990s.
- The sale of council houses to tenants has reduced the stock of local authority housing provision, since money received from the sales is not used to build new houses.
- Homelessness appears to be a growing social problem. Local authority statistics on the number of households accepted as homeless do not provide a full picture and underestimate the true extent of homelessness.

Single homeless people are generally not seen as being in priority need. As a result, they are not accepted as homeless by local authorities so they do not appear in the statistics. A more complete picture of homelessness is given by figures from the 1991 census:

The annual homelessness acceptance figures are, of course, just a measurement of the local authority response over a year, based on a restricted definition of homelessness. A fuller picture based on 1991 census data suggests that on census day there were

- approximately 110,000 concealed families (such as families having to live with parents)
- 50,000 would-be couples living apart
- 140,000 sharing households
- 100,000 single homeless people in hostels etc.
- 10,000 squatters and rough sleepers
- 22,000 families accepted as homeless and living in hostels and bed and breakfast hotels

This gives a total of 430,000 households who could be described as homeless.

Source: adapted from Ginsburg (1997)

HOMELESSNESS

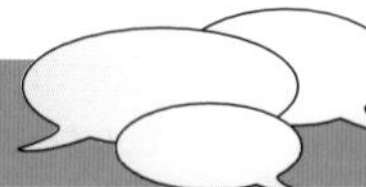

In a small group, discuss the possible reasons why

1 young people might become homeless;
2 the number of homeless people appears to be increasing.

Make a note of two reasons for each.

- Unemployment is a far bigger social problem than official statistics suggest. Official figures do not provide us with a true picture of the extent of unemployment (see Chapter 7). For these reasons, some sociologists believe that if the welfare state is to tackle social problems effectively, then funding should be increased and provisions improved.

ATTITUDES TO SOCIAL SECURITY SPENDING

Members of the public seem to favour spending on some groups more than others. In a survey, respondents were given a list of five benefits and asked to select their two priorities for extra spending. The results are shown in Figure 4.1.

Figure 4.1 Attitudes to social security spending

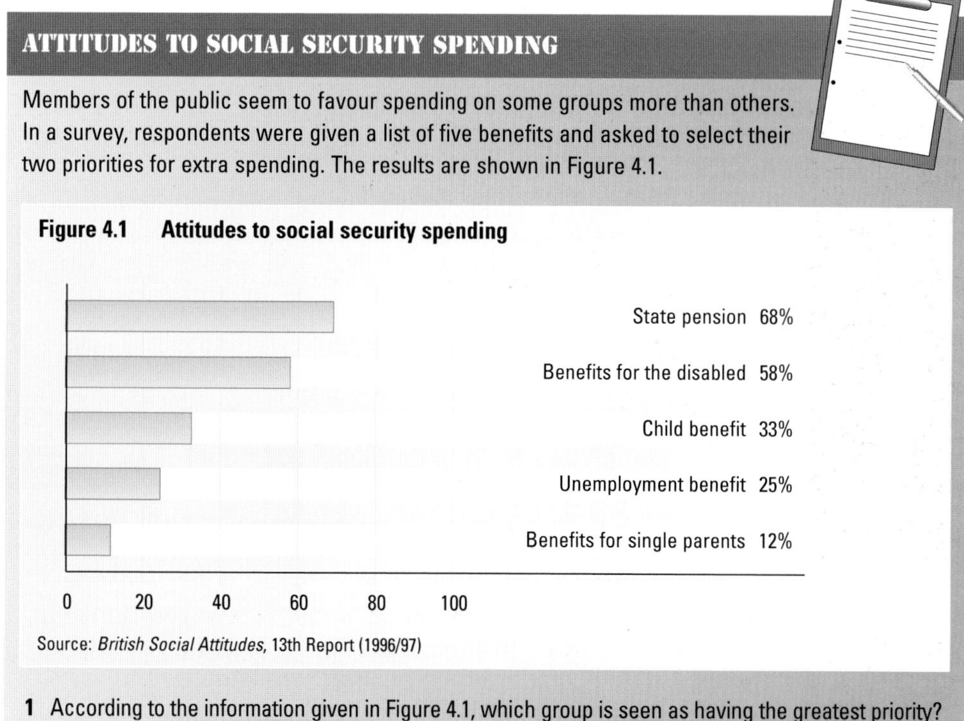

Source: *British Social Attitudes*, 13th Report (1996/97)

1 According to the information given in Figure 4.1, which group is seen as having the greatest priority?
2 To what extent does this information suggest that some groups are seen as more worthy of financial assistance than others?

Other critical views of the welfare state

Yet another view is that the welfare state has actually gone too far and that provision should be reduced.

- Some argue that welfare state provisions may actually discourage people from helping themselves. New Right approaches suggest that the welfare state has created a **dependency culture**, in which people who rely on benefits become so dependent on them that they lose all motivation to work. They claim that state benefits present a disincentive to work – that is, they discourage people from genuinely seeking paid employment. For example, David Marsland (1996) observes that many young men, unemployed since leaving school at the earliest opportunity, and supported in a life of useless idleness by state benefits, family support and a varied stock of regularly used scrounging skills, simply do not want to work.
- New Right approaches suggest that public spending on welfare is wasteful and costly. For example, child benefit is currently paid universally – to all those with children – but critics suggest that it should be given selectively – only to those who really need it. Such approaches stress self-reliance rather than reliance on the state, arguing that people should take more responsibility for themselves.
- Critics suggest that the welfare state reduces the importance of families. One of the traditional functions of the family was to provide social welfare to family members in need, yet today many families no longer perform this function. It is argued that individuals and families must accept more responsibility for their own welfare.

STEREOTYPING

In Britain over the last three decades, there has been a series of **moral panics** (see pp. 301–2) surrounding the crisis in the welfare state in general, and benefit claimants in particular.

A moral panic involves a group becoming defined as a threat to society's interests. Claimants are often presented in insulting and stereotyped ways by tabloids and some politicians. Walker and Walker (1997) argue that, during the 1980s, the Conservative governments attacked the credibility of most groups of benefit claimants: older people were not really poor any more; the unemployed and those with long-term illnesses were not genuine; the young homeless were to blame for their situation, while young people and lone parents should look to their families for support.

The Child Poverty Action Group campaigns against poverty

Millar (1997) identifies the stereotypical figures of the 'single mum' with her 'babies on benefits' who grow up to be 'delinquent youth', partly because the 'absent father' fails to provide support.

Parts of the media seem to encourage 'scroungerphobia' in presenting us with a distorted picture of claimants as idlers and cheats. In 1996, a telephone 'hotline' was launched to encourage members of the public to report benefit fraud. Such media presentations reduce the impact of the arguments of voluntary groups such as the Child Poverty Action Group in their campaign against poverty.

SUPPORT FOR THE WELFARE STATE

Many people continue to support the welfare state. Discuss the possible reasons for this continued support. Make a note of two possible reasons.

WHAT IS THE ROLE OF VOLUNTARY ORGANIZATIONS?

Voluntary organizations are 'voluntary' in the sense that they are non-statutory. Many of them are charities that receive tax breaks, government grants and lottery money in order to carry out their work. Many voluntary organizations provide help that the welfare state is unable or unwilling to supply.

Some voluntary organizations, such as Citizens' Advice Bureaux, the Samaritans, Rape Crisis Line and MENCAP, exist to support and help other people. Some, such as Alcoholics Anonymous and Body Positive North West, exist as self-help groups. Other voluntary organizations have more of a dual role in supporting themselves and others, for example Families Need Fathers and Release (National Legal and Drugs Services).

Examples of voluntary organizations

- **Age Concern** works to improve the quality of life for older people. Local organizations provide community-based services such as day centres, lunch clubs and transport.
- **Barnardo's** works with children, young people and their families who are disadvantaged. It runs community-based projects such as providing day

care centres for young children at risk and supporting young people leaving care.

- **Benevolent Society of St Patrick** gives grants to provide practical help to people of Irish descent who are in need and living in London.
- **Body Positive North West** provides services to those living with or affected by HIV/AIDS in the north-west of England, for example keep-fit facilities and information on HIV/AIDS-related research.
- **Turning Point** provides information, advice, counselling and rehabilitation for those with drug, alcohol or mental health problems.

Voluntary organizations

THE IMPORTANCE OF THE VOLUNTARY SECTOR

- Voluntary organizations may be better equipped than welfare state agencies to deal with particular needs, client groups or issues. Some voluntary organizations have filled gaps in state provision and may be the only provider of a particular service.
- Many voluntary organizations rely in part on the work of unpaid volunteers. It is suggested that volunteers can provide a flexible and responsive service to clients. The Samaritans, for example, provide 24-hour confidential support to people going through a crisis. In 1994, it had 22,000 volunteers.
- Some voluntary organizations are staffed by employees or volunteers who have had direct personal experience upon which they can draw. Within Body Positive, for example, people can use their own experience of living with HIV/AIDS in order to support others.
- Voluntary organizations may act as pressure groups to encourage governments to introduce or change policies. The Child Poverty Action Group (CPAG) is a leading anti-poverty organization that campaigns on behalf of benefit claimants. It also undertakes and publishes research on poverty-related issues. CPAG has been critical of government policies and pushes for policy improvements and for the provision of more resources for people in poverty.

CHECK YOUR UNDERSTANDING

Name two voluntary organizations in Britain, other than those named above, which offer welfare services to people. In each case, explain briefly how they do this. (4 marks)

WHAT IS POVERTY?

Poverty is a controversial issue and there is no single agreed way of defining it. This means that different researchers work with different definitions of poverty.

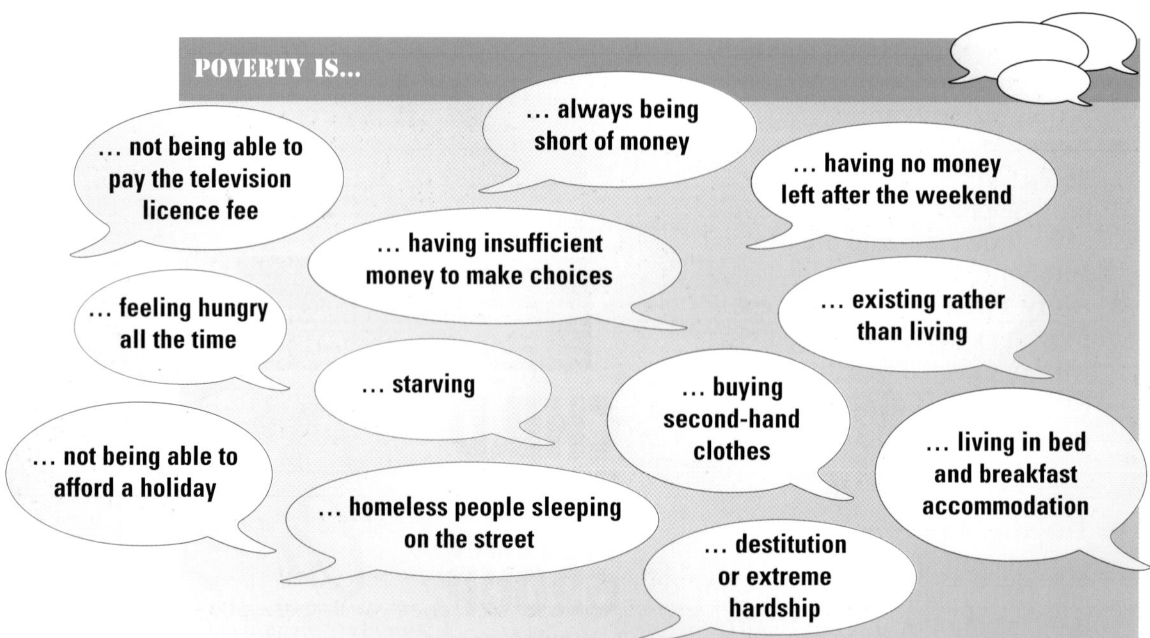

1 In a small group, discuss these statements and decide which are the two most satisfactory and the two least satisfactory examples of poverty. Be prepared to justify your choices.
2 Now attempt to write your own group definition of poverty.

Even though defining poverty has proved difficult, the issue of how we define it is very important for a number of reasons. First, we need to be able to define poverty if we are to identify and measure it. Our definition will affect how we measure poverty, the numbers said to be in poverty, and the extent to which it is said to exist. Second, our definition will influence our views on how poverty should be tackled.

Walker and Walker (1997) argue that the definition of poverty chosen by the state is crucial, first, because it determines to what extent the government accepts that poverty exists, and second, because it influences what policies are adopted to tackle poverty and how the poor will be treated.

Absolute and relative poverty

There are two broad approaches to defining poverty – the absolute and relative approaches. People experience **absolute poverty** when their income is insufficient to obtain the minimum needed to survive. People in absolute poverty do not have access to even the basic necessities of life such as food, clean water, shelter, heating and clothes. Their income is so low that they can barely survive.

The absolute definition is useful in that it allows researchers to measure trends over time. It is criticized, however, because in practice it is very difficult to determine what the 'minimum needed to survive' is. For example, is the minimum dietary requirement just bread and water, or should we include fresh fruit and vegetables? 'Survival' is also relative to such factors as age, climate, and level of activity.

People experience **relative poverty** when they cannot afford to meet the general standard of living of most other people in their society. The income of people in relative poverty is much less than the average for society as a whole, so they are poor compared to others in their society. In affluent or rich

Absolute poverty

Relative poverty

societies such as Britain or the United States, even the poor are well off compared to people in many other societies. Most researchers in Britain today agree that the relative definition of poverty should be used.

What is considered as poverty differs from time to time and from society to society. Using the relative approach means that we will always find poverty in a society in so far as we will find some people who have less than average income.

DEFINING POVERTY

Read through the extract on the right, which gives Peter Townsend's influential view of poverty. Does it provide us with an absolute or a relative view of poverty? Explain your answer.

Individuals, families and groups in the population can be said to be in poverty when they lack the resources to obtain the types of diet, participate in the activities and have the living conditions and amenities which are customary, or at least widely encouraged or approved, in the societies to which they belong.

Source: Townsend (1979) p. 31

STUDYING RELATIVE POVERTY IN THE UK

In a small group, discuss the possible reasons why sociologists usually study relative rather than absolute poverty in the UK today. Note down three of these reasons.

SOCIAL EXCLUSION

During the 1980s and 1990s, a distinction has been drawn between poverty and **social exclusion**. Poverty refers to a lack of material resources, particularly income. Social exclusion is a broader concept that refers to being shut out or excluded from society's social, economic, political and cultural life.

Forms of social exclusion:

- Social exclusion – homelessness, dependence on benefits
- Economic exclusion – unemployment
- Political exclusion – people are less likely to take an interest in the political process
- Cultural exclusion – lack of recreation and leisure.

The EU in its Second European Poverty Programme defined people as poor where 'their material, cultural and social resources are so limited as to exclude them from the minimum acceptable way of life in the member state in which they live.' Social exclusion certainly plays an important part in lives marked by poverty.

Source: adapted from Melanie Phillips, 'Who are the poor?', *The Observer*, 21 April 1996, p. 5

Robert Walker (1997) believes that while the use of the term poverty encourages the practice of blaming the poor, the term social exclusion stresses society's role in excluding certain people from full participation.

The shift in focus from poverty to social exclusion has been influenced by the European Union (EU), whose definition of poverty centres on social exclusion and powerlessness, as the extract on the left illustrates.

The Child Poverty Action Group sees poverty not simply in terms of being short of money, clothing or food. Poverty is also not being able to join a sports club, go out, or send one's children on a school trip. Poverty is experienced in terms of having limited access to decent services such as education, housing and health services.

CHECK YOUR UNDERSTANDING

What are some of the problems associated with defining poverty? (6 marks)

HOW DO WE MEASURE POVERTY?

Britain has neither an official government definition of poverty nor an official measurement of it. This means that in Britain there is no official **poverty line** – a government-approved line that divides those who are in poverty from those who are not. Nevertheless, sociologists have used government statistics to show the extent of poverty.

One way of defining the poverty line, popular between the mid-1960s and the mid-1980s, is to use minimum government social security benefit levels. According to this measure, we would count as poor those people living on or below the state safety net of current benefit rates. Some approaches identify those who live on incomes between 100 and 140 per cent of current benefit rates as living on the margins of poverty.

Walker and Walker (1997) point out that many people live on incomes that are actually below the government's social security benefit rates. For example in 1992, over 4.5 million people lived on incomes below these rates. One explanation for this is that many people who are entitled to benefits do not take them up. In particular, older people are least likely to claim benefits to which they are entitled. A second reason is that many people earn low wages.

A second way of measuring poverty is based on statistics on households below average income. According to this measure, people are in poverty when they live in a household that has an income below half of the average wages. This is worked out at 50 per cent of average income after housing costs have been paid.

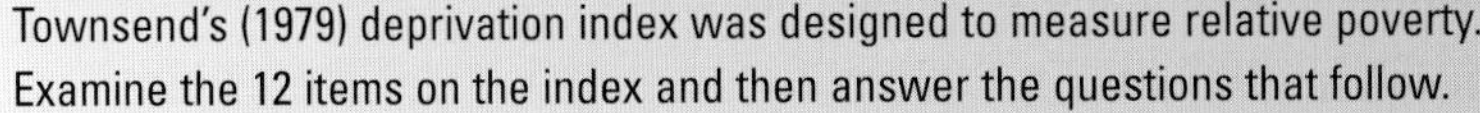

POVERTY IN THE UK

Townsend's (1979) deprivation index was designed to measure relative poverty. Examine the 12 items on the index and then answer the questions that follow.

The deprivation index

	Characteristic	% of population
1	Has not had a week's holiday away from home in the last 12 months	53.6%
2	Adults only. Has not had a relative or friend to the home for a meal or snack in the last four weeks	33.4%
3	Adults only. Has not been out in the last four weeks to a relative or friend for a meal or snack	45.1%
4	Children only (under 15). Has not had a friend to play or to tea in the last four weeks	36.3%
5	Children only. Did not have party on last birthday	56.6%
6	Has not had an afternoon or evening out for entertainment in the last two weeks	47.0%
7	Does not have fresh meat (including meals out) as many as four days a week	19.3%
8	Has gone through one or more days in the past fortnight without a cooked meal	7.0%
9	Has not had a cooked breakfast most days of the week	67.3%
10	Household does not have a refrigerator	45.1%
11	Household does not usually have a Sunday joint (three in four times)	25.9%
12	House does not have sole use of four amenities indoors (flush WC; sink or washbasin and cold water tap; fixed bath or shower; and gas or electric cooker)	21.4%

Source: Townsend (1979) p. 250

1. What percentage of the population had not had an afternoon or evening out for entertainment in the last two weeks?
2. Point 9 indicates that almost seven out of ten people did not have a cooked breakfast most days of the week. To what extent can we see this as evidence of deprivation?
3. Examine points 7 and 11 on the index. To what extent can we see the lack of a Sunday joint and fresh meat as evidence of deprivation?
4. Townsend found that 45 per cent of households lacked a refrigerator. To what extent can we see this as showing deprivation?

BREADLINE BRITAIN

Mack and Lansley (1985) measured poverty in terms of minimum living standards rather than income. In order to establish what the minimum standard of living was, they conducted their Breadline Britain Survey. In the survey, they presented respondents with a range of items and asked them to decide whether they considered each item to be either necessary or desirable. In this way, the Breadline Britain Survey aimed to find out what the general population regarded as necessities as a way of discovering what standard of living was considered unacceptable by society as a whole in 1983.

Mack and Lansley measured poverty as the lack of items that are regarded as necessities by society as a whole. Households lacking three or more necessities were counted as being in poverty.

Over 90 per cent of respondents agreed that the following were necessities (the figures on the right refer to the percentage of the population having the item):

- heating 92
- an indoor toilet (not shared) 98

- a damp-free home 85
- a bath (not shared) 97
- beds for everyone 97

More than 65 per cent of respondents classed the following as necessities:

- enough money for public transport 87
- a warm waterproof coat 88
- three meals a day for children 90
- self-contained accommodation 93
- two pairs of all-weather shoes 84
- a bedroom for every child over ten of different sex 76
- a refrigerator 96
- toys for children 92
- carpets 97
- celebrations on special occasions 93
- a roast joint or equivalent once a week 87
- a washing machine 89

Source: adapted from Mack and Lansley (1985) p. 66

In 1990, Mack and Lansley updated their research and found that one in five people, or 20 per cent of the population, lacked three or more of these items.

THE MINIMUM STANDARD OF LIVING

According to Mack and Lansley's Breadline Britain Survey (1985), what percentage of people

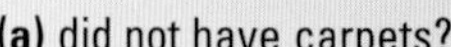

(a) did not have carpets?
(b) did not have a damp-free home?
(c) had two pairs of all-weather shoes?
(d) had toys for the children?

RESEARCHING THE BREADLINE

1 (a) Conduct your own survey using Mack and Lansley's criteria to find out whether these items are seen as necessities or desirables today. You should ask at least ten respondents.

(b) Once you have conducted your survey, write a paragraph summarizing your findings.

2 Mack and Lansley's survey was carried out in 1983.

(a) Do any of the items need to be revised so that they are more relevant to the present?

(b) Suggest whether items could be deleted or added.

CHECK YOUR UNDERSTANDING

Identify and explain two ways in which poverty can be measured. (4 marks)

WHO ARE THE POOR?

Alan Walker (1997) argues that there is evidence in Britain in the late 1990s of desperate poverty on a scale not witnessed since the 1930s. People from some groups are more likely to experience poverty than others. In particular, unemployed people, lone parents and pensioners are more vulnerable compared to other groups of people. Furthermore, different groups may experience poverty in different ways.

The composition of the poor

The graph in Figure 4.2 provides a breakdown of who the people in low-income families were in 1993–5. For example, 38% of people in the lowest income group were from families comprising couples with dependent children. The graph also shows that 38% of people in the population as a whole live in families with dependent children.

PEOPLE IN THE BOTTOM INCOME GROUP

According to th information in Figure 4.2:

1. Which individuals are over-represented in the bottom income group compared to their numbers in the population as a whole?
2. Which individuals are under-represented in the bottom income group compared to their numbers in the population as a whole?

Figure 4.2 People in the bottom income group: by family type 1993–5

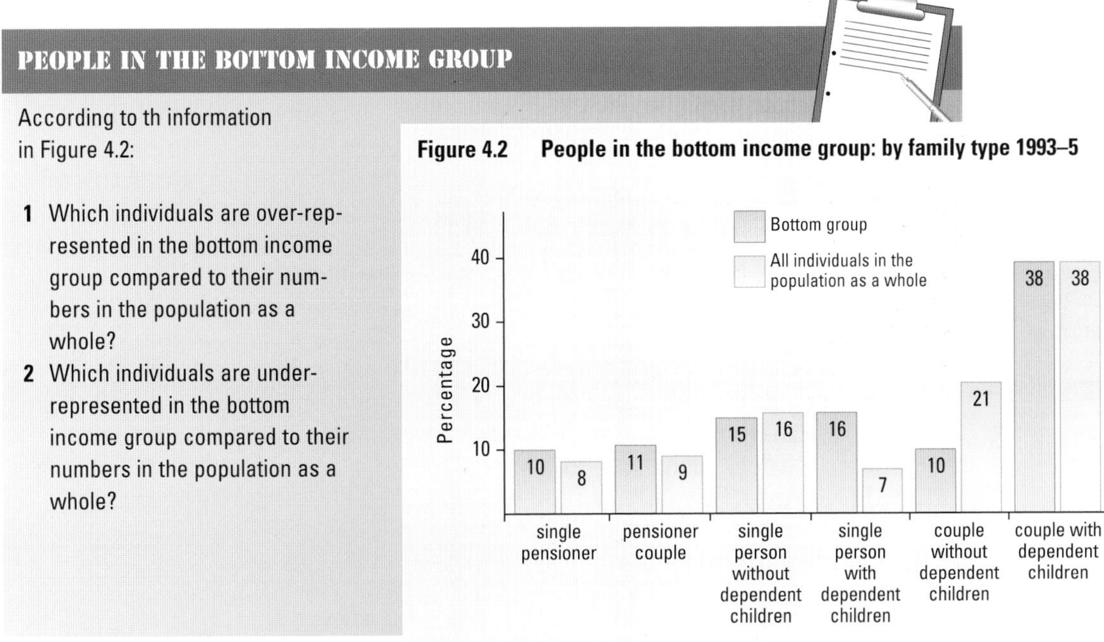

Source: adapted from *Social Trends* (1997), table 5.19, p. 99

Ethnicity and poverty

People from some minority ethnic groups are over-represented in low-income households. For example, Table 4.1 (see p. 102) shows that 64 per cent of people in households with a head of household of Pakistani or Bangladeshi origin were in the bottom income group in 1994–5.

Social Trends (1997) points out that, in examining these statistics on low-income households, we need to consider factors such as the differing rates of female participation in the labour market. For example, among women of working age of Pakistani and Bangladeshi origin, three quarters were not in paid work in Spring 1995. This was twice the rate for women in the Black and Indian ethnic groups.

Poverty is also linked to unemployment rates in that people from the black, Bangladeshi and Pakistani communities are at greater risk of unemployment.

ETHNICITY AND POVERTY

Table 4.1 Distribution of disposable income by ethnic group of head of household in Great Britain (1994–5)

Ethnic group	Bottom fifth (%)	Top four-fifths (%)
White	19	81
Black	27	73
Indian	27	73
Pakistani/Bangladeshi	64	36
Other ethnic minorities	36	64
All ethnic groups	20	80

Source: *Social Trends* (1997), table 5.20, p. 99

According to the information in Table 4.1:

(a) which group is most likely to live in a low-income household?

(b) which group is least likely to live in a low-income household?

When in employment, they are more likely to be in low-paid jobs. Amin and Oppenheim (1992) argue that, in addition to low pay and unemployment, black people face poor housing, increasing homelessness and run-down schools. Amin and Oppenheim see ethnic origin and poverty as being closely connected. The extract on the left provides their explanation of one thread of the link.

> *Since the early 1950s, ethnic minorities have been regarded as a convenient pool of cheap labour which can be used to prop up specific parts of the British economy. Working in unskilled and low-paid work – mainly in manufacturing industry – and facing marginalization through racism and discrimination, people from ethnic minorities have been and continue to be more susceptible to poverty than white people.*
>
> Source: Amin and Oppenheim (1992) p. v

A further point raised by Bloch (1997) is the low take-up of benefits. She suggests that cultural factors come into play attaching shame and stigma to claiming benefits. She quotes research carried out in Leeds which found that, among Chinese, Pakistani and Bangladeshi communities, the stigma attached to claiming benefits sometimes resulted in a decision not to claim.

Children and poverty

The largest group in poverty in Britain in the late 1990s comprises families with children. Figure 4.2 (see p. 101) shows that 54% of people in the bottom income group were from families with dependent children. In particular, children in lone-parent families are disproportionately exposed to poverty. Alan Walker (1997) points out that this means that two generations are being blighted by poverty at the same time.

Women and poverty

In general, women are more likely to experience poverty than men. Millar (1997) points out that the two groups with the highest risk and the longest durations of poverty comprise females: older women living alone and lone mothers. There are a number of reasons for this:

- Women have a longer life expectancy than men so there are more older female than male pensioners living alone. In May 1995 there were just over half a million single women aged over 80 receiving income support.

- Women are more likely than men to be lone parents.
- Women in paid work earn, on average, less than men.
- The responsibility for caring for children and for relatives who are elderly, sick or with disabilities often falls on women. Consequently, women are less likely than men to have earnings from full-time employment.

Millar (1997) suggests that because women are generally responsible for domestic work and childcare, the burden of 'managing' poverty falls mainly upon them. Research indicates that in some couple households, the men may be well off while the women and children are poor. Oppenheim (1993) maintains that women often put the needs of family members before their own and so go without. A woman can be in poverty while other members of her family are not, or she may be in deeper poverty than family members.

People with disabilities and poverty

People with disabilities are more likely to experience poverty because they are more likely to be unemployed. If employed, they are more likely to be in low-paid, low-status occupations. People with disabilities are also more at risk of poverty because they may have extra costs associated with their disability.

Older pensioners

Many people retire with an occupational pension, which means that they enjoy a good standard of living. Older pensioners who are more likely to be solely reliant on the state retirement pension are more vulnerable to poverty.

CHECK YOUR UNDERSTANDING

1. Identify and explain two reasons why some people in the UK with a disability may be at risk of poverty. (4 marks)
2. Identify two reasons why women are more likely than men to be living in poverty in the UK. (2 marks)
3. Identify two other groups whose members are more at risk of poverty. (2 marks)
4. State three ways in which governments have tried to reduce poverty in Britain since the Second World War. (3 marks)

LIVING IN POVERTY

It's cold and damp. We've just got a fire in the children's room which took years to get. I've got bronchitis and so have the children.

Julie

We're getting deeper and deeper into debt. I mean that hurts as well … One week he'll go and tell them that we can't pay, the next week I'll go. There was a time I'd hide if anybody knocked on the door. And if I went to the door, I'd stand there shaking. But now I just stand there and face them and tell them we haven't got the money.

Mrs Ward on loan sharks

The children are always asking for things – they say their friends have this and this … we have to say no, so the kids get upset and we feel upset.

I'm turning into a cabbage here. Sometimes I think I'm going mad in this box of a room.

A resident in bed and breakfast accommodation

Source: quoted in Oppenheim (1993)

People living in poverty face the very real possibility of falling into debt for basic household bills such as water, gas, electricity, rent or mortgage payments.

> *'Life for the poor is constantly having to balance need against cost: to keep the fire on and stay warm but risk not being able to pay the bill, or to keep down the cost and go cold; buy food for tonight's meal or save for the gas bill; buy the birthday present now and miss the rent or the catalogue payment. For poor families, occasions such as birthdays and Christmas, instead of being happy events, give rise to anxiety and guilt as parents recognize that they cannot give their children the sorts of presents being advertised on television.'*
>
> Source: Walker and Walker (1997)

Poverty affects diet. Research shows that parents, and particularly mothers, may go without food in order to feed their children. Research published in 1991 by the National Children's Home studied 354 low-income families with children. One in five parents and one in ten children had gone hungry in the previous month because they could not afford to buy food. The diet of poor families is less nutritious and so less healthy than that of well-off families. Poor people are likely to suffer worse health than richer people.

THE CONSEQUENCES OF CHILDHOOD POVERTY

Malnutrition is no longer just a Third World problem. It is now evident in the UK on a scale not seen since the Thirties. Research from West Yorkshire has found that poor children entering school are 4 cm shorter, and weigh less, than their wealthier peers … Last month, the United Nations reported that the gap between rich and poor is as bad in Britain as it is in Nigeria. More and more children are born into deprivation, at increased risk of early death, stunted growth, mental impairment and chronic ill-health. The problems spill over into truancy and poor achievement.

Source: Heather Mills, 'Life on the brink: Breadline Britain', *The Observer*, 11 August 1996, p. 18

With reference to the extract:

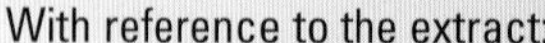

1. Identify three ways in which living in poverty can affect children's health.
2. Identify two ways in which living in poverty may affect children's education.
3. Suggest two reasons why we cannot safely assume that poverty is no longer a problem in the UK.

Alan Walker (1997) points out that:

- in Britain we are now seeing the return of diseases associated with poverty and malnutrition, such as rickets and tuberculosis, which most health experts had hoped were banished for ever;

- estimates suggest that up to 2 million British children are suffering from poverty-related malnutrition;
- three in every four children in care come from families living on income support;
- there is a higher infant mortality rate (the number of infant deaths per 1,000 live births per year) in the poorest households compared to the richest. As many as 2,000 children die in infancy in England and Wales because they are unlucky enough to be born into a poor family rather than a better-off one.

In a report for the Child Poverty Action Group, Oppenheim (1993) argues that poverty means going short materially, socially and emotionally. She suggests that it is not what is spent that matters, but what isn't.

POVERTY AND LIFE CHANCES

'Poverty means staying at home, often being bored, not seeing friends, not going to the cinema, not going out for a drink and not being able to take the children out for a trip or a treat or a holiday. It means coping with the stresses of managing on very little money, often for months or even years. It means having to withstand the onslaught of society's pressure to consume ... Above all, poverty takes away the tools to create the building blocks for the future – your "life chances". It steals away the opportunity to have a life unmarked by sickness, a decent education, a secure home and a long retirement. It stops people being able to plan ahead. It stops people being able to take control of their lives.'

Source: Oppenheim and Harker (1996) p. 5

In a small group, discuss what Oppenheim and Harker (1996) mean by the statement that poverty 'takes away the tools to create the building blocks for the future – your "life chances"'.

Now make a note of the outcome of your discussions.

CHECK YOUR UNDERSTANDING

1 How might poverty affect the life chances and status of individuals in society? (6 marks)

2 Identify two groups who are at risk of poverty and, for each, briefly explain the consequences of living in poverty. (6 marks)

THE LIFE CYCLE OF POVERTY

Official statistics provide us only with a snapshot, for example of households below average income at any one point in time. The idea of the life cycle of poverty is important because it provides more of a moving picture. It highlights movement into and out of poverty over time and suggests the possibility that we may move into and out of poverty at different stages in our lives. Many more of us experience poverty at some point in our lives than is indicated by the statistics.

Figure 4.3 The life cycle of poverty

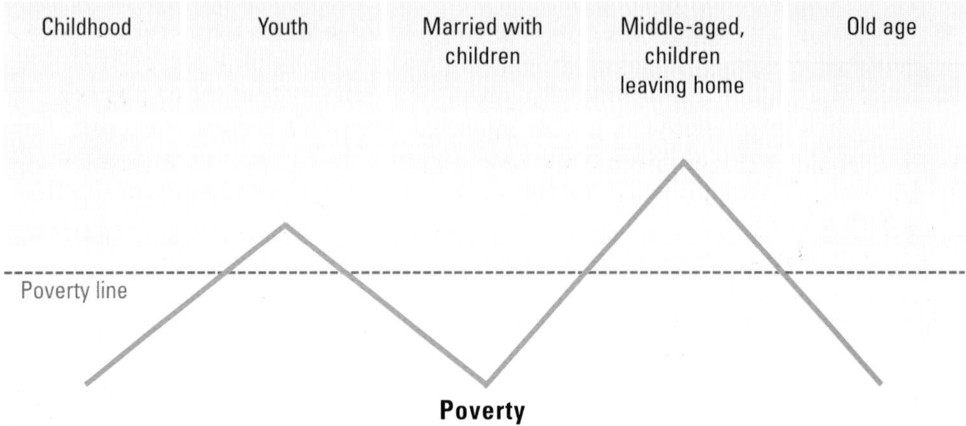

Source: Jorgensen et al. (1997)

CHECK YOUR UNDERSTANDING

1 Explain briefly what is meant by the 'life cycle of poverty'. (2 marks)
2 Identify one point in the life cycle at which people are more vulnerable to poverty and one point at which they are less vulnerable. In each case, explain briefly why this is so. (4 marks)

DOES POVERTY REALLY EXIST IN BRITAIN?

Some sociologists, politicians and journalists have suggested that poverty no longer really exists in Britain. Discuss the arguments for and against this view.

Now make a note of your conclusion, giving your reasons.

EXPLANATIONS OF POVERTY

Poverty, as we have seen, is difficult to define and measure. Not surprisingly, there are disagreements among sociologists and politicians about what causes poverty and why it continues over time. Some explanations of poverty focus on the poor themselves, while others focus more on the structure of society within which the poor live.

Minority group theory

Minority group theory begins by identifying the different groups in poverty. It then explains poverty in terms of the group characteristics of the poor. Unemployment and low pay, for example, are seen as immediate causes of poverty.

Labour politician and Chancellor of the Exchequer Gordon Brown (1997) identifies the causes of poverty as unemployment, low skills and low wages. In order to tackle poverty at root, he suggests policies to improve skills, educational and employment opportunities.

The poverty trap

Once in poverty, it can be very difficult for people to escape. In effect, people can be trapped in poverty because being poor is expensive.

Housing in poorer areas can be run down. A damp house with badly fitted windows or inadequate loft insulation will be expensive to heat.

Means-tested benefits can create a poverty trap. For example, an employed person who is claiming means-tested benefits could receive a wage increase yet be no better off as a result. This is because he or she has crossed the qualifying threshold of the benefits involved and now earns too much to qualify. If this happens, the individual may actually end up worse off after a wage increase because of the loss of benefit.

"Where I live, the nearest supermarket is in town so I have to get the bus, which costs over £2.00 return. When I'm short of money, which is nearly always, I shop at the corner shop. I know it's expensive but they let me buy a small piece of loose cheese or a few slices of meat. Take things like soap powder, tea or cornflakes. I can't afford to buy the bigger sizes, even though they work out much cheaper."

CHECK YOUR UNDERSTANDING

Explain why it might be difficult for people to move out of poverty. (3 marks)

The culture of poverty

One explanation, popular during the 1950s and 1960s, of the persistence of poverty among some groups pointed to the culture of poverty. According to this view, people from the poorest section of society are socialized within the subculture of poverty, which means that they are unable to take up the opportunities open to them and so break free from poverty. The poor develop a way of life, a set of values and attitudes to cope with their poverty which include the following:

- Enjoy life today, as it is not likely to get any better! You may as well accept your situation, you can't do much about it, so live for the moment and don't worry about the future.
- With means-tested benefits, the amount of your savings may affect your entitlement to benefit and how much you receive. You may as well spend these savings now so that you will be able to get means-tested benefits – there is no point in saving up.

The very values that poor people develop to help them cope with their situation also prevent them from escaping poverty, for example by saving or staying on at school. They become trapped in poverty. Through socialization within families, such values are passed on from parents to their children, so poverty persists over time from generation to generation.

According to this explanation, the policy to remove poverty would consist of educating and training children to compensate for their home values. The culture of poverty explanation can be criticized as follows:

- it shows how people adapt to poverty, but it does not explain what actually causes poverty in the first place;
- it seems to blame the poor for their situation.

The cycle of deprivation
Linked to the culture of poverty, this explanation was popular during the 1960s and 1970s. It focuses on how poverty 'breeds' from one generation to the next.

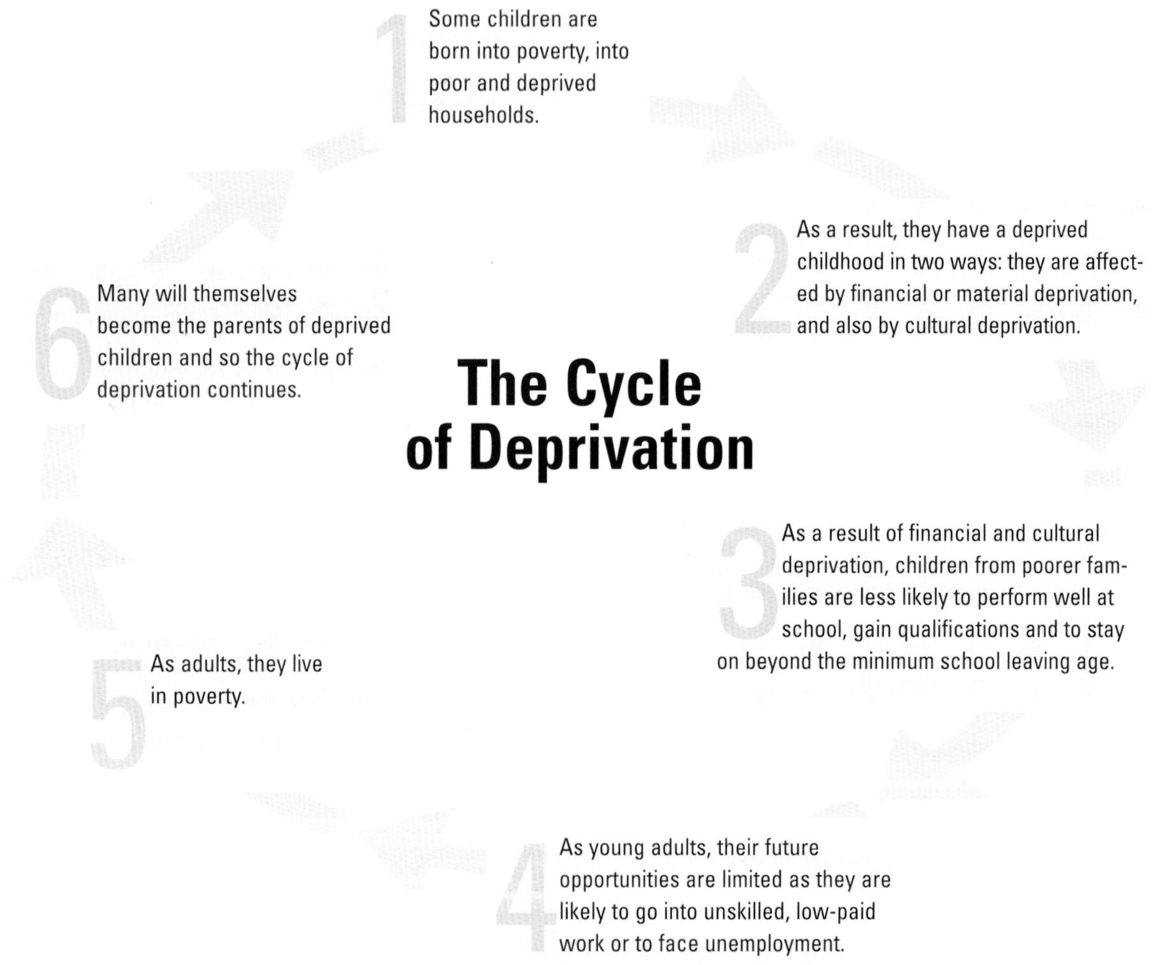

The Cycle of Deprivation

1 Some children are born into poverty, into poor and deprived households.

2 As a result, they have a deprived childhood in two ways: they are affected by financial or material deprivation, and also by cultural deprivation.

3 As a result of financial and cultural deprivation, children from poorer families are less likely to perform well at school, gain qualifications and to stay on beyond the minimum school leaving age.

4 As young adults, their future opportunities are limited as they are likely to go into unskilled, low-paid work or to face unemployment.

5 As adults, they live in poverty.

6 Many will themselves become the parents of deprived children and so the cycle of deprivation continues.

- Financial or material deprivation – lack of money – means that their diet will be inadequate, so poverty may result in the children's ill health. Housing may be inadequate and, at the extreme, the family may live in hostels or bed and breakfast accommodation.
- Cultural deprivation means that the children's background does not provide them with the resources to perform well at school. They have less parental encouragement and a poorer educational experience than children from more affluent, or well-off, backgrounds.

The policy to remove poverty according to this explanation is to employ social workers and to use the local authority provisions to help children to break out of the cycle.

Critics, however, suggest that this explanation may describe how deprivation continues over time from one generation to the next, but it fails to explain why some groups fall into poverty in the first place. Critics argue that deprivation should be treated as a structural phenomenon, arising as a consequence of the economic and political organization of society, rather than an individual or family phenomenon. (See page 111 for structural explanations of poverty.)

CHECK YOUR UNDERSTANDING

State one example of a feature of material deprivation and one example of a feature of cultural deprivation. (2 marks)

New Right approaches

More recently, New Right approaches have attempted to explain poverty in ways similar to the culture of poverty and cycle of deprivation. New Right approaches identify the emergence in Britain of an underclass, a group whose attitudes and values are different to those of mainstream society.

Charles Murray (1996) focuses on the individual behaviour of those he sees as the 'undeserving poor'. Reflecting upon his childhood experience in the USA, Murray describes the underclass in the first extract on the right.

He focuses on three symptoms of the underclass: crime, births outside marriage and economic inactivity among men of working age.

According to New Right approaches, the 'undeserving poor' remain in poverty because the welfare state encourages them to depend on state provision. Critics suggest that New Right approaches blame the victim. Others reject the very idea of an underclass, as illustrated by the second extract here.

> *'Their homes were littered and unkempt. The men in the family were unable to hold a job for more than a few weeks at a time. Drunkenness was common. The children grew up ill-schooled and ill-behaved and contributed a disproportionate share of the local juvenile delinquents.'*
>
> Source: Murray (1996)

> *'Kempson (1996) has recently reviewed the findings from over 30 studies of how people cope on low incomes. She finds no sign of an "underclass" of poor people with different attitudes and aspirations from the mainstream. What she does find is much evidence of people struggling hard to manage on what they have, and to improve their situations.'*
>
> Source: Millar (1997) p. 104

The inadequacies of the welfare state

Some sociologists believe that the social security system often fails to meet people's needs. Many people who are entitled to benefits, for example, do not claim them. One viewpoint, suggested in the following extract, is that benefits are simply too low:

> **There is agreement among academics, nutritionists, paediatricians and the Conservative government's own advisors that benefit and income support levels are too low and that not enough is being done to help families out of poverty. Yet the government refuses to accept that poverty exists in the UK. Peter Lilley, Social Security Secretary, maintained in 1996 that poverty was a problem only for the Third World. However, Professor Townsend, an authority on poverty, quotes the DSS's own figures to show that, since the Conservatives came to power in 1979, the number of children in households with an income only half that of the poorest 10 per cent has risen from 860,000 to 1,180,000.**
>
> Source: adapted from Heather Mills, 'Life on the brink: Breadline Britain', *The Observer*, 11 August 1996, p. 18

Amin and Oppenheim (1992), in their study of ethnicity and deprivation, argue that the social security system itself has often been discriminatory. Social security policies have failed in a number of ways to protect ethnic minority communities. For instance, the NI contribution principle discriminates against people with work patterns interrupted by unemployment. They point out, further, that many people from ethnic minorities are not receiving the benefits to which they are entitled. The welfare state has failed to remove poverty, so it should be reorganized to do the job that it was set up to do.

REACHING THE PEOPLE

Discuss the possible reasons why welfare services may not reach the people they are intended to help. Now note down three important points raised during your discussion.

Government policies

Inequality and relative poverty increased in Britain during the Conservative governments between 1979 and 1997. Millar (1997) suggests that government policies have largely failed to prevent poverty and have sometimes made the situation worse, citing examples such as the freezing of child benefit through most of the 1980s and the abolition of the minimum wage. Similarly, Labour politician Roy Hattersley (1997) suggests that former Conservative governments' policies were responsible for increasing inequalities in Britain:

The very rich – far from being a thing of the past – are richer than they have ever been. Over the years between 1979 and 1983–4, the income of the richest 10 per cent of society increased by almost 60 per cent. At the same time, the income of the poorest 10 per cent (after housing costs were taken into account) fell in real terms. Margaret Thatcher was the most redistributive Prime Minister in British history: her government took from the poor and gave to the rich. The poor are still with us today and in greater numbers.

Source: adapted from an essay by Roy Hattersley, former deputy leader of the Labour Party, in *The Guardian*, 26 July 1997

Structural explanations of poverty

Some explanations of poverty focus on the individual's inadequacies or the problems faced by people such as material or cultural deprivation. Structural explanations of poverty, however, reject the focus on individuals and groups and examine instead the way in which society is structured. According to this view, poverty results from the inequalities that are built into society.

Marxists argue that capitalist society is based on social divisions between the bourgeoisie and the proletariat – the capitalist class and the workers. The workers are dependent upon wages from paid labour. Those who cannot work for wages cannot support themselves and so constitute the poor. It is in the capitalists' interests to keep wages down. In a society based on a minority group making a profit out of the rest, it is inevitable that some people will be poor.

Marxists argue that poverty works to the advantage of the employers or bourgeoisie; for example, if those in employment demand higher wages then employers can threaten to replace them with workers from among the unemployed. The fear of poverty can serve to discipline the workers.

According to Marxists, the only way to remove poverty is to have revolutionary change in society and to replace capitalism as an economic system with communal ownership of factories, land and capital. This would ensure that nobody was exploited and it would end poverty. Critics argue, however, that if we examine societies that have gone through such social change, we will still find poverty, inequality and differences in the distribution of income and wealth.

CAN POVERTY AND INEQUALITY BE ELIMINATED?

Oppenheim (1997), in *Britain Divided*, ends her discussion of the growth of poverty and inequality on a positive note. According to her, the international picture suggests that some other countries have been much more successful at containing poverty and inequality. Oppenheim points to the many small-scale local projects that tread new ground in tackling poverty. She also highlights the importance of groups from the voluntary sector, such as the Child Poverty Action Group, in keeping issues related to poverty and inequality on the political agenda.

The Big Issue is one example of a project designed to provide vulnerable people with opportunities to earn money.

The Big Issue was set up in 1991 to give homeless people the chance to make an income. It campaigns on behalf of homeless people and highlights the major social issues of the day. It allows homeless people to voice their views and opinions.

To become a vendor you must be homeless or vulnerably accommodated. However, we recognize that for many homeless people, being housed is only the first stage in getting off the streets. Therefore if a rehoused vendor needs to continue selling *The Big Issue* in the North we may allow them to do so.

Vendors buy the magazine for 35p and sell it to the public for 80p. All vendors receive training, sign a code of conduct, and can be identified by badges with photos.

Source: *The Big Issue in the North*, No. 182, 27 October–2 November 1997, p. 3

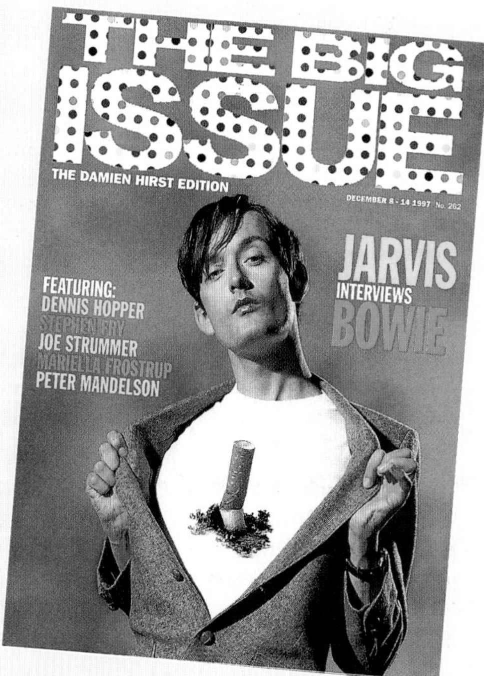

SUMMARY

In this chapter, we have covered the following points:

- The term welfare state describes a system in which the state takes responsibility for protecting the health and welfare of its citizens, and for meeting social needs. Under the post-war Labour government (1945–50) a system was set up so that in return for insurance contributions paid while in work, people would be entitled to draw out benefits when they were unable to work.
- The welfare state provides services in relation to education, training, health, housing and social security.
- Sociologists argue about how successful the welfare state has been. Those who believe it has been successful see it as playing a vital role in providing educational opportunities for all and a fairer distribution of income and wealth. Those who believe it has been less successful claim that the system is under great strain and that it falls well short of providing sufficient support to all who need it. Critics from the New Right argue that welfare state provisions encourage over-dependency on benefit and discourage some people from genuinely seeking to take care of themselves.
- Additional help is provided for needy groups by voluntary organizations and charities such as Mencap, Age Concern and the Samaritans. Some organizations have filled gaps in state provision and are the only provider of a particular service. Voluntary organizations also act as pressure groups to encourage government action and operate as centres for research.
- Poverty is a complex issue. There are two broad ways of defining it:
  - Absolute poverty – this is when people do not have access to even the most basic necessities of life such as food, clean water, shelter and clothing.
  - Relative poverty – this is when people fall below an agreed minimum standard of living of most people in a particular society.
- Poverty can be measured in terms of income level or in terms of an agreed minimum standard of living (e.g. having such items as a refrigerator or a warm waterproof coat).
- Sociologists have found that people from certain groups in society are more likely to experience poverty than others. For example, people from ethnic minorities, women, children and people with disabilities are disproportionately exposed to poverty.
- Sociologists have put forward various explanations of what causes poverty. These include the culture of poverty and cycle of deprivation theories, which claim that children born into poverty enjoy fewer opportunities than more affluent children. Consequently, they fail to break out of poverty as adults and go on themselves to become parents of deprived children. Other sociologists claim that the government does not do enough to help families out of poverty and that benefits are too low.
- Sociologists also argue about whether or not poverty and inequality can be eliminated.

EXAMINATION QUESTION 1

Study **Item A**. Then answer the questions that follow.

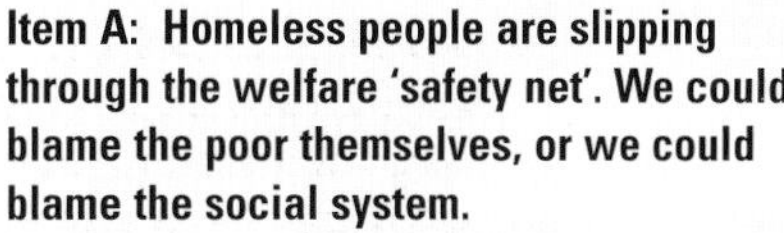

Item A: Homeless people are slipping through the welfare 'safety net'. We could blame the poor themselves, or we could blame the social system.

(a) **(i)** According to **Item A**, whom might we blame for the problems of the homeless? (1 mark)

(ii) According to **Item A**, why are people becoming homeless? (1 mark)

(iii) Identify one kind of help which might be given to the homeless person in the picture. (1 mark)

(b) **(i)** Identify one difficulty which people with disabilities face in Britain today. Explain why this is so. (3 marks)

(ii) Suggest one way in which the government can help to overcome the difficulties faced by people with disabilities. (1 mark)

(c) **(i)** Explain what is meant by 'relative poverty'. (2 marks)

(ii) Why do sociologists have difficulty in measuring the amount of poverty in Britain? (2 marks)

(d) **(i)** State an example of a voluntary organization concerned with the welfare of people. Briefly describe what it does. (3 marks)

(ii) Suggest one advantage of having voluntary organizations as well as the welfare state. (1 mark)

Source: SEG GCSE Sociology, Summer 1996, Foundation Tier, Paper 1, Section B, Question 8

EXAMINATION QUESTION 2

1 What explanations might sociologists offer for the existence of poverty in Britain in the 1990s? (10 marks)

Source: SEG GCSE Sociology, Summer 1997, Higher Tier, Paper 2, Section C, Question 7

BIBLIOGRAPHY

Amin, K. and Oppenheim, C. (1992) *Poverty in Black and White*, Child Poverty Action Group.

Bloch, A. (1997) 'Ethnic inequality and social security', in A. Walker and C. Walker (eds), *Britain Divided*, Child Poverty Action Group.

Brown, G. (1997) 'Why Labour is still loyal to the poor', *The Guardian*, 2 August 1997.

Charities Digest 1996 (1995) Waterlow Information Services.

Fraser, D. (1984) *The Evolution of the British Welfare State, 2nd edition*, Macmillan.

Ginsburg, N. (1997) 'Housing', in A. Walker and C. Walker (eds), *Britain Divided*, Child Poverty Action Group.

Jorgensen, N. et al. (1997) *Sociology: An Interactive Approach*, Collins Educational.

Mack, J. and Lansley, S. (1985) *Poor Britain*, George Allen and Unwin.

Marsland, D. (1996) *Welfare or Welfare State?* Macmillan

Millar, J. (1997) 'Gender', in A. Walker and C. Walker (eds), *Britain Divided*, Child Poverty Action Group.

Mills, H. (1996) 'Life on the brink: Breadline Britain', *The Observer*, 11 August, p. 18.

Murray, C. (1996) 'The emerging British underclass', in R. Lister (ed.), *Charles Murray and the Underclass: The Developing Debate*, Institute of Economic Affairs.

O'Donnell, M. and Garrod, J. (1990) *Sociology in Practice*, Thomas Nelson & Sons.

Oppenheim, C. (1993) *Poverty: The Facts*, Child Poverty Action Group.

Oppenheim, C. (1997) 'The growth of poverty and inequality', in A. Walker and C. Walker (eds), *Britain Divided*, Child Poverty Action Group.

Oppenheim, C. and Harker, L. (1996) *Poverty: The Facts, 3rd edition*, Child Poverty Action Group

Smith, G., Smith, T. and Wright, G. (1997) 'Poverty and schooling: choice, diversity or division?', in A. Walker and C. Walker (eds), *Britain Divided*, Child Poverty Action Group.

Townsend, P. (1979) *Poverty in the United Kingdom*, Penguin Books Ltd.

Walker, A. (1997) 'Introduction: the strategy of inequality', in A. Walker and C. Walker (eds), *Britain Divided*, Child Poverty Action Group.

Walker, R. (1997) 'Poverty and social exclusion in Europe', in A. Walker and C. Walker (eds), *Britain Divided*, Child Poverty Action Group.

Walker, C. and Walker, A. (1997) 'Poverty and Social Exclusion', in *Developments in Sociology*, Volume 13, Causeway Press.

CHAPTER 5

Families and Households

In this chapter, we will explore and attempt to answer the following questions:

1. **What is the family?**
2. **What different types of families and households exist in Britain today?**
3. **How do sociologists approach the study of families and family life?**
4. **What do historical approaches tell us about changes in families and households in Britain over time?**
5. **What can we learn about families and households from cross-cultural evidence?**
6. **How have relationships within families changed over time?**
7. **What are the contemporary trends in marriage and divorce in Britain?**
8. **What are the current trends in families and households?**
9. **What is the future for families and households?**

Happy families!

At some stage in our life most of us will live in a family unit. This is why the family is very significant in our society. However, even though we are likely to have personal experience of family life, this does not mean that it is an easy topic for sociologists to study. This is because we can all experience difficulty in separating the **facts** about families from our own experience of them and our own personal **beliefs** about them.

Here are just a few examples of people's beliefs about families and family life:

- Children brought up by one parent are worse off than those brought up by both parents.
- Gay men and lesbian women should be allowed to adopt children.
- Children need firm discipline from their parents. An occasional clip round the ear does them no harm at all.
- Mothers with young children should not work in paid employment.
- Unmarried couples should not live together. They should marry first in order to show their commitment to each other.
- A married couple should not have to stay together if they no longer get along, even if there are children involved.
- Free abortion should be available to all women on demand.

These sorts of issues are hotly debated by sociologists, politicians and the media. Such issues can arouse strong feelings because they involve judgements not only about how we live but about how people think we *should* live.

WHAT IS THE FAMILY?

Initially, the answer to this question might seem obvious. One possible – but very narrow – definition of the family is that it consists of **a married couple and their children who all live together**.

Once we begin to probe this definition, however, the task of defining the family becomes much more difficult.

DEFINING THE FAMILY

The definition of the family given above implies that a family is a group based on marriage, blood ties and shared residence. It can be criticized because it is not broad enough to include all the family types that exist in Britain today.

In a small group, discuss and note down:

1 the family types that are not included in this definition;
2 your own definition of the family that includes all the possible family types.

When we begin to look more closely at the idea of the family, the picture becomes much more complicated. It is very difficult to devise an adequate definition which includes all of the possible variations. Sociologists disagree on how to define the family. Some prefer to use the term **'families'** rather than 'the family', recognizing that a variety of different household arrangements and family types exists in modern Britain.

WHAT DIFFERENT TYPES OF FAMILIES AND HOUSEHOLDS EXIST IN BRITAIN TODAY?

Sociologists distinguish between **nuclear**, **extended**, **lone-parent** and **reconstituted** families. They also recognize that many people live in 'households' rather than in families.

Households

A household consists of either one person who lives alone or a group of people who live at the same address and who share one meal a day or facilities such as a living room. People living in a household are not necessarily related (by blood or marriage) to one another. For example, a household could consist of unrelated people, such as a group of students who share a residence, a lesbian couple who live together, a single person living in a bedsit, or a family group. A family household is one in which family members live in the same home, but a household does not necessarily contain a family. Some sociologists prefer to describe their work in this area as the study of 'households' rather than of 'the family' because they recognize that many people do not live as part of a family.

The nuclear family

A nuclear family consists of a father, mother and their child or children. It contains only two generations and family members live together in the same household.

The 'cereal packet' nuclear family: mum, dad and their children

The extended family

An extended family contains relatives from beyond the nuclear family, who live together in the same household. A family may be extended horizontally, for example with the addition of the husband's brother or the wife's cousin. In this case the family would still consist of just two generations.

Alternatively, it may be extended vertically, for example with the addition of the wife's parents, in which case the family will contain three generations.

The lone-parent family

A lone-parent family consists of one parent and a child or children.

The reconstituted family

A reconstituted family is usually referred to as a 'step family' and consists of parents and children. While both adults are the children's social parents, in that they bring the children up, they are not both their biological parents. A reconstituted family might come about as the result of a previously widowed woman with two children marrying a previously divorced man with one child.

FAMILY AND HOUSEHOLD TYPES

Most of us live in some sort of household but not all of us live in a family unit. Select five of your relatives or friends but do not include more than one person from any one household.

1 For each relative or friend, state what type of family or household they live in. It may be useful to begin with yourself.

Relative or friend	*Family or household type*
1	
2	
3	
4	
5	

2 What is the most common family or household type that you have identified?

Alternatives to the family in Britain today

In contemporary Britain, not all households are based on family ties and not all children are brought up in families. Some children may be brought up in the care of the local authority and may live in children's homes run by the social services. Alternatively, children in care may live with foster parents. About 65 per cent of children and young people in care are fostered and a small number live in voluntary sector homes and hostels.

It is important that we recognize that some people live neither in traditional families nor in households. Homelessness is a growing social problem in contemporary Britain and many homeless youngsters live on the city streets, sleeping in hostels or night shelters.

Alternatives to the traditional family

CHECK YOUR UNDERSTANDING

1 Explain what is meant by the term 'household'. (2 marks)

2 Identify and describe two types of family or household that can be found in Britain today. (4 marks)

3 Explain why some sociologists prefer to use the term 'families' rather than 'the family'. (2 marks)

HOW DO SOCIOLOGISTS APPROACH THE STUDY OF FAMILIES AND FAMILY LIFE?

During the 1940s and 1950s, the nuclear family was viewed by many sociologists in very positive terms as an important and necessary part of society. Such approaches, however, provide us with a rather rosy and optimistic view of family life. Recent approaches see things rather differently as they focus much more on the negative aspects of families and family life.

The positive approach to the study of the nuclear family

Some sociologists believe that the nuclear family plays an important role because it performs a number of essential **functions**, both for individuals and for society as a whole. This view, known as the **consensus** or **functionalist approach**, starts off from the assumption that people and society have basic needs that must be met if society is to function smoothly.

THE NEEDS OF INDIVIDUALS

1 Identify three things that individuals need in order to survive. You could, for example, consider people's physical, emotional or financial needs.
2 Does the nuclear family meet any of these needs? If so, state briefly which needs are met and explain how the nuclear family meets them.
3 If the needs you listed are not met by the nuclear family, explain briefly how they are met in ways other than through the nuclear family.

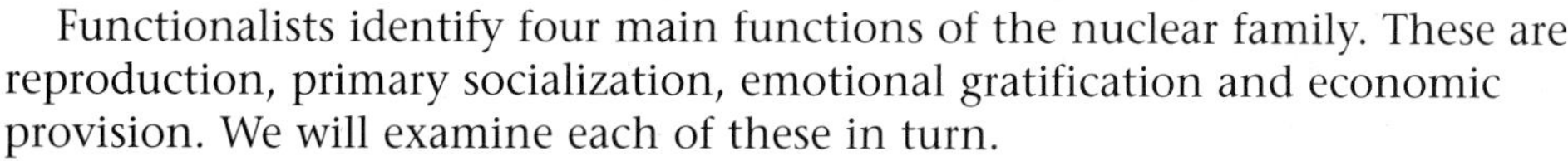

Functionalists identify four main functions of the nuclear family. These are reproduction, primary socialization, emotional gratification and economic provision. We will examine each of these in turn.

Reproduction

Society obviously needs new members if it is to survive. The nuclear family has an important role in procreation and childbearing. The family reproduces the human race and the future workforce. It also helps to regulate adult sexual behaviour. This is because the nuclear family is based on monogamy (marriage between one man and one woman). Consequently, married people are expected to have only one sexual partner, and extra-marital sex is viewed with disapproval.

Primary socialization

Society needs to ensure that new members will support its norms and values. Through the primary socialization process, which takes place within the nuclear family, we learn the culture and way of life of our society. In so doing, we learn how to fit in and how to conform. In this way, the family also acts as an agency of social control. The effects of not having undergone the process of primary socialization can be seen in case studies such as the wolf children (see p. 33).

Emotional gratification and nurture

Most of us need stable relationships with, and support from, other people. The nuclear family supplies us with emotional and psychological support and comfort. It is a place of safety and security.

Economic provision

We all need financial support, food and shelter, particularly if we are young, elderly or sick. The nuclear family meets these needs.

IS THIS IMAGE OF THE NUCLEAR FAMILY FALSE?

Since the 1950s this rosy image of the nuclear family has been heavily criticized as unrealistic and outdated. For example, in practice the four functions outlined on p. 119 are not necessarily carried out adequately or effectively by all families.

1 In a small group, take each function in turn and suggest two reasons why families might not fulfil that function.
2 Make a note of your reasons.

The New Right approach

The New Right approach of the 1980s and 1990s can be seen as a recent reworking of the earlier optimistic approach of functionalism. Like the earlier approach, it believes that the nuclear family is the preferred family type. It suggests that if children are to develop into stable adults, they are best brought up by two married parents. This is because the children of two parents are thought to do better educationally, physically, psychologically and socially than the children of single parents. The New Right approach is therefore seen by critics as an attack on gay and lesbian rights, single parenthood and fatherless families.

The New Right approach believes that family values are important. Jewson (1994) identifies four main aspects of family values:

- Family values are based on the view that there is a normal family type, comprising a married couple bringing up their natural children.
- Supporters of family values believe that the woman's role within the family is that of carer and nurturer, while the man's is that of breadwinner and protector.
- Family members have a duty to provide for each other and should take on the burden of looking after the old, sick, unemployed or homeless.
- Supporters of family values tend to oppose gay and lesbian rights, sexual freedom, certain types of sex education and (especially in the USA) abortion.

The New Right warns us that family values are declining and that this has placed the family in crisis.

FAMILY VALUES

1 Which family type do you think supporters of family values would see as the ideal?
2 Suggest briefly how supporters of family values might view:
   - the increase in divorce;
   - the increase in lone-parent families;
   - mothers who work in full-time paid employment.
3 Do supporters of family values seem to promote a growth or a reduction in the role of the welfare state?

FAMILIES WITHOUT FATHERHOOD

Although not part of the New Right, Halsey (1992) shares with it concerns about fatherless families. Read through the extract and then answer the questions that follow.

Divorce, separation, birth outside marriage and one-parent families as well as cohabitation and sex outside marriage have increased rapidly. This has meant that the children from parentally deprived homes (in which parents do not take on personal, active and long-term responsibility for the social upbringing of their children) are thereby disadvantaged. On the evidence available, such children on average tend to die earlier, to have more illness, to do less well at school, to suffer more unemployment, to be more prone to crime and finally to repeat the cycle of unstable parenting from which they themselves have suffered.

One consequence of family breakdown is the emergence of a new type of young male, who has not had a male breadwinner role model. He no longer feels the pressure felt by previous generations of males to be a responsible husband, father and adult.

Source: adapted from Halsey (1992)

1 Explain in your own words what the author means by 'parentally deprived homes'.
2 State three ways in which, according to the extract, children from these homes are disadvantaged.
3 Briefly explain how, according to the extract, family breakdown has affected some young men.

STAYING TOGETHER

1 Should a married couple with young children have to stay together if they no longer get along?
2 Note down two good reasons why you think they should stay together and two reasons why you think they should not.

How do critical approaches view families and family life?

So far, we have examined views of families and family life which suggest that the nuclear family is beneficial and desirable.

A second view, however, sees things rather differently. A number of sociologists have a critical view of the modern family and they focus on the **negative side** of family life. They point to the incidence of domestic violence and the abuse of family members within the home to show that the family is not necessarily a safe haven. Critics of family life point to the emotional conflict that can exist between family members, leading to stress, frustration and even mental health problems. This shows the dysfunctional or dark side of family life.

The negative side of family life

WHEN PARENTS ROW

Read through the following newspaper extract and then answer the questions:

SHOULD I STAY OR SHOULD I GO?

Mary MacLeod, director of research at Childline, reports frequent calls from children upset by parental arguments. 'We often have calls from children lying in bed listening to their parents rowing. They are upset by their helplessness to do anything about it, or even say they don't like it. But they are not generally calling about any old row. It has usually been going for months, or even years, and they desperately want to make it better.'

MacLeod reports that children also say that, when their parents have been rowing, they take out their feelings on the children. 'They get told off more and the parents are generally shorter-tempered.' Emotional neglect of children is another danger in homes where parents are consumed with anger. While their parents are rowing or preoccupied by conflict, the children may effectively be abandoned.

Source: Rickford (1996)

1. Identify three ways in which, according to this article, children can be affected by parental conflict.
2. With reference to the extract, write a paragraph criticizing the optimistic functionalist approach to the nuclear family.

The conflict approach

The conflict approach is particularly critical of the family as an institution. Marxist sociologists see capitalist society as based on conflict; that is, class conflict between the capitalist ruling class and the proletariat. The family is one of the institutions through which social inequality is reproduced over time from one generation to the next. For example, through the family set up, the rich are able to pass on wealth to their family members. In this way, the social class system is reproduced from one generation to the next. Educational advantage is also passed down through families. For example, people from wealthy backgrounds can afford to pay the fees to send their children to public schools. In addition, conflict sociologists argue that through socialization processes in the family, working-class people may learn to accept their position in an unequal society.

The feminist approach

Feminists are also critical of the family. They accept that biological differences exist between women and men. They argue, however, that many differences are actually created by society. The family contributes to the creation of these differences through primary socialization processes. We can see this in the way that girls and boys are dressed and the toys they are given. Within the family, young children learn how they are expected to behave not only as individual people, but also as males and females. A young girl who sees her mother doing the cooking, cleaning and washing up may well assume that such tasks are part of a woman's role. A young boy who is encouraged to help his father with home improvements or to wash the car may think that this is part of a man's role.

Feminists argue that families are patriarchal, which means that they are based on male power and dominance over women. The males within families (husbands, fathers and brothers) benefit while the females lose out. In the 1970s Bernard (1976) argued that there were really two marriages in every marital union, his and hers, and that the two did not necessarily coincide. The husband gained more from his marriage than the wife did from hers. (See p. 128 for a discussion of the domestic division of labour.)

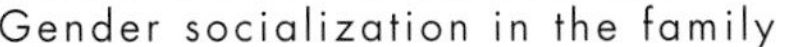
Gender socialization in the family

PARENTS' EXPECTATIONS OF DAUGHTERS AND SONS

Many people, including parents, often treat female and male babies differently, for example in the way they are dressed and in the toys they are given.

1 Discuss reasons why baby girls and baby boys are often treated differently.
2 Should parents have different expectations of daughters and sons, e.g. regarding how much housework they do, how much freedom they have and what time they have to be home in the evening?
3 Write a paragraph explaining your view on whether parents should have different expectations of daughters and sons.

Domestic violence within families

Some critical approaches highlight the apparent increase in violence within the home in order to show that families are not necessarily safe havens for their members.

CHECK YOUR UNDERSTANDING

1 Identify and describe two ways in which families may contribute to the well-being of members. (4 marks)
2 Identify four potentially negative aspects of family life. (4 marks)

VIOLENCE IN THE HOME

Read through the following extract and answer the questions.

Domestic violence describes violence against women in the family; it also includes the physical, psychological or sexual abuse of children; violence between brothers and sisters and the abuse and neglect of the elderly.

During the late 1980s and 1990s the media have concentrated our attention on numerous cases of domestic violence. Much publicity has been given to women who have killed their male partners and to horrific cases of child murder and abuse.

One view is that abuses against women and children are symptoms of the crisis in the family caused by the decline in moral standards and family values this century. A second view argues that there has not really been an increase in family violence. In fact, historians have suggested that the scale of family violence has declined gradually since the late nineteenth century as a result of campaigns to improve the status of women and children. Rather, the media, the public and experts are now paying it much more attention. The problem of domestic violence has been rediscovered.

Source: adapted from Clarke (1997)

1. Of the approaches discussed (functionalist, New Right, conflict and feminist), which approach do you think supports the view that the crisis in the family is caused by the decline in family values?
2. We have seen that early approaches focused on the functions of the family, two of which are emotional gratification and nurture. Using the information in the extract, write a paragraph to show that these functions are not always fulfilled.
3. Explain in your own words what the author means by 'the problem of domestic violence has been rediscovered'.

WHAT DO HISTORICAL APPROACHES TELL US ABOUT CHANGES IN FAMILIES AND HOUSEHOLDS IN BRITAIN OVER TIME?

As we would expect, historical evidence shows that families and households have changed over time. Sources suggest that the process of industrialization, which began around the mid-eighteenth century, had a significant effect on family structure. The industrial revolution involved the development of factories in which goods were produced, the growth of industrial cities and towns, and the growth of new transport systems.

In order to examine how these changes affected families, we first need to look at pre-industrial families and we can then compare them with contemporary families.

Pre-industrial families

It used to be thought that the extended family was typical of pre-industrial Britain. More recently, however, sociologists and historians have rejected this view. Evidence suggests that before the industrial revolution there was not one main family type that existed everywhere as the norm.

- **The extended family** was one type of family to be found in pre-industrial times. Evidence suggests that, before industrialization, many families in various parts of Europe were of the extended type.

- **The nuclear family** was also to be found before the industrial revolution. A historian named Laslett studied the parish records of 100 villages in sixteenth- to nineteenth-century England. He argues that the average family was relatively small and that most households during this time contained an average of 4.75 people. Laslett concludes that nuclear families existed widely in pre-industrial England – in fact, they were the norm. Only 10 per cent of households contained kin beyond the nuclear family and this figure is the same as in 1966.

Laslett (1965) points out that in the period he studied the average age of brides was 24 and the average age of grooms was nearly 28. Life expectancy was in the low thirties. Few families, therefore, could live as three-generational extended families.

Early industrial families

Anderson (1971) studied census data on Preston, an early industrializing cotton town in Lancashire, for the year 1851. He found that 23 per cent of households contained kin beyond the nuclear family and that there was an *increase* rather than a decrease in family size at this time. This was because jobs were being created in Preston's cotton industry and so relatives from the countryside migrated to the town to live with family members who were already there.

According to Anderson, it seems that working-class families became *more* extended during the early stages of the industrial revolution.

Families in the twentieth century

Young and Willmott (1957) studied family life in Bethnal Green, in the East End of London, during the mid-1950s. Among their working-class sample, they found that the extended family flourished. For example, many young couples began their married life living with one set of parents. Family ties were strong and 43 per cent of daughters had seen their mothers within the last 24 hours. Young believes that, even today, although family members may be separated geographically, many still remain in close contact with their family of origin, for example via telephone calls. Furthermore, official statistics show that, in 1995, 69 per cent of respondents who did not live with their mother saw or visited her at least once a month.

WHAT CAN WE LEARN ABOUT FAMILIES AND HOUSEHOLDS FROM CROSS-CULTURAL EVIDENCE?

Often, the nuclear family is seen as normal and natural while other family types are seen as deviant. Cross-cultural evidence, however, reminds us that different forms of family and household exist in different cultures. If we examine households around the world today, we will find a range of household organizations and personal relationships that are not based on the nuclear family. In different cultures, people have alternative lifestyles and children are brought up in various ways.

What are some of these household arrangements?

Communes and kibbutzim (plural of kibbutz) are important examples of alternatives to the nuclear family household.

A commune

A kibbutz

Communes

Communes were popular during the 1960s and 1970s, especially in the USA, and some still exist today. In broad terms, a commune is a group of people who share living accommodation, possessions, wealth and property. It is difficult to generalize about communes because they do vary but usually each adult has his or her own room and young children share a room.

Communal households try to achieve equality in terms of the status of women and men, adults and children. Kanter (1979), who has conducted research into communes, describes one in America which named its cat as head of the household on official forms rather than singling out one individual person.

Kibbutzim

About 3 per cent of Israel's population live in kibbutzim. A kibbutz consists of a group of people who live together communally, with shared ownership of land and factories. Originally, all children lived and slept separately from their parents in the children's quarters. They were looked after by 'kibbutz mothers' and saw their biological parents for a few hours every day. More recently, however, this has changed and on some kibbutzim children now live with their biological parents up to the age of 15 when they move to the teenagers' houses.

Each family has its own apartment but meals are eaten in the communal dining hall. All children born in the same year are raised and educated together, spending the day in the children's houses. In longer-established kibbutzim, multi-generational families exist.

LIFE IN A COMMUNE OR KIBBUTZ

Identify two advantages and two disadvantages of life in either a commune or a kibbutz.

Families in modern China

In an attempt by the Chinese authorities to control population growth, couples in China are, by law, allowed to have only one child. In the cities, couples are encouraged to sign a one-child pledge in return for privileges such as an extra month's salary per year until the child reaches the age of 14. If the couple do have a second child, the privileges are withdrawn and penalties such as demotion or dismissal from work may be imposed. A woman who has an abortion is entitled to a holiday with pay. All methods of birth control are free. Some pregnant women, known in the press as 'birth guerillas', hide out in the countryside until their baby is born. Male children are preferred and there are reports in the press of female infanticide – the practice of killing female infants soon after birth.

During the 1980s, an increasing number of children were abandoned, partly as a result of the one-child population control policy. Many children, particularly females, end up in state-run orphanages. Chinese government statistics show that the majority of these children end up dying in the orphanages.

Historical evidence from India and the USA

The Nayar people

Historical evidence suggests that household arrangements and personal relationships have taken many forms in the past. Among the Nayar people of Kerala, India in the eighteenth century, for instance, the family group consisted of brothers, sisters and the sisters' children. The Nayar were a warrior group and the men were absent for part of each year because they were hired as mercenaries. Before reaching puberty, a Nayar female was involved in a ritual marriage ceremony after which she could have a number of lovers. Each female had her own room where she might be visited at night by one of her lovers. She did not live with her husband but with her kin group – her mother, brothers and sisters. Children were brought up by, and lived with, their mother's kin group rather than in a nuclear family. Descent was traced through the female line.

The Oneida Community

The Oneida Community, based in New York State between 1848 and 1880, is an interesting example of a group which had an alternative form of marriage and family life. This community aimed to live by Christian moral standards. Oneidans rejected personal wealth and private property. Items such as clothes, watches and children's toys were jointly owned. All members were housed under one roof in the communal home, each having his or her own room. Marriage was based on group marriage and it was believed that all members of the community should love each other and not live as monogamous couples.

The community practised 'scientific breeding' of children, which meant that only a limited number of women and men were selected as 'suitable' biological parents. When a child was born, it was reared by its birth mother for the first 15 months. Later, it lived in the children's section of the community home, where it was brought up with the other children. All adults were expected to love all children and to treat each child as their own. Children were expected to treat Oneidan adults as they would their own parents. In effect, children, sexual partners and property were shared.

LOOKING AT DIFFERENT HOUSEHOLD GROUPS

Identify three differences between the nuclear family and:

1 the Nayar people;
2 the Oneida community.

HOW HAVE RELATIONSHIPS WITHIN FAMILIES CHANGED OVER TIME?

Sociologists are interested in examining what happens within families. In particular, they are keen to explore role relationships between family members; between parents and children, and between adult partners. In doing so, they touch upon issues of gender and age divisions within families.

Evidence suggests that role relationships have changed over the last 100 years and are still undergoing change today. Changes, however, have not occurred at the same pace or to the same extent through all sectors of society, and so role relationships today may vary according to social class and ethnicity.

Changes in the domestic division of labour

Some sociologists argue that one important change within families is that of the move towards greater gender equality. It has been suggested that the domestic division of labour – who does what within the home – is more equal today as men are now much more involved in housework and childcare than they were in the past.

Segregated conjugal roles during the early twentieth century

During the early part of the twentieth century, conjugal roles (those of husband and wife) within the home were segregated or separate and unequal. In general, married women were expected to take the main responsibility for housework and childcare. Married men were expected to be the main wage earner.

Women's roles differed, however, according to social class. In addition to housework and childcare, many working-class women went out to work or took on paid work from home, e.g. taking in laundry, in order to survive. Among the middle class, on the other hand, the wife was not expected to undertake paid work. She supervised the work of the household employees such as the maids, the governess and the nanny. Families were male-dominated and both working- and middle-class husbands were expected to provide for their family.

MEN AS 'HOUSEHUSBANDS'

Do you think that men are less suited to childcare and housework tasks than women? Explain your answer.

THE PERFECT WIFE?

Read through this extract, which is taken from a 1950s home economics textbook. It gives advice to women on how to be the perfect wife. Write a paragraph explaining what it tells us about conjugal roles at that time.

How to look after your husband

Have Dinner Ready

Plan ahead – even the night before – to have a delicious meal on time. This is a way of letting him know that you have been thinking about him and are concerned about his needs. Most men are hungry when they come home and the prospects of a good meal are part of the warm welcome needed.

Prepare Yourself

Take 15 minutes to rest so you will be refreshed when he arrives. Touch up your make up, put a ribbon in your hair and be fresh looking. Be lively and interesting. His boring day may need a lift.

Minimize All Noise

At the time of his arrival, eliminate all noise of washer, dryer, dish-washer or vacuum. Try to encourage the children to be quiet. Greet him with a warm smile and be glad to see him.

Make Him Comfortable

Speak in a low, soft, soothing and pleasant voice. Allow him to relax.

Listen To Him

You may have a dozen things to tell him but the moment of his arrival is not the time. Let him talk first.

Source: adapted from *The Big Issue* (Ireland), No. 74, 30 July 1997

The symmetrical family

Young and Willmott (1973) published research findings which suggested that the **symmetrical family** was now the typical family form in Britain. The symmetrical family was one in which gender role segregation did still exist, but at the same time there was more equality than in the past. Although women still took the main responsibility for housework and childcare, men were spending an equivalent amount of time on home-related tasks.

The family was seen as symmetrical because the husband and wife made a similar contribution to the home even though each might carry out different tasks. Their relationship was now more democratic or equal. Compared with the past, gender roles, decision making and leisure activities were shared more. The husband was more likely to help with housework and childcare and the family was home-centred. There was, for example, now more interest in DIY and home-based entertainment. Relationships between spouses were warmer and more caring.

INVESTIGATING HOUSEWORK AND CHILDCARE

How might you investigate the distribution of housework and childcare further? You will need to consider the following:

- What are your research aims?
- Who would your population consist of, e.g. couples or female partners only?
- What sampling technique would you use?
- How large would the sample need to be?
- Which research technique would you use and why?
- What sources of secondary data could you use?

RESEARCHING HOUSEWORK AND CHILDCARE

1 Design a questionnaire to find out whether childcare and housework tasks are equally shared today. In wording the questions, you will need to think about the nature of your population – whether this is made up of couples or women only.

2 Carry out the survey on a sample size of 10.

3 Make a note of your three most significant findings.

How do we explain the move to symmetry?

Let's assume for the moment that Young and Willmott were correct in identifying the move to greater symmetry in gender roles. We now need to identify possible reasons for this change.

Some sociologists have pointed to wider social changes that help to explain the changes in gender role relationships.

- The rise in feminism since the 1960s has had an impact on role relationships. Feminists have fought for equal opportunities for women and men, e.g. at work and in education. Feminism has influenced many women's attitudes and has led them to reject the traditional housewife role.
- More effective forms of contraception have resulted in women having fewer children. Families can now be planned, therefore women can combine motherhood with paid employment and a career. Many women are financially independent and have more equality and status, both inside and outside the home, than in the past.
- There has been an increased interest in home life generally, e.g. in DIY and home-based leisure pursuits such as computers and satellite television. This has meant that men are more likely to spend time at home and to become more involved with their family.
- As a result of increasing male unemployment, many husbands have become more involved in domestic tasks. Jane Wheelock (1990) conducted research into the effects of male unemployment on who does what tasks at home. She found that men undertook more housework and childcare when they became unemployed.

Is the symmetrical family reality or a myth?

Feminists reject the idea of symmetry. Oakley (1974) is critical of studies such as Young and Willmott's and is not convinced by their evidence. For example, a husband who washes up at least once a week is regarded by them as helpful in the home. Oakley argues that occasional help from the husband, such as ironing his own trousers on a Saturday, is regarded as a sign of a 'good' husband. From her own research, Oakley found little evidence of symmetry. In fact, even women in paid employment still do most of the work at home.

Some feminists argue that family life is still patriarchal, by which they mean male-dominated and unequal. For example, Jan Pahl (1989), in her study of money and power in marriages, interviewed 102 married couples with dependent children in Kent. She found that husbands were more likely than

WHO DOES WHAT AT HOME?

The data in Table 5.1 is based on the findings of a survey and shows how many hours mothers and fathers spend on various household tasks per week. The survey found that mothers who also worked outside the home still spent more time on household tasks than they spent in their paid place of work. These women spent 53 hours a week on average on household tasks.

Table 5.1 Hours spent on household tasks by parents: by gender, August 1996

United Kingdom	Hours and minutes per week *Fathers*	*Mothers*
Cooking/preparing meals	2:50	13:30
Cleaning	2:00	13:15
Washing and ironing clothes	0:55	9:05
Spending time just with the children	5:05	8:45
Shopping	2:50	5:50
Washing up	2:00	3:40
Driving children to school	1:45	2:55
Gardening	3:00	2:00
Sewing/mending clothes	:10	1:20
Other household tasks	2:25	1:40
All household tasks	**23:00**	**62:00**

Source: *Social Trends* (1997)

According to this information:

1 On average, how much more time per week do mothers spend doing household tasks than fathers?
2 On which household task did mothers spend most time?
3 On which household task did fathers spend least time?
4 If women are in paid employment, are they likely to spend significantly less of their time on household tasks?
5 Is the symmetrical family a reality or a myth in the 1990s?
Write a paragraph explaining your answer.

wives to be dominant in decision making. Pahl did argue that, compared with 30 years ago, more couples now share decisions concerning the spending of the household income. She points out, however, that there are still many marriages in which the husband controls finances and the wife's access to money is very limited. Women and children can live in poverty even though the man with whom they live has a good income.

CHECK YOUR UNDERSTANDING

1. Explain the terms 'symmetrical family' and 'domestic division of labour'. (4 marks)
2. Identify and explain two ways in which conjugal roles within families may have changed in the last 25 years. (4 marks)
3. Identify and explain two possible reasons for these changes in conjugal roles. (4 marks)

DO YOUNGER PEOPLE CONFORM TO GENDER STEREOTYPES?

Table 5.2 How often young people perform certain household tasks: by gender, 1992–93

England and Wales — Percentages

	*A	USR	N	D
Males				
Cleaning own room	42	48	9	-
Making the bed(s)	34	47	18	0
Washing own clothes	14	33	52	-
Household shopping	11	54	34	-
Cleaning rest of house	8	66	25	-
Looking after younger children	4	37	32	27
Making meals for others in family	3	57	37	3
Females				
Cleaning own room	64	33	3	0
Making the bed(s)	56	34	9	0
Washing own clothes	38	36	26	-
Household shopping	30	41	20	-
Cleaning rest of house	28	64	8	-
Looking after younger children	24	7	19	20
Making meals for others in family	22	61	15	2

*Always; Usually, Sometimes or Rarely; Never; Does not apply

Source: *Social Trends* (1997)

We often assume that younger people are less likely to conform to gender stereotypes than older people. The evidence in Table 5.2 gives some indication of whether or not traditional gender roles are filtering down to the younger generation.

1. According to this information:
   (a) Which task did approximately one in ten males and three in ten females always do?
   (b) Which two tasks were males and females more likely always to do?
   (c) Which task were both males and females most likely never to do?
2. To what extent does this evidence suggest that young males and females make a similar contribution to household tasks? Give examples from the information to support your views.

Changes in the relationship between parents and children

The relationship between parents and their children has changed over time. During the nineteenth century, children's experiences and life chances varied significantly according to their age, gender and social class (see p. 40). Middle-class children, for example, were often looked after by paid employees such as a nanny. Working-class children, especially boys, were expected to work in paid employment from an early age.

Details from the 1841 census show that in towns around Lancaster more boys than girls aged 10–14 were employed in paid work. The textile industry in Lancashire provided the greatest number of jobs for children, who were, for example, employed as cotton mill workers, spinners and weavers. There was a wider range of jobs for boys than for girls.

Few children under the age of 10 worked in paid employment. According to census figures for England and Wales, in 1851, 36.6 per cent of boys and 19.9 per cent of girls aged 10–14 worked. By 1911 these figures stood at 18.3 per cent for boys and 10.4 per cent for girls. Many girls were involved in unpaid work at home, for example in housework and child minding, but this was not officially recorded in the statistics.

It is possible that poverty prevented many parents from sending their children to school. Well into the twentieth century, many working-class parents seem to have viewed education as a barrier to their children's paid employment. Many sent their children out to work as soon as they could and relied on the children's income.

Following the introduction of the Education Act (1918), however, all children had to attend school until the age of 14. Young and Willmott point out that only then did childhood come to be officially recognized as a separate stage in human life.

Children at work in the nineteenth century

Contemporary parent–child relationships

Today, relationships between parents and children are usually closer and warmer than in the past. As children, we are seen as important members of the family household, are listened to and taken more seriously. There is less emphasis on discipline and more on freedom and children's rights. Relationships are less authoritarian and more child-centred. The average family size is smaller than at the beginning of the twentieth century, so individual children are likely to get more attention from their parents.

Childrearing is no longer motivated by economic factors. The minimum school leaving age was raised to 16 in 1976 and although young people today may obtain part-time paid employment before they are 16, the number of hours they can work is restricted by law. This means that young people are financially dependent on their family for longer periods, particularly if they continue into further and higher education. Youth unemployment can also make it more difficult for young people to gain independence from their families. This can lead to potential conflict and stress within families.

Older people within families

The age structure of the population has changed during the twentieth century. People are living longer and the proportion of middle-aged and older people has increased, while the proportion of younger people has reduced – we now have an ageing population (see p. 355).

Caring for the youngest family members

This is having an impact on families. Older people are able to provide support and care within many families. For example, if retired people live close to their daughter and son-in-law, they may provide help with childcare during school holidays and after school.

Elderly people in need of care may also be looked after by family members and, in practice, this responsibility often lies with adult daughters. If women are caring for an elderly parent, in addition to looking after their own children, this can make it more difficult for them to work in full-time paid employment. They may experience role conflict when the demands and responsibilities of the roles of employee, mother and adult daughter come into conflict with each other (see p. 31).

Social class, ethnicity and role relationships

Some sociologists argue that role relationships within families vary according to social class. Popular images suggest that working-class families are male-dominated. There is some evidence to suggest that, in general terms, middle-class conjugal relationships are more equal than working-class ones. Other evidence, however, seems to suggest that working-class fathers are more involved in childcare than middle-class ones.

Similarly, popular beliefs suggest that Asian families are based on unequal, male-dominated relationships. Westwood and Bhachu (1988) challenge such beliefs, suggesting that popular images of 'the Asian family' are often based on prejudice or prejudgments. In reality, there are ethnic differences among Asian people in Britain, for example according to religion and social class. This makes it very difficult to generalize about 'the Asian family'. Westwood and Bhachu point out that Asian families are, in fact, British families and are a major source of strength and resistance against the racism of British society.

CHECK YOUR UNDERSTANDING

Identify and explain two changes that have occurred in relationships between parents and children during the twentieth century. (4 marks)

WHAT ARE THE CONTEMPORARY TRENDS IN MARRIAGE AND DIVORCE?

Different forms of marriage

Serial monogamists

In Britain today, marriage is based on monogamy, which means that it is possible to be married to only one person at a time. Monogamy is the accepted form of marriage in Britain and is backed by the law. Bigamy (marrying someone when already married to another person) is a criminal offence. Monogamous marriage is also supported by the Christian religion.

Serial monogamy occurs when a person enters into a marriage then divorces, remarries, divorces, remarries, and so on. Elizabeth Taylor, Henry VIII, Joan Collins and Picasso are all famous examples of serial monogamists.

Polygamy occurs when a person has more than one husband or wife

Polygyny

at the same time and is therefore illegal in Britain.

Polygyny occurs when a man has two or more wives. This was acceptable within the Mormon religion in Utah in the USA during the nineteenth century because Mormons believed that polygyny had been ordained by God. Brigham Young, a Mormon leader, had 27 wives and 56 children. In practice, however, only a minority of Mormon men practised polygyny. Polygyny was outlawed in Utah by the Mormon General Conference of 1890. Despite this, there is evidence to suggest that the practice continues there today, for example, Alex Joseph (pictured) had 13 wives at the last count.

In some societies, Muslim men are allowed to marry up to four wives, but only under certain conditions. The first wife, for example, has to give her permission and all wives must be treated equally and fairly. In such societies, a woman may have it written into her marriage contract that she should remain the only wife.

Polyandry occurs when a woman has more than one husband. It is less common than polygyny. Polyandry occurs, for example, in Tibet. Unlike polygyny, polyandry can serve as a means of male contraception; if a female is pregnant then she can continue to have sexual relations with all her husbands without risking further pregnancies.

CHECK YOUR UNDERSTANDING

Give two reasons why you think monogamy is the accepted form of marriage in Britain today. (2 marks)

Changing trends in marriage

The decline in the marriage rate

The marriage rate refers to the number of marriages per 1,000 people per year. The marriage rate in the UK has declined from 7.1 marriages per 1,000 people in 1981 to 5.9 marriages per 1,000 people in 1993.

Since the 1960s, the number of people marrying for the first time in the UK has decreased. In 1961, there were around 340,000 first marriages in the UK, but by 1994 there were only 208,000 first marriages. At the same time, the number of remarriages has increased, and the UK still has one of the highest marriage rates in the European Union (see p. 137).

People are getting married at a later age

The average age at first marriage for men and women in the UK has risen (see p. 136).

The increase in cohabitation

Official statistics show that, in Britain, the proportion of all non-married women aged between 18 and 49 who are cohabiting (living with their partner) has doubled since 1981 to 25 per cent in 1995–6. Data from the 1991 census shows that similar numbers cohabit among the white and black population, but that people from Indian, Pakistani and Bangladeshi cultural backgrounds are much less likely to cohabit.

LOOKING AT MARRIAGE

Average age at first marriage

	1971	1993
Men	24	28
Women	22	25.8

Suggest two possible reasons why:

1 People are now getting married at a later age.
2 Women usually marry men who are older than them.
3 Fewer people are getting married.

COHABITATION

1 In a small group, discuss the advantages and disadvantages of a couple living together before marriage.
2 Discuss the possible reasons why more people are choosing to cohabit rather than marry.
3 Make a note of three possible reasons for the increase in cohabitation.

The increase in live births outside marriage

Out of all live births in England and Wales in 1971, 8 per cent were outside marriage. By 1981, this figure had risen to 12 per cent and, by 1991, 30 per cent of all live births were outside marriage. Out of all live births in 1995, over a third (around 34 per cent) were outside marriage.

Often, non-marital births occur within a stable parental relationship. In 1995, approximately four-fifths of non-marital births were registered jointly by both parents. This means that both parents' names were entered on the baby's birth certificate. Of these, four-fifths of the parents were living together at the same address.

BIRTH OUTSIDE MARRIAGE

1 Discuss the possible reasons why many couples choose to have children outside marriage.
2 Make a list of three possible reasons that you have identified.

Marital breakdown and divorce

We have seen that patterns of family life seem to be undergoing change at the present time. Perhaps one of the most significant changes is the increase in marital breakdown. Broadly speaking, there are three types of marital breakdown:

- 'empty shell' marriages;
- separation; and
- divorce.

While the first type may not lead to eventual marital break up, the latter two do.

An 'empty shell' marriage is one in which the couple still live together but the marriage has effectively broken down. In practice, the husband and wife no longer have a sexual or emotional relationship. A Roman Catholic couple, for example, may have a relationship which has broken down but they will stay together because they feel that divorce is unacceptable. It is very difficult to estimate the number of empty shell marriages because they are not recorded officially as statistics.

Separation involves both marital breakdown and break up. Legal separations are recorded in the official statistics. Some couples, however, separate by informal agreement and so their marital break up does not appear in the official statistics.

Contemporary trends in divorce

A divorce is the legal termination of a marriage. The term 'divorce rate' refers to the number of divorces per 1,000 people per year. The UK divorce rate has risen dramatically and, in 1993, the number of divorces per 1,000 of the population reached 3.1; seven times the number of divorces in 1961.

The divorce rate varies between ethnic groups. According to statistics from the 1991 census, for example, divorce is less common among South Asian Britons than in other groups. Young women of Indian descent are more likely to experience divorce than young women of Pakistani or Bangladeshi descent.

MARRIAGE AND DIVORCE IN THE EUROPEAN UNION

Table 5.3 Marriage and divorce rates: EU comparison, 1981 and 1993

Rates per 1,000 population

	Marriages		Divorces	
	1981	1993	1981	1993
United Kingdom	7.1	5.9	2.8	3.1
Denmark	5.0	6.1	2.8	2.5
Finland	6.3	4.9	2.0	2.5
Sweden	4.5	3.9	2.4	2.5
Belgium	6.5	5.4	1.6	2.1
Austria	6.3	5.6	1.8	2.0
Netherlands	6.0	5.8	2.0	2.0
France	5.8	4.4	1.6	1.9
Germany	6.2	5.5	2.0	1.9
Luxembourg	5.5	6.0	1.4	1.9
Portugal	7.8	6.9	0.7	1.2
Greece	6.9	6.0	0.7	0.7
Spain	5.4	5.0	0.3	0.7
Italy	5.6	5.1	0.2	0.4
Irish Republic	6.0	4.4	..	..
EU Average	6.1	5.3	1.5	1.7

Source: Eurostat

According to the information in Table 5.3:

1 What was the average marriage rate in the EU in 1993?
2 Of the 15 countries listed, which had higher marriage rates in 1993 than 1981?
3 Which country had the highest divorce rate in 1993?
4 How many EU countries had a higher divorce rate in 1993 than in 1981?

How do we explain the increase in divorce?

Changes in the law

Changes in the law have made divorce easier, quicker and cheaper to obtain than in the past. Following the Divorce Law Reform Act (1969), which came into effect in 1971, an individual could petition for divorce on the grounds of 'irretrievable breakdown of marriage' as a result of separation, desertion, adultery or unreasonable behaviour. Further legislation in 1984 allowed couples to request or petition for divorce after only one year of marriage, rather than three as previously. Legal aid facilities became available, which made divorce cheaper. By contrast, in the Republic of Ireland people have only been able to petition for divorce since February 1997.

Changes in attitudes

Changes in attitude have meant that divorce has become more socially acceptable. Some members of the Royal family, for example, have separated and divorced.

Secularization

This refers to the decline of religion in society. (For more on religion, see Chapter 11.) Statistics suggest that the Christian churches, in particular, are attracting fewer members today compared with 20 years ago.

Many people now choose to have a civil ceremony in a registry office rather than a church wedding. This means that fewer people take sacred vows before God to stay together 'till death us do part'. The religious barrier to divorce is therefore weaker today.

Changes in the social position of women

Women are more likely than men to petition for divorce; almost three-quarters of divorce petitions in 1995 were filed by women. Today, more women are in paid employment so they are now more economically independent than in the past. With the availability of welfare benefits, women with children will not be destitute as a result of divorce. They may be eligible for a number of state benefits with which to support their family.

Media influence

The media tend to emphasize the importance of 'romantic love', which means that people may enter marriage with unreasonably high expectations. As an increasing number of marriages do not fulfil such aspirations, more divorces occur.

ROMANTIC LOVE

1 State two ways in which romantic love and sexual attraction are emphasized by the media.
2 Identify two advantages and two disadvantages of marriage based on romantic love.

Media representations of romance

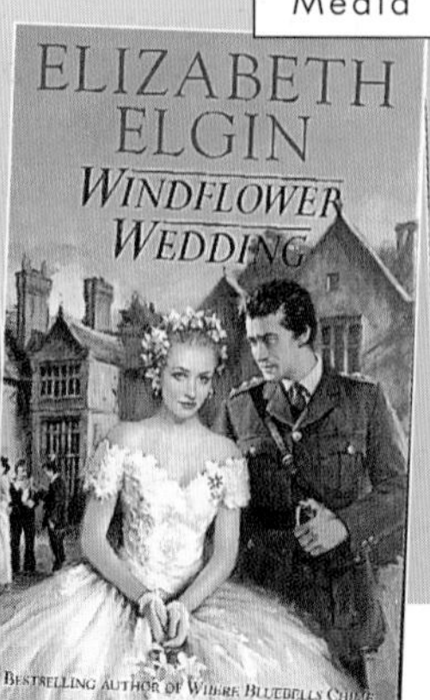

Why is remarriage so popular?

Although the divorce rate is increasing, many divorcees remarry. In 1961, 9 per cent of all marriages were remarriages where one partner or both partners had been divorced. In 1981, this figure stood at 31 per cent and by 1991 it had risen to 34 per cent. According to official statistics, men are more likely to remarry than women.

The popularity of remarriage can be explained as follows:

- It is argued that those people who seek a divorce are not rejecting the institution of marriage itself. Rather, they are rejecting one particular partner. This would account for the high rates of remarriage among divorcees. People still value a happy marriage and hope to succeed in another relationship the second time round.
- Divorcees with young children may want to find a partner to help them in the task of bringing up their children.
- People may remarry for companionship.
- In the past, marriage gave status, particularly to women. This is not so true today but in many ways marriage remains the norm – it is the conventional thing to do.

THE EFFECTS OF DIVORCE

1 In a small group, discuss the consequences of divorce for the individuals involved and for society as a whole. You could include in your discussion the effects of divorce on the number of single-parent families, the remarriage rate and the incidence of poverty.
2 Note down three significant consequences of divorce which were identified during your discussion.

CHECK YOUR UNDERSTANDING

1 Give four reasons for the increase in the divorce rate in Britain over the past 40 years. (4 marks)
2 Identify and explain two consequences of this increase. (4 marks)
3 Explain two reasons for the popularity of remarriage among divorcees. (4 marks)

WHAT ARE THE CURRENT TRENDS IN FAMILIES AND HOUSEHOLDS?

Over the last few decades, families and households in Britain have been changing in a number of ways. We have already noted some of these changes, for example in role relationships and marriage and divorce rates. Other important trends in families and households are examined below.

The apparent decline in the nuclear family

If we look at official statistics we can see that the percentage of households that are made up of nuclear families (couples with dependent children) is declining. This marks a decline in the 'traditional' or 'cereal packet' family, as Figure 5.1 shows. (See p. 140.)

THE NUCLEAR FAMILY IN DECLINE

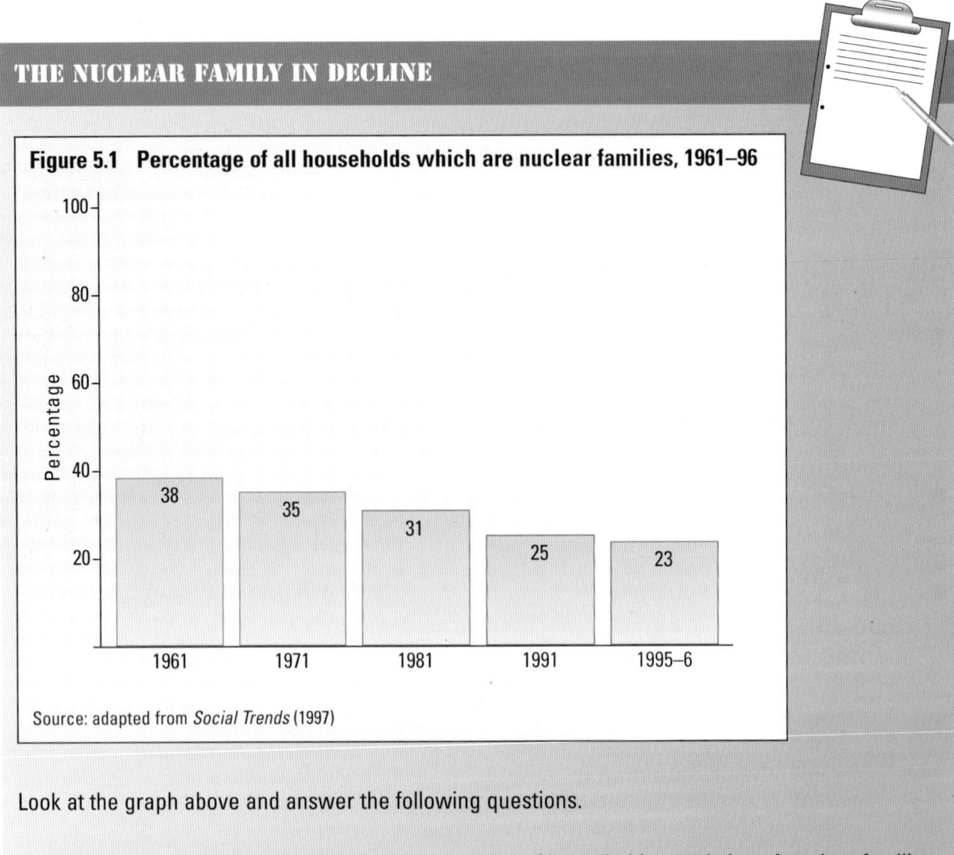

Figure 5.1 Percentage of all households which are nuclear families, 1961–96

Source: adapted from *Social Trends* (1997)

Look at the graph above and answer the following questions.

1 By how many percentage points did the proportion of households consisting of nuclear families decline between 1961 and 1991?
2 What percentage of households did not consist of nuclear families in 1995–6?

The significant increase in the number of lone-parent families

Some lone-parent families come about because a couple separate or divorce, or because one of the partners dies. Other lone-parent families occur when a woman decides that she would like to bring up a baby on her own without having a long-term relationship with the baby's father.

In Britain between 1971 and 1995, the percentage of all families with dependent children, which were headed by lone parents, rose from 8 per cent to 22 per cent. Lone-parent families with dependent children made up 2 per cent of all households in 1961, 6 per cent in 1991 and 7 per cent in 1995–6. Lone-parent families are usually headed by females. Around 5 per cent of single parents are female teenagers.

Jewson (1994) points out that there is evidence that African–Caribbean communities have a higher than average proportion, and Asian communities a lower than average proportion of lone-parent families. He warns us, though, that it is important to avoid stereotyping as the majority of African-Caribbean households with children contain two parents.

One reason for the increase in the number of lone-parent families is that it is now more socially acceptable for single women to have children. A second explanation is the increase in families headed by divorced or separated mothers. Each year, however, many lone mothers will form new partnerships and cease to be lone parents.

LONE-PARENT FAMILIES

Between 1961 and 1991, what was the percentage increase in households consisting of lone-parent families with dependent children?

THE CONSEQUENCES OF LONE-PARENT FAMILIES

As we have seen, the number of lone-parent families has increased.

1 In a small group, discuss the possible consequences of this increase for:
   - marriage;
   - family life;
   - demands on the welfare state.
2 Note down three possible consequences of the increasing number of lone-parent families.

CHECK YOUR UNDERSTANDING

Identify and explain two reasons for the increase in the number of lone-parent families headed by unmarried women since the 1970s. (4 marks)

The increasing significance of reconstituted families

According to data in *Social Trends* (1997), in Britain in 1991 around half a million step-families contained dependent step-children.

The increase in one-person households

Over the last 25 years there has been a significant increase in the number of people living alone in Britain, as Figure 5.3 shows. (See p. 142.) In part, this increase is explained by the changing age structure of the population. People are living longer so there is an increasingly large number of elderly, one-person households.

The decline in the fertility rate

In the UK there is a trend towards women having fewer children. They are tending to have children at a later age and an increasing number of women choose not to have children.

The increase in abortion

The number of abortions has, in general, increased since the 1970s. Single women are more likely than married women to end pregnancy in abortion. Of all the pregnancies in 1994, 4.3 per cent inside marriage ended in legal abortion, and 15.2 per cent outside marriage ended in legal abortion.

Figure 5.2 Percentage of conceptions leading to legal abortion (England and Wales)

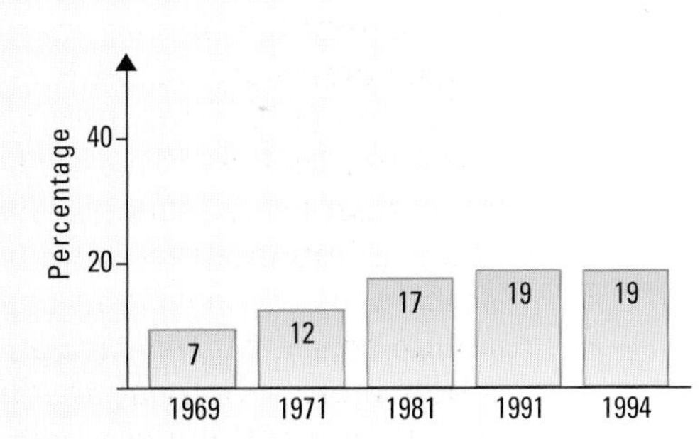

Source: adapted from *Social Trends* (1997)

ONE-PERSON HOUSEHOLDS

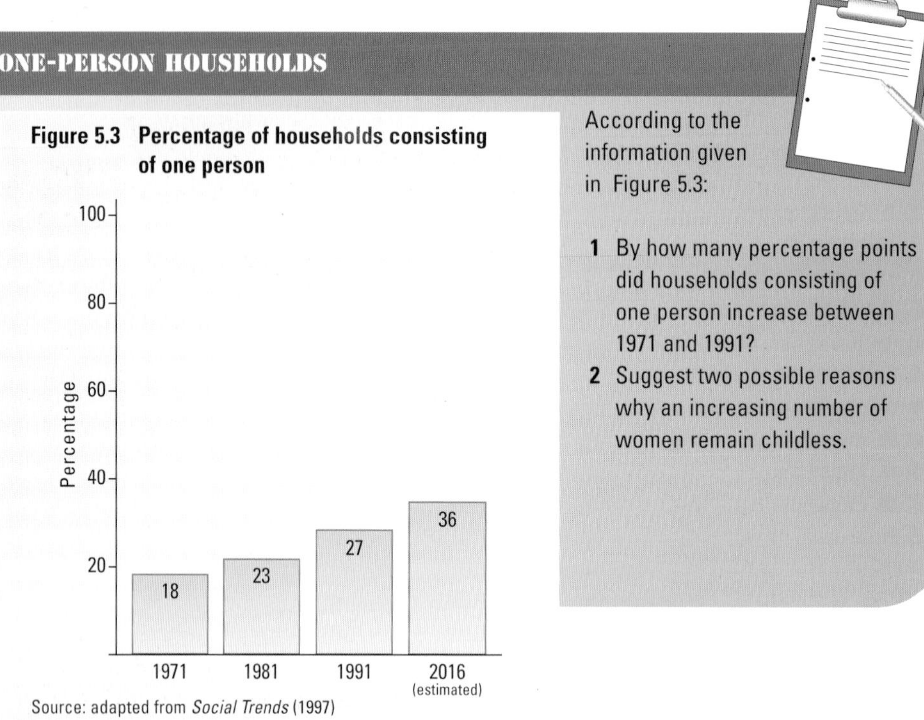

According to the information given in Figure 5.3:

1. By how many percentage points did households consisting of one person increase between 1971 and 1991?
2. Suggest two possible reasons why an increasing number of women remain childless.

LOOKING AT ABORTION

Read the newspaper extract and then discuss the following questions.

1. Discuss this case study and identify reasons for and against the woman going ahead with the abortion.
2. Make a note of two reasons for and two against the woman having an abortion.

A Scottish couple separated in April 1997 after a stormy marriage lasting less than two years. They have one daughter. The woman is pregnant and wants an abortion, but her husband does not want her to have one. He is taking the case to court, trying to claim custody of his wife's foetus so preventing his wife from having an abortion. There is a clash between the woman's right to have the abortion and the man's attempt to prevent her from doing so.

Source: adapted from *The Guardian*, 21 May 1997

The increase in dual-worker families

As a result of the increasing proportion of married women now working, there has been an increase in dual-worker families in which both partners are in paid employment. In 1973, 47 per cent of women with dependent children were working but by 1988 this figure had risen to 56 per cent (see Chapter 7).

WORKING MOTHERS

1. Some people believe that women with young children should not work in paid employment. Do you agree with this view? What are the arguments for and against it?
2. Note down three important points that were raised during your discussion.

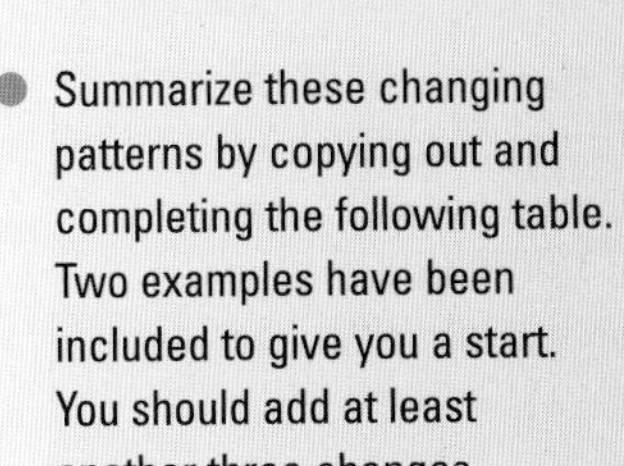

CHANGING PATTERNS IN FAMILIES AND HOUSEHOLDS

We have examined many changing patterns in families and households, e.g. the increasing number of one-person households and the declining birth rate.

- Summarize these changing patterns by copying out and completing the following table. Two examples have been included to give you a start. You should add at least another three changes under each heading.

Changing patterns in families and households

Increase in	Decrease in
Number of one-person households	*The birth rate*

FAMILIES AND ETHNICITY

Immigration has added to the diversity of family types found in Britain. Immigration from South Asia, for example, has increased the importance of the extended family. Statistics from the 1991 census suggest that there are more three-generation households among South Asian groups in Britain than among other groups. At the same time, Indian, Pakistani and Bangladeshi households had approximately double the proportion of households consisting of a nuclear family when compared to black or white groups. This means that we should avoid generalizing about South Asian families because they differ, e.g. according to social class and religion.

Immigration has added to the diversity of family types

CHECK YOUR UNDERSTANDING

1 'Perhaps the most remarkable thing about families in Britain today is that they are all so very similar.' To what extent do you agree with this view? Give reasons for your answer. (10 marks)

2 Suggest two reasons why the family may be undergoing change today. (4 marks)

MIXED-RACE RELATIONSHIPS

Read through the following extract and answer the questions.

Race Barriers Toppled by the Power of Love

A report published in May 1997 gave details of a growing trend towards mixed-race relationships. Among British-born Caribbeans, half the men and a third of the women now live with a white spouse or partner. Almost half of 'Caribbean' children have one white parent. Mixed-race relationships are also increasing among Indians and African Asians, who have traditionally married within their communities. Nineteen per cent of British-born Indian and African Asian men and ten per cent of the women had a white partner, although there were few such relationships among Pakistanis and Bangladeshis.

The issue of mixed-race relationships remains controversial. Among some black people, marrying white people was seen as a betrayal of community identity. The study found some evidence of hostility about relationships between the races.

One of the report's authors noted that arranged marriages among younger British Asians were in decline.

Source: adapted from Ford (1997)

According to this extract:

1 Are British-born Caribbean women or men more likely to live with a white partner?
2 Which ethnic groups were least likely to have a white partner?
3 What is happening with arranged marriages among younger British Asians?

WHAT IS THE FUTURE FOR FAMILIES AND HOUSEHOLDS?

Some media sources, politicians and sociologists have suggested that the family as an institution is under threat or in crisis. Some have gone so far as to suggest that the family is dying out or even dead. They point to a range of evidence:

- the increase in the divorce rate;
- the increase in non-marital births;
- the increase in abortion;
- the increase in lone-parent families;
- the apparent increase in child abuse and domestic violence;

They also suggest that the family has failed to stem anti-social behaviour among its members: it does not operate effectively as an informal agency of social control.

Other sociologists believe that the family plays a less important role in society today compared to its role during the early nineteenth century. It has 'lost' a number of functions, such as its health and social welfare function. For example, in the past, family members looked after relatives who were sick, elderly or unemployed. With the growth of the welfare state and the NHS, the care of the elderly, sick and unemployed is now expected to be undertaken by the state, for example through provision of pensions, hospitals, benefits and social workers.

It is also argued that the family has lost its educational function. Until schooling became compulsory, the family was responsible for educating children and teaching them important skills. Today, we start school at the age of 4 or 5.

Before that, some of us attended nursery from an earlier age. This means that the role of families in educating the young has become less important.

Other sociologists accept that families are undergoing change but reject the idea that the family is dying. They argue that:

- Most people do get married and have children.
- Marriage rates remain high.
- The increasing divorce rate indicates that people have high expectations of marriage.
- Remarriage rates are high.
- The family system as a whole is tough and resilient.

FAMILY V. FRIENDS

Family or Friends?

Although there are plenty of indications that the traditional image of the family is a thing of the past, 'British Social Attitudes' data from 1996 contained research which indicated that people still tend to regard families as much more important than friends. The research found that only about 13 per cent of those questioned agreed with the statement 'I would rather spend time with my friends than my family'. Also, 76 per cent disagreed with the statement 'On the whole my friends are more important to me than my family.'

Source: adapted from Denscombe (1997)

Read the extract and then write a short paragraph to explain what light it throws on the debate about the death of the family.

DOES THE NUCLEAR FAMILY STILL MATTER?

In a small group, discuss whether the nuclear family is less important today than in the past. In what ways is it more or less important?

CHECK YOUR UNDERSTANDING

State two reasons why some sociologists believe that the family is less important today than in the past. (2 marks)

Medical advances and parenting

Throughout the twentieth century there have been important developments in science and medicine. Recent medical advances have had an important impact on reproduction and parenting.

- Developments in contraception mean that women can choose whether and when to have children.
- Middle-aged men have always been able to father children. Now, women can give birth into their mid-fifties. This opens up new possibilities for women: they could pursue a career and delay having children, or they could have a second family after divorce.

- It is now possible for a couple to have a baby with the help of a surrogate mother (a woman who bears a child for them). Either the surrogate mother's own egg is fertilized by the other woman's partner or a fertilized egg from the other woman is implanted in the surrogate's womb.
- *In vitro* fertilization (which takes place in a test tube) is now commonplace. A future possibility is that the healthy eggs of young women will be frozen and stored for use when they are older and ready for a career break.

SUMMARY

In this chapter, we have covered the following points:

- **The term 'family' is difficult to define adequately because there are a number of different family types. The term 'families' is more useful because it recognizes the variety or diversity of types.**
- **This diversity includes the nuclear family, the extended family, the lone-parent family and the reconstituted family. Many of us live in households rather than in families. Immigration has added to the overall diversity.**
- **Some sociological approaches view the nuclear family optimistically as an essential part of society.**
- **Other approaches are critical and associate families with conflict and frustration.**
- **In the past, a range of family types and households has existed.**
- **Cross-cultural studies show us that, today, in different parts of the world, different family and household arrangements exist.**
- **There is some evidence to suggest that relationships within families are becoming more equal. It is important, however, not to exaggerate the move towards equality.**
- **In broad terms, the marriage rate is declining while the divorce rate is increasing.**
- **Families are currently undergoing change as more options become available for personal fulfilment.**
- **Despite some suggestions that the family is dying, this seems unlikely to be true.**
- **Recent medical advances have had an impact on parenting and reproduction.**

EXAMINATION QUESTION 1

To what extent have the roles of husbands and wives changed in the last 40 years? (10 marks)

Source: SEG GCSE Sociology, Summer 1997, Higher Tier, Paper 2, Section C, Question 8

EXAMINATION QUESTION 2

Study **Item A**. Then answer **all** parts of the question that follows.

Item A Families with step-children

Many families now contain children from previous marriages.
The pie chart shows the different types of families with dependent children in 1991.

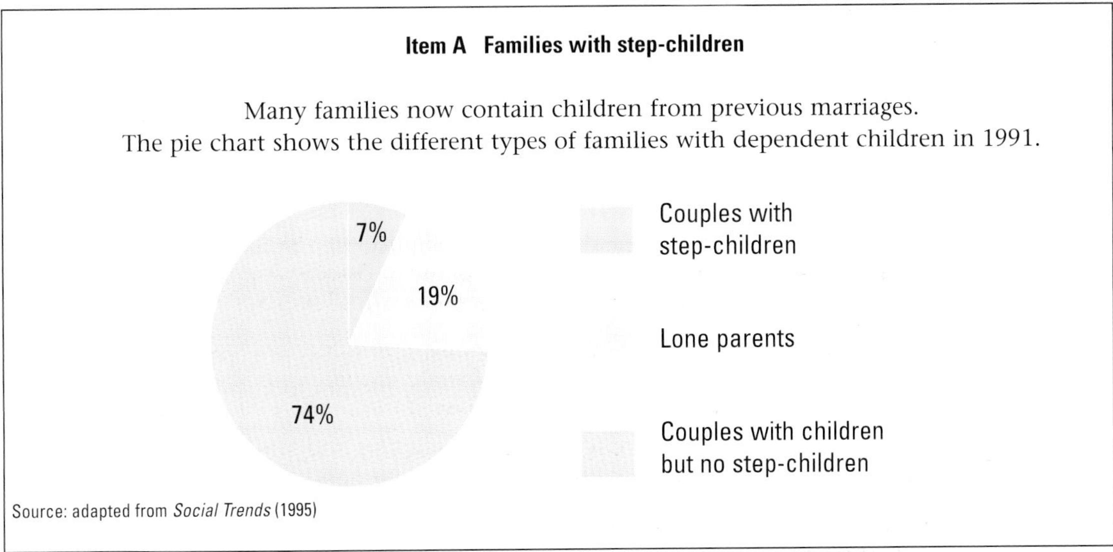

Source: adapted from *Social Trends* (1995)

(a) According to the information given,

(i) what was the most common type of family with dependent children? (1 mark)
(ii) what percentage of families included step-children? (1 mark)
(iii) what percentage of families were lone-parent families? (1 mark)

(b) (i) Identify one form of family other than lone-parent families. (1 mark)
(ii) Identify and explain one role that the family performs in society. (3 marks)

(c) (i) Describe one way in which the role of women has changed in the last 50 years. Suggest one reason why this has occurred. (2 marks)
(ii) Describe one way in which the relationships between parents and children have changed in the last 50 years. Suggest one reason why this has occurred. (2 marks)

(d) (i) What is meant by 'role conflict'? (2 marks)
(ii) Describe with an example one way in which mothers who work outside the home may experience role conflict. (2 marks)

Source: SEG GCSE Sociology, Summer 1997, Foundation Tier, Paper 1, Question 5

BIBLIOGRAPHY

Anderson, M. (1971) *Family Structure in Nineteenth-century Lancashire*, Cambridge University Press.
Ariès, P. (1973) *Centuries of Childhood*, Peregrine.
Bernard, J. (1976) *The Future of Marriage*, Penguin.
Case, J. and Taylor, R.C.R. (eds) (1979) *Co-ops, Communes and Collectives*, Pantheon Books.

Clarke, J. (1997) 'Domestic violence revisited', *Sociology Review*, Volume 6, No. 4, (April) pp. 32–3.
Coleman, D. and Salt, J. (eds) (1996) *Ethnicity in the 1991 Census*, Volume 1, HMSO.
Denscombe, M. (1997) *Sociology Update*.
Ford, R. (1997) *The Times*, 22 May.
Halsey, A.H. (1992) in N. Dennis and G. Erdos, *Families Without Fatherhood*, The IEA Health and Welfare Unit.
Jewson, N. (1994) 'Family values and relationships', *Sociology Review*, Volume 3, No. 3.
Jorgensen, N. (1996) 'Coming to terms with the family?', *Sociology Review*, Volume 5, No. 3.
Kanter, R.M. (1979) 'Communes in cities', in J. Case and R.C.R. Taylor (eds) *Co-ops, Communes and Collectives*, Pantheon Books.
Kephart, W.M. and Zeller, W.W. (1991) *Extraordinary Groups*, St Martin's Press.
Laslett, P.K. (1965) *The World We Have Lost*, Methuen.
Munro, R. and Rigsby, J. (1996) *Death By Default*, Human Rights Watch.
Oakley, A. (1974) *The Sociology of Housework*, Martin Robertson.
Pahl, J. (1989) *Money and Marriage*, Macmillan.
Peach, C. (ed.) (1996) *Ethnicity in the 1991 Census*, Volume 2, HMSO.
Rickford, F. (1996) 'Social change: Should I stay or should I go?', *The Guardian*, 27 March, p. 22.
Social Trends 24 (1994) Office for National Statistics and HMSO.
Social Trends 25 (1995) Office for National Statistics and HMSO.
Social Trends 26 (1996) Office for National Statistics and HMSO.
Social Trends 27 (1997) Office for National Statistics and HMSO.
The Big Issue (Ireland) (1997), No. 74, 30 July.
Westwood, S. and Bhachu, P. (1988) 'Images and reality', *New Society*, 6 May, pp. 20–2.
Wheelock, J. (1990) *Husbands at Home*, Routledge.
Whitelegg, E. et al. (eds) (1982) *The Changing Experience of Women*, Blackwell Publishers.
Winstanley, M. (ed.) (1995) *Working Children in Nineteenth-century Lancashire*, Lancashire County Books.
Young, M. and Willmott, P. (1957) *Family and Kinship in East London*, Routledge and Kegan Paul.
Young, M. and Willmott, P. (1973) *The Symmetrical Family*, Routledge and Kegan Paul.

CHAPTER 6

Education

In this chapter, we will explore and attempt to answer the following questions:

1. **What is education for?**
2. **What is learned – formal and informal education.**
3. **The education system in Britain:**
   - **What changes have taken place in Britain's education system?**
   - **How is the education system organized in contemporary Britain?**
   - **Should education be provided by the state or by the independent sector?**
   - **What have been the effects of recent changes in the education system?**
4. **How can we explain different levels of educational achievement?**
   - **How can social class affect achievement?**
   - **How does gender affect educational attainment and subject choice?**
   - **How can ethnicity affect educational attainment?**

Is this what education is for?

The education system is a key institution in society. We spend a large part of our early lives in it and some of us go on to make it our career. Clearly, education can have an important influence on us as individuals and on our future lives. One task of the sociologist is to understand what role education plays in society and how this role may have changed over time.

Sociologists studying education have raised a number of interesting issues, for example:

- Do we all have an equal chance to succeed in school or are our chances of success already decided before we even enter the education system?
- Do we actually learn anything useful in school?
- How do changes in government policy on education affect the student?

We will attempt to address these and other issues in this chapter.

WHAT IS EDUCATION FOR?

Initially, we need to examine the role that education plays in society. There is a lot of disagreement among sociologists over this question.

Functionalist sociologists examine institutions in terms of the positive role they play in society as a whole. So, for functionalists, education is seen as performing a beneficial role in society.

Marxist sociologists, on the other hand, examine society in terms of the struggle between powerful and less powerful groups. They argue that the powerful groups in society (the ruling classes) use the education system to impose their own beliefs and values on the rest of society. From this point of view, education would be seen as having a beneficial role only for certain groups. (More details on the Marxist view can be found in Chapter 3, on Stratification and Differentiation.)

According to these different viewpoints, what, then, is the role of education?

The economic role – teaching skills for work

For functionalists, schools and colleges teach the **skills and knowledge** necessary for work in a modern, technical, industrial society, for example literacy, numeracy, and computer technology. Vocational courses aim to train young people for the world of work. In this way, education prepares young people for their future occupational roles.

For Marxists, education is seen as **reinforcing the class system**. Thus children from less powerful groups (the working classes) learn the skills necessary for lower-status occupations, while the children from more powerful groups (the middle and upper classes) gain the qualifications needed for higher-status occupations.

THINKING ABOUT THE FUTURE

Make a list of all the subjects you are studying.

1 For each subject, explain how it could be useful in preparing you for your future working life.
2 Do you think the education system really teaches the skills and knowledge necessary for work in a modern industrial society? Explain your answer.

The selective role – choosing the most able people for the most important jobs

Functionalists see the education system as a sieve, grading students according to their ability and placing individuals in occupational roles best suited to their talents and abilities. This process is based on the functionalist belief that all individuals have equal opportunities in their school career. In this way, those who achieve high qualifications are seen as the most able and are therefore rewarded with higher pay levels and higher status in society. This is known as a **meritocratic** system.

Marxists, on the other hand, do not believe that the education system provides equal opportunities for everyone. They argue that it is designed to benefit the powerful groups. They claim that both teachers and schools reject working-class children and that working-class children therefore underperform.

From the Marxist point of view, the education system is not seen as meritocratic because it does not offer an equal opportunity to all groups in society.

LOOKING AT OCCUPATIONS

The list of occupations on the right has been ranked in terms of qualifications required.

1. Identify what qualifications each of these occupations would require. Do the jobs requiring more qualifications pay more than those requiring fewer qualifications?
2. How else could we rank occupations, other than by qualifications needed? Rewrite the list using another method. Explain which you think is the best method of deciding on the importance of occupations.
3. Do you think people who get high qualifications always gain the more skilled, better-paid jobs?

1. doctor
2. lawyer
3. bank manager
4. teacher
5. nurse
6. typist
7. supermarket cashier
8. pop singer
9. refuse collector

The socialization role – teaching norms and values

For functionalists, education also plays a role in teaching the values and norms of society to each new generation. School is seen as an **agent of socialization**, through which young people learn a common culture, beliefs and expectations. The education system 'knits' children from different backgrounds into a flexible whole.

Marxists, on the other hand, see education as socializing individuals into accepting the values of the powerful groups. For example, the stress placed on the importance of hard work in schools and colleges is seen as preparing the future **workforce** for accepting hard work as normal when it enters the workplace.

Social control – teaching acceptance of rules and authority

Functionalists argue that for society to run smoothly there must be some means of regulating people's behaviour and activities. Schools act as an **agent of social control** by teaching rules such as obedience and punctuality.

Social control operates at two levels: the formal and the informal. In this way, people learn to conform to rules and authority in later life.

Social control

Formal	Informal
discipline of staff (e.g. during lessons)	through general school life (e.g. peer-group pressure)
punishments	learning to live and work with others
school rules	

VALUES AND BELIEFS

1 In a small group, decide what values and norms are being learned in the following situations:

2 To what extent do you think that we exit the education system with a set of shared values and beliefs? Make a note of your conclusions.

For Marxists, social control in schools and colleges is seen as reflecting social control in the wider society, which benefits the powerful groups. For example, the importance of obeying a teacher in school is seen as preparation for obeying a boss in the workplace.

THE ROLE OF SCHOOLS IN SOCIAL CONTROL

In a small group, discuss the following points:

1 Do you agree that schools succeed as agents of social control?
2 Give some examples to show how they may not be successful.

The political role – teaching people to be effective citizens

According to functionalists, people learn about society through education. In this way, they accept the political system and are able to exercise their voting rights wisely at election time.

Marxists disagree, suggesting that only certain political opinions and ideas are tolerated in education – radical ideas are rejected or ridiculed. In this way, the political ideas of the powerful groups come to be accepted by individuals.

FUNCTIONALIST V. MARXIST

1 In a small group, discuss the functionalist and Marxist views of the education system.
2 Make a list of arguments for and against each point of view.

CHECK YOUR UNDERSTANDING

1 Identify one way in which schools teach children to become part of society. Explain with one example how this is done. (3 marks)
2 Identify and explain two functions of schools in Britain today. (4 marks)

WHAT IS LEARNED – FORMAL AND INFORMAL EDUCATION?

It is important to note that the education system, consisting of schools, colleges and universities, is not the only arena of learning. Learning also takes place informally through the socialization process (see pp. 32–50).

The education system provides students with **formal learning** through the **official curriculum**, which includes all those subjects studied in lessons, for example maths, history, and so on. But students also learn through the **'hidden curriculum',** which refers to the learning that takes place outside particular subjects or lessons as part of general school or college life. The hidden curriculum of a school may be very different from that of a college, but it will generally involve learning rules, routines and regulations. Students may learn such things without necessarily realizing they are learning them. This is known as **informal learning**.

What is the importance of the hidden curriculum?

The hidden curriculum reflects society's **values** and prepares students for their place in society and their future work role, in the following ways.

Hierarchy

Schools are hierarchical institutions. Any hierarchy can be illustrated in the shape of a pyramid: each layer of the pyramid has more power than the one below it, with the layer at the top having the most power of all. So, in a school, the headteacher is at the very top of the pyramid and the students are at the bottom.

The hierarchy in school can be seen to reflect the hierarchical structure of society at large. In the workplace, for example, a hierarchy may exist between a manager and a trainee.

(Chapter 3, on Stratification and Differentiation, looks in more detail at hierarchy in society.)

Headteacher
Deputy heads
Heads of year
Heads of department
Classroom teachers
Students

The school hierarchy

The importance of competition is learned through the exam system

Competition

Schools encourage competition between students, for example in sport or for exam results. Society is also based on competition, for jobs, material possessions or status, for example. So schools reflect the value that society places on competition and prepare students for their place in a competitive society.

Social control

The hidden curriculum – of rules, regulations, obedience and respect for authority – is one mechanism of social control that reflects those operating in society at large. In effect, students learn to accept society's social controls while they are in the education system.

Gender role allocation

There is a link between expectations, subject choice and gender in school and gender role allocation in the wider society. Job segregation begins at school. For example, teachers may expect girls to be less good at science than boys. This may discourage girls from entering science-based careers.

Lack of satisfaction

Critics of schools claim that much of the school day is taken up with boring and meaningless activities. Students have little say in the content of the subjects they study or in the overall organization of the day. Equally, following the same timetable, week in, week out, may lead to a sense of boredom and powerlessness.

Schools, it is argued, prepare students for boring, meaningless and repetitive jobs. In this way, there is a link between students' experience of school and many employees' experience of work.

CHECK YOUR UNDERSTANDING

1. Explain what sociologists mean by the 'hidden curriculum'. (2 marks)
2. Explain what part the hidden curriculum plays in the socialization of a child. (3 marks)
3. Identify and explain three ways in which the hidden curriculum may reflect society's values. (6 marks)

THE EDUCATION SYSTEM IN BRITAIN

There have been a number of major changes and developments in Britain's education system over the years. We will look here at the most significant ones.

Before 1870

Before 1870, the education system was not formally organized in the way it is now. People's access to educational provision depended to a large extent on their position in society. For example, church-run charity schools were available to the poor, while the rich could afford private tutors or could send their children to private school.

The 1870 Education Act

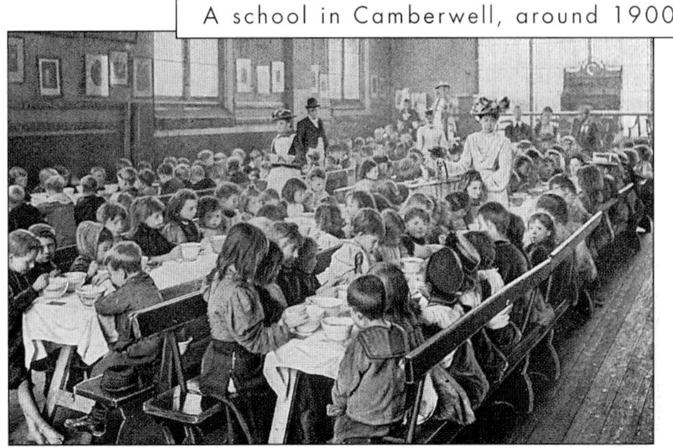
A school in Camberwell, around 1900

The 1870 Education Act tried to ensure that some basic education became available to all children from the ages of 5 to 11. It led to the general acceptance of the idea that revenue from state taxation should be used to pay for schooling. This was the start of the link between the state and education that exists today. Between 1870 and 1944, the education system was firmly based on social class. Three types of school were available:

1. elementary schools for the working classes up to the age of 14;
2. fee-paying grammar schools for the middle classes with a limited number of scholarships available to working-class boys;
3. expensive fee-paying public schools for the upper classes.

The 1944 Butler Education Act

The background

During and after the Second World War there was widespread debate over what sort of society Britain should be. It was felt that the talents of the nation were not being fully used and that the education system should be reformed in order to allow individual talent to flourish. It was also felt that Britain needed a better-educated workforce in order for its economy to be competitive. (This desire to educate a workforce to meet the needs of the economy has also influenced some of the changes in the education system in recent years.)

The aims

The 1944 Act aimed to give all pupils an equal chance to develop their talents and abilities in a system of free, state-run education. A new, three-stage structure was created:

1. primary – up to the age of 11, including infant and junior stages;
2. secondary – from 11 to 15 (school leaving age was raised to 16 in 1976);
3. further/higher – education beyond the school leaving age.

The tri-partite system

11-plus exam
(taken at age 11; designed to test ability and potential of student)
Based on this, students were placed in either:

SECONDARY MODERN	SECONDARY TECHNICAL	GRAMMAR
general education for less academic	practical education, e.g. crafts, skills	academic education for more academic
(approx. 75% of students)	*(approx. 5% of all students)*	*(approx. 20% of all students)*

The main changes were in the organization of the secondary sector. The aim here was to introduce a meritocratic system where children would receive an education based on their own academic ability, rather than on the ability of their parents to pay. The result was the **tri-partite** system. Children's ability was tested at the age of 11 by the '11-plus' exam. Based on the results of this exam, children went to one of three types of school, each of which was designed to meet their needs (as illustrated in the table above).

Pupils at a comprehensive school

1965: the start of the comprehensive system

The Labour government decided in 1965 to ask Local Education Authorities (LEAs) to reorganize secondary education so that all students, regardless of academic ability, attended the same type of school. This became known as a 'comprehensive' school, and still exists in this form today. By 1986, approximately 90 per cent of secondary school pupils were attending comprehensives.

Why are comprehensives thought to be a good idea?

- Comprehensive schools were introduced in response to what some saw as the failings of the tri-partite system, which often simply reflected social class backgrounds, with more middle-class children in grammar schools. Instead, comprehensives are based on the principle of one type of school for everyone.
- Social reasons – as children of all abilities and from different social classes attend the same school and mix, so social barriers are broken down.
- Educational reasons – they are designed to cater for children of all abilities. There is no entrance examination or selection such as there was in the '11-plus', so no child is labelled as a 'failure'. This is seen to be fairer to many, and particularly to late developers.
- Comprehensives are said to provide pupils with more opportunity to achieve success according to their ability.
- Economic reasons – comprehensives are larger, so more subjects and more facilities are available. They are seen as cheaper to fund and run.
- Each school has a specific 'catchment area' – a particular area or neighbourhood from which pupils are drawn. This has established the principle of local schools enrolling local children of all abilities and providing them with the same opportunities.

What are the problems with the comprehensive system?

No choice

- It is argued that comprehensives limit parental choice. Each student is expected to go to the nearest school in the area, no matter how good or bad that school's reputation.

Educational factors

- It is argued that less academically able students are held back by the more able, particularly in mixed-ability groups (that is, where children of all abilities are taught in the same classroom). Teachers' attention and time might be torn between meeting the needs of the very bright as well as of less able students.
- The education of bright working-class children may suffer if they go to the local comprehensive rather than to the local grammar school.

- Comprehensives accept lower standards. This criticism is related to social class as comprehensives contain a mixture of classes with a range of values and attitudes. The grammar school, on the other hand, was largely middle class and so would reflect middle-class standards only.

Do comprehensives break down class barriers?

- Comprehensives are not really of mixed social class as they are based on a local neighbourhood; for example, inner-city comprehensives are usually working class and suburban ones are usually middle class.
- Some argue that most comprehensives are not really comprehensive at all because, for instance, they stream or band students within the school according to ability. Critics claim that streams reflect social class differences.
- In other words, the comprehensive system simply reproduces the old tri-partite system, but in one school.

How is the education system organized in contemporary Britain?

The answer to this question is more complicated than it seems at first. There is a range of different types of schools and colleges in Britain, some of which are provided through LEAs in each area of the country, while some are financed by charging attendance fees. However, we can broadly describe educational provision in the following ways.

Pre-school education

This refers to the care and education of children under the age of five. It may take a variety of forms, such as:

- **day nurseries**, which may be provided through the local authority or by voluntary or private means;
- **playgroups**, which provide care and learning experiences mainly for 3- to 5-year-olds;
- **nursery education**, which may be provided in nursery schools or in nursery classes attached to primary schools.

Primary education

This refers to infant and junior schools, which are usually co-educational (that is, they take both girls and boys) and tend to take any student from a particular area. Most primary education is provided by the state (or public sector) through the LEA. However, some schools at this level are private and fees must be paid.

Secondary education

This refers to schools that take students from the ages of 11 to 16 (from 12 in Scotland), although some may also provide sixth-form education up to the age of 18. Most secondary education is provided by the state in comprehensive schools where no fees are paid. However, some secondary education is provided by private fee-paying schools, by grammar schools, independent church schools and by a minority of state schools that have 'opted-out' of, or left, LEA control (known as grant-maintained schools).

Further and higher education

This refers to education beyond the compulsory age of 16. From 16 to 18, students can study for a range of qualifications (e.g. A levels, Advanced GNVQs, Scottish Highers) at sixth-form colleges or further education colleges, or go on to skills training courses. At 18, students may then be qualified to go on to higher education and study at a university. Many adults choose to return to education, taking courses at further education colleges or universities.

Should education be provided by the state or by the independent sector?

This has been an area of debate for many years. At present, Britain has a mixture of state and independent provision, with the vast majority of children attending state schools.

TYPES OF SCHOOLS

Examine the following statistical information.

Table 6.1 School pupils (by type of school)

United Kingdom	1990/91	(Thousands) 1994/95	1995/96
PUBLIC SECTOR SCHOOLS			
Nursery	105	85	84
Primary	4,955	5,255	5,335
Secondary			
modern	94	90	79
grammar	156	184	182
comprehensive	2,844	3,093	3,130
other secondary	300	289	280
All public sector schools	8,433	8,996	9,096
INDEPENDENT SECTOR SCHOOLS			
Pupils aged 10 and under	266	262	268
Pupils aged 11 and over	347	338	335
All independent schools	613	600	603

Source: adapted from *Social Trends* (1997)

There is some dispute about the educational significance of average class size and pupil/teacher ratios but these are widely regarded by parents as key indicators of the quality of education ... In 1994/95 the pupil/teacher ratio for public sector schools was around twice that for non-maintained (independent) schools at 19 and 10 pupils per teacher, respectively.

Source: Social Trends (1997)

1. What type of state (or public sector) school do most secondary school pupils attend?
2. In which sector do the highest number of pupils attend?
3. According to the information given, what might be one advantage of attending an independent school?

The independent sector

These are schools that charge fees. This sector is made up of:

- **private schools** – all schools that charge fees;
- **public schools** – these are the older and more famous independent schools, such as Eton, Harrow or Rugby.

In 1995 there were 2,000 independent schools, of which about 200 were public schools. Attendance in the independent sector accounts for around 7 per cent of all schoolchildren. As the name suggests, independent schools are not subject to the same rules as the state sector schools. For example, they do not have to teach the National Curriculum.

A state school and an independent school

Because of the high tuition fees paid, opponents of independent schooling have claimed that they allow the children of the rich to receive a separate and particular kind of education that gives them certain advantages over state-educated children. For example, ex-public school pupils are far more likely to go on to the top universities, such as Oxford or Cambridge, and to occupy the most important positions in our society.

In this way, opponents argue, the rich and powerful can pass on privileges to their children through the independent education system.

Why are independent schools favoured by some parents, politicians and educationalists?

- They have a lower teacher–pupil ratio than state schools, which means that classes are smaller and pupils receive more attention from the teacher.
- Resources and facilities are often better than in some state comprehensive schools.
- Many independent schools have an academic culture, in which academic achievement is emphasized and examination results are good. Pupils are said to be highly motivated and may go on to university.
- Parental input is high in terms of fees, support and expectations.
- Independent boarding schools are said to benefit from the full immersion of staff and students in school life.

Why are state schools favoured by some parents, politicians and educationalists?

- State schools are free – they are not based on the ability of parents to pay the sometimes high fees of private schools. Some critics argue that it is not morally right to have a private education system to which only the rich have access as this reinforces inequalities in society based on wealth.
- State schools are more socially mixed. Independent schools are seen as elitist and socially divisive.
- State schools may provide a route of upward social mobility for pupils from poor families. Fee-paying schools are less likely to do so.
- Pupils do not have to travel so far on a daily basis if they attend a local state school. Private school pupils may have to travel relatively long distances, or live away from home altogether.

THE PROS AND CONS OF THE INDEPENDENT SECTOR

In a small group, read the following summaries of the main arguments for and against the independent sector:

- *Independent schooling maintains privilege based on social class position; that is, it can only be afforded by the rich. It is used by the rich to give their children a headstart. Education should only be provided through a properly funded state system to ensure that everyone has access to the same levels and quality of education.*
- *Independent schooling is similar to private health care in that people should be able to spend their money however they choose. If they can afford to send their children to an independent school, then, in a free society, this option should be available to them.*

Using these summaries and other information in this section, list arguments for and against the following statement: 'Education should be provided only by the state.'

WHAT HAVE BEEN THE EFFECTS OF RECENT CHANGES IN THE EDUCATION SYSTEM?

The 1988 Education Act

Some major changes were introduced as a result of the 1988 Education Act brought in by the Conservative government.

The National Curriculum and testing

The National Curriculum was introduced in September 1989 in all state schools in England and Wales.

It established a number of **core subjects** (English, maths, sciences), which all students aged 5–16 must study, and also a number of **foundation subjects** (for example history and geography), which must be studied to Key Stage 3.

Science is now compulsory for all pupils up to GCSE level

In addition, students' progress is assessed at the end of **key stages**, at the age of 7, 11, 14 and 16. At 7, 11 and 14, students are assessed formally by their teachers and by national tests in the core subjects. Sixteen-year-olds are assessed by means of the GCSE examination.

The aim here is to measure students' performance against national targets for each key stage. In this way parents and schools can be informed as to whether a child is performing above or below the expected level for their age. Measures can then be taken to improve the performance of children who are below the expected level, as well as the performance of schools whose students fall below the national targets.

One aim of the National Curriculum has been to provide greater equality of education for all by ensuring that all pupils take the same subjects. Science, for example, has traditionally been a boys' subject but it is now compulsory for *all* pupils up to GCSE level.

ASSESSING STUDENTS' PROGRESS

1. In a small group, discuss the idea of assessing students' progress at the end of key stages.
2. Make a list of the possible benefits and problems of testing 7-year-olds and using the results as a measure of their ability.

Local management of schools (LMS)

Under LMS, all state sector schools have been given responsibility for managing their school budgets and staff. This has had the effect of weakening the role of the LEAs, which traditionally had had more control over budgets and staffing arrangements in schools.

City technology colleges (CTCs)

These are a new type of school designed to meet the increasing emphasis on developing the skills needed for industry and the economy. They are part state and part privately funded and offer a curriculum that specializes in technical and scientific education.

Grant-maintained schools (GMSs)

This development has allowed any LEA school to apply for self-governing grant-maintained status and to receive direct grants from the government rather than being funded through LEA budgets. This process is sometimes known as 'opting out'. This allowed the school to have almost total control over the management of its budget, staffing decisions, priorities for spending, and so on. These schools also had the right to introduce the selection of pupils through entry exams.

By January 1996, over 19 per cent of secondary school pupils attended a GMS in England. In total, there were 642 grant-maintained secondary schools.

Increased competition and choice

The 1988 Act introduced the principles of choice and diversity in educational provision. The idea here is that parents should be able to choose the type of school they prefer for their children from a range of options (comprehensive, grammar, GMS, independent). Schools must now produce a prospectus and publish exam results and National Curriculum test results, as well as a comparison between the school and national results. Increased parental choice has led to schools having to compete with each other for students.

TYPES OF SECONDARY EDUCATION

> **There will be three categories of secondary education in Britain: private schools for the rich, 'opted-out' government schools for the less rich but clever, and local council schools for the poor and rejected ...**
>
> Source: Simon Jenkins, *The Times*, 29 June 1994

Consider quote above, and answer the following questions.

1 Do you agree that 'clever' students should have access to a different type or quality of education? What might be the benefits of this and what might be the problems? Explain your answer.
2 Explain what the effects might be of the situation Simon Jenkins is suggesting.

School league tables

School league tables were introduced to provide information about the performance of schools. They allowed parents to make comparisons between schools more easily. The aim was to create more competition between schools, with the assumption that this would lead to higher standards. Schools that appear successful in league tables become oversubscribed, with many parents wanting to send their children there.

Vocational education and training

This area is sometimes known as 'the new vocationalism' because of the range and number of new initiatives that are being made available to provide vocational (or work-related) qualifications and training.

This development has reflected the growing importance of the view that the education system has to provide the skills and expertise needed by industry and the economy in the modern world far more effectively than it used to.

A range of qualifications now exist, from work-based National Vocational Qualifications (NVQs) to the introduction in 1992 of General National Vocational Qualifications (GNVQs), which have provided a vocational counterpart to GCSEs and A levels.

Linked to this, government has sought to ensure that skills training is targeted at school-leavers by placing 16-year-olds on training programmes for vocational skills or work experience; that is, unless they have a job to go to or are continuing in education.

Is the 'new vocationalism' useful?

Supporters of these changes argue that they will lead to a more skilled, better-qualified workforce that will allow Britain to be more competitive. Also, NVQs and GNVQs provide another kind of qualification for those who are less academic.

Opponents argue that the emphasis on skills training disguises the fact that the problem is not that young people lack the necessary skills for work but, rather, that there is no work for skilled young people to do.

Vocational qualifications are seen by critics as being similar to the ideas of the tri-partite system in that students who are not seen to be academic are considered failures and are pushed into lower-status vocational training.

Developments in further education

At 16, young people must decide whether to:

- remain in education;
- go into training; or
- seek employment.

In recent years there has been a clear trend to remain in full-time education. The government is committed to raising the number of young people remaining in full-time education or training after the age of 16. This is because, in order for Britain to remain competitive and prosperous in a global economy, it needs a highly educated and well-trained workforce.

Competition has been encouraged in the further and higher education sectors. All further and higher education colleges 'opted out' of LEA control and are funded instead by government, through funding councils such as the Further Education Funding Council (FEFC) and the Higher Education Funding Council (HEFC). In effect, colleges became separate businesses, in competition with each other for students to increase their funding.

SEEKING FURTHER EDUCATION

Examine the following statistics.

- Around three-quarters of those aged 16–18 in England were in education and training at the end of 1995.
- While the proportion of 16-year-olds in education and training increased only slightly between the end of 1990 and 1995, the proportion of 18-year-olds increased more, especially for females.
- Between 1990/91 and 1994/95, the number of students enrolled in full-time higher education in the United Kingdom increased by 55 per cent and the number in full-time further education by 60 per cent.
- For undergraduate courses, in 1994/95 there were around twice as many enrolments by men than in 1970/71 and just over four times as many enrolments by women.

Source: *Social Trends* (1997)

1 Identify the general patterns in the statistics.
2 How would you explain these patterns?

The funding councils monitor colleges' performance against targets set for recruitment, exam performance, and so on. In this way, as with schools, supporters hope that these measures will result in improved quality of provision in the sector.

CHECK YOUR UNDERSTANDING

1 Identify and explain two reasons for the introduction of comprehensive schools. (4 marks)
2 Identify and explain two advantages of comprehensive schools, compared with private schools. (4 marks)
3 Explain how the introduction of the National Curriculum might improve the education system in the UK. (6 marks)
4 State one important change in the education system since 1979 and explain how this change may have increased or decreased educational opportunities. (4 marks)

HOW CAN WE EXPLAIN DIFFERENT LEVELS OF EDUCATIONAL ACHIEVEMENT?

Certain groups appear to perform relatively badly within the educational system, for instance when measured in terms of examination results and entry to higher education. Such groups are said to **underachieve** educationally.

The nature–nurture debate: is it our genes or is it our social environment?

Nature

This theory suggests that the explanation for educational success and failure lies with **intelligence/heredity**. The more extreme view sees intelligence as largely inherited; that is, as genetic. Educational success and failure are seen as reflecting the different ability levels we are born with.

Nurture

This theory suggests that the explanation for educational success and failure lies with the **social environment**. Educational achievement is related to social factors such as class, gender, ethnicity, peer groups, family and school organization.

NATURE V. NURTURE

In a small group, discuss these two views.

1 Which would you support and why?
2 Make a note of arguments for and against these views that come out of your discussion.

How have sociologists tried to explain different levels of educational attainment?

Research into educational attainment has gone through various stages.

- During the 1960s and 1970s **social class** was seen as an important influence on people's lives, so much of the research examined social class and how it could affect achievement levels.
- While many of the ideas and findings developed at this time may still be of use, it is important to recognize that many significant changes have taken place in British society since this research was done. For example, the

way in which the education system is organized has changed, as well as the nature of social class itself (see Chapter 3).

- Later research, in the 1980s and 1990s, focused on a growing interest in the importance of **gender** and **ethnicity** as influences on people's lives. Consequently, research into educational achievement has reflected this.
- Many of the areas of importance identified during research on social class, such as parental encouragement and teachers' attitudes, have been re-examined from the point of view of gender and ethnicity. For example, differences in the treatment of male and female students by teachers has been examined.
- It is important to remember, then, that the focus of sociological research changes over time and that research will always require updating.

How can social class affect achievement?

The term 'social class' is one way of describing a person's position in society. An individual's social class is usually determined by looking at their occupation or at their parents' occupation. Statistics tend to show that the higher a student's social class background is, the greater the chance of that student's achieving high educational qualifications.

Sociologists have put forward a number of explanations for the relative underachievement of working-class pupils. Such explanations can be divided into:

- the influence of home environment/background;
- the influence of the school environment.

How can the home environment affect educational achievement?

A range of explanations has been put forward in answer to this question, based on individuals' home background or environment.

The material environment/material deprivation

In spite of 'free schooling', there is still an obvious connection between the material conditions of the home and educational achievement.

The Child Poverty Action Group has stressed the **costs** of school uniforms, sports kits and special materials, for example, which often result in poorer children being kept away from school or being sent home. There is a stigma attached to children who are treated in this way.

Living conditions – poor housing, overcrowding, lack of privacy or quiet places to do homework adversely affect performance at school (Douglas 1967). These conditions are more likely to apply to working-class children. In addition, research has revealed that absenteeism is higher among such children.

Many working-class areas, especially in the inner cities, may lack **pre-school facilities**, such as nursery schools and playgroups.

Halsey, Heath and Ridge (1980) showed that a high percentage of working-class children (75 per cent) left school at the first possible opportunity. Lack of **maintenance grants** for secondary school pupils was seen as a major obstacle to 'equality of opportunity'. As a lower priority was accorded by working-class parents to their daughters' education, this obstacle is very much greater for working-class girls.

On the other hand, middle-class children may have a headstart as their higher social class position and income may lead to better-quality housing and a greater availability of books and study facilities at home, for example their own room or the ability to afford private tuition.

WHAT CAUSES UNDERACHIEVEMENT?

For each of the factors listed, explain how they could lead to educational underachievement:

- lack of new school uniform or sports kit;
- lack of privacy or quiet place in the home;
- poor diet, e.g. no breakfast before arriving in school;
- poor attendance through illness;
- not having attended a nursery school.

Parental attitudes and expectations

While material conditions seem to be of great importance in a working-class area, parental attitudes seem to be a more important factor in more prosperous areas.

The government Plowden Report (1967) and sociological research by Douglas in the same year both stressed the importance of parental attitudes in determining educational success.

Table 6.2 Middle class v. working class

Middle-class values	Working-class values
1 Desire for control over their lives.	**1** A more passive attitude with a fatalistic acceptance of other people being in control.
2 Emphasis on future planning.	**2** Emphasis upon present or past.
3 'Deferred gratification' – being prepared to make sacrifices now in order to fulfil future ambitions; investing for the future. Sacrificing money and time now to ensure a better future (e.g. staying on at school or going to college/university).	**3** 'Present gratification' – living for the moment with little attempt to plan for the future or get a job.
4 Individual achievement stressed – by their own efforts, individuals will improve their position.	**4** Collective action stressed – working people will achieve improvements by sticking together (e.g. trade union activities).

Some researchers have suggested that middle-class parents socialize their children into one set of values while working-class parents socialize their children into a different set of values.

It has been suggested that **middle-class values** contribute to the development of ambition, disciplined study and individual striving for success among middle-class children. These are values which are highly thought of by teachers in school. This may be due to the mainly middle-class backgrounds of teachers. **Working-class values** are less likely to lead to such success as there is an emphasis upon present gratification and a tendency to accept one's position fatalistically. Thus, middle-class parents are more likely than working-class parents to provide their children with attitudes that contribute to educational success.

Middle-class parents' knowledge of how to 'work the system' may also be an important factor in their children's success – how to hold their own in disagreements with teachers about the teaching of their children; how to fight sexual discrimination; knowing what books and periodicals to buy and having the money to buy them.

It is argued that middle-class parents expect more from their children and are more interested in their progress, for example as measured in school visits.

THE INVOLVEMENT OF PARENTS

In a small group consider the following points:

1 Are school visits and parents' evenings a useful way to measure parents' interest in their children's education? List reasons why this might be a good method and also any possible problems with this approach.
2 What method(s) would you use to measure whether or not parents were encouraging their children? Make a note of the method(s) chosen and list any possible problems with your approach.

Cultural deprivation

We have already examined the view that working-class children underachieve at school as a result of **material deprivation**. In addition, it may be that working-class children and those from some ethnic minority groups may suffer as a result of **cultural deprivation**.

It is suggested that schools are white, middle-class institutions and therefore white middle-class culture dominates. Children from middle-class homes will be advantaged in schools as their upbringing will provide them with a better opportunity for academic success. For example, family visits to a library or museum will encourage interest in learning and introduce children to key elements of general knowledge and research skills more quickly. Middle-class families are more likely to make such visits. The middle-class home is seen as a place where books, CD-ROMs and educational toys are the norm. The working-class child, it is argued, is less likely to receive this kind of upbringing.

Material deprivation?

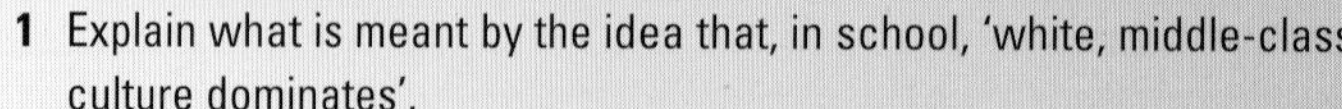

WHAT IS 'WHITE, MIDDLE-CLASS CULTURE'?

1. Explain what is meant by the idea that, in school, 'white, middle-class culture dominates'.
2. Describe how this idea could explain working-class underachievement.

We have already looked at explanations of working-class educational underachievement that stress the influence of the home environment. We now need to look at explanations of working-class underachievement that stress the influence of the school environment and the way the school is organized.

How can a school affect achievement?

How can teachers' judgements and expectations affect achievement?

Teachers are unavoidably involved in making judgements and classifying pupils. These judgements often affect a child's chances of educational achievement. Bernstein (1960) observed that infant teachers in working-class areas tended to judge students on their reactions to the commands and questions made by the teachers, while in middle-class areas teachers were more interested in students who took initiatives.

Bernstein further speculated that infant school teachers tend to encourage independence among middle-class children, but expect working-class children simply to react to what they are told to do.

The 'halo' effect

Several studies have noted the effect of teachers' expectations on their students' performance and also on the actual teachers' assessments of the students' performance.

Teachers tend to judge children who are well behaved as 'bright', while they tend to be more questioning about the good performance of those children who are less well behaved. This is known as the **'halo effect'**: students are typecast on the basis of early impressions based upon their appearance, clothing, manners, speech and school records about their homes. Teachers, in effect, **label** students.

Many sociologists suggest that teachers' assessments of students tend to reflect the teachers' views of what middle-class and working-class pupils should be capable of, rather than their *actual performance*.

LABELLING STUDENTS

1. Describe four ways in which teachers give labels to students.
2. For each of the four ways chosen, explain why working-class students may be more likely to receive negative labels.
3. Some students may try to 'reject' the label they are given. Identify and explain one way in which this might happen.

If teachers have low expectations of working-class children, this may affect the actual progress of the children in a number of ways. For example, the teacher may make fewer attempts to encourage a child's interest in a subject.

Equally, if the teacher sees the student as only being capable of reaching a certain level of academic achievement (perhaps based on the results of IQ tests), he or she may see no point in trying to develop the student's performance any further. This is known as a **'self-fulfilling prophecy'**.

TESTING THE SELF-FULFILLING PROPHECY

Read the following details of a study by Rosenthal and Jacobson, called *Pygmalion in the Classroom* (1968). The study was designed to test the theory of the self-fulfilling prophecy.

> *Teachers in an elementary school in California were told by the researchers that they had identified a number of students – the 'spurters' – who were likely to make rapid academic progress. The teachers were led to believe that the spurters had been identified as a result of high scores in IQ tests.*
>
> *In reality, the spurters had simply been selected randomly by the researchers and did not display any greater ability than their classmates. However, a year later it became clear that the spurters had, indeed, made significantly greater progress than the other students.*
>
> *Rosenthal and Jacobson concluded that the progress of the spurters was a result of the teachers' expectations of them. These higher expectations had been communicated to the students and they had come to believe in the teachers' 'prophecy' about them.*

In a small group, make a note of your answers to the following questions:

1. In what ways could the teachers have communicated their high expectations to the spurters?
2. What do you think happened to the other students who were not labelled as spurters?
3. If you were a parent of a child at that school, how would you have felt about the research?
4. Can you think of any other factors that could have influenced the spurters' achievements, other than the teachers' 'prophecy'?
5. Having considered the study by Rosenthal and Jacobson, do you think the self-fulfilling prophecy is a useful theory in trying to explain educational underachievement?

The idea of a 'self-fulfilling prophecy' has been used to explain how differences between students may be made more significant than the simple measure of classifying children as 'dull' or 'clever'. Students are often under pressure to bring their own 'self-image' into line with the teacher's judgement of them. What is the point in trying to improve your maths if the teacher has told you that you are hopeless in the subject? Even if the student resists the teacher's assessment of them, they might still find it difficult to improve their performance because the teacher may deem it a waste of resources to spend time trying to improve a performance that he or she has already judged to be irredeemable. In effect, the student is forced to accept the teacher's 'prophecy' about them.

Again, it is thought that working-class students are more likely to receive a negative 'prophecy' from teachers, whereas middle-class students will receive a more positive one.

Effects of streaming

Streaming into different-ability groups, based upon an assessment of general ability, can be seen as an ideal way in which to meet the educational needs of individual students. For example, students will receive a level of work that is appropriate to their needs and abilities and will be working alongside students of similar ability – this may help to avoid the stigma of being seen as 'bottom of the class'. Equally, teachers will be able to produce materials and lessons that meet the needs of the students more effectively, as they know what ability range they are to teach.

However, streaming may have undesirable effects, similar to the self-fulfilling prophecy mentioned above. For example:

- Students in the lower streams tend to have their confidence damaged and this may result in them not trying to improve their position.
- Even when students are not disheartened, teachers may devote less attention to the students in the lower stream than to those in the higher stream.
- Streaming is often linked to social class, with a disproportionately higher number of lower-stream students being drawn from the working class.
- Transfers between streams are rare in practice.

Some schools have sought to overcome the known problems of streaming by having **mixed-ability groups**, or else they have sought a compromise by having **subject setting**. With the introduction of the National Curriculum, some research suggests that streaming is on the increase as schools 'set' students according to their ability to achieve different levels of the curriculum.

STREAMING

In a small group, discuss the following points:

1 Explain how streaming could affect a student's exam performance.
2 How would you explain why a higher number of lower-stream students come from working-class backgrounds?

The school 'counter-culture' and peer-group pressure

The school 'counter-culture'

Studies by Hargreaves (1967), of an English boys' secondary modern school, and by Lacey (1970), of a grammar school, suggest that one of the effects of streaming is to lead to the development of a school subculture which is opposed to the learning objectives of the school.

Hargreaves argued that the lower-stream secondary modern schoolboys tended to reject the academic values and standards of behaviour expected by the school, which had labelled them as 'failures'. The boys had evolved a 'counter-culture' which laid stress on defiance of teachers and the carrying out of daring exploits. Lacey found a similar counter-culture in the lower streams of the grammar school he studied. The evidence seemed to point to the fact that streaming led to pupils being put off any form of learning that the school put forward.

COUNTER-SCHOOL SUBCULTURE IN ACTION

Examine the following extract, which deals with female counter-school subculture.

Girls' deviance in school does not always take different forms from the boys, but it is treated and perceived differently by teachers and other students. Young women's deviance is often seen in relation to their sexuality …

… girls could and did cause as much (if not more) trouble than boys in school, but … this disruption took different forms, and was seen to pose less of an acute discipline problem. 'Good girls' were those who caused minimal disruption in class and were relatively quiet. These same students were not necessarily more academic or pro-school than their deviant peers. Some were simply 'keeping their heads down', and resisting teachers' demands in more subtle, less obvious ways …

It was not always possible to identify a particular group of girls as 'deviants' or troublemakers who were always opposed to school and academic work and destined for factory jobs. It was equally difficult to find 'good' girls who were pro-school and hoped to go on to college or office jobs. The situation was far more complex than analyses of male counter-school subcultures might lead one to expect.

Berni, for example, saw herself as a troublemaker, and when I talked to her in the fifth year, she was hanging around with a group of other white working-class girls: all of whom saw themselves as troublemakers.… They distanced themselves from the 'swots' and 'pets' who wanted to stay on, and had a low opinion of the 'snobs' who wanted to get office jobs. Berni and her friends talked about these distinctions:

Shelly:	*Well there's three that usually don't laugh or mess around.*
Jenny:	*Three at the front, you know, very serious.*
Shelly:	*Oh pets,* (laugh) *don't tell them, Jenny, you're supposed to be a friend.*
Berni:	*They don't laugh. I've never seen 'em laugh. They take life too serious, they should be laughing like us* (laugh).
CG (author):	*Are they going to stay on?*
Shelly:	*Yeah, a lot of them stop on, I can't wait to get away though, I'm bored me.*
Berni:	*They're posh too, snobs wanna do office jobs. We're the troublemakers* (laugh).

Yet Berni went straight into an office job immediately after she left school. It seemed there was no clear link between pro- and anti-school attitudes, friendship groups in school and young women's subsequent jobs.

Source: Griffin (1985)

In a small group, discuss the following points:

1 In what ways might female counter-school subcultures be different to those of males?
2 Is the idea of the school counter-culture a useful way of trying to explain female working-class underachievement?
3 Make a note of your conclusions.

School organization

A well-organized school with good teachers tends to have better results than a poorly organized school. For example, a study by a research team led by Michael Rutter in 1979, based on a sample of Inner London secondary schools, found that schools taking children from similar backgrounds achieved very different results.

The schools with the best results had certain things in common:

- They were well organized, with strong leadership.
- Teachers were dedicated and well prepared.
- There was a strong emphasis on academic achievement.
- Praise and encouragement of students was emphasized, rather than criticism and punishment.

In this way, the quality of the school is thought to play a role in improving student achievement in general.

IS A WELL-ORGANIZED SCHOOL THE ANSWER?

1 In a small group, discuss whether or not a well-organized school can compensate for other unsatisfactory school or home background factors in affecting the educational achievements of different social classes.
2 Note down any points made for and against this idea.

Which is more important – the home or the school?

HOME V. SCHOOL

In a small group:

1 Create two lists of relevant factors, one headed 'home factors', the other headed 'school factors'.
2 For each set of factors, rank them in order of 'most important' or 'most useful idea' to 'least important' or 'least useful idea'. Be prepared to explain your choices.
3 Do you consider home factors or school factors to be the most important influence on achievement levels between social classes? Make a note of the reasons for your choice.

CHECK YOUR UNDERSTANDING

1 Identify and explain two ways in which home background could influence educational achievement. (4 marks)
2 Identify and explain two possible effects of streaming in schools. (4 marks)
3 Identify and explain one way in which teachers could affect a student's achievement at school. (2 marks)
4 To what extent is the education system likely to help to reduce inequality between social classes? (9 marks)

How does gender affect educational attainment and subject choice?

What are the patterns in statistics?

Official statistics reveal some differences in educational achievement based on gender.

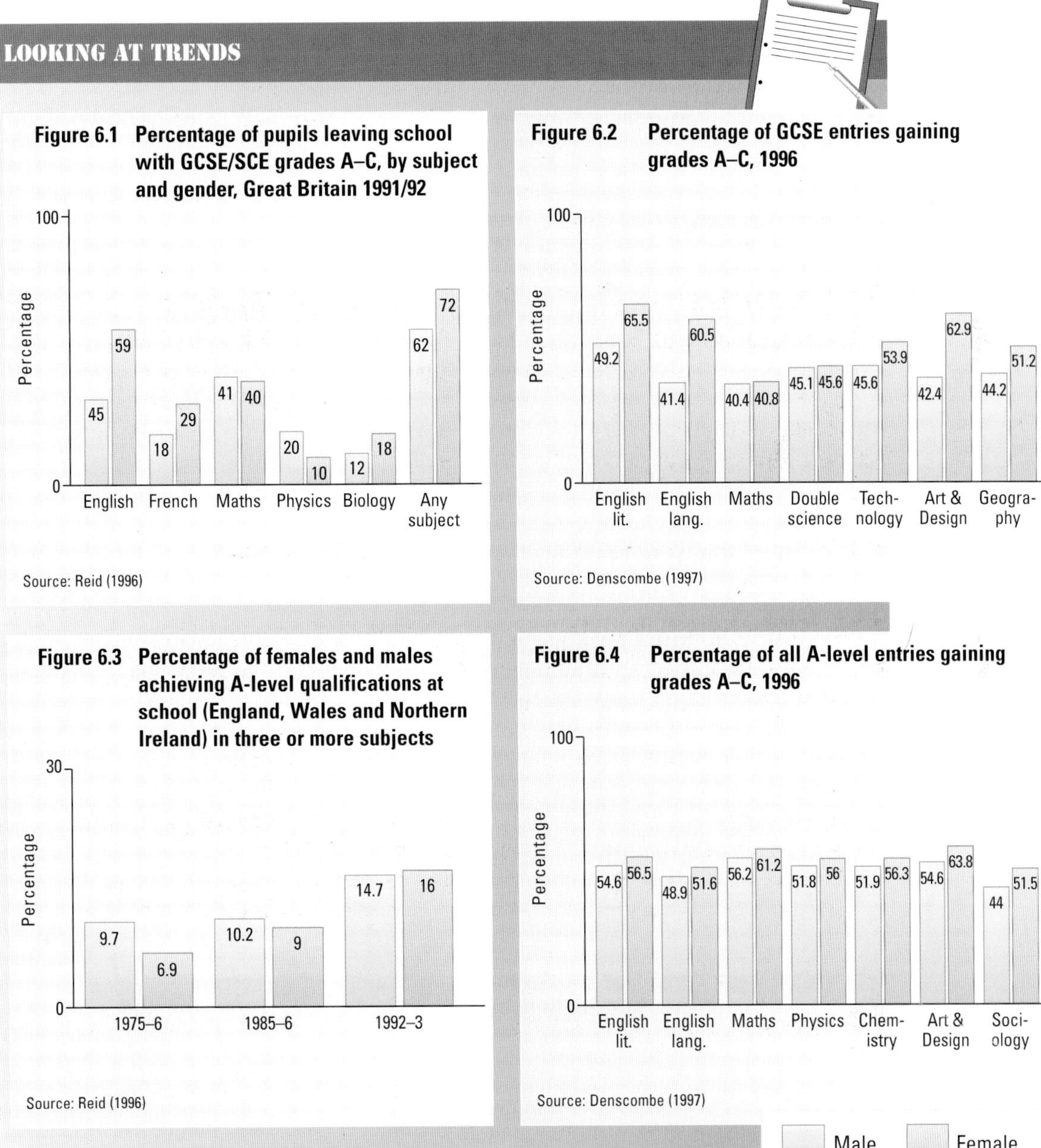

Using the statistics in the figures above:

1 Outline the trends in achievement levels between female and male students at GCSE and A level.

2 Make a list of factors or ideas that might explain these trends in achievement.

Are there different patterns in attainment and subject choice between males and females?

Girls are more academically successful, for example:

- The percentage of girls with five or more GCSEs at grades A–C has increased from 45.8 per cent in 1992/3 to 47.8 per cent in 1993/4, while the percentage for boys was 36.8 per cent in 1992/3 and 39.1 per cent in 1993/4.
- At A level, in 1993/4 30.4 per cent of girls achieved two or more A/AS passes compared to 25.4 per cent of boys.
- The proportion of women attending higher education is now greater than the proportion of men.

Source: DFE *Statistical Bulletin* (May 1995)

How can we explain these patterns?

The feminist movement

The feminist movement has led to changing attitudes towards women's roles and also to their expectations of career opportunities. Boys were always expected to go on to work and to support a family. Girls were not expected to succeed academically. Instead, they were expected to make marriage and motherhood their primary concerns. Feminism has helped to challenge these ideas and to give girls greater confidence in their abilities.

In a recent report, Helen Wilkinson states that:

> *... women's aspirations and their image of themselves have profoundly altered in the past quarter of a century ...*

Wilkinson describes a generation of confident, assertive, ambitious women with goals and expectations far beyond those of earlier generations, partly as a result of earlier gains made by the women's movement.

> *Seventy-nine per cent of the women surveyed say that they want to develop their careers or find employment, while only 50 per cent regard having children as a goal. Less than a quarter of young women between 18 and 24 feel that a woman needs a stable relationship to be fulfilled.*

Source: Wilkinson (1994)

FEMALE ACHIEVEMENT

Outline and explain how the ideas expressed in the extract help us to explain greater female achievement in exam results and university attendance.

Changing job opportunities

Basic changes in the types of work available to them may have encouraged women to gain more educational qualifications. In the future, it is predicted that more women than men will be working. It is also predicted that there will be further decreases in traditionally 'male' jobs in manufacturing and engineering, but a continued increase in 'female' jobs in service industries.

Have changing media images affected young women's aspirations?

Some researchers also argue that the skills seen as most desirable by employers are those traditionally associated with women, for example flexibility, team-work and good communication skills.

Wilkinson's study also suggests that women are feeling more optimistic about the future and that they are also more ambitious and more interested in qualifications than men. Some researchers have suggested that, in effect, women are on the brink of overturning the traditional position of men in both education and the workplace.

Legal changes

The Sex Discrimination Act (1975) makes sex discrimination in education illegal.

Equal opportunities policies

Awareness has been raised as a result of equal opportunities policies in schools and colleges. For example, Alison Kelly's research (1981) demonstrated that science was a 'male' subject as a result of textbook images, male role models and the dominance in the classroom of male teachers and male students. As a result, national projects such as GIST (Girls into Science and Technology) and GATE (Girls and Technology Education), were set up to try to encourage girls' participation and success in science and technical subjects.

In addition, training packs for teachers were developed to look at aspects of the hidden curriculum and teachers were encouraged to make their resources more 'girl-friendly'. In some cases, LEAs developed detailed equal opportunities policies for their schools and provided funds to appoint advisers in this area. In these ways, many factors that were seen as barriers to female students' achievement (such as the greater levels of attention given to male students in the classroom) have been addressed.

The introduction of the National Curriculum

The National Curriculum has meant that girls and boys in both primary and secondary schools have equal access to the same subjects. In addition, some subjects are compulsory for all students. For example, both boys and girls must now take science at GCSE level. This is seen as an improvement on the previous situation where students could choose not to do a science.

While some researchers have argued that this has led to improvements in girls' performances in science and technology, others have argued that it has not helped to encourage girls to choose these subjects at A level or degree level.

GIRL POWER IN SCIENCE

Read the following extract.

Putting the 'phyz' into physics for the girls

Scientists appealed yesterday for a laboratory version of the Spice Girls to break down the obstinate imbalance between the genders in pre-university physics.

Despite formidable role models and encouragement from new curriculum guidelines, the annual congress of the Institute of Physicists heard that many young women still lack the confidence to tackle a subject notoriously seen as too difficult.

A special session on Girls and Science Education heard that GCSE grades among young women have recently shown a marked rise, with girls getting more A and A-star grades than boys in parts of the country.

But progress appeared to falter after the age of sixteen, with only one in four of A-level physics candidates being girls.

'It seems to be a matter of confidence,' said Catherine Wilson, education officer for the Institute. 'Even the girls who've done very well at GCSE start to falter when faced with the next challenge. We need a Phyz Girls group to get across the message – you can do it. Don't leave it to the boys.'

Source: *The Guardian*, 26 March 1997

Girl power!

1 Explain why girls may appear to lack confidence in a science subject such as physics.
2 Using the extract, explain what the consequences of this might be.
3 Suggest ways in which this situation could be improved.

An all-female lesson

MAKING A CHOICE OF SUBJECTS

Carry out some research on student subject choices.

1 Select a sample of students who either have made, or will be making, choices about subjects.
2 Use questionnaires or unstructured interviews to find out what factors may influence their choices.
3 Try to use your results to explain differences in subject choice between male and female students at both A level and degree level

Single-sex schooling

Some researchers have seen single-sex schools as benefiting female students' achievement levels. In particular, they are thought to help to improve girls' performance in traditionally 'male' subject areas such as maths.

Another theory which has been tried out in a small number of schools is that of single-sex classrooms. The idea here is that female and male students are taught separately for certain subjects in an attempt to remove the disruptive influence of boys.

ARE SINGLE-SEX SCHOOLS BEST?

Read the extract and, in a small group, consider the following questions

1. Discuss the possible benefits and problems of single-sex schools and classrooms. Make a list of your points.
2. Reach a decision as to whether single-sex schools and classrooms are a useful way of influencing achievement levels between the sexes.

At the beginning of this school year, Osborne brought back single-sex classes. The girls, he assumes, '... will blossom while the boys, who badly need help to make them like school more, will have teachers who will put down peer group pressure.

You will also take their audience away. Even eleven-year-old boys are saying that they aren't concentrating because they are paying so much attention to girls. We're open to accusations that we're neglecting the social mixing, but we're fostering the extra-curricular activities ...'

Source: *Weekend Guardian*, 22 October 1994

Why is the performance of male students not improving at the same rate as that of female students?

Statistics suggest that the achievement levels of males are remaining static, while female achievement levels are increasing. Harris's research into the attitudes of 16-year-olds from mainly working-class backgrounds has shown that:

- Boys are thought to be suffering increasingly from low self-esteem and poor motivation.
- Boys seem to be less willing to struggle to overcome difficulties in understanding their work.
- Boys are less likely to work consistently hard than girls and are more easily distracted. In areas such as coursework, boys found it more difficult to organize their time effectively.
- Girls are more willing to do homework and also to spend more time on it.
- Girls give more thought to their futures and to the importance of qualifications in achievement of this, whereas boys do not seem as concerned.

Source: Harris et al. (1993)

WHY DO SOME MALE STUDENTS UNDERACHIEVE?

In a small group, discuss the explanations given for male underachievement.

1. Which ones do you agree or disagree with? Make a note of these.
2. Discuss and make a note of at least two other possible explanations.
3. Take each explanation in turn and try to suggest why it is happening.

CHANGING PATTERNS ACCORDING TO GENDER

In this section we have examined the changes in patterns of achievement according to gender. While female students still seem to choose 'female' subjects at A level and degree level, it is clear that they are now outperforming males in all areas and that this may lead to some important changes.

Using the information in this section, describe three possible consequences of the changing patterns in attainment according to gender.

CHECK YOUR UNDERSTANDING

1. Identify and explain three reasons why male and female students often choose different subjects in higher education. (6 marks)
2. Female students are outperforming male students at GCSE and A level. Identify and explain two reasons for this. (4 marks)

How can ethnicity affect educational attainment?

What do the statistics tell us?

Statistics show that educational achievement is, to some extent, related to ethnicity. Students from some ethnic backgrounds tend to underachieve educationally; that is, they do not achieve their full potential and tend to perform relatively poorly in examinations.

A study by Inner London Education Authority (ILEA) of O-level results in 1987 showed the following relationship between ethnicity and educational performance:

- Groups performing above ILEA averages included children from Greek, Indian, African and Pakistani backgrounds. Children from Indian families fared best.
- Groups performing below ILEA averages included children from Bangladeshi, African-Caribbean, English, Scottish, Welsh and Turkish backgrounds.

- Children from English, Welsh, Scottish and African-Caribbean families fared worst.
- The patterns showed that, in all ethnic groups, girls out-performed boys.

A study of 24 secondary schools in Bradford between 1983 and 1987 confirmed some of the ILEA findings, but also showed a marked improvement in black (African-Caribbean and Asian, but mainly Asian) pupil performance compared with white. The research in Bradford took account of the possible influence of the social class background of the students in the study by looking at whether students qualified for free school meals.

In 1991, Nuttall and Goldstein conducted a study of GCSE results for the Association of Metropolitan Authorities, based on six London boroughs' 1990 examination results. As with the ILEA study, pupils from Indian and Pakistani families continued to do better than those of African-Caribbean, English, Scottish, Welsh or Irish origin.

Are there any problems with using such statistics?

A number of points can be made here:

- Very few statistics are available that examine the patterns nationally.
- Many studies are only small-scale, based on one area, e.g. London.
- Many studies use categories to classify ethnic groups that are too general, e.g. the term 'Asian' does not allow us to see differences in achievement levels between Indian, Pakistani and Bangladeshi students.
- Most of the statistics produced do not allow us to examine the possible influence of social class background.

However, as Ivan Reid states:

> *... the general picture to emerge is that Asian children perform similarly to, or somewhat better than, their white classmates, while West Indians perform less well in primary and secondary schools.*

Source: Reid (1996)

EDUCATIONAL ATTAINMENT AMONG ETHNIC GROUPS

Examine the following tablem which is based on data from the Swann Committee (1985), the most extensive study to date on ethnicity and educational attainment.

Table 6.3 Ethnicity and educational attainment

Qualification	Asian	W. Indian	Others
1 A level or more	13	5	13
5 higher-grade GCE/O or more	17	6	19
No graded results	19	19	19

Source: Reid (1996)

1. Identify the patterns in educational attainment for different ethnic groups.
2. Identify and explain three criticisms that could be made of the statistics from the Swann Committee.

How can we explain the relationship between ethnicity and educational achievement?

As with social classes and female and male students, it is clear that factors other than nature or genetically inheritaged abilities may be more important in explaining the relative success or failure of different ethnic groups. Indeed, the Swann Committee, which was appointed by the government to examine the position of ethnic minorities in the education system, ruled out IQ as a cause of differences in attainment.

We can examine two main areas of influence: the home and the school.

The home

These explanations stress the importance of home background and culture to educational success.

Social class background

Some sociologists argue that the explanation is to be found in the socio-economic status (that is, the social class) of the group under study. In the ILEA study, for example, the Bangladeshi children who underachieved tended, on average, to be from lower socioeconomic backgrounds than other groups.

The Swann Committee (1985) pointed out that some ethnic minority students suffered as a result of social and economic deprivation. In this way, many of the factors affecting the attainment of working-class students may also affect some ethnic minority students. In other words, there is a kind of 'doubling up' of factors. Thus, some of the differences in achievement between ethnic groups may simply reflect social class differences.

Cultural differences

This view suggests that the cultures of some ethnic minority groups may be different to 'mainstream' culture. This may affect students' achievement because schools are seen to be institutions where white, 'mainstream' norms and values dominate.

The **language** spoken at home may also be an important factor affecting achievement. Some children who have only recently arrived in the UK may speak English as a second language and, as a result, they may be disadvantaged at school. Creole, a dialect spoken by some African-Caribbean students, may not be seen as acceptable in certain schools and this may lead to students feeling less confident about written and oral work thus affecting their achievement levels.

Parental expectations

Some sociologists have argued that educational success and failure can be explained by the level of encouragement received from parents or guardians. From this point of view it has been argued that parents from some ethnic minority groups are less interested in their children's education than parents from other groups. However, there is plenty of evidence to suggest that this view is inaccurate.

A study by ILEA in 1987 reported that Indian families put pressure on their children to succeed and that this affected their performance in a positive way. In a number of areas African-Caribbean parents established Saturday schools because they were worried about their children's under-achievement. Indeed, Ken Pryce's study of the African-Caribbean community in Bristol in 1979 showed that parents had very high academic aspirations for their children.

IS SCHOOL DOMINATED BY A WHITE, MAINSTREAM CULTURE?

Expectations about clothing may not take into account some minority cultures' norms and values

Teaching staff may not be from minority groups

In a small group, examine the photographs here and note down your conclusions as to how these aspects of school life may affect the achievements of some ethnic minority students.

The holidays celebrated may not be those of some minority cultures

The types of food available may not meet the needs of all minority cultures

THE EFFECTS OF POSITIVE PARENTAL INVOLVEMENT

Read the following extract:

In 1982 Rutter and his team, in their much publicized DES report, found that black pupils, and in particular black girls, were more likely to stay on at school after the fifth year in order to gain qualifications equivalent to their white peers.

The main reason for this, they suggest, was the greater commitment to education that they witnessed among West Indians. Rutter et al. argued that the parents' positive involvement in the education of their children was what helped the West Indian pupils to overcome the social deprivation and the negative schooling that they were more likely to experience.

Source: Mirza (1992)

1. What do you think Mirza means by 'the social deprivation and the negative schooling that they were more likely to experience'?
2. Explain what you think the role of the parents of West Indian students may have been in overcoming these problems.

The school

These explanations stress the importance of the school environment to educational success.

The type of school attended

Some research suggests that the main factor in explaining differences in educational attainment is not a student's ethnic background or culture but, rather, the school attended.

Smith and Tomlinson (1989), in a study of 18 comprehensive schools, identified a range of important influences within the school, including the quality of teaching and the resources available, as well as the attitudes and policies relating to providing equal opportunities within the school. They concluded that ethnic minority students who went to good schools would do as well as white students in these schools.

WERE SMITH AND TOMLINSON CORRECT?

Smith and Tomlinson's research has been criticized in a number of ways:

- the size of the sample;
- the failure to include a mix of schools with both large and small numbers of students;
- the sample was not nationally representative;
- some schools had large numbers of African-Caribbean students and some had small numbers.

In a small group:

1 Explain why the points listed have been used as criticisms of the research of Smith and Tomlinson into the influence exerted by the type of school attended.
2 Try to note down some other possible problems associated with research into this area.

Labelling and teacher expectation

Some sociologists argue that teachers have **stereotyped** views and expectations of students, which are influenced by the child's ethnic origin. These stereotypes may also reflect gender differences. For example, teachers may have higher expectations of Asian pupils – they are considered to be capable and hardworking – with Asian girls seen as quiet and passive.

Research also shows that teachers believe that children from an African-Caribbean background are less academic than those from other ethnic backgrounds, with African-Caribbean boys being seen as more disruptive. Teachers expect less, so black students do not receive as much encouragement as other students. In this way, the teachers' labels may lead to a self-fulfilling prophecy through which the students' educational achievement is affected (see p. 169).

The hidden curriculum

Some sociologists explain ethnic underachievement in terms of the hidden curriculum.

For example, it is argued that subjects that students study are **biased** towards a white European culture. History, for example, has been criticized for presenting the view that Europeans 'discovered' Africa and for ignoring the contributions and lives of black people. Some books may present stereotypical images of black people, or they may ignore black people altogether.

TEACHERS' LABELS AND STEREOTYPES

Consider the following extract from an interview with Asian and African-Caribbean students. David and Deborah are African-Caribbean, Hameeda and Parmjit are Asian.

David: *Teachers had different stereotypes for Asians and West Indians. Basically, the Asians were seen as good and we were seen as bad.*

Deborah: *That's true. And at our school there was a further division between Asian girls and black girls. There's no way that a black girl would be encouraged to do the good subjects. It was music and sport for us.*

Hameeda: *But it's like we said before. That probably happens when there's a lot of West Indians but at my school the Asians were the main group and the teachers had all the usual stereotypes, the bad stereotypes. The men teachers were very sexist, but the women teachers as well thought, 'An Asian, it must be an arranged marriage.' That's all they ever think of.*

Parmjit: *It was the same for me but mainly the problems came from the teachers. There was a lot of pressure on me. The science teacher, a man of course, always gave me as an example of neatness. My mum or my friends wouldn't agree. But when he gave examples of other things, like one day he was talking about lime on the soccer pitch and he said he was surprised I knew anything about it. He actually said, 'How would you, an Asian girl, know about male knowledge?'*

Source: Mac an Ghaill (1992)

1 What do the comments of David and Hameeda tell us about the usefulness of the general term 'ethnic minority' when looking at teachers' labels and stereotypes?
2 Deborah states that she was encouraged to do music and sports. Why do you think teachers selected these particular subjects?
3 Hameeda states that teachers stereotyped Asians as 'bad' in her school and David says West Indians were stereotyped as 'bad' in his school. What might this tell us about the attitudes of some teachers?
4 What points do Deborah, Hameeda and Parmjit make about the different stereotypical labels given to female students?

Racism

This may take different forms within the school environment (for example some teachers and students may hold racist attitudes), and may be both intentional and unintentional.

A less obvious area of concern for some researchers has been the role of discrimination in the process of setting, streaming and option choices (Tomlinson 1987). Here, as a result of teachers' attitudes, some black students may be more likely to be placed in lower sets or streams and to be entered for lower-level papers in exams.

It is argued that many black pupils may feel rejected by the school. As a result, they may reject the school in turn and, consequently, not achieve their full academic potential.

UNFAIRNESS IN BOOKS

Consider the following extract based on work with primary schoolchildren.

There are a wide range of stereotypical images in books

Some 6-year-olds in a different class took a book called *Dressing Up* from the 'Breakthrough to Literacy' scheme. They analysed this book first by counting the numbers.

'Me and Eleanor was looking at the Dressing Up *book and we found out that there was twelve brown and thirty-nine white and it is not fair.'*

They made some more sophisticated observations. They noticed that white children were featured most prominently in the activities described and were actually shown doing the dressing up.

'In all the pictures it is always the white person is always dressing up.' 'There can be brown firemen as well.'

They also noticed that on several occasions black children were portrayed in a servicing role.

'The black person is being kind of the servant in both the pictures. It wouldn't be fair if they just changed places, helping each other would be fair or do it yourself.'

These observations about books also contain statements about the injustice of a situation in which one group benefits at the expense of another. Primary-age children have a strong moral sense and a sense of blatantly 'unfair' situations.

Source: Burgess-Macey (1992)

1 What points do the children make in their analysis of the reading book?
2 Explain how these images could influence teachers' and students' treatment of ethnic minority groups.
3 Note down some ideas as to how the stereotyped ideas and values being passed on through the hidden curriculum could be challenged.

Examples of research in this area include:

- Cecile Wright (1992) found that Asian children may face discrimination based on exclusion from discussion work as a result of teachers' assumptions about their language abilities.
- Wright also found, during research into primary classrooms, that African-Caribbean males may be more likely to receive negative attention and criticism from teachers, even in situations where peers of other ethnic origins shared in an offence.
- A report from the Commission for Racial Equality, called *Learning in Terror* (1988), identified racial harassment within schools as well as attacks on the way to and from school as major areas of concern. One example given was the stabbing to death of Ahmed Iqbal Ullah by a fellow 13-year-old white pupil at a Manchester school in 1986.
- Scott Fleming, in a case study on sport and ethnicity (1993), found that some aspects of South Asian culture – such as observing prayer times during the day – were seen as 'problems' by PE teachers, leading to students being regarded as unable to play in team matches.

RACISM IN SCHOOLS

Iftikhar: *The whole education system is racist. In fact I think it's probably the most important influence on black people. You can look at how there are no blacks in textbooks and library books. History is from a narrow English or European perspective. Black kids are put into the lowest classes. Our language, our culture is excluded. The teachers have no respect for us. This all happened at our school and it happens in all schools in this society. They are preparing us for the worst jobs.*

Source: Mac an Ghaill (1992)

Read the extract and then, in a small group, note down answers to the following questions.

1. Using the extract and the text, identify the range of different ways in which racism may be taking place.
2. For each area you have identified, explain the types of response students may make and how this might affect attainment levels in school.
3. Explain what you think Iftikhar means when he says, 'They are preparing us for the worst jobs.'
4. For each area, explain how you might seek to combat this form of racism.

A lack of black teachers

Research by the Commission for Racial Equality (1988) has shown that teachers from ethnic minority backgrounds are significantly under-represented in schools in Britain. As well as this, they may be less likely to be in positions of authority and may be confined to teaching certain subjects, in particular offering language support to classroom teachers.

Some sociologists feel that this situation can influence the school experiences of ethnic minority students.

HOME V. SCHOOL

In a small group:

1. Read through the various factors that sociologists feel may affect the attainment of ethnic minority groups and rank these in order of importance.
2. Decide which is of greater influence – home or school factors. Note down an explanation for your choice.

DO WE NEED MORE TEACHERS FROM ETHNIC MINORITY GROUPS?

In a small group, read the following extract.

Experiences such as these led African-Caribbean boys to identify their relationships with teachers as a special difficulty. Samuel, a 7-year-old African-Caribbean child at school B, talked of what he perceived to be the teachers' unfair treatment of other African-Caribbean pupils:

Samuel: *I always get done and always get picked on ... I want to go to a black school with all black teachers, it's better. I want to go to a school with just black people.*

Researcher: *Why?*

Samuel: *Because when you go to a school with white people they give you horrible food and you're always picked on when you don't do nothing. When it's white people, they just say stop that and stop doing this.*

Researcher: *Are you saying that you would like some black teachers here [in the school]?*

Samuel: *Yes.*

Source: Wright (1992)

1. Note down the reasons Samuel gives for wanting black teachers in his school.
2. Why else might it be useful to have more teachers from ethnic minority backgrounds in schools?
3. Why do you think teachers from ethnic minority backgrounds are under-represented in schools in Britain?

CHECK YOUR UNDERSTANDING

1. Identify and explain two ways in which home background may influence the achievement of ethnic minority students. (4 marks)
2. Identify and explain two ways in which teachers might influence the educational attainment of ethnic minority students. (4 marks)
3. Explain two ways in which the hidden curriculum might influence the school lives of ethnic minority students. (4 marks)

SUMMARY

In this chapter, we have covered the following points:

- Sociologists are interested in understanding the role that education plays in society.
  - Functionalists argue that the educational system plays a positive role in society by preparing students for the occupational roles best suited to their abilities. They see the system as being an open and meritocratic one with a key role to play as an agent of socialization.
  - Marxists do not believe that the education system provides equal opportunity for all. They argue that it is designed to benefit the privileged groups in society and to reinforce existing inequalities.
- The education system provides students with both formal and informal education. Formal education takes place through the official school curriculum (for example in maths, English or science). Informal education refers to education which takes place outside particular subjects (for example through school rules, routines or expected codes of behaviour). Informal learning is also known as the `hidden curriculum' and often reflects the norms and values of society at large.
- Over the last 150 years there have been many changes in the British education system. In 1870 education was made compulsory for all 5- to 11-year olds. In 1947 a tri-partite system with three different educational pathways (academic, vocational and technical) was introduced for children aged 11 to 15. The aim was to introduce a meritocratic system through which children would receive an education appropriate to their academic ability, rather than based on their parents' ability to pay school fees. In 1965 the comprehensive system was introduced in which all students, regardless of academic ability, attended the same type of school.
- In contemporary Britain, most primary education (5–11) is provided by the state through LEAs. Most secondary education (11–16 or 11–18) comes from state comprehensive schools. There are also some schools that select pupils according to their academic ability (for example grammar schools), private fee-paying schools and others that have opted out of LEA control (grant maintained schools). Education beyond the compulsory age of 16 is provided by state-funded further education colleges and universities.
- At the moment, Britain has a mixture of state and independent education provision, with the majority of children attending state schools. Some sociologists argue that independent, fee-paying schools should be abolished because they are unmeritocratic and reinforce social class divisions.
- Since the late 1980s the education system has undergone major change. In 1989 the Conservative Government introduced the National Curriculum. All pupils in England and Wales now study a number of core subjects and are assessed formally in national tests at the ages of 7, 11, 14 and 16. The aim of the National Curriculum is to provide greater equality of opportunity for all children and to highlight schools where performance is falling below national targets. A number of other changes have also been introduced, these include local management of schools, city technology colleges, school league tables, and a new range of vocational qualifications such as NVQs and GNVQs.

- **Sociologists try to understand and explain different levels of educational achievement among different social groups.**
  - **Statistics show that the higher a student's social class background, the greater his or her chance of achieving high educational qualifications. Children from more privileged backgrounds in general have better facilities at home, receive more help and encouragement from their parents, and tend to be labelled as more able by their teachers in school.**
  - **Gender also affects educational attainment and subject choice. Up to the age of 18, girls are more academically successful than boys in all subject areas. Sociologists have put forward various arguments to explain boys' under-performance. At A level and degree level, girls are less likely than boys to study subjects such as physics and technology.**
  - **Statistics show that educational achievement is, to some extent, influenced by ethnic background. Students from some ethnic minority backgrounds tend to underachieve and not fulfil their potential. However, it is important to note that attainment levels vary from one ethnic minority group to another and are also influenced by other factors such as social class background and the fact that English may be the second language of some ethnic minority students.**

EXAMINATION QUESTION 1

There are many factors that influence how well pupils do at school. Describe and explain some of these factors.

You may wish to include:

- home background
- type of schooling
- the effects of teaching groups, peer groups and the expectations of teachers.

Source: NEAB GCSE Sociology, Summer 1996
Tier P, Section C, Question C7

EXAMINATION QUESTION 2

Study **Items A** and **B**. Then answer the questions that follow.

Item A Percentage of Year 11 students achieving five or more A–C grades in their GCSE examinations

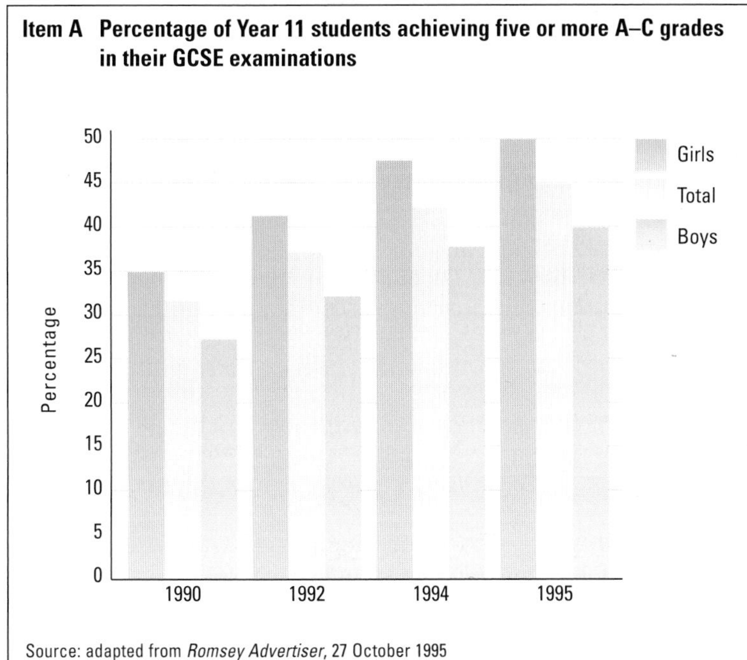

Source: adapted from *Romsey Advertiser*, 27 October 1995

Item B Number of students enrolled in Higher Education in the UK on different types of first degree course (thousands)

	Males	Females
Arts	55	112
Sciences	158	85
Social Studies	70	72
Other	46	58
All	**329**	**327**

Source: adaptedf from *Social Trends* 1995

(a) Study **Item A**. According to the information given:

- **(i)** what percentage of girls achieved five or more A–C grades in their GCSE examinations in 1995? (1 mark)
- **(ii)** what was the trend in levels of achievement of all candidates from 1990 to 1995? (1 mark)

(b) Study **Item B**. According to the information given:

- **(i)** how many males were enrolled on first degree science courses? (1 mark)
- **(ii)** what was the balance between the total numbers of males and females on all first degree courses? (1 mark)

(c) State **two** roles that are carried out by educational institutions in Britain. (2 marks)

(d) **(i)** What do sociologists mean by the 'hidden curriculum'? (1 mark)

- **(ii)** What part does the 'hidden curriculum' play in the socialization of a child? (3 marks)

(e) **(i)** State **one** significant change in the education system since 1979. (1 mark)

- **(ii)** Explain how this change may have increased or decreased educational opportunities. (3 marks)

Source: SEG GCSE Sociology, Summer 1997,
Higher Tier, Paper 2, Question 2

BIBLIOGRAPHY

Bernstein, B. (1960) 'Social class and linguistic development – a theory of social learning' in Halsey, Flood and Anderson (1961), *Education, Economy and Society*, Free Press.

Burgess-Macey, C. (1992) 'Tackling racism in the classroom' in Gill, Mayor, Blair (eds) *Racism and Education – Structures and strategies*, Sage.

Denscombe, M. (1997) *Sociology Update* (January), Olympus Books.

Douglas, J.W.B. et al (1967) *The Home and the School*, Panther.

DFE, *Statistical Bulletin* (May 1995).

Fleming, S. (1993) 'Schooling, sport and ethnicity', *Sociology Review*, Volume 3, No. 1.

Gill, Mayor and Blair (eds) (1992) *Racism and Education – Structures and Strategies*, Sage.

Griffin, C. (1985) *Typical Girls?*, Routledge and Kegan Paul.

Halsey, Heath and Ridge (1980) *Origins and Destinations*, Clarenden Press

Hargreaves, D. (1967) *Social Relations in a Secondary School*, Routledge and Kegan Paul.

Harris, S. et al. (1993) 'Schoolwork, homework and gender', *Gender and Education*, Volume 5. No. 1

Kelly, A. (1981) *The Missing Half: Girls and Science Education*, Manchester University Press.

Lacey, D. (1970) *Hightown Grammar: The School as a Social System*, Manchester University Press.

Mac an Ghaill, M. (1992) 'Coming of age in 1980s England', in Gill, Mayor and Blair (eds), *Racism and Education – Structures and Strategies*, Sage.

Mason, D. (1995) *Race and Ethnicity in Modern Britain*, Oxford University Press.

Mirza, Heidi Safia (1992) *Young, Female and Black*, Routledge and Kegan Paul.

Reid, I. (1997) 'Education and inequality', *Sociology Review*, Volume 6, No. 2.

Reid, I. (1996) 'Educational statistics for the UK' (1993 edn) reproduced in *Sociology Review* (November).

Skellington, R. and Morris, P. (1992) *Race in Britain Today*, Sage.

Smith, D. and Tomlinson, S. (1989) *The School Effect: A Study of Multi-Racial Comprehensives*, Policy Studies Institute.

Social Trends 25 (1995) Office for National Statistics and HMSO.

Social Trends 27 (1997) Office for National Statistics and HMSO.

Tomlinson, S. (1987) 'Towards AD 2000: The Political Context of Multi-cultural Education', *New Community XIV*, (1/2) (Autumn).

Wilkinson, H. (1994) 'No Turning Back: Generations and Genderquake', *Weekend Guardian*, October.

Wright, C. (1992) 'Multi-racial primary school classrooms', in Gill, Mayor and Blair (eds), *Racism and Education – Structures and Strategies*, Sage.

CHAPTER 7

Work, Unemployment and Leisure

In this chapter, we will explore and attempt to answer the following questions:

1. **Work and employment**
   - **What is work?**
   - **Is housework work?**
   - **Why do people work in paid employment?**
   - **What are the different types of employment?**
   - **How does paid work influence our non-working lives?**
2. **Understanding technological developments at work**
   - **What is involved in mechanization and automation at work?**
   - **What are the critical views of such technological developments?**
3. **Equality and inequality at work**
   - **What is the influence of gender and ethnicity on job opportunities and career choice?**
   - **What are the social implications of retirement?**
4. **Work and organizations**
   - **What are trade unions?**
   - **What is the role of trade unions?**
   - **What do we mean by industrial relations?**
   - **What are the different forms of industrial action?**
5. **Unemployment**
   - **How do we measure unemployment and what problems are involved in this?**
   - **Which groups are more likely to experience unemployment?**
   - **What are the regional variations in unemployment?**
   - **What are the causes of unemployment?**
   - **How does it affect individuals and society?**
6. **Leisure**
   - **What is leisure?**
   - **How do we spend our leisure time?**
7. **The future**
   - **What is the future of work and leisure?**

WORK AND EMPLOYMENT

What is work?

If we were asked to explain what is meant by 'work', this might initially seem like a fairly straightforward task. Work, after all, is a distinctive and clear-cut activity. Work refers to our job or occupation. We think of work as both a **place** where we go in order to do our job (the workplace, such as a school, an office or hospital), and as an **activity** that we do there (such as teaching, computer programming or nursing). An important aspect of work is that it is paid activity and, unless we are self-employed, our pay and conditions are set out in a legal contract.

Sociologists have increasingly come to recognize, however, that it is not so easy to define work and that definitions that concentrate solely on paid employment are too narrow. They have tried to put forward a broader account by identifying work done within both the formal and the informal economy. The **formal** economy includes official, paid employment. Those of us who are employed within the formal economy receive from our employer a weekly or monthly pay slip, which records how much we have been paid, along with other information such as how much tax we have paid and our national insurance contributions. The self-employed also work within the formal economy but receive payment direct from customers and must pay tax on this to the Inland Revenue themselves. Self-employed people are also obliged to pay their own national insurance contributions.

If we work within the **informal** economy, our work is not officially recorded. The informal economy can be divided into three distinct parts: the hidden, domestic and communal economies.

The **hidden** economy includes work done for cash in hand, which is not recorded on an official pay slip. For example, a retired machinist who works from home, earning a modest income by altering clothes for friends and acquaintances who pay in cash, is working within the hidden economy. People involved in organized crime are also part of the hidden economy.

The **domestic** economy includes DIY work done within the home and also unpaid housework and childcare, which is mainly done by women.

The **communal** economy includes unpaid work such as voluntary work for a charity or unpaid work for a pressure group.

WHICH ECONOMY?

Examine the following examples of work. For each, state whether the work is part of the formal, hidden, domestic or communal economy. Briefly explain your answers.

- unpaid work in a Help the Aged charity shop;
- working as a freelance photographer;
- baby-sitting for the couple down the road on a Saturday night, while saving for a holiday;
- helping out as a favour in the family shop when it's short-staffed;
- working as a shop assistant in a big London store;
- selling off stolen goods to mates in the local pub;
- decorating the dining room for a friend of a friend during the weekend for cash in hand;
- working as a self-employed market trader;
- a bank manager having lunch on Friday with a business investor;
- door-to-door canvassing for a political party in the run-up to an election.

CHECK YOUR UNDERSTANDING

State two differences between working for an employer and doing voluntary work. (2 marks)

Is housework work?

Many of us think of unpaid housework and paid employment as very different activities. We don't think of housework as real work. Similarly, some sociologists have focused their studies of work on men and paid employment within the formal economy. In overlooking housework and work done within the informal economy, they have neglected the experiences of many women.

Researching housework

Ann Oakley (1974), an important feminist sociologist, conducted a small-scale study of housewives entitled *The Sociology of Housework*. In her research, she treated housework as work. She found that housework was just as boring, mundane and monotonous as some forms of factory work. Oakley saw housework as having **low status** despite the fact that, on average, such workers work for 77 hours per week. She linked this low status to the fact that most housework is done by women.

A woman's work is never done!

INVESTIGATING HOUSEWORK

Carry out two unstructured interviews with women to find out how they feel about housework. You could, for example, find out whether they enjoy some tasks or whether they see all housework as dull. Do they believe that housework has low status? Do they feel that they should be paid for doing housework? (See p. 194.)

In planning your interviews, you will need to think carefully beforehand about the topics you want to cover, but bear in mind that an unstructured interview allows you to probe and to ask extra questions during the interview.

THE TRUE VALUE OF HOUSEWORK

Read through the following newspaper extract and answer the questions.

For the first time official statisticians have tried to put a value on the contribution that unpaid work – mainly housework – makes to the economy. Women put in nearly twice as much time as men on unpaid work. Depending on whether this effort is valued at average pay rates or at the low rates typical of the catering and childcare industries, it is worth somewhere between £341 billion and £739 billion, or between 56 per cent and 122 per cent of conventionally measured national output.

Catering in the home forms the equivalent of a £140 billion a year industry, with a wage bill that would be around £60 billion if the home cooks were paid the same average hourly wage as employees in the commercial catering sector.

Source: *The Independent*, 7 October 1997

1 In a small group, discuss whether housework should be considered as work.
- Is it employment?
- Should people get wages for housework?

2 List the points for and against viewing housework as work.

Why do people work in paid employment?

People work in paid employment for a number of different reasons. Sociologists have identified four of the most important reasons: for job satisfaction, for money, for company and friendship, and also for status and identity. Of course, most people work for a mixture of these motives, not just for one alone. Let's examine each of the four motives in turn.

Intrinsic satisfaction

It seems clear that, for some people, there is more to their employment than simply the money they earn from doing it. When people find their job interesting, take pride in their work or feel fulfilled by it, their job satisfaction is **intrinsic** to the job, which means that it is found **within** work. A nurse, skilled craft worker or barrister, for example, may find satisfaction within employment. Those who are free to use their creativity to the full at work are likely to find it satisfying.

The economic motive

Some people do not enjoy their job at all and work solely for the money. For example, they might find their job dull or stressful but feel forced to continue in it because they rely on the income that it provides.

When people regard their work as boring or unfulfilling, they gain little job satisfaction and may therefore compensate by finding pleasure in spending their income on leisure activities, clothes or holidays. If this is the case then we can say that their satisfaction is **extrinsic** to their job, which means that it is found **outside** employment.

It is important to bear in mind, however, that a substantial number of people are employed in low-paid jobs and they may have to spend virtually all of their earnings on basic necessities.

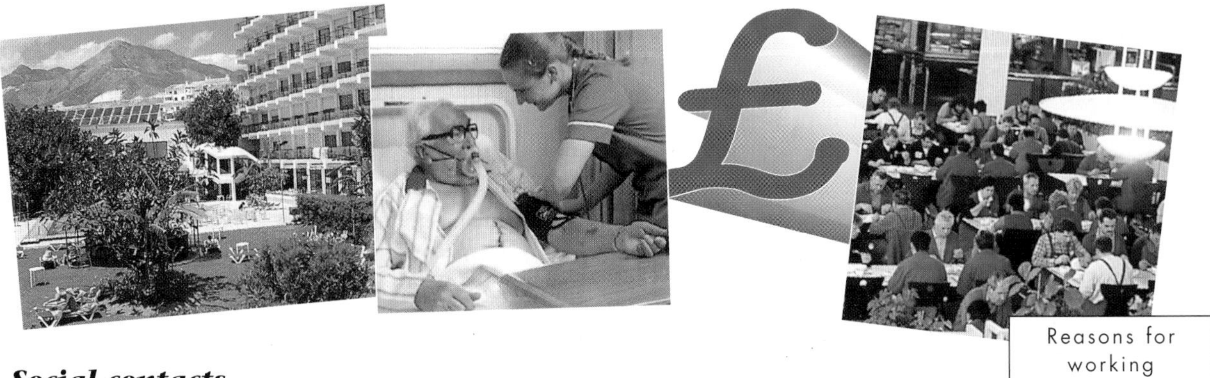

Reasons for working

Social contacts

Many people value the friendships and relationships that they form through work. They enjoy being in the company of colleagues and workmates. One consequence of retirement and unemployment is that people miss out in terms of friendships developed at work.

Status and identity

Paid employment can be a source of status and prestige. People in professional jobs, such as university professors, hospital consultants or judges, may enjoy the status that they get from their work. Some men may derive their masculine identity from being in paid employment and taking on the role of breadwinner for their family. If a man's self-esteem is connected to contributing money to the running of the household, then his job is likely to be important to him.

GIVING UP WORK

1. Do you think most people would give up their jobs if they could afford to do so?
2. If you inherited a large amount of money or won a fortune on the National Lottery, would you still wish to find paid employment? What would your decision depend on?
3. Note down three relevant points, made during your discussion, concerning why people work.

CHECK YOUR UNDERSTANDING

1. Many factors may provide job satisfaction. Describe and explain two possible factors. (4 marks)
2. Give two other reasons why people go out to work. (2 marks)

What are the different types of employment?

Paid employment falls into one of three groups.

- **Primary sector** employment involves collecting or extracting natural resources and raw materials. Agriculture, fishing and mining are examples of primary industries.
- **Secondary sector** employment involves manufacturing – converting raw materials into manufactured goods such as furniture.
- **Tertiary sector** employment involves providing a service to others – such as teaching, hairdressing, catering and financial services.

Primary, secondary and tertiary sector employment

In recent years, employment in Britain has shifted from manufacturing to services. It is possible to categorize jobs according to whether they involve manual or non-manual work. We can divide manual work into skilled, semi-skilled and unskilled work according to the degree of skill involved. The introduction of new technology in manufacturing has resulted in far less demand for unskilled labour.

Within non-manual work, we can distinguish between routine non-manual workers and those in managerial and professional occupations. The number of non-manual and professional jobs has increased since the 1960s and employment has shifted from manual to non-manual occupations (see Chapter 3).

How does paid work influence our non-working lives?

Our paid work influences our lives outside work in a number of ways. Our occupation largely determines our status, income and the degree of choice that we have in leisure pursuits. Our job may influence our family life and even our health. In this way, work affects our **life chances** – the opportunities open to us to experience success and economic rewards.

Our job may influence our **family life**. People who work anti-social hours, such as night or shift workers, may see little of their family and partners on a day-to-day basis. Some occupations demand great commitment from workers in terms of time. Long-distance lorry drivers and flight attendants may have to spend lengthy periods of time away from their homes and families. Extended supermarket opening hours may mean that employees spend less time with their families. Senior managers in industry often have to travel to business conferences or work late hours.

For most of us, our **standard of living** depends on the income that we receive from paid employment. A quick glance at the 'situations vacant' section in a couple of newspapers shows that salaries and wages can vary enormously. While many jobs (for example stacking shelves in a supermarket) pay less than £4 an hour, others (for example senior sales director in a manufacturing industry) pay more than £40,000 per year, which works out at over £20 per hour. A tiny minority of 'fat cats' who hold top positions in industry earn more than £2,000,000 per year. The lower the income, the lower the standard of living.

There is a vast difference in the rates of pay for different jobs

SALES MANAGER
circa £40,000 + bonuses

Dynamic sales manager required to develop measurable sales strategies from inception to implementation and lead its business growth into the 21st century.

Previous sales experience, with a strong background in the management and training of sales teams, is vital.

Applications in writing by 16 April.

ASSISTANT REQUIRED

Busy high-street retailer requires a general assistant for immediate start. Duties include stock-taking and shelf-stacking, as well as some till operation.

Salary: £6,450

Our job may affect our **health**. Some jobs, such as demolition work and many jobs in the construction industry, are potentially more dangerous than others. There is a close link between certain types of illness and particular occupations. For instance, asbestosis is a lung disease that we now know results from inhaling tiny particles of asbestos. Many people who worked with asbestos in the past have suffered ill health.

Repetitive strain injury (RSI) results from using particular muscles in repeated movements over a prolonged period of time. People who work on computer keyboards are particularly susceptible to RSI.

Danger Lurks at the Cleaners

Have pity on the assistant who disappears behind the curtains in the dry cleaners to fetch your clean suit or dress. Forgive him or her if the buttons are broken, or the stain on the collar still shows.

The people who clean your clothes may be risking cancer of the voice box, gullet, mouth and even stomach.

Recent research suggests that exposure to a solvent used in dry cleaning may cause this cancer.

Source: adapted from *The Times*, 11 September 1997

CHECK YOUR UNDERSTANDING

Explain two ways in which a person's job may affect his or her non-working life. (4 marks)

UNDERSTANDING TECHNOLOGICAL DEVELOPMENTS AT WORK

What is involved in mechanization and automation at work?

Over the last 250 years, society has experienced enormous technological changes linked to the processes of industrialization, mechanization and automation. These changes have had a significant impact on work, in particular on types of employment and levels of job satisfaction.

The industrial revolution, which began around 1750, marked the start of the process of industrialization in Britain. The production of goods was increasingly based in factories in towns and cities. Over time, production in the factories became **mechanized**, which means that goods were now mass produced with the help of machines rather than just relying on the physical labour of factory workers. Mechanization benefited the customer, who bought the finished goods because production costs were relatively low and so the goods were cheaper than when they were produced by factory workers.

The introduction of more and more advanced forms of mechanization in factories meant that, although people were not completely replaced by machines, they were often needed only for certain tasks. Workers were required to switch the machines on, to keep them running and to repair them when necessary.

In many factories, mechanization became linked to a production system based on a **division of labour**. Imagine a factory that produced savoury pies. Rather than one worker making the whole pie from start to finish as someone might do at home in their own kitchen, factory production now expected different workers to carry out different tasks. Some workers operated machines that made the pastry, some weighed out amounts of pastry to make the pie lids or bases, while others rolled out the pastry lids and bases, and so on until each pie was finished. Each worker had a specific task to do in connection with the production, packing and distribution of pies. A particular worker was no longer involved in the whole production process from start to finish.

ASSEMBLY LINES AND THE DIVISION OF LABOUR

Workers in the motor-locksmith's workshop of one of Germany's largest early car factories

In car production during the 1940s and 1950s, workers were positioned alongside a moving assembly line where they were engaged in simple, repetitive tasks. The workers produced parts of the car rather than the whole car.

Read through the following extract and answer the questions.

> *Jobs on production lines were broken down into smaller parts and shorter cycles. Cath Smith used to make curtains and upholstery in the trim section of the Standard car factory in Coventry. When she started, each girl made an entire piece of upholstery on her own sewing machine. When the conveyor belts were introduced in 1937 this changed.*
>
> *'When the conveyors came in they were marked off, and the girls would sit along the conveyor. Probably there were about twenty-eight in the gang I worked on, fourteen facing that way, fourteen facing up this way. The first two girls would pick the work up and do probably the first three rows of fluting. The next two girls would do so many more rows of fluting. The next two girls would finish the fluting off. Then two youngsters took the work off the conveyor and marked it round the board. They put it back on the conveyor and the next set of girls would be putting on what we call piping and ending. Those girls finished the job off.'*
>
> Source: Pagnamenta and Overy (1984)

1 With reference to this information, explain what is meant by a division of labour.
2 How do you think working on a production line was likely to affect levels of job satisfaction?

One advantage of production based on a division of labour was that production costs were reduced because the process was now faster and cheaper than before. This resulted in lower prices. One disadvantage for the worker lay in the boredom of doing repetitive tasks and the lack of job satisfaction, possibly leading to high staff turnover and absenteeism. Another disadvantage was that traditional skills, such as weaving and shoemaking, were lost.

Robots spray-painting in a car factory

Today, increased **automation** has meant machinery now automatically controls the complete process of making a product. Whereas, in the past, a team of workers might be employed to paint cars, now robots can spray-paint cars on an assembly line and only a few people are needed simply to supervise the machines.

Developments in **information technology (IT)** mean that the production process can now be controlled by computers. The use of sophisticated computers has reduced the need for human mental and physical labour.

Automation and computerization are replacing both unskilled manual labour (for example in factories) and skilled mental labour (for examples in banks and offices). Where once we had to queue in a bank to conduct our business with a bank clerk, computer technology now allows us to have 24-hour access to an increasing range of 'hole in the wall' banking services. In addition, computers now aid the design of a range of products such as cars and aeroplanes.

The advantages of automation

One advantage of automation

- One advantage of automation is that unpleasant and dangerous tasks can now be done by machines, which makes the working environment safer.
- The quality of goods and the standard of services are improved because human error is reduced.
- New jobs are created in computer technology in service industries, which provide employment opportunities for skilled workers.
- Developments within IT mean that more and more people can work from home, using electronic forms of communication such as e-mail to stay in touch with their head office.

What are the critical views of such technological developments?

Although technological development has many admirers, it also has its critics. They point out that while it may be cheaper to automate jobs than to employ people, automation replaces workers, leading to unemployment. Some critics suggest that employees engaged in supervising machines may gain little job satisfaction from their work.

Critics argue that developments in technology and computerization have led to **deskilling**, which means that the skills required in many jobs have become less complex. As a result, many employees in manufacturing and the service sector are left with mundane, repetitive tasks. Deskilling reduces job satisfaction in that it takes away pride and interest in work. For example, cashier work in a bank has been deskilled as a result of computerization.

An alternative view, however, emphasizes the **reskilling** created by new technology. Rather than downgrading skills, new technology has created the need for new skills. Office workers, for example, will now gain new skills and training in the use of new office technology, and tasks that once took up a lot of time, for example typing out long contracts, can now be done in a fraction of the time using word processors.

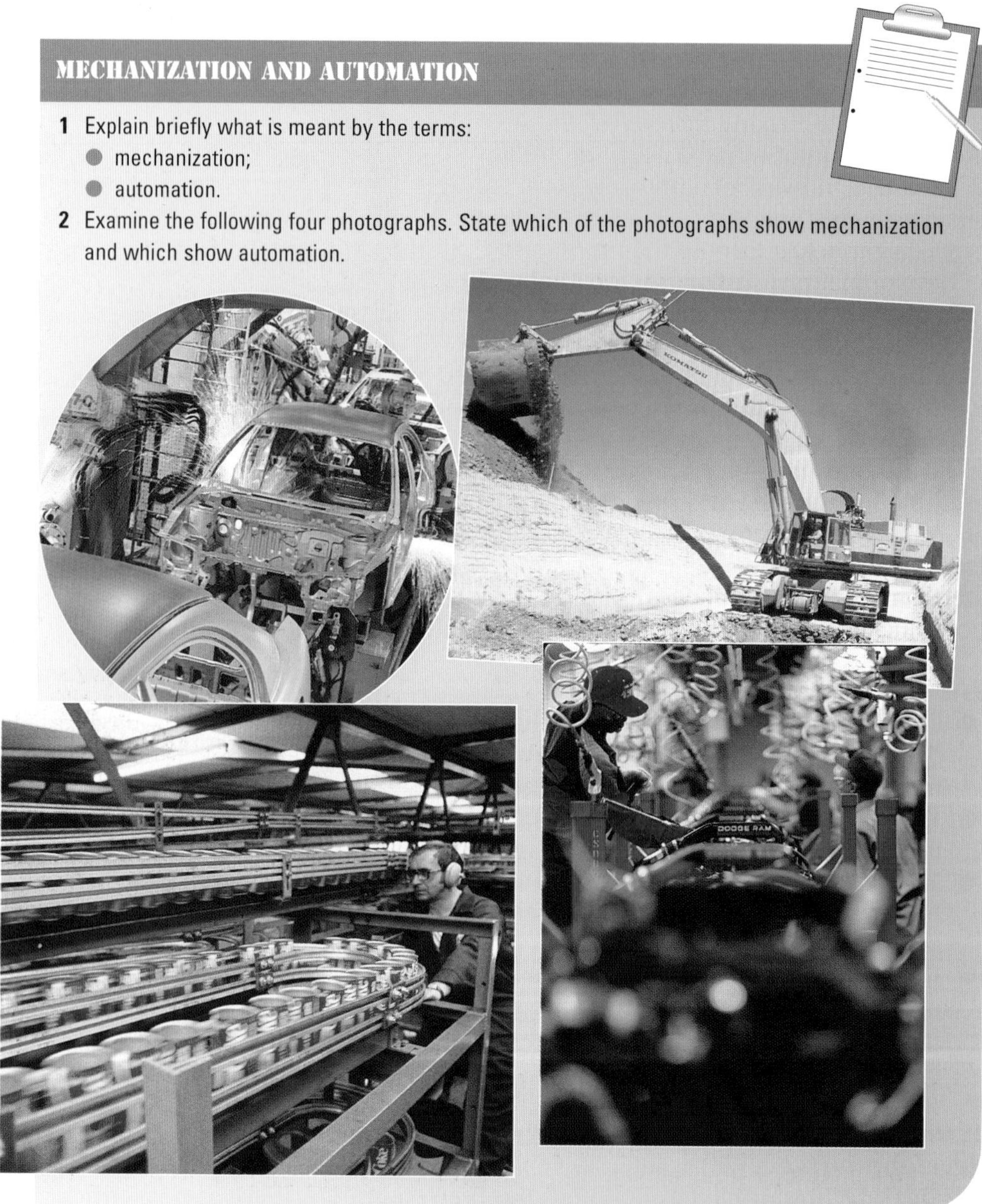

MECHANIZATION AND AUTOMATION

1 Explain briefly what is meant by the terms:
- mechanization;
- automation.

2 Examine the following four photographs. State which of the photographs show mechanization and which show automation.

Alienation at work

It has been suggested that while some people experience intrinsic job satisfaction, others may gain little enjoyment from their work.

Karl Marx (1818–83) felt that many industrial workers in the nineteenth century were **alienated** from their work. By this he meant, firstly, that they lacked control over, and did not benefit from, the products of their own labour. Secondly, they were alienated from their work tasks in that they gained no intrinsic satisfaction from their work; work was a means to an end rather than an end in itself.

Later writings on the experience of alienation emphasized the powerlessness, meaninglessness, isolation and lack of fulfilment experienced by employees at work. In practice, however, the degree of alienation felt by workers would have varied from job to job.

NEW TECHNOLOGY AT WORK

Read through the following newspaper extract and answer the questions.

Stress Gets the Blame for Sick Offices

In a study of several large government and private sector offices in Glasgow, Dr C. Baldry of the University of Strathclyde pointed to one effect of new technology and work practices. They allowed managers to oversee – and oppress – office staff in ways that could not have been conceived of 20 years ago. They could monitor how quickly staff processed work, look at whatever an employee had on his or her computer screen, listen in to telephone calls made to customers, and they could tell instantly how quickly sales were being made. 'It used to be that you could not really monitor office work,' said Dr Baldry. 'Not any more – the staff know they are being watched.' Such pressure can lead to stress and high sickness and staff turnover rates.

Source: Schoon (1997)

Could new technology lead to increased stress at work?

1 According to this information:
- How has new technology increased management's control of the workforce?
- How do some staff respond to the increased pressure at work?

2 Does this extract suggest that new technology has led to an increase or decrease in job satisfaction? Briefly explain your answer.

Some features of alienation

- **Lack of power** – workers have no power or control over the work process. They feel that they have no influence and are of little importance at their place of work.
- **Lack of meaning** – workers feel their work has no meaning or purpose.
- **Isolation** – workers may feel cut off from communication with others, for example in routine office or factory work.
- **Lack of fulfilment** – workers feel they are not using or developing their full abilities nor achieving their potential. As a result, they are not fulfilled in their work and achieve little satisfaction from their job.

Formal responses by employers to the problem of employee alienation at work

Formal responses are an attempt by employers and management to reduce such feelings of alienation and to increase job satisfaction among workers.

- Employers could provide employees with higher wages to compensate for boring work and so increase extrinsic satisfaction.
- Employers could try to create a sense of community and 'belonging' among the firm's workers so that they will feel valued by management. This could be done, for example, by providing a pleasant working environment and good welfare provisions.

- The rigid division of labour could be abolished so that workers do a complete job from start to finish. For example, this might involve scrapping car assembly lines altogether and replacing them with teams of workers who build whole cars. Alternatively, job rotation schemes would provide workers with more varied tasks.
- Share ownership schemes, in which employees own company shares, or profit-sharing schemes could be introduced to increase employee commitment.
- Worker participation could be strengthened by having elected representatives from the workers in the management team where they will have some involvement in decision making.

MORE EQUALITY AT SANYO

At Lowestoft in Suffolk, the Japanese company Sanyo produces televisions. Management and shopfloor workers all wear the same uniform and have a daily meeting to discuss production. Their Personnel Manager says: 'We have common conditions of service for everybody. We try to get rid of the traditional irritants, whereby office staff have different conditions, hours of work, holidays and procedures from shopfloor workers. So we all clock in and out, and we all have the same holidays.'

Source: Pagnamenta and Overy (1984)

Read through the extract on the left.

- Explain how Sanyo has attempted to reduce the differences between office and shopfloor workers.

Informal responses from employees

Employees respond informally to alienation at work in a number of ways. One response is to limit output so that only a 'reasonable' amount of work is done. Daydreaming, practical jokes and humour alleviate boredom and help to pass the time at work. 'Skiving', taking unauthorized or extended breaks and absenteeism can amount to 'survival strategies' in the face of tedious and alienating work.

INCREASING JOB SATISFACTION

1 In a small group, discuss some of the ways in which employers can try to make work fulfilling and satisfying for employees.
2 Make a note of the three most realistic ways discussed by your group.

CHECK YOUR UNDERSTANDING

There have been rapid changes in technology over the last 20 years. State two ways in which such changes may have affected people's lives at work. (2 marks)

EQUALITY AND INEQUALITY AT WORK

Women, men and work

Women make up an increasing proportion of the workforce and today more women are returning to work after having children than 20 years ago. Yet despite legislation passed over a quarter of a century ago, such as the Equal Pay

Act and the Sex Discrimination Act, women's and men's positions in the labour market remain unequal. Many women are employed in low-paid jobs. On average, women earn less than men; in 1995, women's hourly earnings were 80 per cent of the earnings of men.

WOMEN IN THE LABOUR FORCE

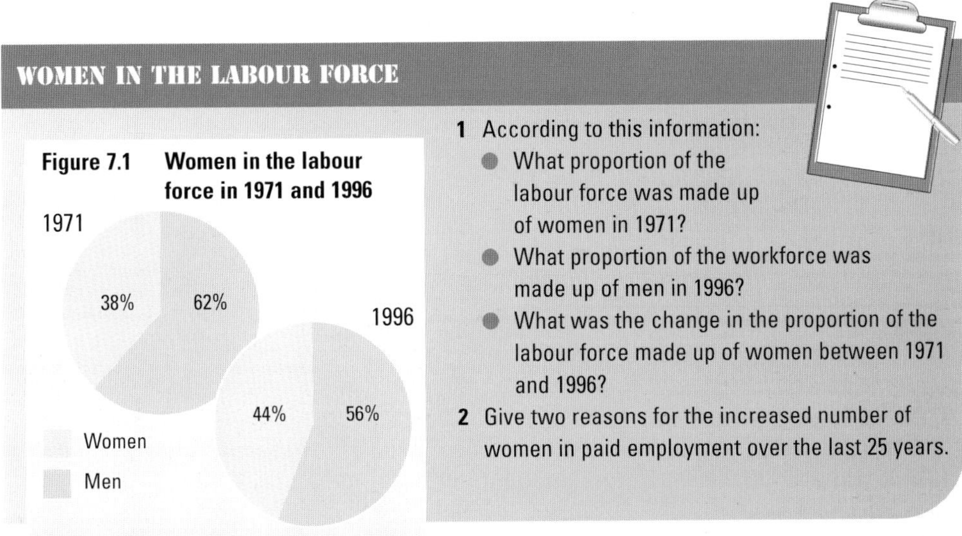

Figure 7.1 Women in the labour force in 1971 and 1996

Source: adapted from *Social Trends* (1997)

1. According to this information:
   - What proportion of the labour force was made up of women in 1971?
   - What proportion of the workforce was made up of men in 1996?
   - What was the change in the proportion of the labour force made up of women between 1971 and 1996?
2. Give two reasons for the increased number of women in paid employment over the last 25 years.

WOMEN, MEN AND PART-TIME WORK

Look carefully at Figure 7.2 and answer the following questions.

1. According to this information, of those people who are in work:
   - Which age group is most likely to work part time?
   - Which age group shows the biggest difference in the percentage of women and men working part time?
   - What percentage of men work part time?
   - Which gender is more likely to work full time?
   - What percentage of women aged 25–44 work full time?
2. Explain in a couple of sentences why such a high proportion of those aged 16-19 work part time rather than full time.
3. Give two reasons why women are more likely than men to have part-time jobs.

Figure 7.2 The percentage of people in work (employees) who were working part time: by age and gender, spring 1996

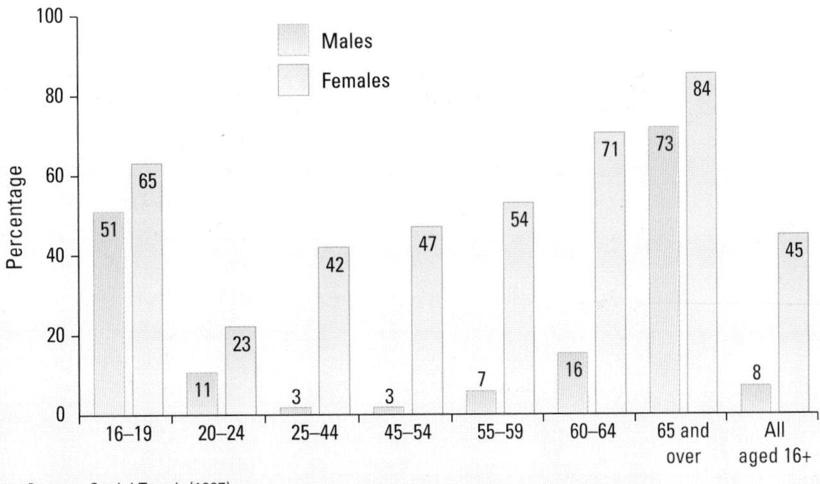

Source: *Social Trends* (1997)

WOMEN, CHILDREN AND PAID WORK

Table 7.1 Economic activity status of women in the UK: by age of youngest dependent child, spring 1996 (%)

	Age of youngest dependent child			No dependent children	All women aged 16–59
	0–4	5–10	11–15		
Working full time	17	22	34	47	37
Working part time	31	43	41	24	29
Unemployed	5	5	4	4	5
Inactive – not seeking work	46	30	21	25	29
Total	**99**	**100**	**100**	**100**	**100**

Source: adapted from *Social Trends* (1997)

1 According to the information in Table 7.1:
- What percentage of women worked full time in 1996?
- Which group is most likely to be economically inactive or not working?
- Which group is most likely to work full time?

2 If women take time out of paid work in order to care for young children, how might this hinder their promotion prospects later?

When women and men are in the same occupation, women are less likely to be in the top posts. It is argued that women are held back by a '**glass ceiling**', which serves as an invisible barrier to promotion. West (1997) uses the term **vertical segregation** to show that, within the same occupation, women and men are found in jobs at different levels. Women tend to be found in lower- or middle-level jobs, while men tend to hold the higher-grade and senior management posts.

Frequently, men and women simply do not work together in the same occupations. Some sociologists use the image of '**invisible walls**', which segregate or divide female and male occupations. For example, far more men than women become firefighters and far more women than men become infant school teachers. In 1996, around half of all female workers in the UK were concentrated in three occupational groups: sales, personal services such as hairdressing, and clerical and secretarial occupations.

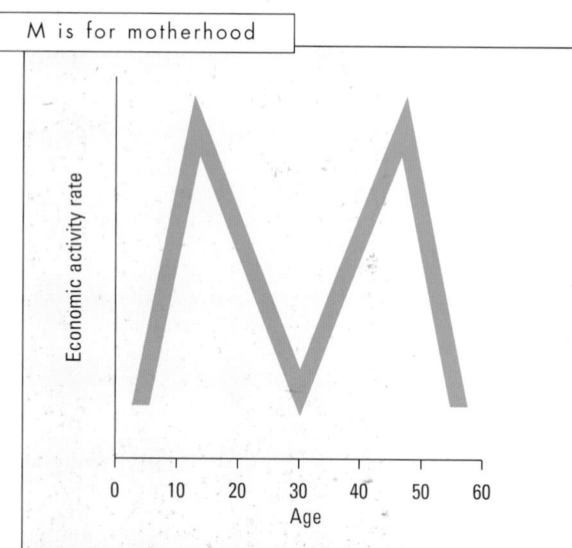

In 1996, over a quarter of female employees, but only a twelfth of male employees, worked in clerical and secretarial occupations in the UK. Nearly 20 per cent of male employees, but only 10 per cent of female employees, worked in managerial and administrative posts. Only 3 per cent of female employees worked in crafts and only 4 per cent worked as plant and machine operatives, compared with 17 per cent and 15 per cent of male employees respectively.

INVISIBLE WALLS

Write a paragraph to describe the patterns shown in Figure 7.3.

Figure 7.3 Female employees in various occupations, as percentage of total employees (1995)

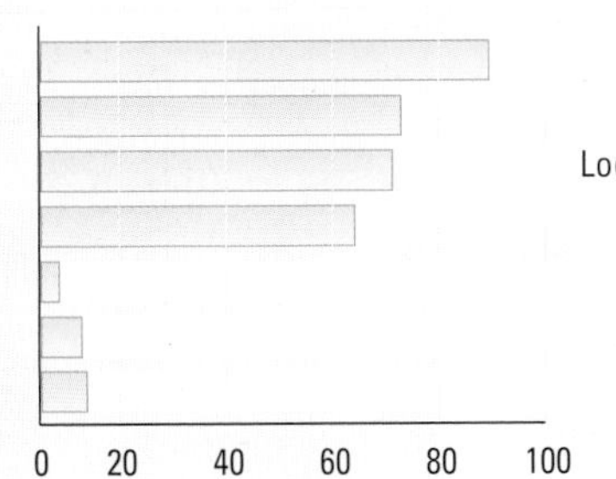

Source: adapted from West (1997)

JOBS FOR THE GIRLS!

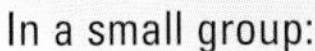

In a small group:

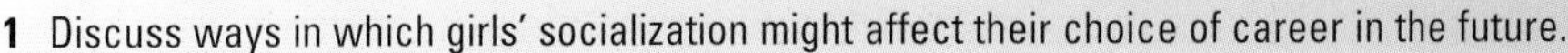

1. Discuss ways in which girls' socialization might affect their choice of career in the future.
2. Discuss why women today might be more likely to enter jobs that have been traditionally thought of as men's jobs.
3. Make a note of three significant points raised during your discussion.

What are the reasons for the unequal position of men and women in the labour market?

One explanation for the persistence of inequality at work is that of **sex discrimination** within the workplace. This means that women are treated less favourably than men because they are women.

A survey called *Working Women in the City* (1997) investigated the thoughts of women and men who work in major financial institutions in the City of London.

The survey found that:

- 87 per cent believed that discrimination against women still exists;
- 59 per cent thought that there is a glass ceiling;
- 25 per cent of women felt that they had been passed over for promotion;
- 82 per cent believed that motherhood hinders women's careers;
- 64 per cent would like, or would not be hostile to, a woman boss;
- 68 per cent said that success is becoming easier for women in the City.

Source: Buckingham (1997)

Working in the City

A second explanation is offered by Dunscombe and Marsden (1995), who argue that women in paid employment bear the burden of working a **'triple shift'**. In addition to paid employment, they are engaged in domestic labour and 'emotion work'.

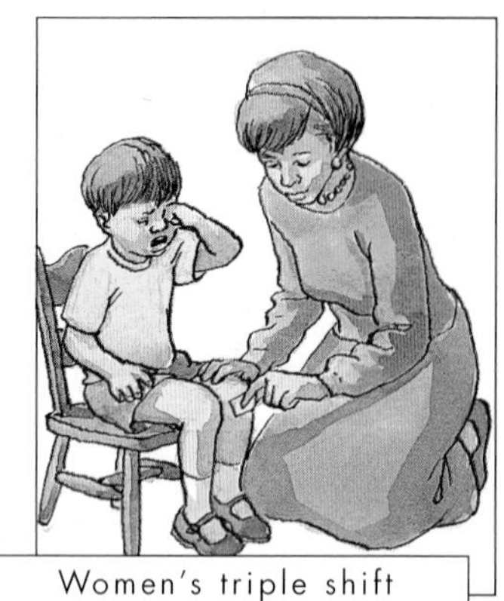

Women's triple shift

Linked to this is the burden of women's **caring responsibilities** for family members who have disabilities or who are elderly or frail. Although many men do act as carers, their participation in employment is less affected by this than that of female carers. This means that women face obstacles that equal opportunities legislation alone cannot tackle.

A third explanation focuses on **childcare provision**. Some critics argue that Britain has poor childcare provision for the under-5s compared to other European countries. If this is true, it might act as a barrier, preventing women with young children from working in full-time paid employment. The Daycare Trust, a national childcare charity, suggests that childcare in Britain is more expensive than anywhere else in Europe.

CHECK YOUR UNDERSTANDING

1. State two reasons why women in the UK tend to earn less, on average, than men. (2 marks)
2. Explain in full two reasons why employment opportunities for women and men seem to be unequal. (6 marks)

Ethnicity and work

Research has shown that job levels for many members of minority ethnic groups are lower than those of white people with similar qualifications. Studies suggest that most minority ethnic groups are doubly disadvantaged. Firstly, they have less chance of actually getting a job compared to British-born whites with similar qualifications (see p. 207). Secondly, they have less chance of getting secure, well-paid employment.

Explanations for the unequal labour market position of some minority ethnic groups

One explanation is that of racism and **discrimination** in recruitment practices. To discriminate on racial grounds means to treat a person less favourably because of their race. Banton (1994) refers to a series of studies in which job

MEN, ETHNICITY AND SOCIOECONOMIC CLASS

The information in Figure 7.4 suggests that, in general, the experience of some minority ethnic groups is better than others. For example, while 6.8 per cent of all male workers are in social class 1 (that is, professional occupations), 17.6 per cent of male workers from a Chinese ethnic background are in social class 1.

It can be seen from the figure that most ethnic minorities do not suffer significant discrimination and that this problem mostly affects African-Caribbean and, to a lesser extent, Bangladeshi men.

According to the information in Figure 7.4:

1 Which group is most likely to have men in the top occupational grouping?
2 Which group is least likely to have men in the top occupational grouping?

Figure 7.4 Percentage of male workers in social class 1 by ethnic group

Total	6.8
Ethnic group:	
African-Caribbean	2.4
Bangladeshi	5.2
Chinese	17.6
Indian	11.4
Irish born	6.9
Pakistani	5.9
White	6.7

Source: adapted from Peach (1996)

applications were submitted in the names of people whose qualifications were similar but who appeared to be of different ethnic origin. The idea behind such research was to see if the applicants' ethnic or national origin influenced deci-

Racial Discrimination in the Medical Profession

It has often been alleged that racial discrimination occurs in the UK medical profession but such claims have not been based on firm evidence. A study published in the British Medical Journal *in March 1993, however, provides some support for claims of racism. The authors, who are both doctors, sent off pairs of application forms that were more or less the same except for the names. The forms were sent off for 23 senior house posts advertised in May 1992. The authors found that the NHS hospitals were twice as likely to put applicants on a shortlist for interview for medical jobs if they had an Anglo-Saxon rather than an Asian name.*

Source: Denscombe (1994) p. 41

sions about whom to interview. Such studies have discovered that at least 20 per cent of employers in the UK discriminate against applicants from Asian or Caribbean backgrounds.

A second explanation is that, once recruited, black people are discriminated against in the workplace.

RACIAL DISCRIMINATION IN THE WORKPLACE

SOCIAL WORKER'S AWARD

A black education social worker who complained of race discrimination after a staff regrading exercise has accepted £30,000 in an out of court settlement.

The woman took her case to an industrial tribunal claiming race discrimination. She complained that white staff received higher grades than black employees regardless of qualifications or experience. The woman has a master's degree and a teacher's certificate, yet white staff with only nursery qualifications were awarded higher grades.

Source: *The Guardian*, 28 June 1996

- With reference to the information given in the extract, explain what is meant by race discrimination.

CHECK YOUR UNDERSTANDING

1 Identify and describe two ways in which some minority ethnic groups may experience discrimination in employment. (4 marks)

2 State two possible reasons why minority ethnic groups do not have equal opportunities in employment. (2 marks)

RETIREMENT

Throughout the nineteenth century and well into the twentieth, the vast majority of older people did not retire from paid employment. Retirement is a relatively recent development. Most people retire in their sixties, but some retire in their fifties.

One of the major social trends in Britain over the last 20 years is that of the sharp fall in the proportion of older people in paid employment. There has also been a significant increase in life expectancy in Britain – people are living longer. This means that many people who leave work early can expect to spend a substantial proportion of their lives, possibly 20 to 30 years, outside of the paid workforce. Indeed, for some people this phase of their life may be almost as long as their working lives, and often longer than their childhood.

Source: Laczko and Phillipson (1991)

What are the social implications of retirement?

Retirement can have positive and negative consequences.

- Many retired people rely on the state pension as their only source of income. If this is the case, they are likely to experience poverty. At the extreme, some elderly people have died from hypothermia because they could not afford to heat their homes.
- Retired people may experience loneliness when they lose touch with social contacts made at work.
- As retired people grow older they may experience ageism as elderly people do not have high status in British society.

- Retired people in their sixties and seventies may have the opportunity to take up new hobbies or to pursue an interest such as travel.
- Some retired people have started up or joined pressure groups in order to campaign on issues about which they feel strongly.
- If retired people are in receipt of a second pension (related to their previous employment), retirement can be a time for them to enjoy leisure activities that they did not have time for while they were working.

Retirement from paid work is not retirement from life!

RESEARCHING RETIREMENT

1. Using resources such as local newspapers, the Yellow Pages and leaflets from organizations such as Help the Aged, make a list of facilities available to retired and older people in your area.
2. Compare your list with that of another member of your group.
3. Write a brief paragraph explaining whether you think sufficient facilities are available locally for retired and older people.

CHECK YOUR UNDERSTANDING

Identify and explain two likely consequence of retirement for an individual. (4 marks)

WORK AND ORGANIZATIONS

Trade Unions are one example of organizations within the workplace.

What are trade unions?

Trade unions are organizations which emerged to represent and defend the rights of workers. As such, they are an example of a protectional pressure group. (See pp. 267–72 for more on pressure groups.)

UNISON

Members:	male 402,426; female 966,370; total 1,368,796.
Main trades and industries:	workers in local government, health care, higher education, transport, water, gas and electricity.
Services:	legal, insurance, holidays, mortgages, welfare.
Further information:	Unison is Britain's largest union. Its policy is to defend all public services and the jobs and conditions of all members.

Musicians Union (MU)

MUSICIANS UNION

Members: male 30,990; female 2,144; total 33,134.

Main trades and industries: people within the music profession.

Services: specialist career advice, health care schemes, sickness and accident benefit, free legal advice and assistance, free pension and personal financial planning, discounted rates for the purchase of instruments and music.

Further information: the union's political fund is provided for parliamentary lobbying on behalf of members in the music profession. The union's main aim is to improve the social and economic status of musicians.

National Union of Lock and Metal Workers (NULMW)

NULMW
NATIONAL UNION OF LOCK AND METAL WORKERS

Members: male 2,211; female 2,089; total 4,300.

Main trades and industries: workers in the lock, key and safe manufacturing industry and metal trades.

Services: in-house free hearing tests, free legal advice service, will service.

Source: *New Statesman* (1997)

What is the role of trade unions?

The idea behind trade unions is that the rights of individual workers can be better protected if they join together with others in a union organization.

Their role is:

- to protect members' rights and support them if they have a problem at work;
- to represent members' interests and to negotiate with management to improve pay and working conditions;
- to negotiate such matters as holidays, hours of work, and health and safety issues;
- to provide services to members. Unison, for example, provides mortgages and welfare services;
- to campaign on issues such as job insecurity and equal opportunities.

How are they organized?

The General Secretary and members of the National Executive Committee are union officials based at national headquarters. They are elected by union members. At regional level, there are full-time paid union officials who support members locally.

At branch level, in the workplace, there is either a shop steward or a union representative. A shop steward is found in blue collar jobs, such as in factories, while a union representative is found in white collar jobs, such as clerical work and teaching. These union officers are unpaid, voluntary representatives who are elected by the workforce of a particular branch. Their role is to support members in the branch.

The bulk of members are people who pay an annual subscription in order to belong to a union.

National headquarters

Regional level

Branch level

The structure of a union

How has union membership changed since the 1980s?

There has been a fall in the membership of trade unions since the peak (reached in 1980), when 53 per cent of the UK workforce were members of a trade union. By 1994 this figure had fallen to 32 per cent. The decrease in membership has been sharper among men than women.

Membership varies widely according to industry. For example, figures for autumn 1995 show that while 52 per cent of UK workers in energy and water supply were union members, only 9 per cent of workers in distribution, hotels and restaurants were members of unions.

Figure 7.5 The fall in union membership

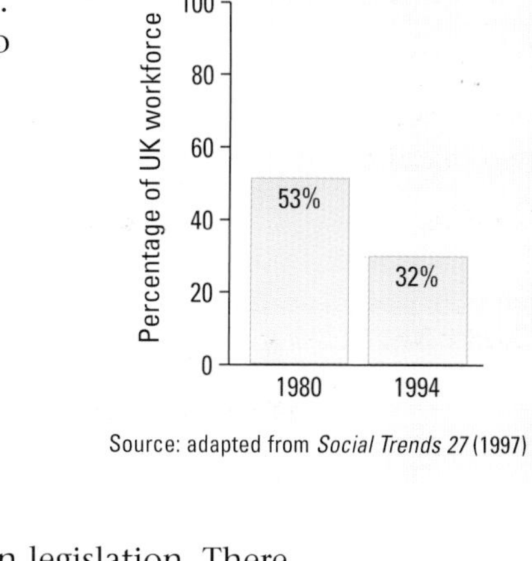

Source: adapted from *Social Trends 27* (1997)

During the early 1980s many members were lost, partly through high levels of unemployment and also because of a decline in employment within the manufacturing industries. Critics of the former Conservative governments also point to their attacks on unionization to explain the fall in membership. More recently, union membership has been negatively affected by the increase in part-time and short-term workers who are less likely to join unions.

In order for unions to increase their power, the following would be necessary:

- a long-term fall in unemployment;
- greater job security, for example less pressure from redundancy and unemployment;
- a hard drive by unions to organize the new sections of the workforce, such as part-time workers;
- the repeal of former Conservative governments' anti-union legislation. There are some signs that this may be under way. For example, in January 1984 the Conservative government announced that workers at Government Communications Headquarters (GCHQ) – known by some as the government spy centre – were banned from belonging to a union or from taking industrial action in the interests of national security. In May 1997 the new Labour government restored the GCHQ workers' right to trade union membership, although the ban on industrial action still stands.

Staff at GCHQ protesting againt the ban on union membership

What do we mean by industrial relations?

Industrial relations concern the relationship between workers and bosses, employees and employers.

One view of this relationship sees workers as wanting high wages and better conditions and employers as wanting greater profits and lower costs, including wages. Because these two groups have different interests, the result has been industrial conflict.

Since Labour won the general election in 1997, there has been more emphasis on all sides working together. Labour feel that workers, employers and government should all co-operate in industrial relations in order to avoid conflict and create a partnership. In September 1997, Tony Blair was the first prime minister in 20 years to address the Trade Union Congress conference and Adair Turner was only the second ever Confederation of British Industry (CBI) leader to address the conference.

What are the different forms of industrial action?

- When we think of industrial action we often think of strikes, possibly because they are often reported in the news. In reality, though, strikes are quite rare. Strike action involves a group of employees temporarily stopping work, for example as a result of disagreements with their employers over pay and conditions. Generally, strikes occur so that workers can express a grievance or defend or gain improvements at work. Official strikes are backed by the trade unions.
- A 'work to rule' means that the workers stick strictly to the rules or conditions of employment. This is sometimes also known as a 'go slow'. In a work to rule, for example, workers may refuse to clock on before official starting times, or to work extra, voluntary hours.
- A sit-in or work-in occurs when the workers occupy the place of work and refuse to leave, for example to protest against compulsory redundancies.
- A lock-out is when managers lock the workers out and won't let them into their place of work.

A number of factors that influence the amount of strike action have been identified:

- Government legislation – former Conservative governments (1979–97) passed a number of laws that limited the power of trade unions to call strikes. This has reduced the number of strikes that occur. Employers can now sack a worker who is on unofficial strike.
- The economy and unemployment rate – when the unemployment rate is high, the bargaining position of unions is weakened. Employers can hire other workers to replace those on strike so the number of strikes will decline, as happened during the 1980s, for example.
- It is argued that boring, routine work that frustrates and alienates the workers is more likely to lead to strike action than interesting, stimulating work.
- Some employees in occupations such as nursing and teaching see their work as a vocation rather than simply as a job. If this is the case, they are less likely to support strike action. Members of the Royal College of Nurses and the Professional Association of Teachers have a 'no strike' policy.
- Immediate causes include wage disputes and disputes over conditions of work.

CHECK YOUR UNDERSTANDING

1. Trade unions have fewer members today than they had 18 years ago. Identify and explain three reasons for this decline in membership. (6 marks)
2. State one task that trade unions perform for their members and explain briefly how this task is done. (3 marks)
3. Identify and explain two ways in which employees may engage in industrial action at work. (4 marks)

WOMEN, MEN AND UNIONS

Men are more likely than women to be actively involved in trade unions.

1. Discuss the possible reasons for men's greater involvement.
2. Make a note of three possible reasons for this.

UNEMPLOYMENT

How do we measure unemployment?

Unemployment

There is some disagreement about how we should measure unemployment.

In the UK, there are two main ways in which unemployment can be measured. These are the official UK measurement and the International Labour Organization (ILO) measurement. It is important to recognize that different ways of measuring unemployment will give different figures.

The official UK measure of unemployment counts those who are claiming and receiving unemployment-related benefits (for example Jobseeker's Allowance). In order to receive unemployment benefit, a claimant must be available for employment and actively seeking work.

The ILO definition of unemployment broadly includes people without a job who are seeking work and are available to start work within two weeks.

MEASURING UNEMPLOYMENT

Table 7.2 shows unemployment rates based on the ILO definition of unemployment. In 1991, for example, 15.2 per cent of economically active males aged 20–24 were unemployed.

Table 7.2 UK unemployment rates for spring 1991 and 1996: by gender and age (%)

Males	1991	1996	Females	1991	1996
16–19	16.4	20.6	16–19	12.7	14.6
20–24	15.2	16.2	20–24	10.1	8.9
25–44	8.0	8.7	25–44	7.1	6.3
45–54	6.3	6.4	45–54	4.6	4.1
55–59	8.4	9.9	55–59	5.5	4.2
60–64	9.9	8.9	60 and over	4.4	..
65 and over	5.9	4.1	All females 16 and over	7.2	6.3
All males 16 and over	9.2	9.7			

Source: *Social Trends* (1997)

According to this information:

1 What percentage of economically active females aged 20–24 were unemployed in 1996?
2 Are unemployment rates higher for men or women?
3 Did male unemployment increase or decrease between 1991 and 1996?
4 Did female unemployment increase or decrease during this time?
5 Which age group is most likely to include people in full-time education who are seeking part-time jobs?

What are the problems of measuring unemployment?

Sociologists point out that official statistics on unemployment tend to underestimate the true level of unemployment.

Measuring unemployment

If we base unemployment figures on the number of people who receive unemployment-related benefits, then we exclude those who are not eligible for unemployment benefits and those who have not registered as unemployed. For example, those who are looking for work but not claiming benefit are not counted. Young people who live at home with their parents are excluded. Many women whose partners have jobs are not eligible for unemployment-related benefits and so they are also excluded from the official UK figures.

This means that it is difficult to assess the true level of unemployment as it depends on how we define unemployment – that is, who we include and exclude.

MOVING THE GOAL POSTS

The author of the following letter questions the validity of unemployment statistics.

I was heartened to read your recent report on the reduction in the jobless total. However, I wonder if this is the result of 'real' jobs being created by our government. Or, is it more likely to be the consequence of their latest change in benefit entitlement? For example, the new Jobseeker's Allowance now only covers a six-month period, whereas before it was paid over one year. During the past 18 years of Conservative government, the 'entitlement to unemployment benefit' goal posts have shifted at least 20 times.

I am probably one of those people no longer reflected in the unemployment statistics. Having been made redundant in 1987, my benefit entitlement ended in 1988/89. Despite many unsuccessful attempts to obtain 'real' permanent employment, I am still dependent on my wife.

Source: adapted from a letter to *The Guardian*, 19 August 1996

- With reference to the arguments put forward by the author of the letter, give two reasons why we should handle unemployment statistics with care.

Which groups are most likely to experience unemployment?

We do not all have the same chance of experiencing unemployment. Members of some groups – particularly younger and older workers, black people and those without qualifications – are more vulnerable to unemployment than others.

The young

Since the mid-1970s, youth unemployment has become a problem. School leavers aged 16–19 who lack experience or qualifications are particularly vulnerable to unemployment. Figures for spring 1996 show that nearly 21 per cent of economically active young men aged 16–19 and nearly 15 per cent of economically active young women aged 16–19 were unemployed.

Older workers

The likelihood of experiencing long-term unemployment (of over one year) increases with age. Figures for spring 1996 show that almost 60 per cent of unemployed men aged 50–64 were experiencing long-term unemployment. Some employers may feel that it is not worth their while to invest money in retraining older workers. Some employers may be 'ageist', which means that they discriminate against people on the basis of their age. Negative ideas about older workers, for example that they are less efficient, may mean that employers are unlikely to recruit them. It has been suggested that some job advertisements try to put older applicants off by stating that the successful candidate will work with a 'young and dynamic team'.

Minority ethnic groups

Among some minority ethnic groups, unemployment is much higher than the national average. Figures from the 1991 census show that African-Caribbean unemployment rates are double the national average. People from Pakistani and Bangladeshi backgrounds experience the highest rates of unemployment at 29 per cent and 32 per cent, respectively. In particular, young black men experience high levels of unemployment. In London in the mid–1990s, 60 per cent of young black men under 25 were out of work. Sociologists have pointed to racism and discrimination as explanations for this.

ETHNICITY AND UNEMPLOYMENT

People from some ethnic minorities are more than twice as likely to be unemployed as whites.

The gap in unemployment rates between whites and ethnic minorities narrowed during the boom times of the late 1980s but has broadened in the 1990s.

Ethnic minorities have been disproportionately hit by job losses in sectors such as the civil service, manufacturing and the NHS.

Reena Bhavnani has studied the position of women in the workforce. She has found much evidence of white women finding jobs more easily than better-qualified women from the ethnic minorities.

Source: *The Observer*, 30 June 1996

According to the information in the newspaper extract:

1. Is unemployment among black women linked to their lack of qualifications?
2. Are black people more likely to experience unemployment during an economic boom or slump?

The less skilled and unqualified

People without qualifications are much more likely to experience unemployment than well-qualified people.

What are the regional variations in unemployment?

Unemployment rates within the UK vary by region. Figures for spring 1996 show that Merseyside was the area with the highest unemployment rate (at 13 per cent), while the city of Glasgow had an unemployment rate of 16 per cent. Northern Ireland also has a relatively high unemployment rate. Generally, inner-city and former industrial areas experience relatively high rates of unemployment, while rural areas are less vulnerable.

In the early 1980s, much unemployment was concentrated in former industrial areas and old manufacturing centres, for example those areas associated with car production, steel and shipbuilding. Extraction industries, such as coal mining, have also been badly hit by unemployment. This has affected some regions more than others: in particular, the north of England, Wales and Scotland have been badly hit.

Parts of southern England have suffered less from unemployment. The south-east of England is geographically closer to Europe, which could be advantageous as the EU is one of Britain's important trading partners. Banking and finance in the service sector have not declined in the same way as manufacturing. They are both linked to the City of London, which is the financial centre of the UK.

It is important to note that, more recently, the south of England has increasingly experienced unemployment as an effect of recession.

What are the causes of unemployment?

There is a link between the introduction of new technology and unemployment in that fewer employees are required in automated industries. High-tech industries are not necessarily big employers. Automation has resulted in the loss of jobs in both unskilled manual employment and, increasingly, in skilled employment, for example in printing, offices, banks and car factories.

The decline of the manufacturing industries has resulted in fewer jobs in manufacturing firms today, compared to the 1970s. Britain faces international competition from countries such as Japan for manufactured products like electrical goods and cars. Competition also comes from the newly industrializing countries where wage rates are low and working conditions are relatively poor, for example Thailand.

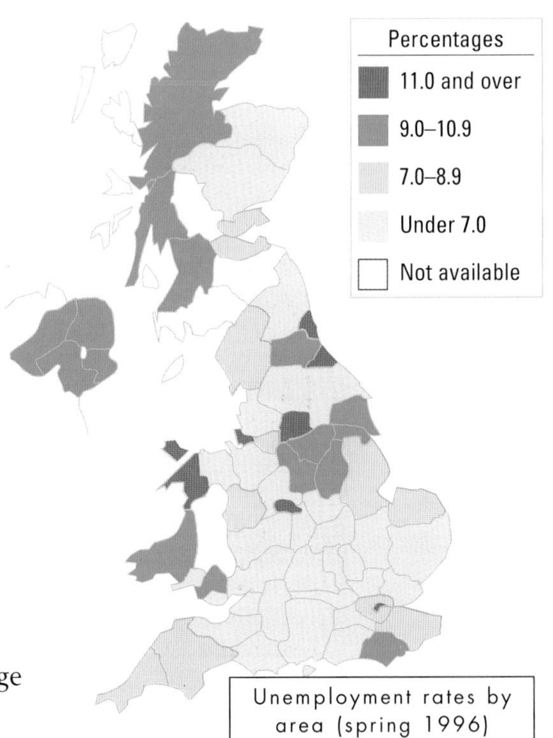

Unemployment rates by area (spring 1996)

INVESTMENT DOWN, UNEMPLOYMENT UP?

Recent research by Cambridge academics suggests that a lack of manufacturing investment in Britain is most closely associated in a causal way with rising unemployment.

Figure 7.6 Investment down – unemployment up

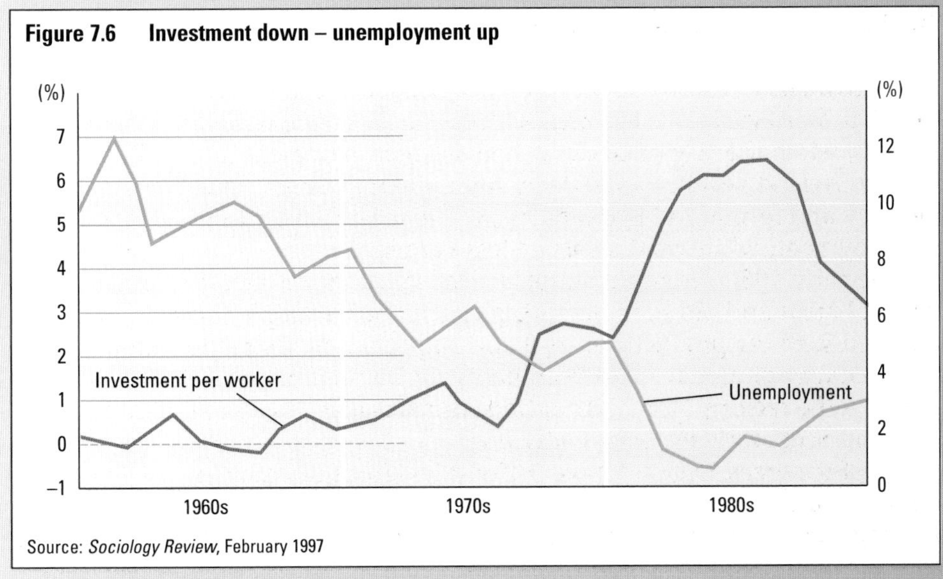

Source: *Sociology Review*, February 1997

Using this information:

1. Describe briefly the changes in the rate of unemployment between the 1960s and the 1980s.
2. Describe briefly the changes in the rate of investment between the 1960s and the 1980s.
3. Describe the link shown between lack of investment and unemployment.

The economic recessions of the 1970s, 1980s and 1990s have resulted in unemployment. In many areas people who lost their jobs during these recessions have never found paid employment again.

How does unemployment affect individuals?

Some of the ill effects of unemployment affect all unemployed people. Deem (1988) suggests that all unemployed people may be affected by poverty, loss of income, lack of status, boredom, too much time on their hands, marriage break up, loss of friends, and loss of identity and aspirations.

If a person loses his or her job (and therefore the income from that job), his or her standard of living and lifestyle will be affected. Leisure is curtailed and luxuries and holidays often become a thing of the past. Unemployed people may become socially isolated because they are cut off from, and lose touch with, former workmates and colleagues. The long-term unemployed are particularly likely to face money problems.

Unemployment may affect not only individuals but also their families. Relationships between partners and between parents and children may be placed under strain. Although all unemployed people face some of the same problems, unemployment affects different groups in different ways. For example, young people's experiences of unemployment will be different to those of older people.

Young people

Unemployed young people may be forced to continue to depend on their parents and this may lead to family tension, conflict and stress. Deem (1988) identified the social and personal difficulties experienced by young unemployed people (see the first extract on the left).

Black people

In addition to facing problems that affect all unemployed people, black people may also face disadvantages that arise from racism, including prejudice, discrimination and poor housing.

Women

If a married woman becomes unemployed, she may be forced to take on a more traditional role within the home. Deem (1988) has identified ways in which job loss affects women (see the second extract on the left).

Men

Particularly for older men, unemployment may result in loss of confidence and of occupational identity. The resulting fall in income hits the middle-aged, who cannot maintain their standard of living and who may feel a sense of failure and a loss of self-esteem. There is a link between illness and unemployment among the middle-aged.

Young people

The nature of these difficulties varies by gender, race, and class. Generally they include things like depression and feelings of listlessness and worthlessness (the 'real people have a job' syndrome), lack of money, social isolation, bitterness about the inability to get a job, and real difficulties in pursuing what are taken to be the 'normal' aspects of becoming an adult, such as getting a place of one's own, marrying, having children, and so on.

Source: Deem (1988) p. 66

Women

Income loss, decline in status, the absence of workmates, a drop in confidence, fewer leisure activities outside the home are all things found by Martin and Wallace (1984) in their study of women made redundant. The idea that women suffer less than men from unemployment because they have another role in the family did not appear to stand up. In most households women's earnings are as vital to the household budget as men's ... and, if anything, women set more store by friendships made at work than do men.

Source: Deem (1988) p. 69

West (1997) argues that unemployment undermines men's status as the breadwinners with responsibility for bringing home the wages. This can threaten men's gender identity, which means that they are then less likely to take on what they see as women's work in the home. This is particularly likely among men from traditional heavy industries and manufacturing, where the sexual division of labour tends to be very marked.

Deem (1988) summarizes the effects of unemployment on men in this extract (right).

Men

In our society having a job is a major part of masculine identity ... Without that job masculinity is more difficult to sustain. Men without jobs cannot be breadwinners ... and this strikes hard at identity, status and friendships with other men, particularly if those men are still in employment. Unemployment puts a strain on sleep, money, health, and relationships.

Source: Deem (1988) p. 72

How does unemployment affect society?

- Unemployment has economic costs for society. Public money is spent on social security benefits rather than being invested in schools and hospitals.
- High rates of unemployment mean greater inequality in the distribution of income between the employed and unemployed, and cause rising levels of poverty. Unemployed people may feel forced to find work in the informal or hidden economy.
- High rates of unemployment weaken the trade unions. Employers can use the threat of unemployment as a 'stick' to keep workers in their place. This may lead to lower wages and poorer working conditions.
- Research suggests that unemployment is linked to scapegoating and racism.

Unemployment and Racism

The number of recorded racially motivated assaults doubled between 1988 and 1993. Many racially motivated incidents are not reported and so are not recorded in the official statistics. The evidence strongly suggests that the incidence of racially motivated violence is closely associated with economic conditions, particularly with the prevalence of unemployment.

Neville Lawrence, the father of Stephen Lawrence, who was murdered in a racially motivated attack in 1993.

Unemployment operates to intensify racism in a number of ways. Firstly, higher unemployment could generate complaints from the indigenous population that black people are 'taking our jobs'. Factual evidence, which shows that such complaints are ill founded, is usually ignored. Secondly, high levels of unemployment are likely to intensify informal racism, which impacts upon black people's lives in the form of verbal or physical abuse. The economically insecure seek weaker scapegoats to blame for the financial problems facing them.

On present evidence it appears that a fatal combination of unemployment, poverty, fear and ignorance is promoting a rising tide of racially motivated violence today.

Source: Bainbridge, Burkitt and Macey (1994) pp. 10–11

- High rates of unemployment are linked to a rise in social problems. Argyle (1996) links unemployment to a higher death rate, a much higher suicide rate, poorer physical health and poorer mental health, leading to problems such as depression and alcoholism among the unemployed.
- Unemployment has been linked to crime as some of the unemployed may turn to crime. Reports on the Brixton disorders in 1981 have linked youth unemployment and crime. More recently, unemployment has been linked to a 'lawless masculinity', as the following extract shows.

Following the riots on outer urban estates in three British cities in 1991, Campbell (1993) argued that unemployment is creating a 'lawless masculinity'. Waged work once provided men with a legitimate escape from the domestic domain but unemployment shatters the difference between the worlds of women and men. Campbell sees the contemporary problems of urban crime and violence as rooted in men's active rejection of fatherhood.

Men choose to resist family obligations as a way of reasserting differences between the worlds of women and men.

Source: West (1997) pp. 143–4

- New Right approaches emphasize the link between unemployment and the underclass. Murray (1990) argues that an underclass has emerged in Britain. One feature of an underclass is that large numbers of healthy, low-income young men choose not to take paid jobs. They drop out of the labour force. Murray believes that work is much more important than just making a living – it is at the centre of life. Without work, it is difficult for us to maintain self-esteem and the respect of others. These young men grow up without being socialized into the world of work. He argues further that when a large number of young men don't work, their communities break down.
- Some communities have developed around a particular industry such as mining and shipbuilding. For instance, working-class communities developed in Yorkshire pit villages in the nineteenth century. The closure of pits and resultant job losses in the late twentieth century has had a devastating effect on these communities. Not only do miners lose their jobs, but high unemployment rates may mean that small businesses go bankrupt, shops close down and people are forced to move.

CHECK YOUR UNDERSTANDING

1. State two reasons why people from some minority ethnic groups are likely to experience unemployment. (2 marks)
2. Name two other groups of people who are likely to experience unemployment. For each, explain why this may be the case. (4 marks)
3. Sociologists tend to treat official statistics with caution. Identify and explain two reasons why we should treat official government unemployment figures with caution. (4 marks)
4. State two ways in which unemployment can affect those people who are unemployed and two ways in which it can affect their families. (4 marks)

LEISURE

What is leisure?

Leisure involves the use of free time in recreational activities that are geared towards personal fulfilment and enjoyment.

In practice, however, it can be difficult to distinguish clearly between work and leisure. One reason for this is that one person's paid work can be another person's unpaid leisure. For instance, professional footballers, photographers, cyclists and chess players earn money doing what others choose to do in their leisure time. This means that definitions of work and leisure may vary from situation to situation.

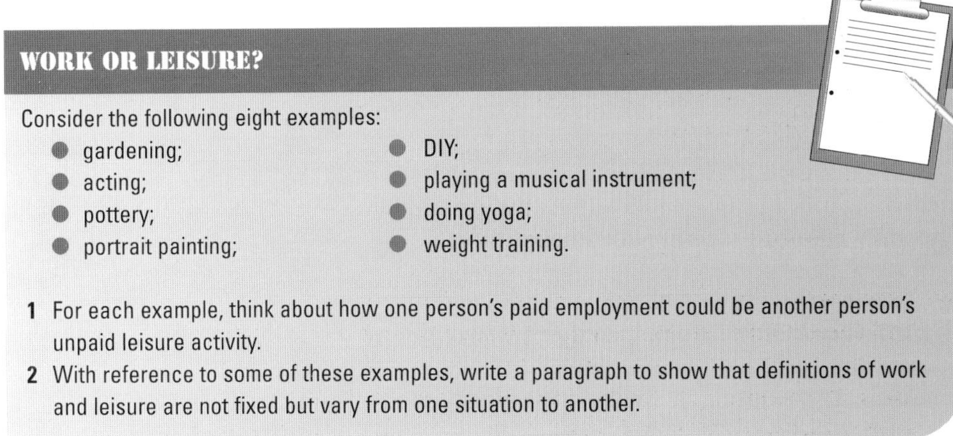

WORK OR LEISURE?

Consider the following eight examples:

- gardening;
- acting;
- pottery;
- portrait painting;
- DIY;
- playing a musical instrument;
- doing yoga;
- weight training.

1 For each example, think about how one person's paid employment could be another person's unpaid leisure activity.
2 With reference to some of these examples, write a paragraph to show that definitions of work and leisure are not fixed but vary from one situation to another.

Leisure and unemployment

Leisure time and unemployment both involve free time: time spent away from work. In this sense, they could both be considered as non-work. Unemployment, however, involves enforced leisure time.

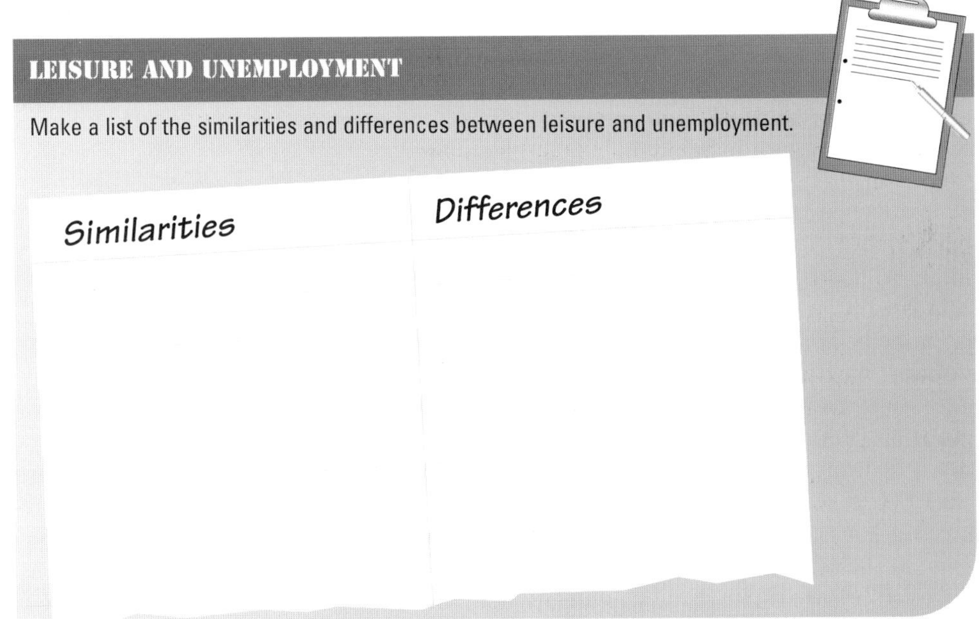

LEISURE AND UNEMPLOYMENT

Make a list of the similarities and differences between leisure and unemployment.

Similarities	Differences

How might unemployment affect our leisure activities?

If you are unemployed, this is likely to affect your leisure activities. Although you may have a lot of free time on your hands, you will not necessarily be able to use this time in leisure activities.

Your choice of leisure pursuits may be restricted by financial factors because most leisure activities must be purchased. Some sporting activities, such as horse riding, skiing and sailing, will probably be too expensive. Gyms can be costly to join and usually require a monthly payment. Going to the theatre or cinema can be expensive. Joining an art class will require payment of a fee and the purchase of equipment and materials. The clothing and equipment required before a person can engage in some leisure pursuits may be prohibitively expensive if you are unemployed.

This means that even though unemployed people may have lots of free time on their hands, compared to those who work seven or eight hours a day, they are least well placed to take advantage of many leisure facilities. They are excluded from work through unemployment and excluded from leisure through poverty.

Being unemployed can be depressing and these feelings of depression may further restrict the degree to which the unemployed engage in leisure pursuits. This may result in unemployed people feeling socially isolated or cut off from contact with others.

Is non-work time necessarily leisure time?

There are 168 hours in a week. If we work on a full-time basis then about 40 hours will be spent at work. Some of the rest of our time will be spent in leisure activities. This still leaves a lot of time that we spend neither on paid work nor on leisure.

A whole range of our activities cannot be considered as either paid work or leisure, for example travelling to work in the morning, eating lunch, washing the dishes or doing jury service for a fortnight (see p. 223).

How do we spend our leisure time?

John Williams (1993) points out that watching television is the most popular of the home-based leisure activities (see p. 305). There are, however, social class differences in how we use our leisure time. According to official statistics, working-class people are keener television viewers, while middle-class people favour more outdoor 'cultural' pursuits such as going to the cinema or theatre or visiting historical buildings. There are also social class differences in people's participation in sporting and physical activity. Middle-class people are more likely to do this than working-class people.

According to official statistics published in 1997, age is also a factor in the popularity of some leisure pursuits outside the home. Going to the pub is a popular pastime with adults in Britain, particularly among those aged under 44. Going to a disco or nightclub is much more popular among younger people than older people. While around 70 per cent of 16–24 year olds go to a disco or nightclub at least once in every three months, only 3 per cent of those over 60 do so. Going to a fast food restaurant is also much more popular among younger people.

In addition to social class and age differences, there are also gender differences in leisure pursuits. For example, while men are more likely to go to a

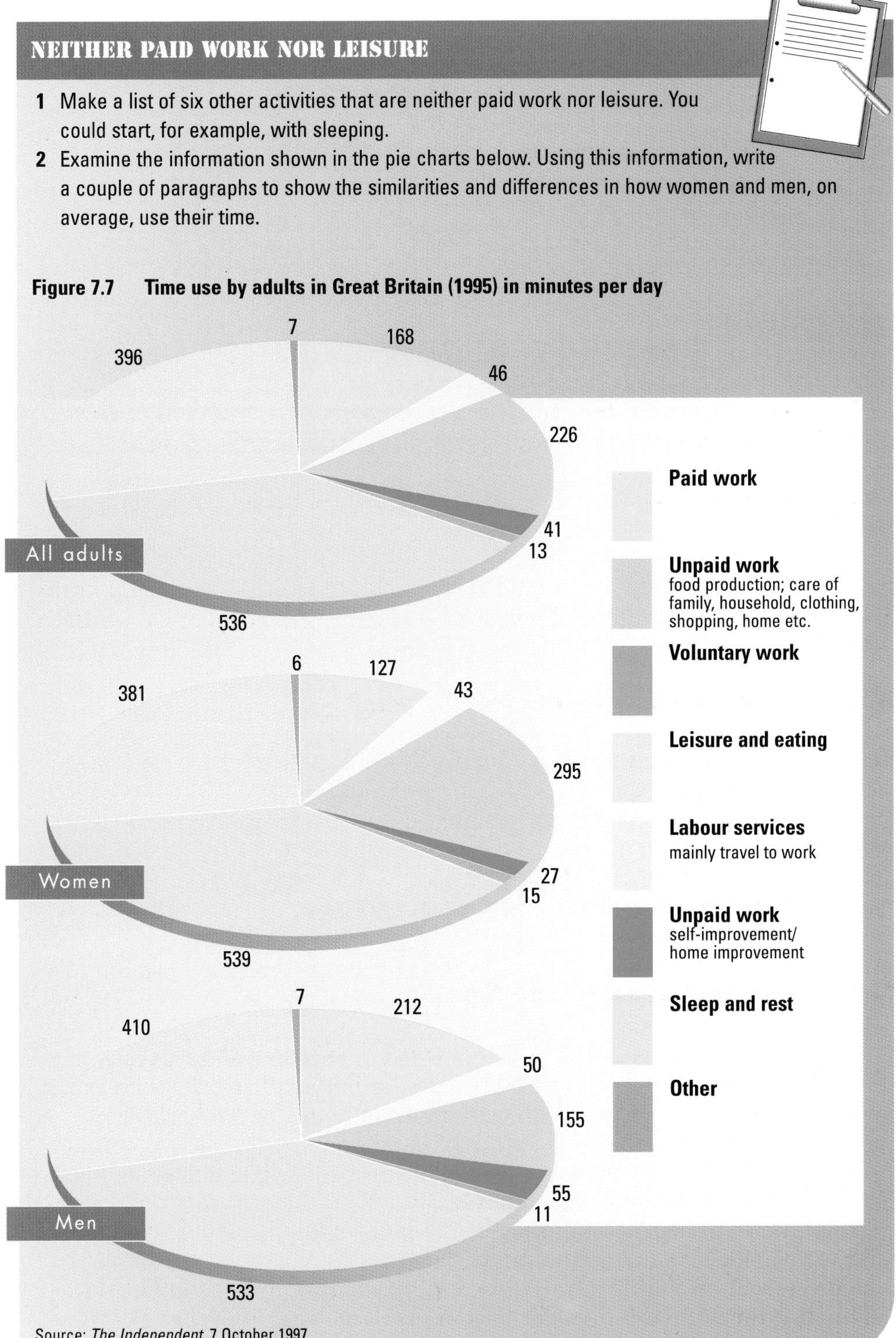

pub or attend a sporting event, women are more likely to visit the theatre or a library. Women have less leisure time than men. Scraton (1992) suggests that the idea of 'free time' and 'time left over' for leisure is meaningless for many women because they have round-the-clock responsibilities. The extract on the following page illustrates gender differences in leisure activities.

Social and sporting venues remain dominated by men. The pub, working men's clubs, snooker hall, rugby and cricket clubs are male domains. Research shows that many women are reluctant to visit cinemas or pubs in city centres. The streets and public transport are problematic for women because of the very real fear of sexual assault and violence. Fear of crime restricts women so they do not go to the leisure centre at night or travel across town to meet friends alone. Young women are often not allowed to do things that their brothers do, because of the protectiveness of parents.

Source: Scraton (1992)

RESEARCHING GENDER AND LEISURE

1 **Devise and carry out a questionnaire to find out whether men and women engage in different leisure pursuits.**

2 **Does fear of crime restrict women more than men when it comes to engaging in leisure pursuits that involve going out alone after dark?**

3 **Make a note of three important findings from your research.**

CHECK YOUR UNDERSTANDING

1 State three reasons why people today might spend more time in leisure pursuits than people 50 years ago. (3 marks)

2 Explain in full how people's jobs may affect their leisure. (4 marks)

3 Give one example that shows that non-work is not necessarily leisure. Explain why this is the case. (3 marks)

WHAT IS THE FUTURE OF WORK AND LEISURE?

An optimistic view is that new technology has the potential to liberate us from work. For instance, new technology could allow us to work shorter hours, which would give us more time for leisure.

Linked to this idea is the view that new technology can allow us to work more flexibly. For example, if we have access at home to facilities such as fax, e-mail and teleconferencing, then working from home becomes a realistic option for those whose work is information-based.

Critics, however, argue that, in reality, flexible working practices are likely to benefit employers rather than employees.

Employers will benefit from the flexibility of part-time, casual, fixed-term and self-employed workers who can be hired and fired as required. Such employees will have little job security and may have to hold a number of jobs at any one time in order to make ends meet. Home-working is not always well paid. Some people who work from home are paid under £3 an hour for boring and repetitive work.

The leisure boom is likely to continue. New jobs are being created in the leisure sector, for example in entertainment, music and tourism.

It is possible that, in future, more and more people will 'downshift'. This involves giving up secure and well-paid jobs in order to live a more simple and less stressful life that is not dominated by work. The following extract gives an example of a family who have downshifted.

Sophie says: *Andrew was made redundant from his desk-top publishing job at the end of the 1980s, so we decided to take the plunge and leave London.*

We'd already thought about changing our lifestyle, though. At the time we lived in Hammersmith and our flat was the only one in our street that hadn't been burgled. When our local newsagent was shot dead, we decided that was it.

Sophie and Andrew Chalmers and their children

We settled for an old mill in Gwent. The nearest road is a mile down the lane but the mill has all mod cons and really is beautiful.

I always wanted to work with Andrew and together we run a magazine for self-employed homeworkers, called Home Run, and we have a readership of about 6,000.

The move was just what I wanted. I was brought up in the country so I had no illusions. It was ideal for our three children, who are aged between six months and six years, and I have more time for my own passions – writing and gardening.

Nothing could tempt me back now. I thought I'd miss my friends but they love visiting us.

Andrew says: *I like to say that we've 'upshifted', not 'downshifted'. Financially, we halved our income but we spend so much less. We've gained freedom, a fabulous environment and a nicer kind of neighbour.*

We could never return to London with its threatening atmosphere and unfriendly people.

Source: *Woman's Own*, 25 August 1997, pp. 23–4

SUMMARY

In this chapter, we have covered the following points:

- **Defining 'work' is not as simple as it first appears. Paid work includes activity in the formal and hidden economy. Unpaid work goes on in the domestic economy (for example, parents looking after young children) and in the communal economy (for example, retired people working in the voluntary sector for charities).**
- **Until the pioneering work of sociologists like Ann Oakley in the 1970s, many people had overlooked work outside the formal, paid environment, especially the work done by women in the domestic sphere.**
- **Sociologists have identified four main reasons why people work in paid employment: for the money, for job satisfaction, for company, for status and identity.**
- **There are three main sectors of paid employment: primary, secondary and tertiary. In the UK, most people are now employed in the tertiary sector.**

- **Our paid work influences our non-working lives, particularly because our standard of living is determined by the income we receive from our work.**
- **Mechanization, automation and technological change have had a huge impact on employment patterns and the type of work people do. Critics of technological developments claim that technology has led to deskilling, alienation and unemployment. Advocates of technology claim that it has led to reskilling and job creation.**
- **More women work today than ever before and more women return to work after having children. Despite this, in 1995, women's hourly earnings were 80 per cent of men's. More women than men work part time and fewer women than men reach senior management grades.**
- **Certain sectors of work are dominated by one or other sex, for example more men than women are machine operatives, but more women than men are infant school teachers. Our choice of career is often determined by socialization and educational opportunity.**
- **Members of some ethnic minority groups find it harder to get paid employment and to enter higher-status jobs. This is due to discrimination.**
- **Trade unions are work-based organisations that represent the rights of workers and promote their interests in relation to pay and working conditions. Unions sometimes take industrial action (strikes, sit-ins, etc.) in order to express grievances. Since the 1980s, union membership has fallen in most industries.**
- **There are various ways of measuring the number of people out of work or unemployed. Different definitions of unemployment will generate different figures. Sociologists argue that official statistics on unemployment tend to underestimate the true level.**
- **The young, the old, minority ethnic groups, the less skilled and the unqualified are more vulnerable to unemployment than others.**
- **Unemployment rates within the UK vary by region. Generally speaking, inner-city, former industrial areas are more prone to high unemployment than rural areas.**
- **Unemployment affects individuals and society in a negative way, contributing to poverty, ill-health, and social problems such as crime.**
- **Leisure is time that we have to spend away from paid and unpaid work. In the UK, the most popular leisure activity is watching television. There are social class, age and gender differences in choice of leisure pursuits.**
- **In the future, it looks likely that more people will work from home, part time and in the leisure sector. The concept of working for the same company all of one's life will become a thing of the past.**

EXAMINATION QUESTION 1

There have been many changes in patterns of employment for adults. Describe and explain some of these changes. You may wish to include:

- part-time and full-time employment;
- types of job satisfaction;
- the effects of new technology on job opportunities.

Credit will be given for appropriate sociological evidence. (25 marks)

Source: NEAB GCSE Sociology June 1996, Tier Q, Section C, Question C9, p. 13

EXAMINATION QUESTION 2

Study **Item A**. Then answer **all** parts of the question that follows.

Item A Percentages of employees in various types of occupation in Britain in 1992

Types of occupation	%
Managerial and administrative	15
Professional	10
Technical	9
Craft	14
Machine operators	10
Personal services	10
Sales	8
Other	24

(a) According to the information given,

(i) which type of occupation has the lowest percentage of workers? (1 mark)
(ii) what percentage of workers worked as machine operators? (1 mark)
(iii) in which type of occupation did 14 per cent of the employees work? (1 mark)

(b) **(i)** Suggest one way in which unemployment may affect an individual's leisure time. (1 mark)
(ii) The level of unemployment may be higher in some parts of Britain than in others. Identify and explain one cause of this. (3 marks)

(c) **(i)** Give one example of a social group in Britain whose members are more likely to be employed in low-paid jobs. (1 mark)
(ii) Identify and explain one cause of this. (3 marks)

(d) **(i)** What is meant by 'alienation'? (2 marks)
(ii) Suggest two ways in which a worker may respond to alienation at work. (2 marks)

Source: SEG GCSE Sociology June 1997, Foundation Tier, Section B, Question 6, p. 7

BIBLIOGRAPHY

Argyle, M. (1996) *The Social Psychology of Leisure*, Penguin Books.

Bainbridge, M., Burkitt, B. and Macey, M. (1994) 'Unemployment and racially motivated violence', *Sociology Review*, Volume 4, No. 2 (November), pp. 10–11.

Banton, M. (1994) *Discrimination*, Open University Press.

Buckingham (1997) 'Still the same old boys' club', *The Guardian*, 4 October.

Coyle, D. (1997) 'At last, the true value of housework is revealed', *The Independent*, 7 October, p. 3.

Deem, R. (1988) *Work, Unemployment and Leisure*, Routledge.

Denscombe, M. (1994) *Sociology Update*, Olympus Books.

Dunscombe, J. and Marsden, D. (1995) 'Women's "triple shift": paid employment, domestic labour and "emotion work"', *Sociology Review*, Volume 4, No. 4 (April).

Laczko, F. and Phillipson, C. (1991) *Changing Work and Retirement*, Open University Press.

Macerlean, N. (1996) 'Workplace: employers still let race colour their judgement', *The Observer*, 30 June.

Murray, C. (1990) *The Emerging British Underclass*, The IEA Health and Welfare Unit.

New Statesman (1997), Trade Union Guide: 'TUC-affiliated trade unions'.

Oakley, A. (1974) *The Sociology of Housework*, Martin Robertson.

Pagnamenta, P. and Overy, R. (1984) *All Our Working Lives*, BBC.

Peach, C. (1996) 'The ethnic question' in C. Peach (ed.) *Ethnicity in the 1991 Census*, Volume 2, Office for National Statistics.

The Guardian (1996) 'Social Worker's Award', 28 June, p. 10.

Schoon, N. (1997) *The Independent*, 10 September.

Scraton, S. (1992) 'Leisure', *Developments in Sociology*, Volume 8, Causeway Press.

Scraton, S. and Bramham, P. (1995) 'Leisure and postmodernity', *Developments in Sociology*, Volume 11, Causeway Press.

Social Trends 27 (1997) Office for National Statistics and HMSO.

West, J. (1997) 'Gender and work: continuity and change in the sexual division of labour', *Developments in Sociology*, Volume 13, Causeway Press.

Williams, J. (1993) 'In focus: the leisure society?' *Sociology Review*, Volume 2, No. 3, (February), p. 34.

Williams, J. (1997) 'In focus: work and the trade unions', *Sociology Review*, Volume 6, No. 3 (February), p. 34.

Fenton, A. (1997) 'We had a big house, smart car, fat salary and we gave it all up', *Woman's Own*, 25 August 1997, pp. 23–4

CHAPTER 8

Crime, Deviance and Social Control

In this chapter, we will explore and attempt to answer the following questions:

1. **What is the difference between crime and deviance?**
2. **Is deviance always illegal?**
3. **When is an act deviant?**
4. **What does the historical evidence tell us about deviance?**
5. **What does the cross-cultural evidence tell us about deviance?**
6. **What are taken-for-granted rules?**
7. **What is social order?**
8. **What is the difference between formal and informal social control?**
9. **What are official crime statistics and why do we need to handle them with care?**
10. **Who commits crime?**
11. **How do we explain criminal and deviant behaviour?**

WHAT IS THE DIFFERENCE BETWEEN CRIME AND DEVIANCE?

Sociologists make the important distinction between criminal and deviant behaviour. A **crime** is an act which breaks the criminal law of a society. **Deviance** refers to behaviour which is disapproved of by most people in a society and which does not conform to a society's norms and values.

DEVIANT BEHAVIOUR

In order to think about the nature of deviance more fully, consider the following ten acts:

- stealing a bottle of milk from a doorstep;
- kerb crawling in the town centre;
- crossing a pedestrian crossing on red;
- drinking a can of lager in the park;
- smoking cannabis on the bus;
- driving at 35 mph in a 30 mph zone;
- attempting to commit suicide;
- 'burping' after a meal;
- taking paper clips home from work;
- being overchanged at the supermarket and keeping the money.

1 Discuss and decide whether you think any of this behaviour is deviant.
2 Of those acts that you have classed as deviant, identify the two most deviant acts and the two least deviant acts. Discuss why you have picked them out.

IS DEVIANCE ALWAYS ILLEGAL?

Deviant behaviour may be illegal but not all deviant acts are against the law. Legal deviance will be considered 'abnormal' in some way by most people in a society. Illegal deviance is criminal and is punishable by the state.

DEVIANCE AND THE LAW

Consider the following:

- murder;
- alcoholism;
- busking on the London underground;
- parking on double yellow lines;
- shoplifting;
- a man dressing in jacket, tie, shirt, bowler hat, boxer shorts, silk stockings and suspenders.

List those acts which

1 are both deviant and illegal;
2 are deviant but legal;
3 are illegal but would not usually be considered as deviant.

CHECK YOUR UNDERSTANDING

1 Explain the difference between legal and illegal deviance. (2 marks)
2 Give two other examples of acts which are against the law but which are not usually considered to be deviant. (2 marks)
3 Give two other examples of deviant acts which are not against the law. (2 marks)

WHEN IS AN ACT DEVIANT?

Many sociologists believe that deviance is **socially defined**. According to this view, whether an act is seen as deviant or not depends on the particular social setting in which it takes place. In order to understand this more fully, consider the example of 'nudity'. There is nothing deviant about nudity in itself. In the bath, shower, bedroom, sauna or as represented in a famous statue, nudity is seen as perfectly acceptable. In a supermarket, at a pop concert or on a football pitch, however, nudity would be seen as deviant. In certain settings and contexts, therefore, nudity is seen as appropriate and fitting. In other situations, however, it would be seen as deviant and might also be illegal.

Sociologists argue that what is considered 'deviant' depends not on the act itself but on how other people react to it; how they see, define and label the act. Deviance, therefore, is defined according to the social setting in which the act takes place – it is socially defined.

WHO AND WHERE

Whether a particular act is considered deviant may vary according to who does the act and where it is done.

1 For each of the following, list at least three acts which, in your school or college, would be
   (a) deviant only if done by the student;
   (b) deviant only if done by the teacher;
   (c) deviant regardless of who does it.
2 Do you think that this list would vary from school to school? If so, try briefly to explain why.
3 Which of these acts would not be considered deviant if they occurred outside the context of your school or college?
4 Write a short paragraph to explain the idea that what is considered deviant varies according to who does the act and where it is done.

Continuing with our example of nudity, a survey carried out in May 1990 found that many respondents felt uncomfortable about seeing mothers breast-feeding in public places such as in restaurants and on trains. This reaction can be contrasted with many people's acceptance of photographs of topless female models found daily in some of the tabloid newspapers.

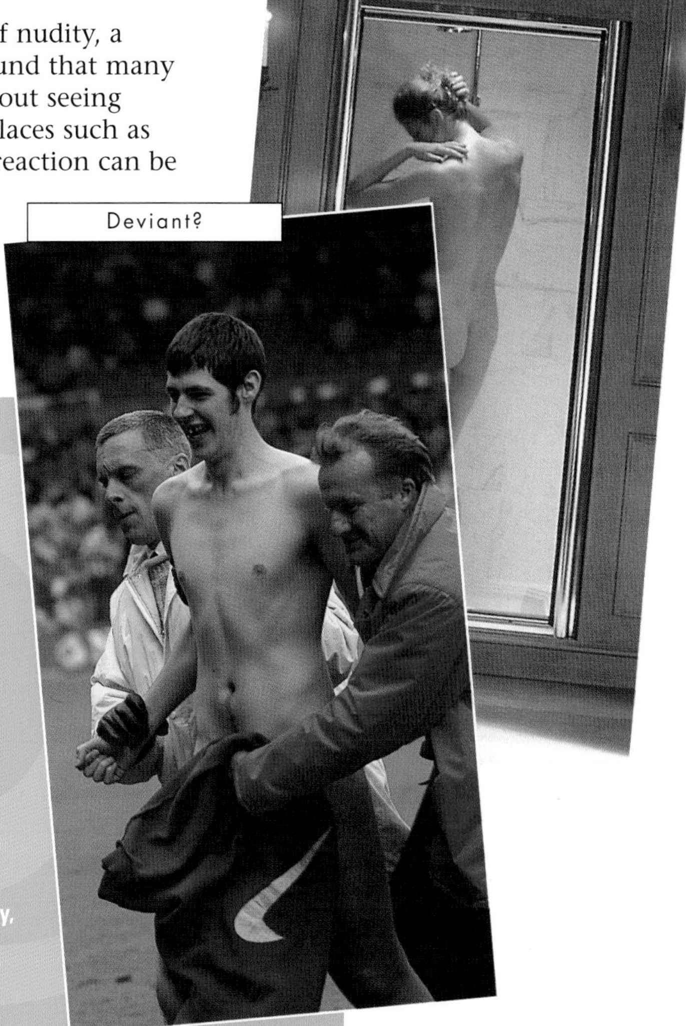

INVESTIGATING ATTITUDES TO NUDITY

Design and carry out a brief questionnaire survey to investigate attitudes towards nudity. You could investigate, for example, whether women and men have different attitudes to 'page three' models. (For guidance on how to design your survey, see pp. 13–17.)

Once you have completed your survey, make a note of three significant findings regarding attitudes towards nudity.

IS THE SAME ACT ALWAYS DEVIANT?

1 Consider the following examples and discuss how they show that what is considered as deviant can depend on the context in which the act takes place.
   - wrestling or boxing and street fighting.
   - murder and capital punishment.
2 Under what circumstances might each of the following be considered appropriate behaviour?
   - spraying CS gas in someone's face.
   - setting fire to someone's drink or pudding.
   - breaking someone's nose.
   - claiming to be Henry VIII, Marilyn Monroe or Elvis Presley.
   - carrying a gun.
   - shooting a person.

Make a note of three important points that arise in your discussion about whether the same act is always deviant.

We have seen that sociologists believe that deviance is socially defined. In order to support this claim, they would point to historical and cultural variations in what is considered deviant behaviour.

WHAT DOES THE HISTORICAL EVIDENCE TELL US ABOUT DEVIANCE?

An examination of historical evidence shows that behaviour classified as deviant can vary over time. The following examples illustrate that norms and values change over time.

1 In the past, human sacrifice was practised within a number of cultures. The Aztec civilization in Mexico during the fifteenth century, for example, offered captive warriors as sacrifices in order to keep the sun alive.
2 Victorian England had some very different standards for what was considered appropriate behaviour compared to those of today. Capital punishment was practised and male homosexuality became a crime.
3 During the twentieth century, in the USA, attitudes towards the consumption of alcohol have varied. During the 1920s, for example, alcohol was banned in some American states. This was known as Prohibition.
4 Attitudes towards suicide have varied over time. Japanese kamikaze pilots during the Second World War dive-bombed and deliberately crashed their planes into enemy ships, resulting in their own deaths.

RESEARCHING CHANGING ATTITUDES TO DEVIANCE OVER TIME

Using your college or school library as a resource, try to find out more background information about one of the five examples listed above. For instance, you could choose Prohibition in the USA and find out why alcohol was banned, exactly how long the ban lasted and why it was lifted. Using your findings, write a paragraph to show how attitudes and beliefs about what is considered deviant vary over time.

5 Since the Second World War, attitudes to divorce, abortion and non-marital births have changed in Britain. The social stigma or disgrace attached to non-marital births, for example, has declined considerably since the 1950s.

WHAT DOES THE CROSS-CULTURAL EVIDENCE TELL US ABOUT DEVIANCE?

Evidence suggests that behaviour classified as deviant can also differ cross-culturally, from one culture to another. The following examples illustrate that norms vary cross-culturally.

- Cultures vary in their expectations regarding appropriate dress.
- In the USA, it is acceptable for the police and members of the public (within limits) to carry guns.

Laws vary regarding the possession of firearms

Appropriate dress?

In summary, sociologists argue that deviance is socially defined and that behaviour classed as 'deviant' can vary historically and culturally. It can also vary according to *who* performs the act and *where* they do so.

WHAT ARE TAKEN-FOR-GRANTED RULES?

Generally, we take much of our behaviour for granted; so much so, in fact, that often we do not think about the unwritten rules that govern many aspects of social life. They are 'taken-for-granted' rules or guidelines on how we are expected to behave in particular settings. We would not, for example, be expected to seek permission before making ourselves a cup of tea or having a bath at home. At the home of a distant relative, however, we would be much more likely to seek permission. Most people would not help themselves to a cup of tea or wander into the kitchen in a restaurant unless they worked there.

Even though we may not always consciously think about the unwritten rules that govern social life, they can still exert a powerful influence over how we behave in specific situations.

BREAKING THE RULES

Look at the following cartoons which illustrate examples of taken-for-granted rules being ignored or broken.

1 Note down two unwritten rules that govern how we are expected to behave at a supermarket checkout queue and two unwritten rules that govern how you would dress for a job interview.
2 Make a list of at least three 'taken-for-granted' rules that you have obeyed today. Explain briefly why you obeyed each rule.

Written rules

Written rules direct people's behaviour in many social settings such as schools, police stations and on public transport. Motor vehicle drivers, for example, are obliged to follow the rules listed in the Highway Code.

WRITTEN RULES

1. Explain briefly why it is necessary that people abide by the following written rules:
   - driving on the right-hand side of the road in France;
   - not smoking on the underground in London.
2. Why might written rules concerning teacher and pupil behaviour in the classroom be necessary?
3. List five of the rules in your school or college and, for each, give one reason why you think the rule is either necessary or unnecessary.

LIFE WITHOUT RULES

1. Think what our lives would be like if there were no rules, or if most people ignored the rules. Does society need rules? Which rules? Why? Who benefits from the rules? Does anyone lose out?
2. Note down the three most important points that were made during your discussion.

WHAT IS SOCIAL ORDER?

For people to live and work together, some degree of order and predictability is needed. It could be argued that social order and predictability are necessary if society is to run smoothly without chaos or continual disruption. In studying social order, sociologists focus on the many aspects of social life that are stable and ordered. Sociologists are interested in finding out how and why social order is achieved and maintained over time. There are two main approaches to explaining the maintenance of social order – consensus and conflict.

The consensus approach

According to the consensus approach, social order and stability depend on co-operation between individuals and groups who work together to the same end. Generally, such co-operation occurs in situations where people believe that they share common interests and goals. Functionalist sociologists, for example, believe that society is based on consensus, by which they mean that broad agreement exists among people on shared norms and values. Such consensus arises from the process of socialization, during which we learn the shared norms and values of our society. Functionalists argue that social order is maintained over time because most people support and agree to abide by the rules.

The conflict approach

A second approach sees society as characterized by a conflict of interests between different groups. Clashes occur because groups do not share common interests and goals. Marxists, for example, identify conflict between the two main social classes, the bourgeoisie and the proletariat. The bourgeoisie are the propertied ruling class and the proletariat are the propertyless working class. Members of the bourgeoisie own the factories that employ the workers (the proletariat). Class conflict occurs because these two groups have opposing interests. The bourgeoisie want to make more profits while the proletariat want higher wages. Social order and stability are generally maintained, however, partly because members of the bourgeoisie have the power to enforce order.

CONSENSUS V. CONFLICT

1 Look at a daily newspaper. Select three articles reporting on issues which have generated conflict between individuals or groups.
2 For each article, state briefly what the source of the conflict is.
3 Do you think that society is, in general, held together by consensus or disrupted by conflict? Write a paragraph explaining your answer.

SOCIAL CONTROL

We have seen that much social life is subject to both written and unwritten rules. The question that we must now ask is: why do most people conform or go along with most of the rules most of the time? Social control refers to the processes by which people are persuaded to obey the rules and to conform.

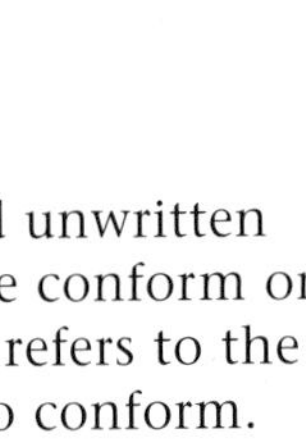

THE PROCESSES OF SOCIAL CONTROL

In order to explore the processes of social control, choose two settings with which you are familiar, for example a football match, a shopping precinct, home.
1 State three rules that operate in each setting.
2 Explain briefly why you stick to each of these rules.
3 If the rules were broken, what would happen to you – the individual – and to society?

In explaining how social control operates, sociologists point to the role of **agencies of social control**. These are the groups and organizations in society that serve to ensure that most people conform and stick to the rules most of the time. Sociologists have identified two distinct types of social control: formal and informal social control.

Formal social control

Formal social control is based on written rules and laws. It is associated with the way in which the state regulates and controls people's actions and behaviour. The agencies of formal social control are those bodies in society which make the laws, enforce them or penalize convicted law breakers:

1 The Houses of Parliament consist of the House of Commons and the House of Lords. They are known as the legislature. Their role as an agency of formal social control is to legislate: to make the laws that regulate our behaviour.

2 The role of the police force as an agency of formal social control is to enforce the law and to investigate crime.

3 The role of the judiciary (the courts) as an agency of formal social control is to deal with alleged offenders and to convict and sentence those found guilty of a criminal offence. The Crown Courts and Magistrates Courts deal with criminal law. The more serious criminal cases, such as murder, rape, robbery and arson, are tried by a judge and jury at a Crown Court. The role of the jury is to find the accused guilty (beyond all reasonable doubt) or not guilty of an alleged offence. If the accused is found guilty, then the judge will impose a sentence based on the severity of the offence. Possible sentences include a probation order, a community service order, a fine or a term of imprisonment. Such sanctions are official and are backed by the state.

4 The role of the prison service, as part of the penal system, is to confine prisoners. Prison, as an agency of social control, punishes convicted law breakers and deters other people from committing crime.

AGENTS OF FORMAL SOCIAL CONTROL

Study these four photographs and state which agency of formal social control is identified in each one.

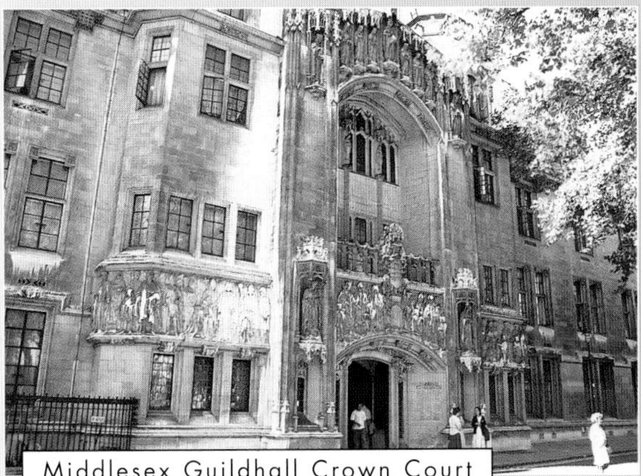

Middlesex Guildhall Crown Court

Santa Fu Prison, Germany

Stoke Newington Police Station

The Houses of Parliament

CHECK YOUR UNDERSTANDING

1 Identify two agencies of formal social control and explain, in each case, how they control people's behaviour. (4 marks)

2 Identify and describe two ways in which society tries to prevent people from becoming criminals. (4 marks)

Informal social control

We have seen that formal social control of people's behaviour and actions is achieved through laws and written rules. Rather than being based on written laws, informal social control is based on informal processes such as the approval or disapproval of others. Informal social control is enforced via social pressure – by the reaction of group members such as families, friends, workmates and bosses. Negative reactions towards individuals who do not conform to the group's expectations include ridiculing them, ignoring them, playing practical jokes on them, gossiping about them, hitting them or using argument to try to persuade them to change their behaviour. Positive reactions include praising them, giving them a gift, promoting them at work or giving them a pay rise.

INFORMAL PROCESSES OF SOCIAL CONTROL

Discuss at least two ways in which informal processes of social control may operate to deal with each of the following:

- a school pupil who is seen as hard working and dedicated;
- a neighbour who works as a prostitute;
- a married MP who is caught committing adultery;
- a teenage girl who rescues a drowning child.

Informal social control and socialization

Socialization (see pp. 32–4) is the process whereby people learn the culture of their society, including the patterns of behaviour considered appropriate in society. Socialization is one way in which people are taught or persuaded to conform to the norms, mores and customs of society.

- Norms are guidelines on how people are expected to behave in particular situations. In the library, for example, people are expected to talk quietly.
- Mores are norms based upon the moral judgements of the social group. Members of some groups, for example, believe sex outside marriage is morally wrong and would disapprove of pre-marital and extra-marital sex.
- Custom refers to traditional patterns of behaviour and belief. Traditionally, in Church of England wedding ceremonies, for example, the bride wears a white wedding dress.

The **agencies of socialization** are those groups or organizations that carry out socialization. In so doing, they attempt to prevent people from becoming deviant or criminal and so operate as agencies of social control. Agencies of socialization include:

- families;
- peer groups;
- religions;
- mass media;
- schools;
- the workplace.

INFLUENCES ON OUR BEHAVIOUR

1 Examine the list at the bottom of page 238. Divide it into two parts: **(a)** those agencies of informal social control which have had an influence on your behaviour, and **(b)** those which have not.
2 Select the two that you think have had the most influence and write a paragraph showing how one of them has influenced your behaviour.

RESEARCHING AGENCIES OF SOCIAL CONTROL

- **Design and conduct a survey to investigate the opinions of students in your class on the influence of family, peer group and religion on their behaviour. You could, for example, focus on finding out whether they believe that these agencies have had an influence on their behaviour and, if so, how.**
- **Make a note of three significant findings from your survey.**

CHECK YOUR UNDERSTANDING

Identify and describe two informal ways of controlling deviance. (4 marks)

OFFICIAL STATISTICS ON CRIME

Official statistics on crime are published by the Home Office annually in *Criminal Statistics, England and Wales*. Sociologists use these statistics as a secondary source of data (see pp. 24–6) to obtain information on a range of crime-related issues, including the numbers of offences recorded by the police, the number of offences cleared up, sentencing patterns, the social characteristics of offenders and victims of crime. Official crime statistics are a cheap and readily available source of data.

Table 8.1 shows the number of notifiable or more serious offences recorded by the police in 1981 and 1995 in England and Wales. In 1981, for example, you can see that 20,000 robberies were recorded and by 1995 this figure had risen to 68,000.

Table 8.1 Notifiable or more serious offences recorded by the police in England and Wales, 1981 and 1995 (thousands)

Type of offence	1981	1995
Theft and handling stolen goods	1,603	2,452
of which: theft of vehicles	333	508
theft from vehicles	380	813
Burglary	718	1,239
Criminal damage	387	914
Violence against person	100	213
Fraud and forgery	107	133
Robbery	20	68
Sexual offences	19	30
of which rape	1	5
Drug trafficking	-	21
Other notifiable offences	9	29
All notifiable offences	**2,964**	**5,100**

Source: adapted from *Social Trends* (1997)

LOOKING AT THE STATISTICS

A wealth of information is available from statistics such as those in Table 8.1. The following activity is designed to help you extract some of this information from the table.

1 State the increase in the number of fraud and forgery offences recorded by the police between 1981 and 1995.
2 State which offences more than doubled between 1981 and 1995.
3 Was there a decline in any type of offence recorded by the police between 1981 and 1995?
4 Which offence accounted for just under half of all offences recorded by the police in 1995?
5 Which type of offence was least frequently recorded by the police in 1995?
6 Does this table take into account the changing size of the population between 1981 and 1995?

Do official crime statistics tell us the whole story?

Although such statistics may appear to be a straightforward measure of the real level of crime, they need to be treated with caution. Crime recorded by the police represents only a partial picture of the total amount of crime committed. A number of issues arise when considering whether official crime statistics tell us the whole story: issues including detection, reporting, recording of crime, and policing. We will examine each of these in turn.

Detection

Are all crimes detected? If a crime has not been detected in the first place, it cannot be reported to the police and so cannot be counted in official statistics. For example, a victim of crime may not be aware that a crime has actually taken place. If a thief takes a £5 note from a wallet containing about £45, for instance, this may pass unnoticed by the owner. Similarly, a victim must define an incident such as a smashed window as criminal damage rather than as an accident if it is to be detected. In addition, some murders have gone undetected for years.

Reporting

Are all detected crimes actually reported to the police? Many less serious offences are not reported to the police and so cannot be recorded by them. Victim surveys show that many people who have been victims of crime do not report it to the police. Serious crime and car theft are more likely than other offences to be reported, but vandalism is less likely to be reported.

The British Crime Survey, which covers England and Wales, gives a more realistic account of the amount of certain crimes than the figures recorded by the police because it involves interviewing a sample of the public about their experiences of crime. However, it only includes offences against individuals and their property.

The British Crime Survey 1994 estimated that, in 1993, 95 per cent of motor vehicle theft was recorded by the police. This is probably because people have to report car theft for insurance purposes. Least likely to be reported were robbery or theft from the person (12 per cent) and vandalism (14 per cent). It is estimated that more than 80 per cent of burglaries that involved loss were reported to the police in England and Wales in 1995, but only 25 per cent of acts of vehicle vandalism were reported. Reasons for not reporting a crime include the following:

- The crime is considered too petty, e.g. theft of an old purse containing £1.50.
- The crime is considered too private, e.g. child abuse within the family.
- It is thought that the police could do nothing or would not be interested.
- The victim suffered no loss.
- The victim may not wish to report the crime to the police because they do not believe that the police will handle it sensitively; this is a possibility with crimes such as rape.
- Where crime is committed and detected at the workplace, employers may be reluctant to make public the fact that they have employed a dishonest person. They may prefer to dismiss the employee rather than involve the police. Crime committed by **white-collar employees** (broadly, those in non-manual jobs) in the course of their employment, such as theft from an employer or fiddling travel expenses, is under-represented in crime statistics.

RESEARCHING CRIME AND REPORTING

1. **Find out from five car owners their reasons for reporting or not bothering to report the following to the police:**
   - **a scratch on their car;**
   - **an attempted break-in to their car;**
   - **theft of their car.**

   Record your answers on paper.
2. **According to your findings, does the proportion of crimes likely to be reported to the police vary according to the offence?**

Recording

Are all reported crimes actually recorded by the police? The police may not necessarily record an act as a crime. They may, for example, consider the reported crime to be too trivial or to be a mistake. The complainant may decide not to proceed with a complaint or the police may decide that there is not enough evidence of an offence having been committed to justify a criminal investigation.

Sociologists argue that official statistics ignore the dark or **hidden figure of crime**, which includes unreported and unrecorded crime. Table 8.2 is based on information from *The British Crime Survey* and shows the percentage of crimes committed which were reported to the police and recorded by them in 1981 and 1995. Only half the crimes reported to the police in England and Wales in 1995 were recorded.

Table 8.2 Percentage of crimes committed which were reported to and recorded by the police in England and Wales, 1981 and 1995

	1981	1995
Crimes committed and reported	36%	46%
Crimes committed, reported and recorded	22%	23%

Source: adapted from *Social Trends* (1997)

THE BRITISH CRIME SURVEY

According to Table 8.2:

1 In 1981 in England and Wales, what percentage of crimes was recorded?
2 In 1995, what percentage of crimes committed was reported to the police?

Policing

Official statistics on crime may tell us as much about police activity as about the crime rate. At certain times of the year, for example, the police may clamp down on specific offences, such as drinking and driving at Christmas. If so, this will affect the numbers of drivers breathalysed and prosecuted. The police in one area may be more strict than another police force in enforcing a particular law. If police in one area are strict about drinking and driving then this will also affect the official statistics. For these sorts of reasons, sociologists handle official crime statistics with care.

PROS AND CONS OF OFFICIAL CRIME STATISTICS

Make a list of:

- the advantages of official crime statistics;
- the disadvantages of official crime statistics.

TRUANCY STATISTICS

1 Schools are expected to publish statistics on their truancy rates. What problems are involved in producing accurate statistics on truancy in schools?
2 You will need to think about how to define an act of truancy. How will you measure it? How much truancy would go unrecorded and why?
3 Note down three important points made in your discussion.

CHECK YOUR UNDERSTANDING

1 Identify and explain three reasons why the recorded rate of crime may not include all crimes committed. (6 marks)

WHO COMMITS CRIME?

According to official statistics, there is a relationship between involvement in criminal activity and social characteristics such as age, gender, social class and ethnicity.

Age

Statistics suggest that young people are more likely to engage in criminal activity than older people. In 1995, nearly 40 per cent of offenders found guilty of, or cautioned for, an indictable (serious) offence in England and Wales were aged 14–20.

THE AGE AND GENDER OF OFFENDERS

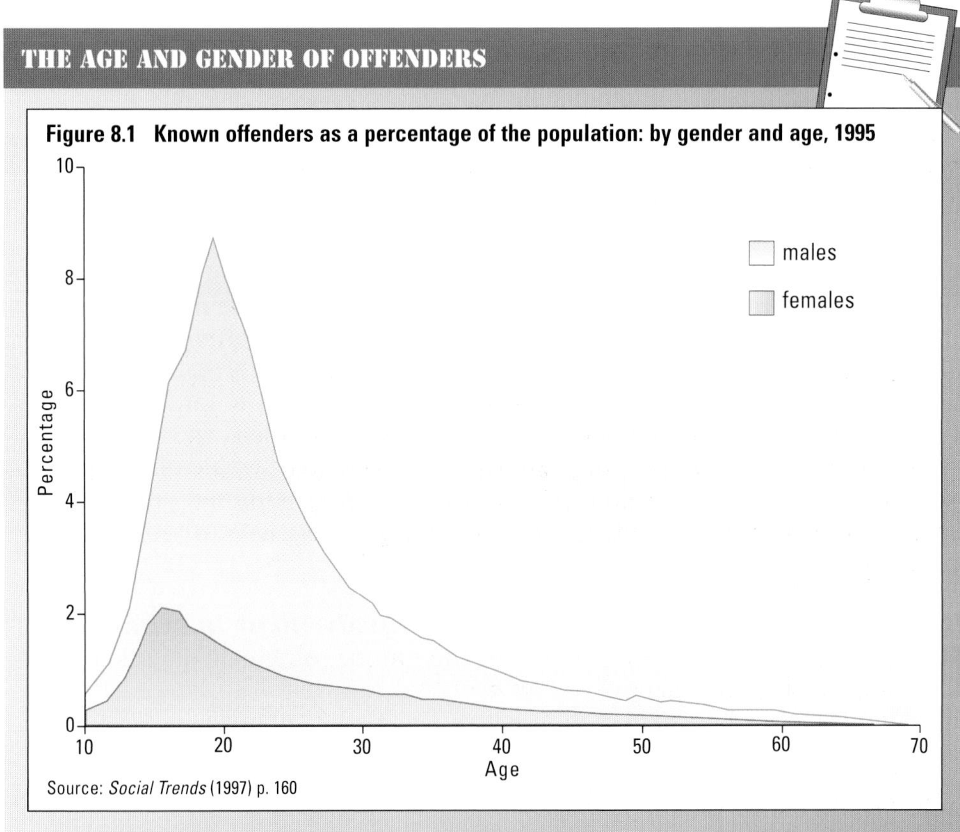

1 According to the police figures in Figure 8.1, what was the peak offending age for males in England and Wales in 1995?
2 What was the peak offending age for females?
3 Who was more likely to commit an offence: a 16-year-old female or a 40-year-old male?
4 These statistics tell us about the age and gender of known offenders. What do the statistics fail to tell us?

How do we explain these patterns?

- Peer group pressure may serve to encourage some young people to engage in criminal activity.
- Young people may seek excitement, which could lead them into trouble with the police.
- It may be that a breakdown of control over young people at home and school has occurred.

Gender

Statistics suggest that males are more likely to offend than females. The male crime rate in England and Wales is well over four times higher than the female crime rate. In 1995, 395,200 males and 84,400 females were found guilty of, or cautioned for, indictable offences. Female offenders are more likely to be involved in theft and handling stolen goods than in other indictable offences. In 1995, over 70 per cent of female offenders were found guilty of, or cautioned for, theft and handling of stolen goods.

Although females are less likely to offend than males, statistics suggest that the number of female offenders in the UK is increasing.

Girls and boys are socialized differently

How do we explain women's lesser involvement in crime?

It may be that women tend to be less involved in crime than men because girls and boys are socialized differently. In general, girls are expected to be more passive and boys more active. Boys and men are often expected to be macho and 'tough'. Such expectations, based on gender, may lead them into conflict with the police and into criminal activity such as alcohol-related crime.

It may be that females have less opportunity to commit criminal offences than males. Young girls, for example, tend to be more closely supervised by their parents than young boys. Women often have more domestic responsibilities than men.

It may be that those in authority connected with law enforcement hold stereotyped beliefs about women and men. A stereotype is an exaggerated and distorted view of a social group, for example that female offenders are 'sad' rather than 'bad', so they are more in need of help than punishment. Consequently, female offenders may be treated more leniently than males within the criminal justice system.

How do we explain women's increased involvement in crime?

There was an increase of 160 per cent in the number of female offenders who received prison sentences of over four years but less than life between 1986 and 1991. One possible explanation is that the media, as an agency of socialization, have had an impact on women's roles. There are now more varied female role models represented in the media. Films, for example, increasingly show assertive female characters who are every bit as strong and resourceful as men. The changing position of women in society means that they are less tied to the home. They now have similar legal and illegal opportunities to men.

Ethnicity

Statistics show that black men are over-represented in the prison population relative to their numbers in the population in England and Wales as a whole. Table 8.3 shows that for every 10,000 ethnic Indian, Pakistani and Bangladeshi men, there are 24.3 in prison compared to 19.4 per 10,000 white men.

Victim surveys show that there is a link between ethnicity and the likelihood of being a victim of crime. Data in *Social Trends* (1996) indicates that people from African-Caribbean backgrounds were twice as likely to be victims of burglary in England and Wales in 1993 than white people. They are also more likely to be victims of assault.

How do we explain these patterns?

We could take the prison statistics at face value and see them as reflecting the true level of crime within each ethnic group. This would involve arguing that there are more black men in prison per 10,000 population because they commit more serious crimes. If we assume for the moment that this is the case, then one possible explanation is that higher proportions of black men experience unemployment, so the level of crime is linked to poverty and deprivation.

An alternative approach, however, is to reject the idea that the statistics reflect the true levels of crime. The statistics can be seen as a reflection of policing methods and bias in the criminal justice system (see page 258). A number of sociologists have suggested that black people are more likely to be targeted, prosecuted, convicted and sentenced for longer periods of time than people from other ethnic groups.

LOOKING AT PRISON POPULATIONS

1. Of the males, which ethnic group has the highest prison population rate per 10,000?
2. Of the females, which ethnic group has the lowest prison population rate per 10,000?
3. Does the prison population consist largely of men or women?

Table 8.3 Prison population by ethnic group in England and Wales, 1992 (rate per 10,000 population aged 14 and over)

Ethnic group	Male	Female	All
White	19.4	0.5	9.6
West Indian, African, Guyanese	144.0	9.9	76.7
Indian, Pakistani, Bangladeshi	24.3	0.4	12.4
Other/not described	72.1	5.4	38.3
All ethnic groups	22.0	0.7	11.0

Source: Denscombe (1995) p. 40

Social class

There is evidence to suggest that working-class people are over-represented in the prison population. If we take the statistics at face value then it could be argued that:

- Most people desire success and affluence. Working-class people have relatively fewer opportunities to succeed through legal channels. They are consequently more tempted to turn to crime.
- Working-class subculture and values may stress deviant behaviour, which may bring status within a particular peer group.

Alternatively, the statistics may reflect bias within the criminal justice system, as the law is more strictly enforced against working-class people. Crimes committed by powerful groups are under-recorded (see p. 269).

Area

In general terms, the crime rate in inner-city areas is higher than in rural areas and the suburbs. Data from *The British Crime Survey 1995*, for example, shows that the risk of being a victim of crime varies from area to area.

Table 8.4 Risk of being a victim of crime in England and Wales, by type of area, 1995*

Type of offence	Inner-city	Non-inner-city
Household offences		
Burglary	180	90
Vehicle vandalism	145	95
Vehicle thefts	150	95
Personal offences		
Assaults	140	95
Robbery/theft from person	185	90

* Indices: national average = 100

Source: adapted from *Social Trends* (1997)

CRIME RATE AND AREA

Examine the figures in Table 8.4 (p. 245), then answer the following questions.

1 According to these figures, is the risk of burglary lower in inner-city areas or non-inner-city areas?

2 Where is risk of robbery almost twice the national average?

How do we explain these patterns?

- Inner-city crime may be linked to greater unemployment, poverty and deprivation in urban areas compared to the suburbs.
- There could be more opportunities to commit crime and more temptations in the city; for example, there are more department stores and cars.
- It may be that cities are more anonymous, so there is less chance of detection than in rural areas. Generally, rural areas have higher clear-up rates for crime than inner-city areas.
- Statistics may, however, reflect different policing methods. In rural areas, the police may be more likely to deal informally with those offenders who commit less serious offences.

Self-report studies

Self-report studies are confidential surveys that ask people to tick off, from a list, those deviant and criminal acts in which they have been involved. Such studies confirm that crime and deviance are not restricted to one particular social class, ethnic group or gender.

CHECK YOUR UNDERSTANDING

1 How would you explain the fact that there are far fewer women than men in prisons in England and Wales? (5 marks)

2 Explain why there appears to be less crime in rural areas than in urban areas of the UK. (5 marks)

3 Identify and explain two reasons why official crime statistics may be misleading. (4 marks)

HOW DO WE EXPLAIN CRIMINAL AND DEVIANT BEHAVIOUR?

The causes of criminal and deviant behaviour have been explained in terms of biological and social factors.

Biological explanations

Lombroso, a nineteenth-century Italian doctor and criminologist, believed that criminals were born and could be identified by physical features such as their large jaw size, high cheek bones, big ears and extra fingers, toes and nipples! He believed that crime and deviance could be explained in terms of genetically determined physical characteristics.

Though we may feel today that such biological explanations of crime are dated, the following extract from a newspaper article describes the case of a young man in the USA who, his lawyer argues, was born to kill.

Natural born killer! Do your genes make you a criminal?

In 1991, Tony Mobley, aged 25, walked into a pizza store and casually shot the manager in the neck after robbing the till and joking that he would apply for the job vacancy when the man was dead.

Now Mobley is waiting on Death Row and his last chance of a reprieve rests with a plea from his lawyer that the murder was the tragic consequence of a genetic predisposition. The genes of Tony Mobley, his lawyers argue, meant he was born to kill.

Source: adapted from *The Independent on Sunday*, 12 February 1995

ASSESSING BIOLOGICAL EXPLANATIONS

1 Do you agree that a person could be born a criminal? Explain your view.
2 Can you think of any other factors that might explain why a person turns to crime?

Make a note of three important issues raised during your discussion.

Sociological explanations

Sociologists reject biological explanations of behaviour. They explain involvement in crime and deviance in terms of **social** factors such as socialization patterns, peer pressure and the opportunity structure.

Socialization

Juvenile delinquency (crime committed by those aged 17 and under) has been explained in terms of family background and home environment. Delinquents may have been inadequately socialized into the norms and values of society. Delinquents may have learned criminal norms and values in the family and may have had criminal role models. To some extent, young people's attitudes to crime will be influenced by those of their parents.

The proud parents?

The influence of the peer group

Some sociologists have explained both juvenile and adult crime in terms of the values of a particular subculture and the influence of the peer group as an agency of socialization.

The extract on the right is taken from Parker's (1992) study of downtown male adolescents, known as 'the Boys', who lived in Roundhouse in Liverpool. The Boys valued being seen as coming from an area with a reputation for toughness.

Believing they come from one of the toughest areas in town holds great advantage for the Boys. They gain dignity and stature and a sense of importance from such an image. Hence some comments made by 'the boys' from another area about not wanting 'no trouble with you lot' is seized upon and repeated continuously till everyone has bathed in the glory.

Source: Parker (1992) p. 33

Deviance among young people may be linked to **school subculture** and peer group influences at school. Paul Willis (1977) studied a group of 12 non-academic, white working-class 'lads' in a Midlands school. The 'lads' were anti-school and part of a counter-school culture which involved completely opposing the values of the school. They opposed authority and rejected the conformist boys in the school, who they referred to as the 'ear 'oles'.

The opportunity structure

Some sociologists have explained both juvenile and adult crime in terms of the level of both legal and illegal opportunities available to the individual. In areas where the levels of employment and educational opportunities are low, people may turn to illegal means to achieve success.

The extracts on the left are from Williams's (1989) study of a teenage drug ring in New York City.

These studies took me to the Bronx, Harlem and Washington Heights – areas of high unemployment and diminishing resources, especially for young people. But while quality entry-level jobs were disappearing, illegal opportunities were emerging with considerable force because of the growth of a powerful and profitable multi-national drug industry.

The Cocaine Kids, and many of the kids coming behind them, are drawn to the underground economy because of the opportunities that exist there. The underground offers status and prestige – rewards they are unlikely to attain in the regular economy – and is the only real economy for many.

Source: Williams (1989) p. ix

Marxist explanations

Marxists explain crime by examining the type of society in which we live. They are critical of capitalist society, in which a small group of very wealthy people – the bourgeoisie – own the means of production (such as land, factories and big businesses) and exploit poorer working-class people – the proletariat – in order to make as much profit as possible.

Capitalist society is based on values such as materialism (valuing material possessions), consumerism (wanting more and better consumer goods such as cars and designer clothes) and competition between individuals to achieve such possessions and consumer goods (keeping up with the neighbours). The media, it is argued, continually reinforce these values through advertising in magazines, in television game shows and even Hollywood films based on the lives of the super-rich. Given such a society, it is likely that some people will attempt to obtain material goods through any means, including illegal means.

Marxists are critical of the laws that are enforced in a capitalist society. Many laws, they argue, are made by, and in the interests of, those who own property, so it is not surprising that many laws relate to the protection of private property. Marxists argue that, given such a legal system, it is likely that working-class people will be caught breaking the law while crimes committed by the powerful bourgeoisie may frequently go undetected.

Labelling theory

According to official statistics, there is a relationship between crime and social factors such as age, gender, class and ethnicity. Labelling theory attempts to explain both how and why certain people (such as working-class boys, black people) come to be labelled as deviant or criminal. A label is like a sticky tag; it can be attached to an individual or group.

Cicourel (1976) carried out participant observation with police and probation officers in two Californian cities in the USA in order to study day-to-day police, probation and court activities. He focused on juveniles and found that the way in which a particular juvenile was viewed by officials had a significant impact on how that individual was dealt with. The decision as to whether or not to bring an individual to court was largely influenced by the probation officer's view of **'the typical delinquent'**. A delinquent type, in the view of officials, is from a low-income, broken home, has a bad attitude toward authority, a poor school performance and ethnic group membership. If an individual's background fits that of 'the typical delinquent' then this particular person is more likely to be charged and, if found guilty, to be labelled a delinquent.

According to Cicourel, the middle-class white boy is less likely to be seen as a typical delinquent. He is, therefore, more likely to receive a warning rather than be charged with a criminal offence. So, according to Cicourel, a delinquent is one who has been labelled as such. To be labelled as a delinquent is more the result of the reaction of other people – such as probation and police officers – than it is of the individual's actual behaviour.

LABELLING THEORY IN ACTION

Ben, a middle-class boy, and Bill, a working-class boy, are stopped for shoplifting. They are not together and do not know each other. According to labelling theory and Cicourel, what is likely to happen to each boy and why?

DO WE KNOW THE TRUTH?

Using Cicourel's ideas, write a paragraph to show why official crime statistics on juvenile law breakers cannot be taken at face value.

Stereotyping

Labelling is often linked to stereotyping. Members of some groups are labelled and treated according to a stereotype which is an exaggerated and distorted view of them. People with mental health problems, for example, are often labelled and treated according to stereotypes. Research published in June 1997 by MIND (the mental health charity) showed that people who suffer from mental health problems can be subject to the 'mad, bad and dangerous' stereotype.

Labelling may lead to a self-fulfilling prophecy (see p. 169):

- A young woman is publicly identified and labelled as a 'drug addict'.
- As a result, she is rejected by her family, loses her job and her home, and comes to regard herself as deviant.
- She turns to shoplifting as a way of financing her drug dependency, thus becoming involved in further crime and deviance.
- She now meets others in the same situation, which leads to involvement in a deviant subculture and lifestyle.

The cause of deviance is not, according to this view, in the action but in the reaction of others to it.

CHECK YOUR UNDERSTANDING

1 A juvenile delinquent is someone aged 17 or under who breaks the law. What explanations have sociologists given for juvenile delinquency? (8 marks)

2 Identify and describe fully one social factor that might lead people to become criminal. (4 marks)

3 Identify and explain two reasons why some people do not always obey the law. (4 marks)

SUMMARY

In this chapter, we have covered the following points:

- **A crime is an act that breaks the law. Deviance is behaviour which the majority of people disagree with, or which goes against the norms of a society.**
- **Deviant acts can be – but are not always – illegal.**
- **Following on from this, whether or not a behaviour is defined as deviant depends on the social setting in which it takes place.**
- **Historical evidence points to the fact that society's view of what constitutes deviant behaviour has changed over time.**
- **What is classified as deviant behaviour varies from one culture to another.**
- **In all societies there are some taken-for-granted rules of behaviour and other rules that are written down.**
- **Social order is necessary for society to run smoothly. Functionalists believe that social order is based on consensus. Marxists believe that social order is based on the power of the ruling class over the working class.**
- **Social control is based on both formal written-down rules and on patterns of behaviour that we learn through socialization.**
- **Official crime statistics are produced in the UK by the Home Office. The official statistics refer only to recorded crime. Not all crime is detected by the police or reported by the victim, so the official statistics do not tell the whole story.**
- **The official statistics suggest that criminal activity is more commonly found in certain groups in society, for example more men commit crime than women.**
- **The causes of criminal and deviant behaviour have been explained in terms of biological and/or social factors. Sociologists focus on social factors.**

EXAMINATION QUESTION 1

How do sociologists explain why an action is seen as normal by one group of people yet abnormal or deviant by another? Illustrate your answer with examples. (10 marks)

Source: SEG GCSE Sociology, Summer 1997
Higher Tier, Paper 2, Section C, Question 10, p. 14

EXAMINATION QUESTION 2

Study **Item A**. Then answer **all** parts of the question that follows.

Item A
Distribution of time taken on police activities

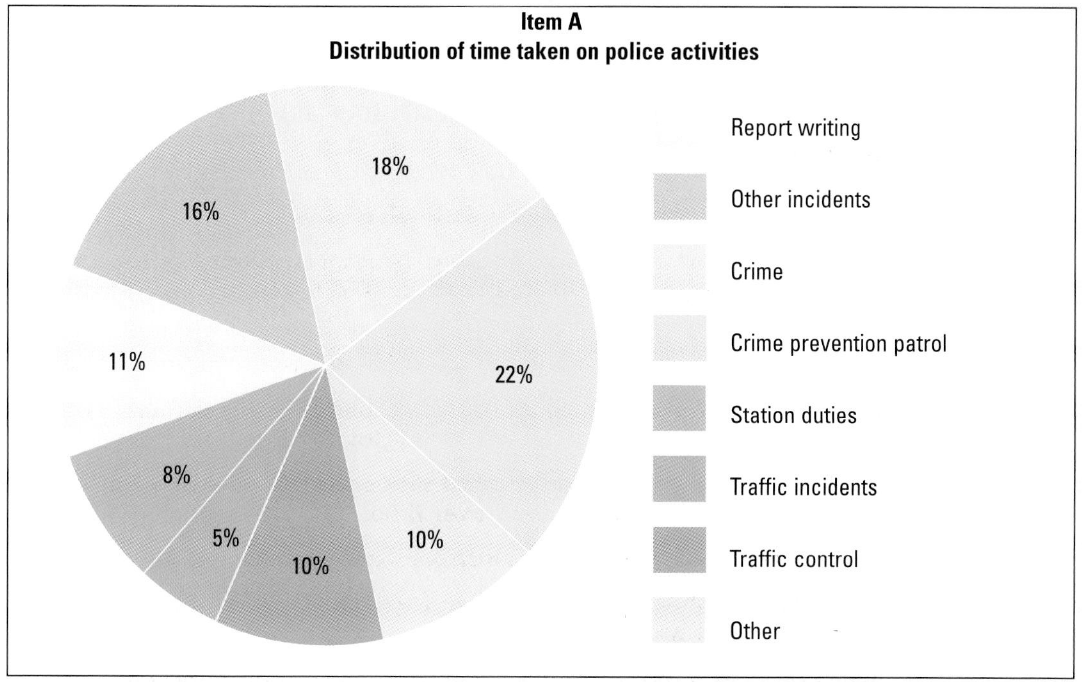

Source: *In Focus: Sociology Review* (September 1994)

(a) **(i)** According to the information in **Item A**, what percentage of police time is spent on crime? (1 mark)

(ii) According to the information in **Item A**, on which police activity is the largest amount of time spent? (1 mark)

(iii) Why might the police carry out this activity? (1 mark)

(b) **(i)** Give **one** example of a punishment used in formal social control. Describe how it might control people's social behaviour. (2 marks)

(ii) Identify **one** group of people who are more likely to experience formal social control than others. Suggest a reason for this. (2 marks)

(c) **(i)** Explain what is meant by 'social deviance'. (2 marks)

(ii) Identify and describe **one** informal way of controlling social deviance. (2 marks)

(d) **(i)** The mass media are said to play an important role in the process of socialization. Describe **one** way in which the mass media do this. (3 marks)

(ii) Identify **one** other agent of socialization. (1 mark)

Source: SEG GCSE Sociology, Summer 1996
Foundation Tier, Paper 1, Section B, Question 9, p. 11

BIBLIOGRAPHY

Cicourel, A.V. (1976) *The Social Organization of Juvenile Justice*, Heinemann.
Denscombe, M. (1995) *Sociology Update*, Olympus Books.
Moore, S. (1996) *Investigating Crime and Deviance*, 2nd edition, Collins Educational
Parker, H.J. (1992) *View From The Boys*, Gregg Revivals.
Social Trends 24 (1994) Office for National Statistics and HMSO.
Social Trends 25 (1995) Office for National Statistics and HMSO.
Social Trends 26 (1996) Office for National Statistics and HMSO.
Social Trends 27 (1997) Office for National Statistics and HMSO.
Williams, T. (1989) *The Cocaine Kids*, Addison-Wesley.
Willis, P. (1977) *Learning to Labour: How Working-Class Kids Get Working-Class Jobs*, Saxon House.

CHAPTER 9

Political Sociology

In this chapter, we will explore and attempt to answer the following questions:

1. **Politics and power**
   - **What is politics?**
   - **What is power?**
   - **What are the sources of power?**
2. **Political systems and power**
   - **What is a democracy?**
   - **How democratic is Britain?**
   - **What is a dictatorship?**
3. **Political institutions and decision making**
   - **What is 'the state'?**
   - **What is the role of elections?**
   - **What part do political parties and pressure groups play in the decision making process?**
4. **Voting behaviour**
   - **What are the different types of voter?**
   - **What factors affect voting behaviour?**
   - **What are the trends in voting behaviour since the 1950s?**
   - **What part do opinion polls play?**
5. **Political socialization**
   - **What is political socialization?**
   - **How does it occur?**

A narrow definition of politics

The Labour cabinet in session on 8 May 1997

Speakers' corner, London

A broad definition of politics

POLITICS AND POWER

What is politics?

When we hear the word 'politics', most of us think of elections, political parties, politicians, the government and Parliament. Many of us tend to see politics as being fairly remote from our day-to-day lives. In taking this attitude, we are adopting a **narrow definition** of politics.

Another equally important way of thinking about politics is to focus much more broadly on the power relationships in society. According to the **broad definition**, politics concerns inequalities in power. Politics is relevant to us in our day-to-day lives because we enter into power relationships in the classroom, at home, at work and with our friends. Our personal relationships are political when they involve power. Domestic violence, child abuse and racist violence can be seen as political in so far as they all involve the exercise of power.

Max Weber

What is power?

There are a number of different ways of defining power. According to Max Weber (1864–1920), one of the most influential early sociologists, power is exercised by an individual or group when they are able to get what they want, despite opposition from others. We have power in so far as we can get others to behave as we want them to. We exercise power when we influence someone even against their will.

What are the sources of power?

According to Weber, power may be based on either **coercion** or **authority**.

- Coercion involves the use of force. We obey because we feel that we have no choice; we are forced into it against our will. Kidnappers, for example, exercise coercive power when they demand and receive the payment of a ransom in exchange for the release of hostages.
- Authority is exercised over us when we willingly obey an individual or group because we see this as the right thing to do. Force is not necessary because we agree to obey. A teacher, for example, exercises authority over students in the classroom when they willingly complete homework and hand it in on time.

Other sociologists are inspired by the work of another highly influential early sociologist, Karl Marx. These sociologists see power as closely linked to social class relationships. Power is held by members of the bourgeoisie who are the property-owning, economically dominant class. Marxists believe that the bourgeoisie use their power to exploit the proletariat – the working class.

Karl Marx

CHECK YOUR UNDERSTANDING

Identify the difference between coercion and authority. (2 marks)

What are the sources of authority?

Max Weber identified three ideal types or models of legitimate authority: **traditional**, **legal rational** and **charismatic** authority. In each, the exercise of power is seen as legitimate or proper by those to whom it is applied. They give their consent.

Traditional authority

Traditional authority is based on custom and tradition. We accept the authority of an individual or group because it is customary for us to do so. The monarchy, for example, exercises authority based on tradition.

Legal rational authority in operation

Legal rational authority

In the case of legal rational authority, we obey an individual or group because of the position that they hold within an organization. For example, the democratically elected president of a nation exercises legal rational authority over its citizens.

In the workplace, the office manager exercises legal rational authority which stems from his or her position within the company. Employees accept that the office manager is authorized to supervise their work each day because this is set out in their job description.

Charismatic authority

In the case of charismatic authority, we obey an individual because we believe that he or she possesses extraordinary personal qualities that inspire us. A charismatic leader is seen as exceptional by others. The authority of some religious leaders, for example, is based on their charisma.

Mahatma Gandhi (1869–1948) can be seen as an example of a charismatic religious leader in India who used his charismatic authority to lead the struggle for India's independence from Britain.

Before the move to democracy in South Africa, Nelson Mandela, a charismatic political leader, led a large popular movement against apartheid. These two examples show that charismatic leaders can act to bring about social change.

Weber recognized that, in practice, things were less clear cut. For example, a teacher exercises legal rational authority but a gifted teacher may also exercise charismatic authority and may act as an inspiration to students.

Charismatic leaders can be a force for change

In this way, as the democratically elected president of South Africa since 1994, Nelson Mandela exercises both legal rational authority and charismatic authority. We should bear in mind, however, that the three types of legitimate authority outlined by Weber are ideal types or models of authority. In practice, things are not usually so clear cut. Real-life authoritative people usually base their authority on a mix of two or even three of these types.

TYPES OF AUTHORITY

For each of the following five pictures, state which type or mix of types of authority are involved. Briefly justify your answer.

POLITICAL SYSTEMS AND POWER

Different societies have different political systems. Some are based on democratic principles.

What is a democracy?

The Houses of Parliament

The word 'democracy' literally means 'government by the people'. In a democratic society, the people hold political power. In Britain, for example, as citizens, we do not govern directly in that we are not given the opportunity to vote on whether we agree with every single proposal in order for it to become law. This would be completely impractical. Instead we have indirect or parliamentary democracy, in which we elect representatives who sit as Members of Parliament (MPs) and govern on our behalf.

If it is felt that the electorate (the voters) should be asked to vote on an important issue, a **referendum** may be held. This involves putting a question to the electorate for a direct yes or no decision. In September 1997, for example, referenda were held in Scotland on setting up a Scottish Parliament and in Wales on setting up a Welsh assembly.

Many countries, including India, the USA, the Republic of Ireland and France, have indirect or representative democracy. This means that they have regular elections, during which representatives are selected by the people. In a democratic system, the government's power is based on legal-rational authority rather than coercion.

DO WE HAVE A SAY IN GOVERNMENT?

In a small group, discuss:

1 some of the ways in which we can attempt to influence political decisions in Britain today;
2 the extent to which you feel that our views influence MPs.

Now make a note of three important points raised in your discussion.

How democratic is Britain?

One important principle of democracy is that we are able to participate in the political process in order to make our views known. In a democratic society, our views count in the process of decision making. In Britain, we can participate and make our views known by:

- voting, e.g. in local, general and European elections;
- starting or joining a political party;
- starting or joining a pressure group and getting involved in its campaigns;
- writing to our MP, Member of the European Parliament (MEP) or local councillor;
- writing to the press.

Critics, however, argue that countries such as Britain cannot really be regarded as democratic. According to this view, certain features of the British political system are not democratic at all, such as the fact that we have:

- an unelected House of Lords;
- a hereditary monarchy.

Critics also point out that, unlike other countries, we do not have a Bill of Rights, which would set out, in written form, our rights as citizens – that is, our fundamental rights and freedoms that cannot be denied to us by government. A further point made by some is that even though people over the age of 18 can vote in elections, many do not bother. In the 1997 general election, for example, only 71.4 per cent of those registered to vote actually did so.

Marxists argue that the real source of power in capitalist societies is economic power. It is members of the bourgeoisie – the economically dominant social class which owns wealth, capital and property – who are really powerful in societies such as Britain and the USA. Poorer people have very little access to economic or political power and therefore these class-based societies are not truly democratic.

DISCRIMINATION

One principle of a fair and democratic society is that of freedom from discrimination. This means that we should not be treated less favourably than any other person because of our ethnicity or gender. A second principle is that of equality before the law; we should all, regardless of ethnicity, age, gender or social class, be treated equally within the legal system.

Equal Treatment For All?

Racial discrimination and violence figure in everyday life for millions of Britons, according to Liberty, the civil rights organization, in a report to be submitted to the UN Committee on the Elimination of Racial Discrimination. The report details incidents of discrimination against Travellers, Jews and Irish people as well as black and Asian people. The police are using powers under the Prevention of Terrorism Act to target black and ethnic minority people.

Addressing the criminal justice system, Liberty says a black or Asian man is 10 times more likely to be stopped and searched by the police than a white man. In its most recent report, the UN Human Rights Committee expressed concern that members of some ethnic minorities are often disproportionately subjected to stop and search practices.

Source: adapted from Stewart (1996)

With reference to this extract:

1 Identify three groups of people who are discriminated against in Britain.
2 Identify one particular way in which some groups are treated differently from the rest of society.

What is a dictatorship?

Under a dictatorship, political power is concentrated in the hands of a dictator: a ruler with absolute authority. Obedience is based on threats or coercion rather than on legal rational authority. Many people obey because they are forced to do so. The government is authoritarian and, in many instances, has total control and power over people's lives. The police force, the mass media and the legal system, for example, are directly controlled by the government. Hitler in Nazi Germany, and Stalin in Russia, are examples of dictators. Military dictatorships – in which high-ranking members of the armed forces hold government positions – exist today in countries such as Nigeria and Burma (Myanmar). Governments that are dictatorships and have total control over most aspects of people's lives are called '**totalitarian**'.

DENIAL OF HUMAN RIGHTS

The following extract describes how human rights are being violated or denied to the citizens of Burma (Myanmar) today. Read the extract and then state five ways in which, according to this information, human rights are denied to the Burmese people.

BURMA – A LAND OF FEAR

For 34 years the people of Burma have been ruled by a military junta or faction which is as tyrannical and secretive as any in the modern era. In February 1996 the UN Commission on Human Rights reported, as it does every year, that the following human rights violations were commonplace in Burma: 'Torture, arbitrary executions, forced labour, abuse of women, politically motivated arrests and detention, forced movement of groups of people from their homes, important restrictions on the freedom of expression and association, and oppression of ethnic and religious minorities ...' Take at random any of the reports by Amnesty International and what distinguishes the Burmese military junta from other modern tyrannies is slave labour.

Source: adapted from Pilger (1996)

The totalitarian school?

The following extract was written by an A-level student in a grammar school. He compares his school to a totalitarian state – one in which people are expected to be completely subservient to the government.

The extract is important because it shows us that politics and power relationships are found in most situations.

Authority rests in the hands of a leader, the Headmaster, who addresses the masses (we, the pupils) daily in Assembly. He has his own symbols of power and authority – for example, his gown, and the school flag used to rally support at sporting and other events. He is the head of an elite, the teachers, whom we can compare to the party to be found in a totalitarian state, who assume unquestioning acceptance of their authority – the party knows what is best for us. There is, too, an official party ideology, as laid down in the school rulebook, with regulations and limitations on how we behave and act.

We also have censorship – freedom of speech is denied, except through officially recognized bodies such as the Debating Society, where members of the party must always be present. We are not allowed to make public announcements without the authorization of teachers. The media, such as it exists in school, through the school magazine and circulated leaflets, is also closely controlled and edited by the party. We have uniforms, marches, curfews, and even a Hitler Youth – the school rugby team (which in our school, it is held by general consensus, exerts a disproportionate influence).

Source: *Social Studies Review* (1990), pp. 68–9

SCHOOL RULES

The writer of the article on p. 259 may not be entirely serious and he has possibly exaggerated some of the school's features. Nevertheless, some schools are stricter and more authoritarian than others. (An authoritarian school is one in which all rules are strictly enforced.)

1 To what extent can your school or college be described as authoritarian?
2 Note down three features of your school or college that might be described as authoritarian and three features that are more democratic.

DEMOCRACY OR DICTATORSHIP?

For each of the following, state whether it is a feature of a democracy or a dictatorship:

(a) elections during which people can vote freely for whichever party they choose;
(b) tight governmental control of the press and television;
(c) freedom of speech and expression;
(d) freedom for organizations (e.g. trade unions) to meet;
(e) the banning of pressure groups;
(f) a legal system and police force that are independent of the government;
(g) rule by one individual or elite group;
(h) the denial of a fair trial.

POLITICAL INSTITUTIONS AND DECISION MAKING

What is the state?

The term 'state' is used to refer to the various institutions that organize and regulate society. The state consists of those institutions that make, implement and enforce laws. The police, the armed forces, the civil service and judges, for example, are all part of the state. It is important to recognize that 'the state' is not just another term for 'the government'. Even though the legal system, the army and the police force are part of the state, they can be (and in many countries are) independent of the government of the day. In the UK, the state covers the geographical areas of England, Northern Ireland, Scotland and Wales.

Table 9.1 The main institutions of the state

Parliament	The civil service	The judiciary
House of Commons and House of Lords	The bureaucracy	The courts
have	*has*	*have*
Legislative power Makes decisions and laws	**Executive power** Advises government ministers, carries out decisions and implements laws	**Judicial power** Law enforcement

The Houses of Parliament consist of an elected House of Commons and an unelected House of Lords. Parliament has an important role in the law-making or legislative process: the government puts forward its legislative proposals in the form of a Bill, which must be passed in Parliament before it becomes law.

An important part of the role of MPs in the Commons is to represent the interests of their constituents.

The role of the civil service is to advise government ministers on policy and to implement or carry out government policy. The civil service is **apolitical**, which means that it is politically neutral, does not take sides and does not involve itself in political debate.

The judiciary consists of judges and the courts. They, along with the police force, are concerned with law enforcement.

Contrasting views of the state

We can identify two broad approaches to the state: the pluralist approach, and the conflict, or Marxist, approach.

According to the **pluralist** approach, a plurality or range of interests and groups exists in society. Political power is spread out among these groups and no single one dominates. Government policies are influenced by many groups in society. The role of the state is to act as an umpire or referee rather than to side with one group over another.

Sociologists from the **conflict** approach point out that those in senior positions in the civil service, the top judges and most army officers are drawn from a narrow social and educational background. They are predominantly from privileged backgrounds sharing the experience of public school and being graduates of Oxbridge (Oxford or Cambridge University). People from schools in the state sector and graduates of the new 'redbrick' universities hold relatively few positions of power. It is argued that those in senior positions within the state form part of a ruling elite in which positions of power and influence are held by members of a small privileged group.

Marxists argue that those in powerful positions within the state are drawn from or serve the interests of the bourgeoisie, the propertied ruling class. Its economic dominance gives it political power and dominance. Marxists believe that state policies generally benefit the bourgeoisie.

The House of Commons has traditionally been composed mainly of white, middle-class, middle-aged men, so we might question whether the Commons can effectively represent the interests and views of all of us.

The 1997 general election saw some changes in the social composition of the House of Commons. The total number of female MPs doubled from 62 to around 120. This means that 18 per cent of MPs are now female. Over 100, or 24 per cent, of Labour MPs are female.

The average age of MPs in the Commons has fallen and the number of relatively young MPs increased after the 1997 election. Some MPs are in their twenties. The social composition of the Commons is certainly changing, but it still does not reflect the social composition of the electorate. For example, only two black female MPs were elected in May 1997.

The number of female MPs has increased slightly since the 1997 general election

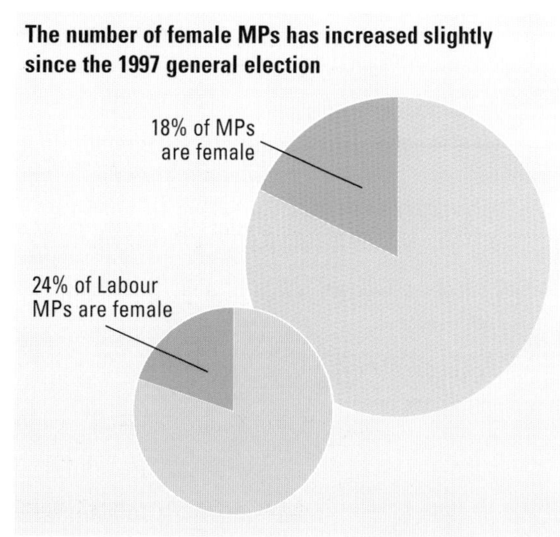

The House of Lords has come under fierce attack in some quarters. Many people believe that it should abolished because it wields political power even though its members are unelected. Many members of the House of Lords are hereditary peers who are there by virtue of birth.

Although unelected, top civil servants potentially hold a great deal of power. They can manipulate ministers and critics suggest that they, in reality, 'run' the country behind the scenes. Senior civil servants are permanently employed in their posts. Government ministers, on the other hand, are temporary appointees who are likely to be shuffled from post to post. Ministers are more likely to lose their posts than top civil servants because, being MPs, they must compete in a general election every five years in order to hold on to their seats.

LOOKING AT JUDGES

How modern is the modern judiciary?

Judges and the 'Old School Tie'

Judges come from a social elite. This fact has been established for quite some time. However, in the late 1990s there might be grounds for expecting some change and for some widening of the social background of judges. Evidence coming from a House of Commons Home Affairs Select Committee in June 1996, though, indicated quite clearly that things are much the same as they were at the start of the 1900s. The Select Committee, which had a majority of Conservative MPs on it, found that:

- *80 per cent of judges had private schooling and went to either Oxford or Cambridge University;*
- *five out of six of the latest appointments as judges follow this pattern of having had private schooling and having been to Oxford or Cambridge University.*

The elitism of the judiciary is further demonstrated by the fact that just:

- *five of the 517 circuit court judges are black or Asian; and only*
- *seven of the 96 high court judges are women.*

Source: Denscombe (1997) p. 24

Judges are powerful, unelected and, as the extract on the left shows, tend to be drawn from a narrow social and educational background.

1. According to this information, how far does the social background of judges reflect that of the wider population?
2. Explain briefly in your own words what is meant by the 'elitism of the judiciary'.
3. To what extent has the social background of judges changed during the twentieth century?

LOOKING AT MPS

1 In a small group, discuss possible reasons why so many of our MPs are middle-class, white men.
2 Make a note of three important points made during your discussion.

IS BRITAIN DEMOCRATIC?

Some sociologists believe that Britain is not fully democratic. For example, we have an unelected monarchy and House of Lords.

1 Conduct an opinion poll to find out whether people believe that:
   - Britain should abolish the monarchy;
   - Britain should abolish the House of Lords.

   Try to ensure that you ask a range of people –male and female, and from different age groups and backgrounds.

2 Write a paragraph to outline and explain your findings.

What is the role of elections?

In Britain a number of different elections are held at different times.

Table 9.2 Types of election in the UK

Type	How often	Elects
General election	Every five years or less	MPs in the House of Commons
By-election	When a Commons seat becomes vacant, e.g. through death or retirement of a sitting MP	MP in the House of Commons
European election	Every five years	MEPs - Members of the European Parliament
Local elections, e.g. county council	Every four years	Local councillors

The electoral system in Britain

In British general elections the vast majority of people aged over 18 have one vote each, which enables them to vote for one candidate. This is known as a 'one person, one vote' system. We cast our votes in a secret ballot in the constituency in which we live.

Elections in the UK are based on the system of **'first past the post'** or 'winner takes all'. A candidate in a constituency needs to get only one more vote than his or her nearest rival in order to be elected as an MP and so get a seat in the House of Commons. One advantage of the present electoral system is that each constituency elects its own MP, whose job it is to represent constituents' interests. Apart from being reasonably straightforward, the first-past-the-post system has the added advantage of ensuring that one political party usually gains sufficient seats to form a government. If two or more parties were to gain a large number of seats so that no party held enough seats to have a working majority in the House of Commons, then there would be a 'hung' Parliament and the parties concerned would have to try to work together in some way.

A problem with the first-past-the-post system, however, is that many MPs will be elected even though more than half of those voting in their constituency did not vote for them. Some MPs are elected with much more support than others. For example, in the May 1997 general election, the Conservative candidate for Teignbridge won by 281 votes, while the Labour candidate for Knowsley South won by 30,708 votes.

The first-past-the-post system works to the disadvantage of those smaller parties whose support is spread out geographically rather than concentrated in a few constituencies. As we currently vote in constituencies, some votes are wasted, such as those cast for candidates who lose, and the surplus or extra number of votes cast for the winning candidate.

Smaller parties would gain more seats from a system of **proportional representation (PR)**, in which a party gained seats according to how many votes it received in Britain as a whole. Critics argue that the first-past-the-post system is actually unfair and undemocratic.

THE VOTING SYSTEM

Let's imagine that, in constituency A, candidates from three parties stood for election. Votes were cast as follows:

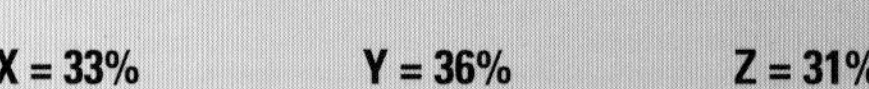

1 Which candidate would become MP?
2 Using this example, explain what is meant by wasted votes.

What is the aim of political parties in Britain?

One feature of a parliamentary democracy such as Britain is that we are free to form, join and become active in the political party of our choice. A political party is an organization that seeks to form a government. With the exception of the Referendum Party and the Prolife Alliance (see p. 267), political parties have policies on a whole range of issues, such as education, welfare, the economy, crime and defence.

Before a general election, each political party publishes its policy proposals in its election **manifesto**. The party that wins the election forms the government. It can then (rightly or wrongly) claim a **mandate** for its policies – that is, it can claim that support for its policies derives from the electorate.

LOOKING AT THE RESULTS OF THE 1997 GENERAL ELECTION

Look carefully at the information below and then answer the questions that follow.

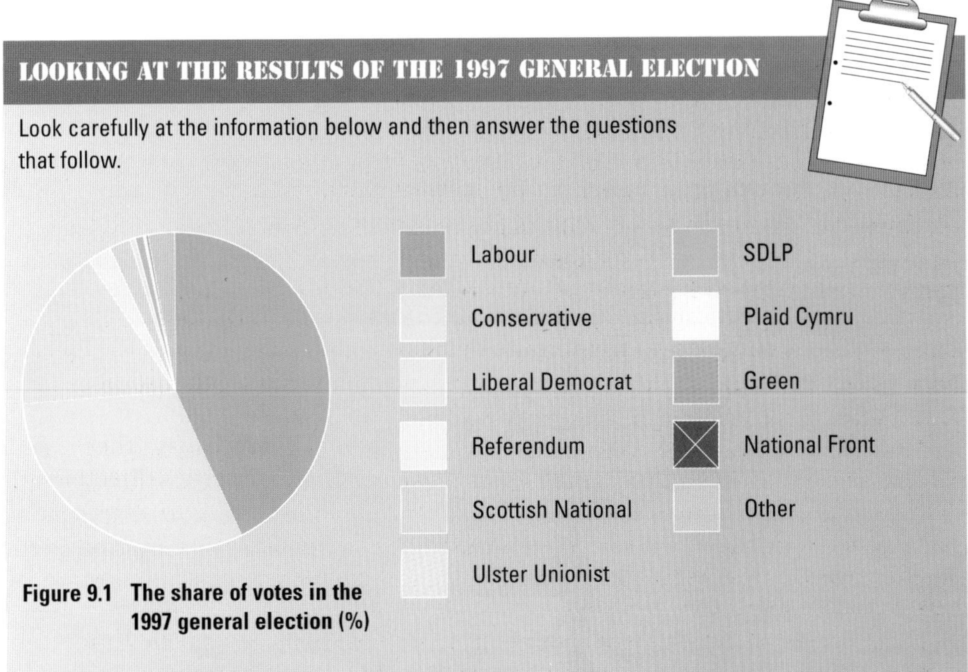

Figure 9.1 The share of votes in the 1997 general election (%)

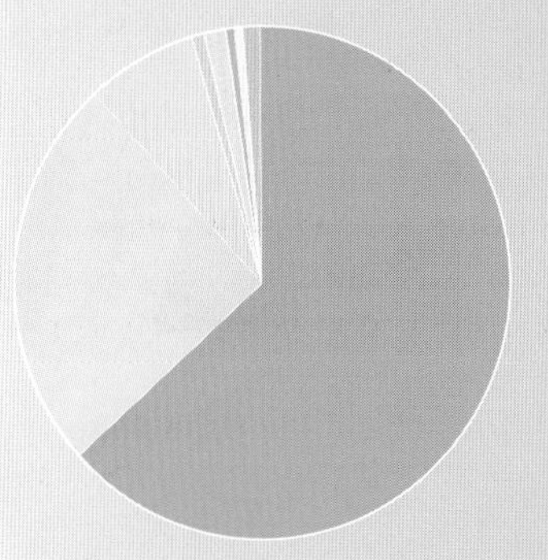

Figure 9.2 The share of seats in the 1997 general election (%)

Table 9.3 Summary of voting in the UK general election, May 1997

	Votes	% share of votes	MPs elected	% share of seats
Labour	13,516,632	43.3	419	63.5
Conservative	9,602,857	30.7	165	25
Liberal Democrat	5,242,894	16.8	46	7
Referendum	811,827	2.6	–	–
Scottish National	621,540	2.0	6	0.9
Ulster Unionist	258,349	0.8	10	1.5
SDLP	190,814	0.6	3	0.5
Plaid Cymru	161,030	0.5	4	0.6
Green	63,991	0.2	–	–
National Front	2,716	0.0	–	–
Other	813,947	2.6	6	0.9
Total	31,286,597	100	659	100

Source: adapted from Clements and Mann (1997) pp. 5–6

1. Which party formed the government?
2. Which party gained 16.8 per cent of the votes?
3. What percentage of seats did it get?
4. Which party gained 811,827 votes?
5. How many MPs did it get?
6. Which party gained just over 30 per cent of the votes but only 25 per cent of the seats?
7. Which party gained 1.5 per cent of seats?
8. Using this information, write a paragraph to show how some parties lose out in the first-past-the-post system, but other parties can gain.

A rough guide to the parties

This is a huge topic and it would be difficult to produce an accurate summary of the policies of all of the political parties in Britain in this volume. Anyone wishing to understand the role, aims and policies of the main political parties in Britain should make a point of studying the political comment and parliamentary news as reported in a good broadsheet newspaper or journal since their policies and priorities change over time in response to changing circumstances. For example, many people who supported the Labour Party in the 1970s and 1980s might not recognize 'New Labour' of the 1990s.

The following provides a thumbnail sketch of some parties' policy proposals around the time of the May 1997 general election. For more detailed information on that election, or more up-to-the-minute details of party policies, you will need to examine other sources, such as the media, or you could even contact the individual parties directly.

THE LABOUR PARTY
(or 'New Labour')

Tony Blair

One big idea: education

- cut class sizes to 30 maximum for 5- to 7-year-olds;
- a year's guaranteed pre-school education for every 4-year-old;
- local ballots (if parents wish) on existing grammar schools;
- 'setting' of pupils by ability;
- accelerated learning for brightest pupils;
- homework centres;
- literacy crusade: 80 per cent of all 11-year-olds to reach the reading age of 11 by 2001;
- failing schools to be taken over by a successful neighbouring headteacher;
- at least six hours a week skills education for 16- and 17-year-olds in work;
- a new student-financing system, with lump sum for maintenance, paid by the state, to be repaid over 20 years through national insurance.

New Labour is currently the largest political party in the House of Commons and so forms the government.

THE CONSERVATIVE PARTY

William Hague

One big idea: welfare

- phase out the basic state pension, replacing it with a weekly state contribution paid into personal pension plans;
- scrap State Earnings Related Pensions Scheme and pay 5 per cent of national contributions into personal pensions;
- new entrants to the job market will start off with a new 'Basic Pension Plus', a funded plan guaranteed to equal the value of the basic state pension;
- explore phased withdrawal of benefits to encourage people to return to work with 'earnings top-up' scheme.

The Conservative Party is currently the second largest party in the House of Commons and so leads the opposition.

THE LIBERAL DEMOCRATS

Paddy Ashdown

One big idea: constitutional reform

With Labour, the Lib Dems are committed to a joint reform plan, including:

- after referendums, set up Scottish Parliament and Welsh Assembly, elected on a proportional system;
- pass a Freedom of Information Act;
- hold referendum on proportional representation (PR) for election of MPs;
- incorporate the European Convention on Human Rights into UK law;
- remove hereditary peers' right to vote as a step towards an elected second chamber.

The Lib Dems are the third largest party in the House of Commons.

Source: adapted from Daniel (1997a) pp. 32–3

In addition to the larger parties, a number of smaller parties exist, including:

- **Referendum Party**, a single-issue party
  Aim: to have a full public debate on the role of Britain in Europe, followed by a referendum. This means that a question on Europe would be put to the electorate for a direct yes or no decision.
- **UK Independence Party**, a single-issue party
  Aim: British withdrawal from the European Union.
- **Prolife Alliance**, a single-issue party
  Aim: to outlaw abortion.
- **The Green Party**
  Aims: withdrawal from the EU; opposition to a single currency; pro-Bill of Rights and PR at all levels of government.

Source: Daniel (1997a) pp. 24–5

RESEARCHING POLITICAL PARTIES

Using your own knowledge and the mass media sources available to you, find out the answers to the following questions:

1. **Who is your local MP and which party does s/he belong to?**
2. **Who is the speaker of the House of Commons?**
3. **Who is the Secretary of State for Education?**
4. **Who is the leader of the Liberal Democrats?**
5. **Where does the Chancellor of the Exchequer live?**

What is the role of pressure groups in the decision-making process?

A pressure group consists of a group of people who share a common concern or interest. The group uses its power to try to influence the government in order to get its views heard and its policies adopted.

Pressure groups can vary enormously, which makes it very difficult to generalize about them. Broadly, there are two types of pressure groups: protective and promotional.

Protective groups seek to protect or defend their members' interests.

Table 9.4 Protective pressure groups

Trade unions	Professional associations	Other groups
Banking, Insurance and Finance Union (BIFU)	Law Society (solicitors)	Automobile Association (AA)
Fire Brigades Union (FBU)	British Medical Association (BMA)	
National Union of Journalists (NUJ)	British Dental Association (BDA)	

Promotional groups seek to promote a cause, to achieve a particular set of changes or to campaign on a specific issue. Examples include:

- Amnesty International
- Anti-Racist Alliance
- Campaign for Press and Broadcasting Freedom
- Campaign for Real Ale
- Child Poverty Action Group
- Greenpeace
- Shelter.

CASE STUDY: AMNESTY INTERNATIONAL – A PROMOTIONAL GROUP

Amnesty International (AI) is a worldwide organization that campaigns for:

- human rights;
- the release of prisoners of conscience – people who have been wrongly imprisoned or who are in prison because of their beliefs;
- fair trials for political prisoners;
- an end to torture and the death penalty.

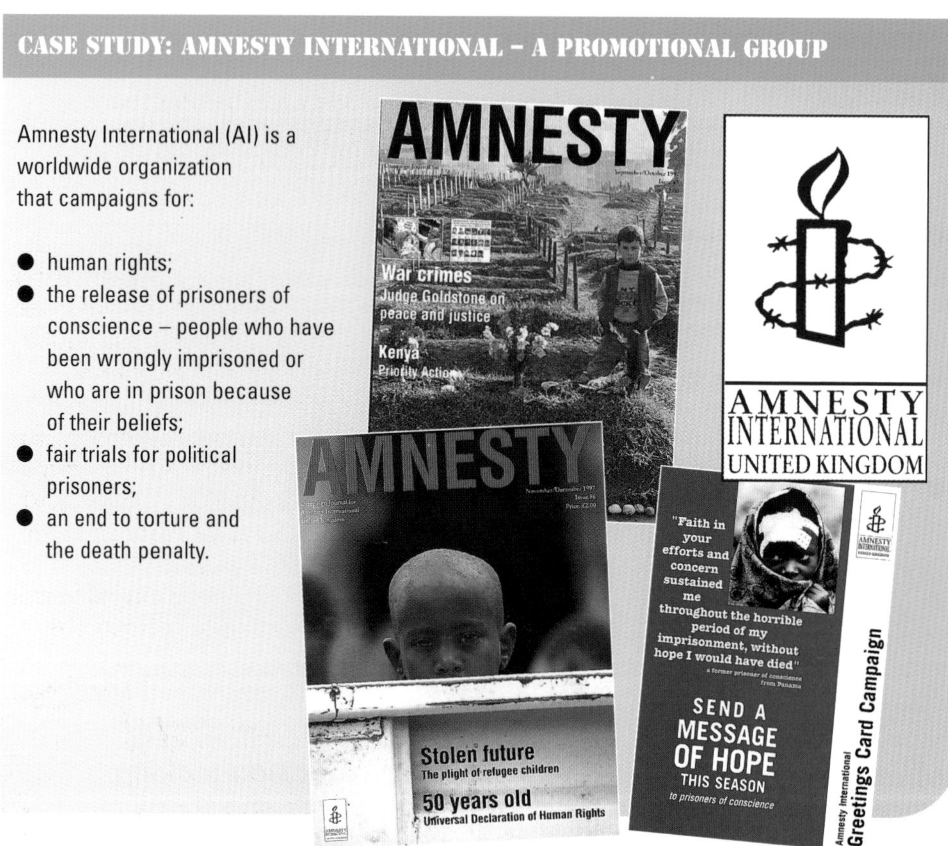

The distinction between protective and promotional groups is not always a useful one. This is because some pressure groups are both protective and promotional. An alternative way of looking at pressure groups is to distinguish between insider and outsider groups.

Insider groups are those that are consulted by government departments, civil servants and ministers in the process of preparing new policy proposals. The Automobile Association, for example, is likely to be consulted on issues concerning road policy. Some groups are consulted automatically, for example the Confederation of British Industry (CBI), so they are in a strong position to influence government policy.

Outsider groups are not consulted automatically because, often, their aims are not recognized by government. On the other hand, some outsider groups are not consulted because although their aims may be recognized by government, their methods of promoting those aims are not. For example, on an issue such as the prevention of cruelty to animals, the government might consult the RSPCA (an insider pressure group) but not the Animal Liberation Front (an outsider pressure group).

Tactics and practices commonly used by pressure groups

Insider groups engage in vigorous campaigning in order to raise their profile and become insider groups in the first place. Having done this, they are then in a favoured position where they will be consulted by government. Although they will continue to engage in campaigning or organizing events to attract publicity and focus attention on their aims, their publicity stunts will usually be legal ones.

Outsider or protest groups are not often invited to give their opinions. Instead, they adopt a variety of campaigning methods in order to try to influence press or public opinion, build up public support and then persuade government to adopt a certain policy or change its position.

Pressure group activity varies according to the aims of the group and their insider/outsider status. Pressure group tactics are varied and a number of possibilities exist. They may:

- Visit MPs in Parliament or write to them. During the passage of legislation, a group can send signed petitions or letters from members of the public to MPs, putting forward its position. The group can also arrange a mass lobby of Parliament, in which a large number of people present their views to MPs in Westminster.
- Sponsor a political party financially. Trade unions contribute money to the Labour Party, providing around half of its annual income. Some big companies make financial contributions to the Conservative Party. Marks and Spencer, for example, donated £40,000 to the Conservative Party in 1996. (Source: 'Jobs and money', *The Guardian*, 19 July 1997, p. 19.)
- Undertake research and provide research findings to the decision makers in the hope that they will respond. Pressure groups are able to provide the government with expert advice on a particular issue.

LOOKING AT PRESSURE GROUPS

The extract below provides an example of research sponsored by a pressure group. (See also page 245.)

1 Which pressure group sponsored this research?
2 According to this information, which group is:
   (a) more likely to end up in court?
   (b) less likely to end up in court?

One Law for the Rich and One Law for the Poor

CHILD POVERTY ACTION GROUP

The Child Poverty Action Group's report published in July 1997, entitled 'Poverty, Crime and Punishment', argues that a two-tier legal system has been established in which the rich are free to commit multi-million-pound white-collar fraud and corruption while the police concentrate on catching the poor.

Law enforcers and politicians are turning a blind eye to white-collar crimes largely because they are considered victimless and are being carried out by wealthy people. People involved in cheating the DSS, on the other hand, are far more likely to end up in court even though the cost of their crime is much less than white-collar offences.

More than £6 billion in unpaid tax was recovered in the year ending April 1995, yet only 357 people were prosecuted – of which just nine were for tax evasion – compared to 9,546 fraud cases mounted by the DSS. Most of these cases involved small amounts of money and saved an estimated £650 million.

Dee Cook, the report's author, concludes: 'In an increasingly divided society, there has been an intensified policing and punishment of poorer individuals and communities. The poor are filtered into the criminal justice system while the rich are filtered out.'

Source: adapted from Bennetto (1997)

- Organize a petition and get as many people to sign it as possible, for example in the summer of 1997, Amnesty International (AI) organized a petition to Jack Straw MP, the Home Secretary, asking the government to end the arbitrary detention of asylum seekers in the UK. AI believe that hundreds of people, fleeing from persecution abroad, are being held in British prisons and detention centres without charge.
- Contact the media directly, for example by writing letters to the press, placing an advertisement in the press, appearing on television.
- Get sponsored by or support from a well-known personality, for example lots of celebrities from the film and music industry, including David Bowie, Skin from Skunk Anansie and Tim Burgess from The Charlatans, who have given their support to Amnesty International.
- Organize a demonstration or protest campaign, for example the action taken against the building of the additional runway at Manchester Airport in 1997.
- A trade union can undertake strike action.
- Undertake non-violent direct action, for example protest groups such as hunt saboteurs disrupting a fox hunt.

Some outsider protest groups, however, engage in illegal activities that may result in the arrest of campaigners, such as:

- the arson of holiday homes in Wales owned by non-Welsh families;
- arson attacks by some animal rights groups;
- obstruction of the highway, e.g. the Greenham Common protesters;
- the anti-poll tax campaign – some protesters had to appear in court for non-payment of the poll tax.

Unconventional but effective protest can be made by pressure groups

Trade union strike action

DIRECT ACTION PROTESTS

Read through the extract below and answer the questions that accompany it.

Britain is believed now to have more grass roots direct action environmental and social justice groups than ever before. A* Guardian *survey conducted with 12 organizations shows that there have been over 500 separate actions against authorities in the past year. The depth of dissatisfaction with the decision-making process and the increasing tendency for people to resort to direct action to assert what they say are their rights is thought to be unique in post-war Britain.*

According to opinion polls, there is increasing public support for direct action protests. A Gallup survey shows that 68 per cent of people believe there are times when protesters are right to break the law.

Source: Vidal and Bellos (1996) p. 5

1. Discuss the possible reasons why more people seem to be getting involved in protest groups.
2. Do you agree that there are times when protesters are right to break the law? When? Why? Why not?
3. Make a note of three important points raised during your discussions.

* 'grass roots' refers to ordinary people.

The role and importance of pressure groups

It is possible to identify two approaches to the question of the role and importance of pressure groups. These are the positive, or pluralist, view and the conflict view.

The positive, or pluralist, view

Pluralists argue that a whole range, or plurality, of views, opinions and interests exists in society. No single group dominates the political process or decision making.

According to the pluralist view, pressure groups play an important role in a democratic society. They are a means by which like-minded people can come together to put forward their views. In this way, all opinions and interests can be heard. Such groups allow us to participate in the political process and to influence the decision-making process.

Pressure groups help politicians to keep in touch with the wishes of the grass roots. Through our involvement in a pressure group or protest movement, we can inform the government of our views in between elections. The former Conservative government was forced to reconsider its policy on the poll tax once it realized the strength of popular feeling against this tax.

Pressure group activity keeps the public informed about important issues and also raises new issues. Environmental groups, for example, have raised our awareness of the dangers of acid rain and damage to the ozone layer, as well as issues to do with transport policy and pollution. As a result of animal rights campaigns, many consumers now check products to ensure that they have not been tested on animals before purchasing them.

Pressure groups often consist of people who are experts in their field. They are therefore in a position to provide government policy makers with expert and informed opinion.

The conflict view

According to the conflict approach, society is based on conflicting interests between different groups. Some groups are much more powerful than others and can dominate the political process and decision making. Some groups' power is based on their ownership of property and wealth. This gives them greater status and they are therefore able to exert more influence on policy makers, possibly behind the scenes. It is argued that governments are more willing (or can be forced) to listen to some groups rather than others, for example the CBI is more influential than the Child Poverty Action Group.

Pressure groups v. political parties

- Pressure groups seek to influence the government but they do not wish to form a government. They do not seek to win electoral power. Political parties, on the other hand, seek to have their MPs elected and to form a government.
- Pressure groups are usually single-issue organizations (for example focusing on human rights or animal welfare), although there is evidence that this is changing. Political parties have policies on a whole range of issues, such as education, welfare, the economy and defence.

CHECK YOUR UNDERSTANDING

1. Briefly explain how a promotional pressure group differs from a protective pressure group. (2 marks)
2. Identify and describe two methods which pressure groups may use to try to influence political decision making. (4 marks)
3. How does a pressure group differ from a political party? (2 marks)

VOTING BEHAVIOUR

The right to vote in elections is an important feature of a democratic society. Sociologists are interested in studying voting behaviour – how people vote and why they vote as they do. It is possible to identify four main types of voter: loyal, floating, abstainers and tactical voters.

What are these different types of voter?

Loyal voters remain loyal to one political party and always vote for that party. Party loyalty, however, appears to be declining. In 1997, for example, many people voted Labour for the first time and 14 per cent of 1992 Conservatives switched to Labour.

Floating voters are those people who vote for one party at one election and another at a later election. They float or switch from one party to another.

Abstainers are those who do not vote at all at a particular election. People may abstain for a number of reasons, including:

- apathy – some people are bored with, or indifferent to, politics – they are simply not interested;
- lack of knowledge may play a part – people do not know enough about the political process;

GENERAL ELECTION TURNOUT

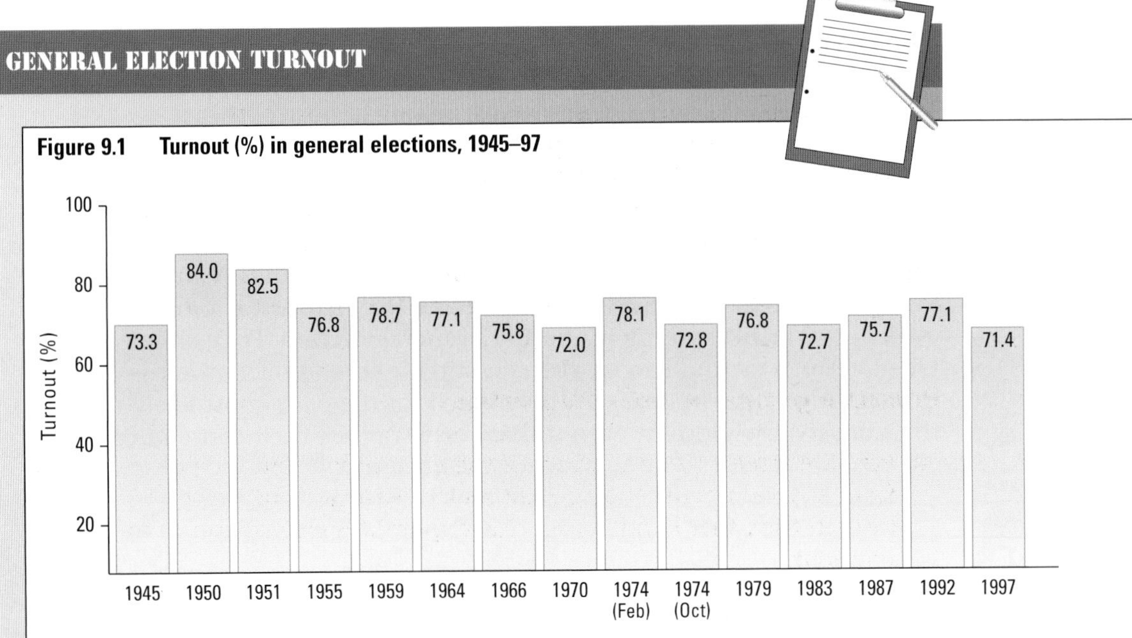

Figure 9.1 Turnout (%) in general elections, 1945–97

Source: Williams (1997a) p. 34

According to this information:

1. In which year were there two general elections?
2. Since 1945, in which general election has turnout been the highest?
3. What percentage of those registered to vote abstained in 1997?

- people may disagree with the policies of all of the parties so they do not vote;
- people may feel disillusioned with politics;
- a person may live in a constituency with a safe seat – one in which a particular party is bound to win. If so, he or she may think that there is no point in voting because the result is a foregone conclusion.

Other people may be prevented from voting because:

- they may be ill or otherwise unable to vote on election day;
- they may not be on the electoral register so they will be unable to vote.

Turnout varies from constituency to constituency. John Williams (1997) points out that in the 1997 general election, in some poorer inner-city constituencies, only slightly over half of those registered to vote actually turned out.

He suggests that little of the 1997 election campaign seemed to be aimed at the plight of the poor.

Rocking the Young into Vote Awareness

Rock the Vote will enlist the help of pop stars to promote awareness of politics and aims to culminate in a Band Aid-style concert in the run up to the 1997 general election.

Adverts in youth magazines and on television will encourage young people to register and then use their vote. They will try to combat a disillusionment with British politics which resulted in 40 per cent of 18–25-year-olds not voting in the 1992 election – either because of non-registration or apathy – compared with about 22 per cent of the population as a whole.

Source: adapted from Bellos (1996) p. 3

WHY DO YOUNG PEOPLE ABSTAIN?

1 In a small group, discuss the possible reasons why young people aged 18–25 are more likely to abstain from voting than any other age group.
2 Make a note of three possible reasons.

Tactical voters are those who adopt a particular strategy in deciding who to vote for rather than automatically voting for their first choice. There was evidence of tactical voting in the 1997 general election. For example, some Liberal Democrat and Labour voters cast their vote to maximize the anti-Conservative vote. In doing so, they voted for the party most likely to defeat the Conservatives locally, even if that party was not their first choice.

CHECK YOUR UNDERSTANDING

Identify and explain two reasons why some people who are entitled to vote in a general election might not do so. (4 marks)

What factors affect voting?

Sociologists are interested in explaining why the electorate votes as it does. A number of factors that influence voting behaviour have been identified. These include social class, gender, age and geography.

Social class

Up until the 1970s, social class was considered to be the single most important influence on voting behaviour in Britain. Support for the two main parties was based broadly on social class. Working-class people tended to vote Labour while middle-class people tended to vote Conservative.

Over the last 25 years, however, the social class structure has changed. This has meant that social class is no longer as strong a predictor of voting behaviour as it was in the past.

Table 9.5 shows the link between class and voting in the 1992 and 1997 general elections. Classes AB and C1 are middle class, while classes C2, D and E are working class. We can see that partly skilled manual workers were more likely to vote Labour, while professional and managerial employees were more likely to vote Conservative.

HOW DIFFERENT SOCIAL CLASSES VOTE

According to the information in Table 9.5:

1 Was there an increase or a decrease in the working-class Labour vote (C2, D and E) between 1992 and 1997?
2 Was there an increase or a decrease in the middle-class Labour vote (AB and C1) between 1992 and 1997?
3 For which party were those in professional and managerial occupations more likely to vote in both 1992 and in 1997?
4 Which social class was most likely to vote Conservative in 1997?
5 Which social classes were more likely to vote Labour in 1997?

Table 9.5 How the electorate voted by social class: 1992 compared to 1997 (%)

	Cons.		Lab.		Lib. Dem.	
	1992	1997	1992	1997	1992	1997
AB – professional managerial	57	42	20	31	21	21
C1 – white collar	41	26	33	47	24	19
C2 – skilled manual workers	38	25	41	54	18	14
DE – partly skilled manual workers	37	21	47	61	15	13

Sources: NOP/BBC exit poll, 1 May 1997; NOP/BBC exit poll, 9 April 1992; Curtice (1997)

From the results of the 1997 general election, we can see that those in professional and managerial occupations were still more likely to vote Conservative. Those in working-class occupations were more likely to vote Labour. In fact, the Labour Party secured support from across all social classes but the gain in support was most marked among white-collar workers.

Age and gender

In the 1992 general election, slightly more women than men voted Conservative and slightly more men voted Labour. In the 1997 general election, however, there was virtually no difference in the way men and women voted. Traditionally, young people have been more likely to vote Labour and older people have been more inclined to vote Conservative. In the 1997 general election, Labour led the Conservatives in all age groups except those over 65.

AGE, GENDER AND VOTING

Table 9.6 The 1997 general election

	Con. %	Lab. %	Lib. Dem. %
Men	31	44	17
Women	32	44	17
First-time voter	19	57	18
All 18–29	22	57	17
30–44	26	49	17
45–64	33	43	18
65+	44	34	16

Source: NOP/BBC exit poll; Williams (1997b) pp. 6-8

1 According to the information in Table 9.6:
(a) Which party were both men and women least likely to vote for?
(b) Which age group was most likely to support Labour?
2 Use this information to show that men and women voted in similar ways in 1997.

Ethnicity

Sociologists point to the important link between ethnicity and voting behaviour. In the 1992 general election, 90 per cent of voters from an African-Caribbean background and 71 per cent of voters from an Asian background voted Labour. This link can be explained partly in terms of social class and also as a result of Labour's image as the party taking an interest in the problems and issues facing black Britons.

THE MINORITY VOTE

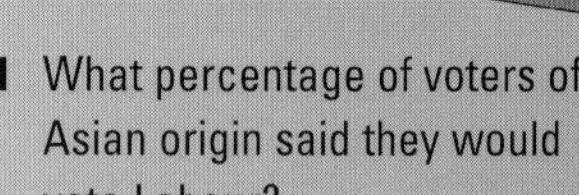

Labour Risks Losing its Grip on an Upwardly Mobile Minority

Research suggests that British Asians, who contribute £5 billion to the economy each year, are shifting their allegiance from Labour as their prosperity grows. Nevertheless, seven out of ten voters of Asian origin still said in a MORI poll that they would vote Labour ... But analysts have also noticed dissatisfaction among young, third-generation Britons from Asian families who feel disenfranchised. Like many young black people, they reject the British political system as racist and will not vote.*

Source: Lee (1997), p. 14

According to this information:

1 What percentage of voters of Asian origin said they would vote Labour?
2 Are British Asians more or less likely to vote Labour as they become more prosperous?
3 Why do many young black people not vote?

* 'Disenfranchised' – little of the election campaign was aimed towards them.

Geography

Voting behaviour is also linked to geography. Traditionally, the Conservative Party has been more popular in the south of England outside London, while the Labour Party has been more popular in the north of England and in Scotland. In the May 1997 general election, this divide became more marked as the Conservative Party lost all of its ten seats in Scotland. It also lost its single seat in Wales.

In general, people living in inner-city areas are more likely to support Labour, while those in rural areas and the suburbs are more likely to vote Conservative. After the 1997 general election, the Conservative Party was left with almost no representation in urban areas. Its support was based mainly in the countryside and some suburbs.

Religion

In some countries religion is an important factor in political life and in voting behaviour. In Northern Ireland, for example, links between religion and politics are important. In England, there is some evidence to suggest that Anglicans are more likely to support the Conservatives and Catholics to support Labour.

Policies

In the 1997 general election, Labour voters were asked by ICM (an opinion polling company) what the most important factors in their decisions to vote were. The results showed that:

- 40 per cent believed it was time for a change of government;
- 39 per cent mentioned policies on health and the welfare state;

VOTING PATTERNS

Figure 9.4 How Britain voted, 1 May 1997

KEY: % of vote — Conservative, Labour, Lib. Dem.

Scotland (SNP)
North East
North West
Yorkshire and Humberside
East Midlands
Wales (Plaid Cymru)
West Midlands
East Anglia
South West
Greater London
South East

Source: Williams (1997a), p. 34

1 Discuss the possible reasons why voting patterns vary from region to region in Britain.
2 Make a note of three possible reasons.

- 36 per cent mentioned policies on education;
- 19 per cent had always supported Labour.

In the run up to the 1992 general election, Heath (1992) emphasized the importance of voters' judgements about the competence of political parties in managing the economy and the welfare state in explaining electoral change.

Studies of voting behaviour indicate that self-interest is important. Many voters vote with their wallets for the party that they see as most likely to bestow prosperity.

Party leaders

John Major was regarded as an asset to the Conservative Party during the 1992 general election. Of the three party leaders on offer at the time (John Major, Neil Kinnock for Labour, Paddy Ashdown for the Liberal Democrats), he was seen by voters as likely to make the best prime minister.

Since Tony Blair became leader of the Labour Party in July 1994, he has been identified by twice as many electors as the person most likely to make the best prime minister.

Party image

In addition to other factors influencing voting behaviour, we must also consider party image – that is, our image of what the political parties stand for. Although such images are not necessarily totally accurate, they do affect the way people view the political parties and their policies.

During the 1980s, the images of the two main political parties were quite markedly different from each other. The Conservative Party was seen as standing for individual freedom, the middle class, law and order, business interests and defence. The Labour Party was seen as the party of the traditional working class, associated with government intervention, a tax and spend economic policy, welfare and trade unions.

During the 1990s, the Conservative Party image has been damaged by various allegations of sleaze. John Williams, writing in 1995, pointed to the appeal and image of 'new Labour'. He stated that polls indicated that people liked Tony Blair and the general direction of the 'new Labour' Party. Such images are partly created by the media and though they may not be accurate, they do help people decide how to vote.

The media

Wagg (1994) points to the changing relationship between politicians and the media. During the 1950 general election, all party leaders refused an invitation to speak on television. No mention of the election was made on television until after the polls had closed.

The link between politicians and the media has now become much closer as politicians recognize the importance of wooing the electorate through the media. The former leader of the Labour Party, Neil Kinnock, appeared in a pop video with Tracy Ullman and, as Prime Minister, John Major was interviewed on Radio 1 by DJ Steve Wright. Political parties now employ media advisors and 'spin doctors' whose job it is to try to 'manage' news.

The role of the mass media is particularly important during general election campaigns. In general terms, we can say that, since 1945, the press have been more supportive of the Conservatives than of Labour. During the 1992 general election campaign, five out of six national tabloid newspapers supported the Conservative Party. *The Sun*'s front page headline read: 'If Neil Kinnock wins today, will the last person to leave Britain please turn out the lights?' Once the Conservative Party's victory was announced, *The Sun* headline stated: 'It's the Sun wot won it'.

The changing face of *The Sun*

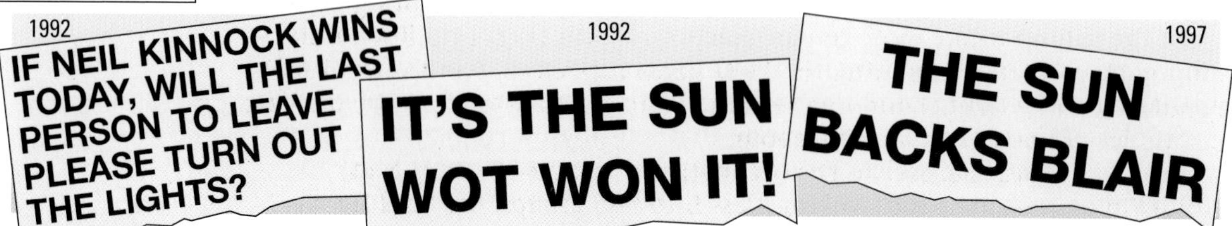

During the 1997 general election, however, newspaper coverage was more in favour of new Labour. For example, *The Sun* announced its support for Blair and new Labour with its 'The Sun Backs Blair' headline, while a total of six national dailies backed the Labour Party.

Research evidence on the impact of the media on voting behaviour during an election campaign is not clear cut. It is also necessary to consider the long-term 'drip, drip, drip' effect of the media rather than just looking at the short-term impact of the media during elections.

Figure 9.5 **Free Press? Partisan support of national daily newspapers by circulation, 1945–92**

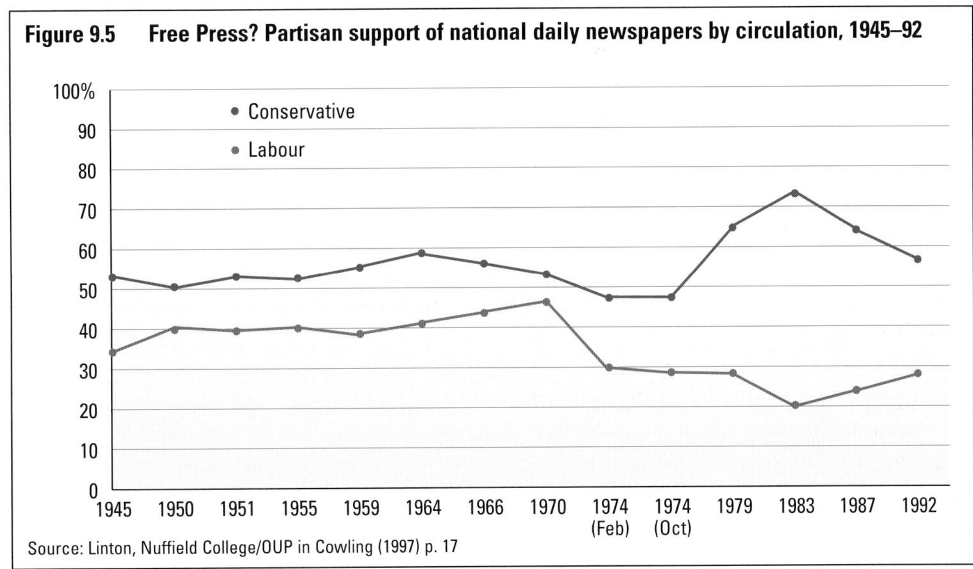

Source: Linton, Nuffield College/OUP in Cowling (1997) p. 17

What are the trends in voting behaviour since the 1950s?

Since the 1950s, a number of trends in support for the political parties can be identified.

Two-party decline

The two major parties, Conservative and Labour, have gradually lost support at elections in terms of the percentage of the electorate voting for them. In the 1950s, the two main parties shared the bulk of votes. In 1951, 96.8 per cent of votes were cast for either Labour or the Conservatives. In the 1955 general election, this figure stood at 96.6 per cent. By October 1974, however, only 76.9 per cent of votes were cast for the two main parties. In 1997, 75 per cent of votes were cast for either Labour or the Conservatives. This means that there has been a rise in **third-party voting**. In 1955, only 3.4 per cent of the vote in Britain went to other parties. By 1987, the Liberals/SDP had 25.2 per cent of the vote, but by 1997 they had only 17 per cent.

Class dealignment

Up until the 1997 general election, the links between class and voting behaviour appeared to be declining. In particular, there had been a decline in the working-class Labour vote. After the 1987 general election, Ivor Crewe (1987) argued that while the Labour vote remained largely working class, the working class no longer remained largely Labour.

This was because changes in the occupational or class structure had resulted in a division of the working class into two groups: the 'traditional'

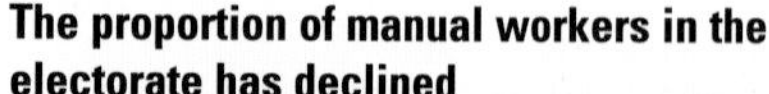
The proportion of manual workers in the electorate has declined

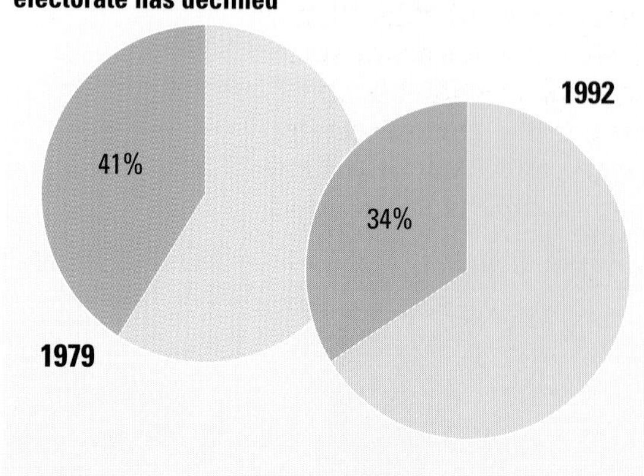

working class, which is shrinking, and the 'new' working class, which is growing. The latter appeared to be more likely to vote Conservative and less likely to vote Labour. As a result of the shrinking of the traditional working class, we can say that the Labour Party's traditional class base is declining. (For more on the contemporary class structure, see Chapter 3 on Stratification and Differentiation.)

Rallings and Thrasher (1997) point out that, between 1979 and 1992, the proportion of manual workers in the electorate declined from 41 per cent to 34 per cent.

A smaller and smaller proportion of the electorate can now be seen as typically working class. This means that Labour's traditional electoral base is being eroded. Despite this, in 1997 the Labour Party won a landslide victory, gaining the support of manual workers and clerical workers. New Labour was successful because it managed to appeal to, and gain support from, a wide social base.

Gender

The links between gender and voting behaviour are declining in that women and men are now voting in similar ways (see p. 275). The gender gap in voting has disappeared.

CHECK YOUR UNDERSTANDING

1 Thirty years ago sociologists believed that social class was important in affecting how people vote. Why might social class be less important in affecting how people vote in general elections in the 1990s? (10 marks)

2 Identify four factors, other than social class, which might affect the way a person votes in an election. (4 marks)

How influential are opinion polls?

Opinion polls are one type of social survey and are used for various purposes.

- Market research companies use opinion polls to find out consumer preferences, for example regarding beer or soap powder.
- Opinion polls are used to find out our views on topical issues, such as the NHS or capital punishment.
- Opinion polls are carried out in order to discover voters' intentions in the run up to elections. These opinion polls are conducted by organizations such as ICM, Gallup, Harris and MORI and the results are published in the press.

In conducting an opinion poll, the questionnaire or survey method is used (see Chapter 2, pp. 9–17). A sample or subgroup of the population is selected for questioning because it would be far too expensive and time consuming to ask everyone's opinion on an issue. The sample must be representative or typical of the population if the results are to be considered reliable.

Opinion polls on voting intentions

The results of opinion polls on voting behaviour are not always reliable. Opinion polls indicated that the Labour Party would win the 1970 general election and that the Conservatives would win the February 1974 general election but these predictions proved to be inaccurate. In the run up to the 1992 general election, some of the opinion pollsters put Labour ahead by a small margin. In the event, the Conservatives were returned to government with a small majority.

> *The polls failed spectacularly in the 1992 general election. Of the 50 polls on voting intention published during the 1992 campaign, 39 registered Labour leads. In the event, the Conservatives scored a 7.6 per cent lead over Labour – a gap of 2.5 million voters. Since then, the pollsters have done much to remedy their 1992 errors.*
>
> Source: Cowling (1997) pp. 16–18

A number of reasons have been put forward to explain why opinion polls can get it wrong.

- Sampling errors – the sample may not be a typical or representative sample of the population or it may be too small.
- People may not respond truthfully, they may change their minds at the last minute or they may not bother to vote on the day.
- The questions asked may be poorly worded.
- Interviewer bias may affect the results.
- Timing – some of those canvassed for their opinion may not yet have decided. They will therefore be registered as 'don't knows'. It has been found that the closer to the general election the poll is done, the more reliable the predictions will be as people are more likely to have made up their minds by then.

Reflecting or directing?

Some sociologists have suggested that the results of opinion polls may affect the outcome of the election rather than just informing about voting intentions. To illustrate this point, let's say that the results of an opinion poll were as follows:

Labour	**40%**
Liberal Democrats	**35%**
Conservative	**10%**
Other	**15%**
	100%

This opinion poll suggests that the Conservative Party has little chance of winning. Mr Blue, who would have voted Conservative, may now switch to the Liberal Democrats in order to try to defeat the Labour Party.

Such voting behaviour is known as tactical voting (see p. 274), in which voters do not vote for the party of their first preference. Instead, they vote for the party which they least dislike in order to keep a third party out.

If an opinion poll suggests that one party is likely to get a large majority, then some of its supporters may not bother to vote. They abstain from voting because the outcome of the election may seem to be inevitable. If this happens on a large scale then the party which was predicted to win may do less well.

When the results of an opinion poll are published, the 'bandwagon effect' may occur. Some of us may jump on the bandwagon and vote for the party which the opinion poll predicts will win. If this happens then the opinion poll has done more than make a prediction – it has actually influenced the outcome of the election.

In the 1997 general election, many of the problems associated with opinion polls seem to have been ironed out. The pollsters' results were considered to be close to the final result. Over 40 surveys were carried out during the campaign and all but two were within three points of the actual outcome.

READING THE POLLS

Examine the information in Table 9.7 and answer the questions.

Table 9.7: Final opinion polls before the 1997 general election (%)

	Lab.	Con.	Lib. Dem.	Other	Lab lead over Con.	Lab lead error
ICM	43	33	18	6	10	–3
Gallup	46	33	16	5	13	0
Final result	44	31	17	7	13	n/a

Source: *The Guardian*, 3 May 1997

1 Which opinion poll company predicted that Labour would have a lead of 13 per cent over the Conservatives?
2 Was this prediction reliable?
3 Which opinion poll company's prediction came closest to Labour's actual final result?
4 Which party did the polls agree would gain a 33 per cent share of the votes?

CHECK YOUR UNDERSTANDING

1 Explain in full two reasons why the results of an opinion poll conducted during a general election campaign may be inaccurate. (4 marks)
2 Sociologists have argued that opinion polls may affect the results of an election. State two ways in which this may happen. (2 marks)

POLITICAL SOCIALIZATION

What is political socialization and how does it occur?

Socialization refers to the process whereby we learn the culture and way of life of our society (see pp. 32–5). An important part of this process involves political socialization, during which we acquire the political attitudes, values and preferences that affect our views on politics, our participation in political activities and the way we vote.

The influences that are directly involved in the process of political socialization include our family, school, workplace and the mass media. They are known as the agencies of political socialization.

Families

Our parents' attitudes can have a powerful influence on us. They can affect our views on political issues, our political values and our voting behaviour. If members of our family are involved in a pressure group such as the Campaign for Press and Broadcasting Freedom, for example, then this is likely to raise our awareness of media issues. If our parents are from Ireland then we are likely to be more aware than others of issues surrounding the conflict in Northern Ireland. If they are actively involved in a trade union at work, then some of their views may rub off on us.

Peer groups

Most of us are influenced to some extent by our peers or friends. The attitudes of peer groups may have an impact on our political views and participation. The extract on the right suggests that although membership of protest groups is open to anybody, in reality members tend not to be drawn from the whole community.

> *Membership of new social movements such as environmental groups, feminist groups, anti-racist groups, anti-war groups, Gay Rights organizations and animal rights groups is usually drawn from a restricted section of the wider community. Generally, members tend to be young people between the ages of 16–30 from the middle class. Many of them are students or unemployed.*
>
> Source: Hallsworth (1994)

The workplace

Workplaces vary in their culture. In general terms, people who work in heavy industries, such as mining and shipbuilding, have traditionally supported Labour. There is some evidence that public sector employees, such as those in social work and teaching, are more likely to support Labour and to oppose the public spending cuts of past Conservative governments.

The media

The media are increasingly important in the process of political socialization because, for most of us, they are our main source of information on political events, issues and personalities. The media set the agenda of public discussion and debate. This means that they decide which issues are important, newsworthy or topical. This gives them a lot of influence. The media create a general climate of opinion within which our attitudes are formed. (For more on mass media, see Chapter 10.)

CHECK YOUR UNDERSTANDING

1 To what extent do the press influence our political opinions and beliefs? (4 marks)

2 Identify and describe two ways, other than through the mass media, in which our political attitudes and beliefs are formed. (4 marks)

SUMMARY

In this chapter, we have covered the following points:

- **Politics is about power relationships within society.**
- **Power can be based on the use of force: coercion. It can also be based on agreement or consent: authority.**
- **Democracy is a system of government in which people choose their rulers or representatives by voting in elections. Sociologists argue about how democratic a nation Britain is, citing our hereditary monarchy and unelected House of Lords as examples of undemocratic institutions.**

- **Dictatorship occurs when a leader or single party obtains complete power, usually by force.**
- **The state consists of those institutions within society which make laws, implement them and enforce them (e.g. Parliament, the civil service, the courts and the police).**
- **Elections provide an opportunity for the adult population to vote for representatives in Parliament – MPs.**
- **Different political parties represent different beliefs and policies on a whole range of issues, such as health, education, the economy and crime control. At a general election, the winning political party can claim that it has the authority (a mandate) to carry out its policies.**
- **Pressure groups also seek to influence government policy and decision making. They are usually single-issue organizations made up of people who share a common concern or interest. They do not seek to win electoral power.**
- **Sociologists are interested in studying how people vote and why they vote as they do. Broadly speaking, voters fall into one of four categories:**
  - **Loyal voters, who consistently vote for the same party.**
  - **Floating voters, who switch parties from election to election.**
  - **Abstainers, who do not vote at all at a particular election.**
  - **Tactical voters, who adopt a particular strategy in deciding who to vote for rather than automatically voting for their first choice.**
- **Various factors influence voting behaviour, including social class background, age, gender, ethnicity, geography and religious belief.**
- **Sociologists have noted a number of broad trends in voting behaviour since the 1950s. These include an increase in class and gender dealignment and a rise in third-party voting.**
- **Opinion polls try to discover people's voting intentions in the run up to elections. The results are not always reliable, for example in the 1992 general election. Sociologists argue about whether opinion polls have any influence on the outcome of elections.**
- **Political socialization refers to the ways in which we acquire our political attitudes. The factors involved in the process include family background, the influence of peer groups, workplace and the mass media.**

EXAMINATION QUESTION 1

(a) What are some of the problems that pressure groups might face in influencing political decisions and public opinion? (8 marks)

(b) How far is the voting system used in a general election in the United Kingdom fair and democratic? (8 marks)

(c) Explain some of the factors that might affect voting behaviour. (9 marks)

Source: NEAB GCSE Sociology, June 1996, Tier Q, Section B, Question 6, p. 12

EXAMINATION QUESTION 2

Study ***Item A***. Then answer **all** parts of the question that follows.

Item A **A demonstration against the M3 link road at Twyford Down in Hampshire, 1993. Many people were against the route and tried to stop the road being built.**

(a) **(i)** According to **Item A**, what are the people in the picture trying to stop? (1 mark)

(ii) According to **Item A**, what form of protest are they using? (1 mark)

(iii) How might their method help them to achieve their aim? (1 mark)

(b) **(i)** Give one reason why one pressure group might be more successful in achieving its aims than another. (1 mark)

(ii) The people in the picture are using one method. Identify and explain one other way in which a pressure group might try to influence a government. (3 marks)

(c) **(i)** What is a political party? (1 mark)

(ii) Give the name of one political party in Britain. Explain why an individual might vote for this party. (3 marks)

(d) **(i)** Describe what is meant by 'an opinion poll'. (2 marks)

(ii) State two reasons why the results of opinion polls might not be accurate. (2 marks)

Source: SEG GCSE Sociology, Summer 1996, Foundation Tier, Paper 1, Question 7, p. 9

BIBLIOGRAPHY

Bellos, A. (1996) 'Rocking the young into vote awareness', *The Guardian*, 15 January.

Bennetto, J. (1997) 'Rich profit from law's poor policy', *The Independent*, 21 July.

Bryman, A. (1991) 'Charisma and leadership', *Sociology Review*, Volume 1, No. 1 (September).

Clements, R. and Mann, P. (1997) 'General election results, May 1 1997', Research Paper 97/49, House of Commons Library, pp. 5–6.

Cowling, D. (1997) 'Swing highs, swing lows', *New Statesman*, 21 March, pp. 16–18.

Crewe, I. (1987) 'Why Mrs Thatcher was returned with a landslide', *Social Studies Review*, Volume 3, No. 1 (September).

Curtice, J. (1997) 'Anatomy of a non-landslide', *Politics Review*, Volume 7, No. 1 (September), pp. 2–8.

Daniel, C. (1997) 'Beyond the fringe', *New Statesman*, 21 March, pp. 24–25.

Daniel, C. (1997) 'What they want to do', *New Statesman*, 21 March, pp. 32–33.

Denscombe, M. (1997) *Sociology Update*, p.24.

Hallsworth, S. (1994) 'Understanding new social movements', *Sociology Review*, Volume 4, No. 1 (September).

Heath, A. (1992) 'Social class and voting in Britain', *Sociology Review*, Volume 1, No. 4 (April).

Lee, A. (1997) 'Labour risk losing its grip on an upwardly mobile minority', *The Times*, 12 April, p. 14.

Pilger, J. (1996) 'In a land of fear', *The Guardian*, 4 May.

Rallings, C. and Thrasher, M. (1997) 'Can Labour win? Voting and general elections', *Sociology Review* , Volume 6, No. 4 (April).

Riley, Mike. (1992) 'Winner takes all', *Sociology Review*, Volume 2, No. 1 (September).

Social Studies Review, (1990) 'Question & answer: politics', Volume 6. No. 2 (November).

Stewart, B. (1996) 'Millions suffer racism, UN told', *The Guardian*, 4 March.

Vidal, J. and Bellos, A. (1996) 'Protest lobbies unite to guard rights', *The Guardian*, 27 August.

Wagg, S. (1994) 'Politics and the media in postwar Britain', *Sociology Review*, Volume 4, No. 2 (November).

Weber, M. (1921) *Economy and Society* (1978 translated edition), University of California Press.

Williams, J. (1995) 'In focus: power and politics', *Sociology Review*, Volume 5, No. 1, (September).

Williams, J. (1997) 'Research roundup election landslide', *Sociology Review*, Volume 7, No. 1 (September), pp. 6-8.

Williams, J. (1997) 'In focus: The 1997 general election', *Sociology Review*, Volume 7, No. 1 (September).

CHAPTER 10

The Mass Media

In this chapter, we will explore and attempt to answer the following questions:

1. **What are the mass media?**
2. **Ownership and control:**
   - **What are the patterns of press ownership?**
   - **How much control do newspaper owners have over content?**
3. **Media content:**
   - **What factors affect how news is selected and presented?**
   - **How are black people and women represented in the mass media?**
   - **How do the mass media represent deviance?**
4. **Media audiences:**
   - **In what quantities are the media used?**
   - **What are the social patterns in listening, viewing and reading?**
   - **What are the effects of the media on the audience?**
   - **How influential are advertisements?**
   - **What is the role of the mass media in the process of socialization?**

WHAT ARE THE MASS MEDIA?

The mass media are those forms of communication that reach mass or large audiences. They include newspapers, magazines, books, television, radio, cinema and all forms of recorded music.

Most of us have at least some contact with the mass media on a daily basis. It would probably be very difficult to avoid the media altogether. Many of us wake up to a radio alarm call in the morning, read a newspaper or magazine over breakfast, listen to a tape on our Walkman on the way to school or work, read a couple of chapters of a best-selling novel over lunch, video-record our favourite television programme, go to see a film in the evening or watch some television before bed.

The mass media are an increasingly important area of sociological study. Let's begin by examining the division between **press** and **broadcasting**.

The press in Britain

'The press' includes newspapers and magazines, which are privately owned and commercially run as profit-making businesses. Newspapers and magazines are financed through advertisements and sales, which means that they are in competition with each other. Some newspapers are published daily, while others appear on a weekly basis. Some, such as *The Guardian* and the *Daily Express*, are produced for a national market, while others, such as the *Manchester Evening News* and the *Liverpool Echo*, are produced and distributed regionally.

Newspapers can be divided into broadsheets and tabloids. The broadsheet newspapers are about twice the size of the tabloids. Broadsheet newspapers, unlike tabloids, are generally seen as high-quality publications.

BROADSHEETS AND TABLOIDS

For this activity your group will need one copy of a tabloid newspaper and one copy of a broadsheet newspaper.

1 Compare the two and discuss the similarities and differences between them.

Do they, for example, each have horoscopes, cartoons and crosswords? Are there sections on famous celebrities, scandal and gossip? How much emphasis is there on international news, politics, fashion and sports? How much space is taken up by photographs and headlines?

2 Now note down three similarities and three differences between the broadsheet and the tabloid newspaper.

Table 10.1 Broadcasting in Britain

BBC	
Television	*Radio*
BBC 1	National (Radio 1, 2, 3, 4, Radio 5 Live)
BBC 2	Local (e.g. BBC Radio Merseyside, BBC Radio Lancashire)
COMMERCIAL BROADCASTING	
Television	*Radio*
ITV (e.g. Granada, Central)	National (e.g. Talk Radio, Classic FM, Virgin 1215)
Channel 4 (SC4 in Wales)	Local (e.g. Piccadilly Key 103, Radio City)
Channel 5	
Satellite and cable television (e.g. Movie Channel, UK Gold, Eurosport, Discovery)	

Broadcasting in Britain

Broadcasting refers to television and radio. In Britain, broadcasting may be publicly or privately funded. Public sector broadcasting operates through the British Broadcasting Corporation (BBC) which is funded by income from the television licence fee.

Commercial broadcasting is funded mainly by advertisers, who pay for commercials which advertise their products. Recently, there has been a move towards sponsorship as a way of financing commercial television. When sponsoring a programme, a company's logo appears at the beginning and end of the televised programme as well as either side of a commercial break. In return for this advertising, the company contributes financially to the programme's production costs.

Satellite and cable television are funded by advertisers and also by paying subscribers.

SPONSORSHIP

If you are a fan of *Coronation Street*, you will have noticed that the Cadbury's logo is now found at the beginning and end of each episode and either side of a commercial break. In pairs, identify and note down at least three other television programmes that receive such sponsorship.

How has media technology developed over the last 20 years?

Over the last 20 years, there have been important developments in media technology.

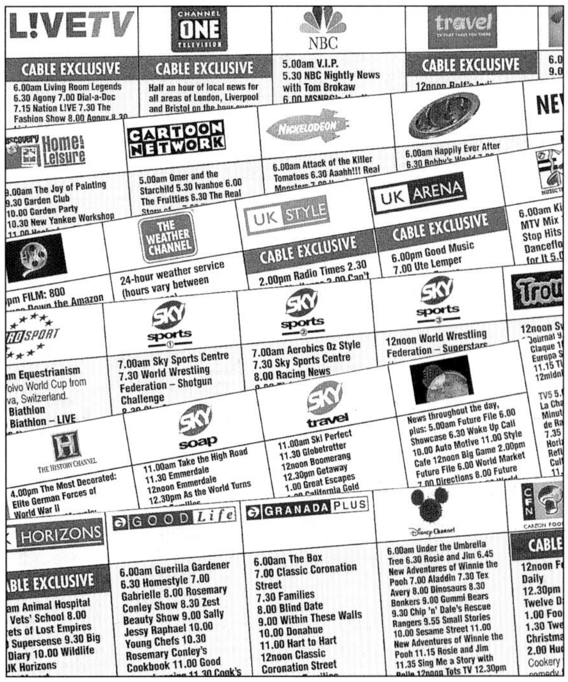

- In 1980, there were only three television channels in Britain: BBC 1, BBC 2 and ITV. These were all terrestrial channels, which means that broadcasts were delivered by ground transmitters rather than by satellite or cable. Since then, the number of channels has increased significantly. In addition to receiving Channel 4 and Channel 5, we can now access what is known as 'New TV'or 'Pay TV'. This includes satellite and cable television for which subscribers pay. Satellite television involves broadcasting via signals which are transmitted by satellite to homes that have a satellite dish aerial. Cable television involves broadcasting via signals which are transmitted by underground cable to subscribers' homes. Having satellite or cable television provides us with a wider choice of channels. Those of us who cannot afford to pay for, or who choose not to subscribe to, cable and satellite television do not have access to new multi-channel television.
- Digital broadcasting is a more recent development that will provide multi-channel television with high-quality picture and sound.
- Viewdata is another important development. Teletext on ITV and Ceefax on BBC give us access to regularly updated news and information on a variety of subjects through our television screens.
- Newspaper production now involves the use of the latest technology such as computerized layout.
- Newer electronic media, such as computers, electronic mail, the Internet and CD-ROM, are likely to transform the nature of the mass media in the future.

MULTI-CHANNEL TELEVISION

1 In a small group, discuss what the benefits of multi-channel television might be to the viewer. Can you think of any disadvantages?
2 Now note down at least two benefits and two disadvantages of multi-channel television.

OWNERSHIP AND CONTROL

What are the patterns of press ownership?

Newspapers in Britain are all privately owned, which means that, potentially, press owners have a lot of influence over content. Let's look at the debate on ownership and control of newspapers in more detail. We'll start off by examining patterns of ownership.

As Table 10.2 shows, eight companies account for the bulk of newspaper sales in Britain. The figures refer to the percentage share of sales for 1995–96. News International, for example, owns Sunday newspapers which represent 37.8 per cent of all Sunday newspaper sales in Britain.

WHO OWNS WHAT?

Table 10.2 National newspaper owners

News International *The Sun, The Times, News of the World* and *The Sunday Times*	Daily 34%	Sunday 37.8%
Mirror Group Newspapers *Daily Mirror, Sunday Mirror, The People* and *Daily Record*	Daily 23.6%	Sunday 29.3%
United News and Media *Daily Express* and *Sunday Express*	Daily 13.9%	Sunday 8.6%
Associated Newspapers *Daily Mail* and *Mail on Sunday*	Daily 13.8%	Sunday 13.0%
Hollinger Inc *The Daily Telegraph* and *Sunday Telegraph*	Daily 7.5%	Sunday 4.2%
Guardian Media Group *The Guardian* and *The Observer*	Daily 2.8%	Sunday 2.9%
Newspaper Publishing *The Independent* and *Independent on Sunday*	Daily 2.1%	Sunday 2.0%
Pearson *Financial Times*	Daily 2.1%	–

Source: adapted from Williams (1996) p. 39

According to the information in Table 10.2:

1 Which two companies together account for over 55 per cent of sales of daily newspapers?
2 Which company publishes the *Sunday Express*?

How much control do newspaper owners have over content?

There is a debate among sociologists about how much control and influence owners of newspapers exercise over the content of their papers. There are two important approaches: the conflict approach and the pluralist approach.

The conflict approach

The conflict approach argues that society is based on conflicting interests between different groups. The owners of newspapers are part of a powerful and wealthy minority group. They are in a strong position to put their own personal views and interests across to the rest of us because, as owners, they are able to control the content of newspapers. They do so in their own interests.

If, for example, a large business concern owns a chain of newspapers, it is likely to encourage the production of news stories and advertisements that support the views of the business world. It is likely to discourage the production of material that is critical of big business. Articles written from the viewpoint of trade unions and environmental groups, for example, are less likely to appear.

On occasions, press owners have intervened directly to influence content. Harry Evans was editor of *The Sunday Times* from 1967 to 1981 and editor of *The Times* from 1981 to 1982. He was allegedly sacked from his post as editor of *The Times* by Rupert Murdoch, the owner, as a result of his (Evans's) political policy.

Supporters of the conflict approach point to the following developments within newspaper companies as evidence to back up their views:

- There has been a concentration of ownership of the press in the hands of a few companies and individuals. This is partly because smaller companies have been swallowed up by media giants.
- There has been a globalization of companies. A small number of massive international companies now have interests in newspapers on a global scale.
- There has been a growth of cross-media ownership. The trend is increasingly for companies to have interests in a range of media so that newspaper owners, for example, also own TV stations, satellite TV channels or radio channels. Mirror Group Newspapers (MGN), for example, owns Live TV and has a 19.9 per cent stake in Scottish TV. MGN also has a 43 per cent stake in Newspaper Publishing, which owns The Independent and Independent on Sunday. United News and Media has a stake of nearly 30 per cent in Channel 5.

This means that a very high proportion of what we see, hear and read comes from a small number of extremely large multinational media empires.

DEVELOPMENT IN NEWSPAPER OWNERSHIP

1 Describe, with examples, two recent developments in newspaper ownership.
2 Some individuals and groups (such as the Campaign for Press and Broadcasting Freedom) express concern over developments in cross-media ownership and believe that government should restrict the growth of media empires. Can you identify two potential dangers of cross-media ownership?

CASE STUDY: RUPERT MURDOCH

- Rupert Murdoch is Chairperson of News Corporation, of which News International is a part. News Corporation now controls about 35 per cent of the national press in the UK, measured in terms of sales. This includes *The Sun, News of the World, The Times, The Sunday Times, The Times* supplements and several evening and weekend newspapers.
- News Corporation is one of the world's largest media companies. It has interests in newspapers not only in the UK but also in Australia, New Zealand and the USA.
- In addition to its newspaper interests, it also has shares in magazines such as *Inside Soap*, HarperCollins book publishers, television films, Twentieth Century-Fox movies, and cable and satellite broadcasting, including a 40 per cent share in BSkyB.

The pluralist approach

According to the pluralist view, a plurality, or whole range, of views and interests exists in society. Unlike the conflict approach, pluralists believe that no one group dominates. The range of opinions is reflected in the whole variety of newspapers and magazines available to us, such as the *Morning Star, The Telegraph, The Sun, Gay Times, Woman's Own, Hi-Fi World, Mojo, The Voice* and *Viz*. Those who support the pluralist approach argue that all points of view and interests are represented within this range.

Pluralists argue that there is no real link between ownership of the press and control of content. Newspapers simply give people what they want. Owners cannot influence the content of newspapers because if they tried to give us what we do not want, we would simply stop buying their product.

According to this view, *The Sun* carries very little international news because its readers do not want this, not because the owners have decided to exclude it.

Pluralism and freedom of the press

The pluralist view supports the idea of freedom of the press. The press is and should be free from the control and interference of owners in the following ways.

- There is freedom to set up new newspapers if existing ones do not meet market demands. Owners cannot simply dictate content but have to give us what we are prepared to buy.
- We, as members of the public, exercise control through our market power. We can easily switch from one newspaper to another if we are unhappy with the content of a newspaper. Many *Sun* readers in Liverpool, for example, stopped buying this newspaper in 1989 because they were offended by the way in which it reported on the Hillsborough Stadium disaster. It was felt that *The Sun* misrepresented the behaviour of Liverpool football supporters and misled readers.
- We can put forward our views on an issue and have them published by writing to the editor of a newspaper.
- On a day-to-day basis, the media professionals, such as journalists and editors, exercise control over content.

OWNERSHIP AND CONTROL

Write a paragraph to summarize:

1 the conflict approach;

2 the pluralist approach.

to the debate on ownership and control of newspapers.

MEDIA CONTENT

One important area of study within the sociology of the media is that of content. Sociologists have, for example, examined the way in which the content of the news on television and in newspapers is manufactured. They have also examined media content in order to explore the images of women and black people that are represented.

The selection and presentation of news

It is easy for us to take the content of news on television and in the press for granted as somehow fixed. Sociologists, however, point out that the news is, in fact, manufactured or made. They focus in particular on the issue of how news is selected and presented.

Selection of news

There is a potentially limitless number of issues, events and viewpoints in society. Sociologists are interested in discovering what sort of issues are selected and included in the media and what sort of issues are excluded. They question why certain issues are selected and covered in the media while others are ignored.

Presentation of news

Sociologists are also interested in examining how the material is presented. Is it presented in a fair and neutral way or in a biased and one-sided way? Two processes employed by the media in the selection and presentation of news content have been identified as **agenda setting** and **norm referencing**.

Agenda setting

This refers to the way the news media tell us what the relevant issues are at any one point in time. Television news programmes, for example, may not tell us what to think but they do influence what we think about. In this sense, they set the agenda of public discussion by including some views, stories and information and excluding others.

Norm referencing

This describes the way in which the news media outline the acceptable boundaries of behaviour. This is done by presenting the behaviour and views of some groups in a positive way and those of others in a more negative way.

Norm referencing

What factors affect how news is selected and presented?

A number of factors that affect what we get to see, hear and read in the news have been identified. As we have seen, one view is that content is heavily influenced by the views of owners. Although this might be the case with some sections of the media, such as newspapers, the BBC is technically without owners; it is 'owned' by the state, so the debate concerning the owners' influence on content is not strictly applicable to the BBC. The second view that we examined, that from the pluralist approach, suggests that one of the most important influences on content is simply consumer demand. In addition to the possible influences of owners and consumers, a number of other factors have been identified.

What are the other influences on content?

Newspaper space and television time

Daily newspapers have fixed amounts of space that must be filled each day. Televised news broadcasts have fixed amounts of time to fill. This means that journalists cannot just sit around waiting for something newsworthy or topical to happen. Instead, editors allocate staff and resources to follow up news items that they think are likely to be worth covering.

News values

Editors allocate staff, space and time to different topics according to the 'news values' of those topics, which are based on how newsworthy the editors think a particular issue or personality is. Oasis, for example, is newsworthy and even trivial stories about the Gallaghers are likely to make news.

On a television news broadcast, items that can be filmed are more newsworthy and so are more likely to be included than ones which are mainly based on interviews and 'talking heads'.

Noel and Liam Gallagher

The role of media 'gatekeepers'

Media gatekeepers are the programme controllers, editors, journalists and owners who decide what to cover and how to present it. They can 'open the gate' to certain issues, events or points of view and 'close the gate' to others. This means that media gatekeepers are in a strong position to set the agenda of public debate and to influence what we think about.

The profit motive as an influence on content

Newspapers exist as businesses and they operate to make a profit. This means that the profit motive will have an influence on content. Press gatekeepers will consider possible stories in terms of whether they are likely to achieve big circulations. Diana, Princess of Wales, was a popular figure and so articles about her are still likely to sell newspapers. The National Lottery has been a source of stories for the tabloids because stories on winners are seen as good for sales.

Advertisements

Advertisements are an important source of revenue for newspapers. The advertisers may have an influence on content in so far as they may withdraw their business if they disagree with a paper's stand on a particular issue.

The state and legal constraints on content

- Governments can control the content of the news media during national emergencies. During the Falklands war in 1982, the then Conservative government censored stories which journalists on the British Task Force sent to the British press.
- A D-notice or defence notice may be issued by the government to news editors asking them not to publish items on particular subjects for reasons of national security. A D-notice is an informal government means of controlling the press coverage of certain issues but, because it is voluntary, it lacks the force of law.

- Legislation can affect the content of the news. In October 1988, for example, the then Conservative government introduced rules for interviewing members of the IRA on television. According to these rules, the voices of members of the IRA could not be broadcast. In September 1994, this broadcasting ban was lifted.
- The media are subject to laws of libel, which prevent the publication of false statements that damage a person's reputation. A number of celebrities, including Elton John, Gillian Taylforth, Jason Donovan and Stephanie Powers, have been involved in libel court cases with newspapers.

LIBEL WIN FOR STEPHANIE POWERS

The American actress Stephanie Powers received an apology in open court yesterday from *The Sun* over a defamatory* article that caused her 'grave distress'.

The star of the long-running ITV series *Hart to Hart* was at the High Court in London to collect more than £70,000 in damages and an estimated £30,000 in legal costs agreed in an out-of-court settlement.

The newspaper had wrongly published allegations that she had sexually harassed and assaulted a former male employee. It was further alleged that she was an alcoholic and had made threats against the employee's life.

Source: *The Times*, 24 April 1996

* A 'defamatory article' is one which attacks a person's reputation.

CHECK YOUR UNDERSTANDING

1 Identify and describe two factors that may influence the content of television news. (4 marks)

2 To what extent can press owners be seen as a major influence on the content of newspapers? (10 marks)

Media imagery and representations

One important area of the study of media content concerns representations. Sociologists are interested in studying the images of social groups, such as black people and women, that are represented in the media. They have done research in different areas of the media according to their own particular interests. Some, for example, have studied gender and television advertisements, while others are more interested in how black people are represented in drama productions. This has resulted in a very interesting but unbalanced collection of findings on media imagery and representations.

How are black people represented in the media?

Research shows that in television drama productions during the 1950s, 1960s and 1970s, black people were either invisible or under-represented. When black people were represented, the media often showed **stereotypes** that were frequently negative. A stereotype is a distorted or exaggerated view of members of a social group. Television programmes during this time often presented black people in stereotypical roles such as criminals. Black people were also presented in a narrow range of roles such as singers, dancers, musicians or sportspeople.

Many viewers, for example, were critical of the way in which students were represented in *Mind Your Language*, a 1970s sitcom set in an English language class. The 'comedy' relied heavily on racial stereotypes and encouraged the audience to laugh at and ridicule people whose first language was not English.

The cast of Mind Your Language

Further research suggests that, during the 1960s and 1970s, news reporting in the media tended to simplify race issues and reported on them in a negative and unbalanced way. Issues that emphasized the problems associated with countries in Africa and Asia, such as famine, poverty and war, were over-reported. In Britain, reports often associated black people with crime, conflict and riots.

Cottle (1994) sees such news reporting in the 1960s and 1970s as effectively hiding the very real problem of racism in Britain. He points out that in the 1970s and 1980s, studies identified how Britain's black population were criminalized in that the media gave the impression that black people were prone to crime. There have been, for example, reports in the media linking black people to mugging, violent street protests and inner-city riots. An important effect of such distorted coverage was that black people came to be defined as a threat to society's values. (See pp. 301–2 on folk devils and moral panics.) The media, however, chose to ignore continuing social inequalities and the growing anger at police harassment and brutality.

Abercrombie (1996), in his discussion of television in the 1990s, believes that there have been considerable changes in the representation of race and ethnicity. More black actors and presenters, for example, are appearing. More important, he argues, black actors are now playing ordinary characters rather than being presented as stereotypes. *The Cosby Show* in America is particularly significant because all of the main characters are black, they are presented in realistic, non-stereotypical ways and they are presented as successful members of upper middle class society. In September 1997, however, the BBC was heavily criticized for its negative stereotyping of Irish people in *EastEnders*.

BLACK ACTORS ON TV

Abercrombie (1996) gives examples of programmes such as *Brookside, EastEnders* and *The Bill* in which black actors play ordinary characters.

Norika from *The Bill*

Mick from *Brookside*

Sanjay from *EastEnders*

1 In a small group, discuss whether you agree that such programmes do present black actors in ordinary roles.
2 Discuss specific examples from recent episodes of these programmes.
3 Now make a note of three significant points made during your discussion.

Xenophobia in the press

Xenophobia refers to the dislike and fear of foreigners. The tabloids have been accused of xenophobia in the way they represent certain issues and events. Their coverage of the European Football Championships in 1996 is a case in point. Before the England v. Germany semi-final match, the *Daily Mirror* used the headline 'Mirror Declares Football War on Germany', while *The Sun* had the headline 'Let's Blitz Fritz'. Such coverage, which harks back to the Second World War, is seen as insulting and offensive.

How are women and men represented in the media?

Sociologists have undertaken research on images of gender in children's books, advertising, television, films and magazines.

During the 1970s, research indicated that the media's representations of women did not reflect the range of roles that they actually played in society. Sue Sharpe (1994) focuses on books and suggests that, since the 1970s, there has been some progress, citing, for example, the appearance of more books that present men and women in a less stereotypical way. She points out, however, that there are still lots of traditional images around.

Recent research highlights the stereotyping of women in a number of media products, including television advertisements, pop videos and magazines. In 1990, Cumberbatch carried out research for the Broadcasting Standards Council on the way in which women and men are represented in television advertisements. The following is a summary of the research findings:

- Nearly two thirds of people in advertisements are men.
- The vast majority of voice-overs in advertisements are male.
- Women in advertisements are more likely than men to be young and blonde.
- Men are more likely than women to be shown in a professional work setting.
- Women are frequently shown with a male partner.

Source: adapted from The Broadcasting Standards Council report (1990)

STUDYING VOICE-OVERS

Over a period of one week, watch a total of 15 television advertisements which have voice-overs.

1. For each of these advertisements, make a note of the product being advertised and the gender of the voice-over.
2. Did you find that the majority of voice-overs were male?
3. Was there any link between the kind of product being advertised and the gender of the voice-over?
4. Write a brief report on your findings and conclusions.

Women in the sports news

Women are invisible in much press and television coverage of sport. When women's sport is reported, it is often trivialized. Women's football, for example, is covered only patchily. John Williams (1997) examines coverage of women's football in television and newspapers today.

WOMEN'S FOOTBALL

And what, generally, of the women's game today? Well, things looked ready for a major take-off as far back as 1989. Then, Channel 4, looking for cheap and 'exotic' alternatives to mainstream sport, showed the Women's FA Cup Final. This was pre-Sky, of course, and fans, 2.5 million of them, a record for sport on C4, gobbled it up. The next season C4 brought coverage from the quarter-finals onwards but also offered too much of the human interest 'aren't they quaint and brave' stuff on board the coach and in the dressing room ...

Now? Well, serious TV coverage has pretty much disappeared. Serie A arrived on C4. The BBC, desperate for soccer action, disgracefully provided the barest highlights of the recent women's World Cup and always around midnight. On Sky you can watch N. Ireland v. Scotland schoolboys live to your heart's content, but no female coverage ... Coverage of the National League in the national press is either rudimentary or non-existent – though* The Times *of course provides copious details of the national public schools football cup. Without media coverage, serious sponsorship for the women's game is pretty much out of the question.*

Source: Williams (1997)

* 'Serie A' refers to the Italian football league.

Read through this extract and write a paragraph to summarize Williams's views on media coverage of women's football.

Newspapers and television do cover women's tennis, but arguably they do so in a way that trivializes the achievements of women players. In the two extracts shown here, Katherine Viner comments on the press coverage of Wimbledon in 1997. Such coverage treats women as sex objects in a way that simply would not happen with men.

You might think that the most impressive thing about world tennis number one Martina Hingis is her ground strokes. But you'd be wrong: the tabloids say it's her bottom. Mary Pierce's hard-hitting forehand? Forget it: let's look instead at her saucy leotards, let's nickname her 'The Body'. Anna Kournikova's volleys? Nah; we'd rather check out the cutesy way she keeps tennis balls in her knickers. We'd rather lust.

Viner asks us to imagine the following report:

Tim Henman, looking saucily resplendent in scrotum-hugging shorts that skimmed his genitals in all the right places, jangled his way to victory on Centre Court yesterday.

Source: Katherine Viner, 'Rock bottom', *The Guardian*, 30 June 1997

Viner argues that what is really going on is an attempt to diminish the power of women players, who can hit a ball hard enough to knock a male commentator's head off!

WOMEN'S TENNIS

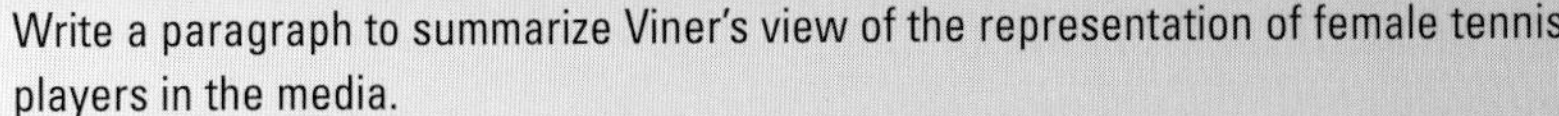

Write a paragraph to summarize Viner's view of the representation of female tennis players in the media.

Gender and soap opera

Abercrombie (1996) points out that one major theme of soap opera is that the soap world is a woman's world. Soaps are based on the world of home rather than the world of work in that much of the action takes place in people's homes. Soap operas also tend to be organized around very strong female characters. Soaps are full of strong women and weak, unreliable or dishonest men. The storylines are largely driven by the feelings or actions of women. This is in contrast to most thrillers or police series, in which men are the central characters who make things happen.

GENDER AND SOAP OPERA

1 In a small group, list as many soap opera characters as you can within five minutes.
2 Once you have done this, go through your list and try to classify each character according to one of the following eight categories.

- Strong female characters
- Weak female characters
- Unreliable female characters
- Dishonest female characters
- Strong male characters
- Weak male characters
- Unreliable male characters
- Dishonest male characters

3 On the basis of your group's work, write a paragraph explaining whether you agree that female soap characters tend to be strong and that male soap characters tend to be weak, unreliable or dishonest.

How do the media represent deviance?

Stan Cohen (1980) argues that the media have been involved in the creation of **moral panics**. An important aspect of a moral panic is that a group becomes defined as a threat to society's values. The group is presented in stereotypical terms by the mass media.

Cohen undertook a case study of the moral panic surrounding mods and rockers during the 1960s. Events in 1964 in Clacton, a small holiday resort on the east coast of England, were the starting point. Easter Sunday in 1964 was the coldest for 80 years. A few groups of bored young people started scuffling on pavements and throwing stones at each other. The mods and rockers factions started separating out. In the extract here, Cohen describes what happened then.

Those on bikes and scooters roared up and down, windows were broken, some beach huts were wrecked and one boy fired a starting pistol in the air. The vast number of people crowding into the streets, the noise, everyone's general irritation and the actions of an unprepared and undermanned police force had the effect of making the two days unpleasant, oppressive and sometimes frightening.

Source: Cohen (1980) p. 29

The incident described by Cohen (see p. 301) was reported in most national newspapers with sensationalist and exaggerated headlines such as:

The phrase 'Wild Ones' was itself taken from a Marlon Brando film that had contributed to a moral panic in America some years earlier. Cohen argues that the media exaggerated the seriousness of the events in terms of:

- the numbers taking part;
- the numbers involved in violence;
- the amount and effects of any damage or violence.

He argued that the media distorted what was actually going on and created a false image of young people and their activities. Cohen describes this process as **amplification**, which involves distortion and exaggeration. Such amplification, Cohen argued, encouraged other young people to behave in the way portrayed by the media. This resulted in further disturbances and led to the public outcry that Cohen termed a moral panic. People reading newspapers and watching scenes on television began to see the mods and rockers as a threat to law and order. The police, responding to the public outcry, acted harshly and this led to further arrests. Cohen's point is that the media can actually increase (amplify) deviance.

Cohen is aware that, today, many younger readers may not even have heard of mods and rockers. He points out, however, that the processes that bring about moral panics remain important.

More recently, moral panics have surrounded:

- raves and warehouse parties;
- lack of discipline in schools;
- road rage;
- alcopops.

CHECK YOUR UNDERSTANDING

1 Identify and explain one way in which the media can influence our views on how much crime there is in society. (3 marks)

2 Choose one social group and explain how the media encourage us to see that group in a stereotyped way. (4 marks)

MEDIA AUDIENCES

The media play an important part in our lives in that virtually everyone has access to the media. At some time most of us watch television, listen to the radio or tapes and read newspapers or books. Sociologists are interested in the audience: how many newspapers are sold each day and which television programmes have the largest audiences.

In what quantities are the media used?

Newspaper sales

Table 10.3 gives circulation figures for ten national daily newspapers, listed alphabetically. There are five tabloid newspapers and five broadsheets.

NEWSPAPER SALES

Examine Table 10.3 and then complete the following tasks.

Table 10.3 National daily newspaper sales

	Average sales, April–Sept 1996
Daily Express	1,220,997
Daily Mail	2,076,951
Daily Mirror	2,443,049
Daily Star	759,344
Daily Telegraph	1,057,017
Financial Times	295,902
Guardian	393,011
Independent	270,608
Sun	4,006,979
Times	733,236

Source: adapted from Denscombe (1997) p. 33

1 Write down the heading 'National Daily Newspaper Sales Figures'.
2 Using the information given, list the ten newspapers in order of sales, starting with the newspaper with the highest sales and finishing with the newspaper with the lowest sales.
3 For each newspaper, state whether you think it is a tabloid or a broadsheet.
4 State whether tabloids or broadsheets have the higher sales figures.

Television viewing

Table 10.4 gives viewing figures for 9–15 June 1997. When more than one episode of a soap opera is broadcast in a week, the highest figure is given. If a programme is repeated (for example *EastEnders* and *Brookside* omnibus editions), the audiences for the first and repeat broadcasts are combined. We can see that 4.41 million viewers tuned in to watch *Absolutely Fabulous*, for example, on BBC 2 during that week.

TELEVISION AUDIENCES

Examine Table 10.4, and then answer the questions that follow.

Table 10.4 Television viewing figures (in millions)

	BBC 1		BBC 2		ITV	
1	*EastEnders* (Tues/Sun)	16.61	*Absolutely Fabulous*	4.41	*Coronation Street* (Wed)	15.63
2	*Driving School*	10.39	*Gardeners' World*	4.16	*Emmerdale* (Tues/Wed)	11.59
3	*National Lottery Live* (Sat)	10.19	*Alexei Sayle's Comedy Hour*	4.14	*The Bill* (Fri)	9.74
4	*Dalziel and Pascoe*	9.54	*The Simpsons* (Fri/Sun)	3.99	*A Touch of Frost*	9.24
5	*Only Fools and Horses*	9.48	*Game On*	3.97	*Home and Away* (Wed)	8.92

	C4		C5	
1	*Brookside* (Fri/Sat)	5.27	*The Beverly Hillbillies*	1.65
2	*Countdown* (Tues)	3.5	*Beatmaster*	1.33
3	*Absolutely Animals*	3.16	*Revenge*	1.25
4	*ER*	3.10	*Hard Evidence*	0.99
5	*Hollyoaks* (Thu/Sun)	2.96	*French Silk*	0.95

Source: adapted from *Radio Times*, 12–18 July 1997

1 One particular type of TV programme came top in three out of five channels. What type was it?
2 Leaving aside programmes that are repeated, which programme attracted the biggest audience of all?
3 Which channel seems to attract the smallest audience?

Social patterns in television viewing

From Table 10.4 we saw that some television programmes attract millions of viewers. The amount of time we spend watching television varies according to social characteristics such as our gender and our age. This point is illustrated in Table 10.5.

TV VIEWING TIMES

Examine Table 10.5 and then answer the questions that follow.

Table 10.5 Television viewing by gender and age in the UK (1995)

	Hours and minutes per week	
	Males	Females
4–15	18:51	17:14
16–24	18:03	20:16
25–34	22:16	25:54
35–44	22:51	25:10
45–54	24:11	26:22
55–64	28:02	31:23
65+	34:29	36:42
All, aged 4 and over	23:45	26:25

Source: *Social Trends* (1997), p. 216

1 Which group watched television for 22 hours and 16 minutes per week?
2 Which group watched television for 31 hours and 23 minutes per week?
3 In which age group did males spend more time watching television than females?
4 Which age group watched least television?
5 **(a)** Which age group watched most television per week?
(b) Explain why you think they did so.

Table 10.5 shows us that there are gender patterns in television viewing. There are also gender patterns in listening and reading. The information in Table 10.6 is based on the percentage of those people aged 16 or over who participated in each activity in the four weeks before interview. We can see, for example, that in 1977, 52 per cent of men interviewed said that they had read a book in the last month. Perhaps not surprisingly, we can see that television watching is Britain's most common home-based leisure activity.

HOW DO WE SPEND OUR LEISURE TIME?

Table 10.6 Participation in home-based leisure activities in Britain (by gender)

	Percentages 1977	1993–4
Males		
Watching TV	97	99
Listening to radio	87	91
Listening to records/tapes	64	79
Reading books	52	59
Females		
Watching TV	97	99
Listening to radio	87	88
Listening to records/tapes	60	75
Reading books	57	71

Source: adapted from Social Trends (1997)

1. According to the data in Table 10.6:
   - What percentage of people watched television in 1993–4?
   - Has listening to records and tapes become more or less popular as a home-based leisure activity?
   - Which activity was far more popular with women than men in 1993–4?
2. Using this information, write a short paragraph to show how important the media are in people's leisure activities at home.
3. How much time do you spend daily on media-related pursuits? In order to answer this question, you will need to complete a time diary, which is a record of how you spend your time. To do this, you should devise a time diary like the one shown, which divides your day into half-hour blocks. At the end of each block of time, record how you spent your time.

SATURDAY

7.00-7.30	*got up, quick wash, went to paper shop to do paper round*
7.30-8.00	*finished paper round, went home*
8.00-8.30	*had breakfast while watching TV*
8.30-9.00	*washed up while listening to the radio*
9.00-9.30	*raining so watched more TV*

At the end of your day, add up the total amount of time you spent on media-related pursuits.

PEOPLE'S USE OF THE MEDIA

1 Devise your own questionnaire to find out about people's participation in media-related activities. In order to do this, you could start off by producing a list of eight media-related activities, such as watching television and going to the cinema. You could then question ten people about whether they have participated in each of the eight activities during the last week.

2 Now write a paragraph outlining your findings.

What are the effects of the media on the audience?

Sociologists, social psychologists, members of the public and politicians have, for a long time, been concerned about the possible effects of the media on their audience.

Films such as *The Wild One* and *A Clockwork Orange* caused concern in the past. *A Clockwork Orange* was released in the UK in 1971. A series of beatings and rapes in England was linked to this film by the police and its director banned the film in the UK. Recently, films such as *Reservoir Dogs* and *Crash* have caused concern in terms of the images represented, their impact on the audience and the possible effects of such images on our behaviour.

Three films that have raised concerns about the impact they have had on their audiences

Such concern is not limited to films. Pornography in magazines and on the Internet is also causing concern. Opponents of pornography in the media are critical of the way in which it represents women as objects. Some critics believe that there is a link between media pornography and rape.

There are three main sociological approaches to the study of the effects of the media on their audience: the hypodermic syringe approach, the uses and gratifications approach, and the idea of decoding. Let's examine each of these in turn.

The hypodermic syringe approach

The hypodermic syringe approach, which compared the media to an injection, was one of the earliest approaches to the study of media effects. The idea is that we receive a daily dose or injection of media messages from television or newspapers which has a direct and powerful effect on our attitudes and behaviour. Much of the early research was carried out in the laboratory using experiments.

Bandura (1963) conducted research with nursery-school children and his findings seemed to support the hypodermic syringe view of the media. In his study, the children were put into four groups. Some of the groups watched a short film showing a large inflated plastic doll being punched and hit with a mallet by an adult. The children were then placed in another room with a number of different toys, including a doll and a mallet. Many of the children who had seen the film copied the behaviour. Such research led to support for the view that television violence could have considerable effects on our behaviour.

More recently, concern has been raised about the effects of films such as *Child's Play 3* and *Natural Born Killers*. It is alleged, for example, that *Natural Born Killers* has led to a spate of copycat murders in the USA.

The hypodermic syringe approach can be criticized, however, because it fails to appreciate that we are able to distinguish real violence from the fictional violence shown in films.

CAN WE BLAME TV?

Read through this short extract on television and the causes of violence and then answer the questions that follow.

TV doesn't make us more violent

Television is not to blame for crime and violence, but has been used as a scapegoat for deep-rooted social problems, according to a recent report from Leeds University. The causes of crime and violence seem much more likely to be found in poverty, unemployment, homelessness, abuse and personality traits.*

Source: Peak and Fisher (1996) p. 159

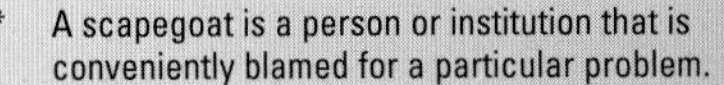

* A scapegoat is a person or institution that is conveniently blamed for a particular problem.

1 According to this extract, how are crime and violence best explained?
2 In your view, does this extract support the hypodermic syringe approach?

THE EFFECTS OF TV VIOLENCE

Study the following newspaper report, then answer the questions that follow.

PROGRAMME THAT MAKES HOME-WRECKING FUN

Every Tuesday afternoon, hundreds of thousands of children glue themselves to a television set to watch an exploding toilet, a duvet that blows out feathers and a toilet roll dispenser that won't stop spewing loo paper.

Last week the parents of two six-year-olds, arrested for destroying the contents of a neighbour's house, blamed their behaviour on the programme, called Finders Keepers. So did the six-year-olds.

'What can you expect when there's a show where children have to look for prizes by ransacking a room?' asked the father of one. 'Kids can't help being influenced when they are bombarded by such programmes' said the other boy's mother.

The programme centres on a high-speed chase through a studio house. Children have to empty drawers and cupboards, overturn beds and ransack the rooms to find hidden tokens. Once they've found the token, the contestants move on to ransack another room and eventually win a prize.

The programme makers say it is unfair to blame the programme. Unlike the parents they are not convinced that there is any connection.

Source: adapted from *Independent on Sunday*, 10 April 1994

1 Write a paragraph to show how this source could be used as evidence to support the hypodermic syringe approach.
2 Do you find the parents' argument convincing? Briefly explain your reasons.

VIOLENT FILMS

1 In a small group, discuss whether:

- violent films may lead to copycat behaviour;
- the likelihood is so great as to justify censorship of films.

2 Now make a note of four important points that were made during your discussions.

The uses and gratifications approach

The uses and gratifications approach focuses on how we, as members of the audience, use the media. It examines the individual needs that are gratified, or met, by the media. Some of us, for example, watch television quiz programmes because they offer excitement, education and the chance for us to try to beat the experts.

McQuail (1987) found that the needs that television most satisfied were for:

- **Information** – we might watch the news or documentaries to find out what is happening in the world; we watch cooking programmes to learn new recipes.
- **Personal identity** – we might watch programmes such as Ricki Lake or Kilroy because they allow us to gain insight into ourselves.
- **Personal relationships** – we could watch a soap opera as a substitute for real-life companionship or as a source of conversation with our friends at school or work.
- **Entertainment** – we watch comedy shows to escape from our problems, to relax or to fill time.

TEEN SOAPS

1 In a small group, discuss why teen soaps such as *Heartbreak High*, *Sweet Valley High* or *Beverly Hills 90210* are popular among some young people.
2 Now make a note of three possible needs that such programmes might satisfy for fans.

The decoding approach

More recently, researchers have become interested in the idea of the audience as decoder. Abercrombie (1996) explains this approach as follows:

> *We are all familiar with the idea of a spy decoding a message from his or her controller. In the same way, the television audience decodes or interprets a message from a TV programme. The difference is that, with a spy message, there is only one possible correct meaning which the spy carefully decodes. In the television message, however, there are several possible meanings and so there are several different ways of decoding the message.*
>
> Source: adapted from Abercrombie (1996)

This approach suggests that the content of a particular television programme has several possible meanings. It may therefore be decoded or interpreted in a number of ways.

Different sections of the audience may decode or interpret the content of a programme differently. The same television programme may be decoded differently by people from different social and cultural backgrounds.

How we decode a particular programme depends on our cultural and social background, our age, gender and ethnicity. How we actually respond to the programme's messages depends on our reading of it.

DECODING TV PROGRAMMES

1 In pairs, choose two of the following television programmes:

- *Neighbours*
- *Teletubbies*
- *News at Ten*
- *University Challenge*
- *Game On*
- *The X Files*
- *TFI Friday*
- *Friends*

2 For each, suggest how it might be decoded by:

- a female doctor aged 36;
- a schoolboy aged 10;
- you.

3 In your discussion, you could focus on how relevant and interesting each of the three might find the programme.

CHECK YOUR UNDERSTANDING

To what extent do you think that the media have a direct and immediate effect on the audience? Illustrate your answer with reference to studies and examples. (10 marks)

Advertising

Much advertising seeks to draw our attention to and promote a product or service in order to sell it to us. In so doing it seeks to influence us and to shape our desires. With the exception of BBC radio and television, advertising is found within virtually all media: in newspapers, at the cinema, and on commercial television and radio broadcasts. It is a significant source of media funding.

Advertising – information or exaggeration?

A positive view of advertising

- Supporters of advertising see it as providing us with consumer information. Through advertising, we learn about new or improved products and services. In this sense, advertising provides a useful educational and informational service. In doing so, it extends our choices.
- Supporters believe that advertising promotes consumption and increases the demand for products, which is good for business and the economy.

A critical view of advertising

- Advertising encourages us to consume products and, in doing so, it encourages us to value material things.
- Advertising can damage the environment by encouraging us to buy harmful products that we don't need.
- Advertisements frequently use exploitative images (e.g. of women) to sell products.

This extract identifies a number of criticisms of advertising:

> *Advertising – a positive social force? I think not. Advertising causes people to buy what they don't need, causes people to throw away perfectly good things, causes poor people to want things they can't afford, and creates unfillable expectations, thus promoting a materialistic society. It encourages half truths and exaggerations.*
>
> *Source: adapted from Dennis and Merrill (1991) p. 185*

How influential are advertisements?

All advertising deliberately tries to influence us. Much of it tries to persuade us to buy a product. Millions of pounds are spent by companies every year in this attempt. It is not clear, however, whether advertisements are effective in their persuasion and a definite conclusion regarding the impact of advertising has not yet been reached.

One view is that although advertising may affect brand choice, this is really all it does. Cigarette advertising, for example, may influence which brand someone buys, but it doesn't influence whether or not we smoke. Estimates suggest that Norway has the highest population of teenage smokers in Europe, yet it outlawed cigarette advertising in 1975.

Early approaches saw the impact of advertisements as being simple and direct – after seeing the advertisement, consumers purchased the product, which led to an increase in sales. This view, like the hypodermic syringe approach, presents the audience as being very passive.

THE INFLUENCE OF ADVERTISING

Ads that turn you off

'More than 40% of Americans actively refuse to buy a product if they do not like its advertising,' says Adweek, the US magazine. The nationwide poll revealed that men and women were equally likely to register their disapproval in such a way, with the 18 to 24-year-old sector likely to be the most militant.

Source: Belinda Archer, *The Times*, 5 February 1997

According to the information in this extract:

1 Do we automatically purchase products after seeing them advertised?
2 How might advertising lead to a decrease in demand for a product?

LOOKING AT ADVERTISEMENTS

Companies spend large sums of money on advertising and aim to ensure that advertisements are best placed to target those customers who are most likely to buy a particular product. This activity enables you to compare the sorts of adverts in a glossy, monthly women's magazine, such as *Cosmopolitan*, with those in a weekly women's magazine such as *Woman's Own*. You will need one copy of a monthly and one copy of a weekly women's magazine.

1 How much space do advertisements take up as a proportion of each magazine? To work this out:
- **As you read through the magazine, identify each advertisement.**
- **Next, measure the total magazine space given to advertisements: for each ad, you will need to measure length × breadth.**
- **Now measure the total magazine space: length × breadth × number of pages.**
- **In order to find the proportion of space given to ads, you will need to work out:**

$$\frac{\text{total advertisement space}}{\text{total magazine space}} \times 100 = \%\text{ of space}$$

2 Is there a marked difference in the amount of space given to advertisements in the two magazines?

3 Is there a difference in the sort of products or services advertised in each magazine? In order to find this out, you could do a counting exercise. Starting with the glossy monthly magazine, place each ad in one of the following categories:
- **Products related to looking after people or the home, such as cooking for others, childcare, shopping for groceries, cleaning the floor, the bath and the oven, dishwashing, dusting.**
- **Products related to personal beauty and hygiene, such as bath soap, hair conditioner, perfume, clothes, make up.**
- **Other: car, computer, holiday.**

4 Did you find evidence to suggest that advertisements are placed to target a particular audience?

More recent studies suggest that we do not simply accept advertisements' images and messages at face value. Instead we are critical and sceptical in our viewing of advertisements. We actively interpret and make sense of advertisement messages.

What is the role of the media in the socialization process?

The media play a significant role in passing on the culture of a society to the next generation. Culture refers to the whole way of life in society, including its norms and roles. As we grow up, we have to learn how to get on with others and how to behave in different social situations. We learn norms of behaviour and social roles.

The media are one source of learning and, as such, they are an important agency of secondary socialization. As young children, we may acquire certain values, attitudes or roles from the media. Film and television characters, for example, may provide us with role models.

We may also pick up messages from the media about how we are expected to behave as males or females. Primary-school reading books in the 1950s and 1960s, for example, presented young children with very traditional images of the roles of males and females. The media, on the other hand, may actually challenge traditional images of gender. One view of the Spice Girls, for example, was that they provided positive role models for young girls in their support of girl power.

Arguably, the media's role as an agency of socialization has become increasingly significant over the last 30 years because they have developed into such an important source of knowledge and information. The danger is, however, that the media provide us with a distorted or biased and one-sided view of the world. Through the process of agenda setting, the media may tell us what to think about. Through norm referencing, the media may encourage us to view some groups much more negatively than others. (See p. 294 for more on agenda setting and norm referencing.)

We should not, however, go to the extreme of seeing people simply as passive puppets or empty vessels waiting to be filled by the media with culture, norms and values. The media are powerful, but different people do experience the media differently. Different audiences respond to content according to how they experience it.

CHECK YOUR UNDERSTANDING

1 How influential is television in the process by which children are socialized today? (5 marks)

2 Identify and describe one other way in which the mass media play a role in the process of socialization. (3 marks)

SUMMARY

In this chapter, we have covered the following points:

- **The mass media are those forms of communications which reach a mass audience. Broadly speaking, the mass media can be divided into two categories: press and broadcasting.**
- **In the UK all newspapers are privately owned. Sociologists argue about how much control the owners exercise. Supporters of the conflict approach believe that a small group of powerful media owners has too much control. Pluralists believe that no one group dominates and that all points of view are represented through the wide range of press available.**
- **What appears in the media is selected. The content depends on what editors and owners decide is interesting or newsworthy. Various factors determine what is selected.**
- **Sociologists examine the way in which ethnic minorities and women are represented in the media and, in particular, at whether certain groups are portrayed in a stereotyped way.**
- **The media can distort or amplify criminal and deviant behaviour in such a way as to cause moral panics.**
- **Sociologists measure the size and type of audience for various types of media and identify consumption trends in terms of social class, gender and age.**
- **The impact of the media on audiences has been disputed. Subscribers to the hypodermic syringe model, for instance, argue that the portrayal of violence on television leads to copycat violence in society. Others argue that there is no evidence to support this.**
- **The influence of advertising has also been disputed. Some people argue that adverts inform, others that they exploit.**
- **The media have a significant role to play in socialization and are a key way in which we learn about culture and the norms and values of society.**

EXAMINATION QUESTION 1

How might our views about levels of crime be affected by media reporting? (9 marks)

Source: NEAB GCSE Sociology, June 1996
Tier P, Part (d), Question B5

EXAMINATION QUESTION 2

How might the media amplify deviant behaviour? (8 marks)

Source: NEAB GCSE Sociology, June 1996
Tier Q, Part (b), Question B5

BIBLIOGRAPHY

Abercrombie, N. (1996) *Television and Society*, Polity Press.
Bandura, A. and Walters, R.H. (1963) *Social Learning and Personality Development*, Holt, Rinehart and Winston.
Broadcasting Standards Council report (1990) 'Sexual stereotyping in advertising'.
Cohen, S. (ed) (1980) *Folk Devils and Moral Panics*, Martin Robertson.
Cottle, S. (1994) 'The news media and "race" – a case of intended and unintended outcomes' in *Social Science Teacher*, Volume 23, No. 2 (Spring).
Dennis, E.E. and Merrill, J.C. (1991) *Media Debates: Issues in Mass Communication*, Longman.
Denscombe, M. (1997) *Sociology Update*, Olympus Books.
Katz, E. and Lazarsfeld, P.F. (1955) *Personal Influence*, The Free Press.
McQuail, D. (1987) *Mass Communication Theory* (second edition), Sage.
Morley, D. (1992) *Television Audience and Cultural Studies*, Routledge.
Peak, S. and Fisher, P. (eds) (1995) *The Media Guide 1996*, Fourth Estate.
Peak, S. and Fisher, P. (eds) (1996) *The Media Guide 1997*, Fourth Estate.
Sharpe, S. (1994) *Just Like a Girl* (new edition), Penguin.
Social Trends (1997), Office for National Statistics and HMSO.
Trowler, P. (1996) *Investigating Mass Media*, Collins Educational.
Williams, G. (1996) *Britain's Media – How They Are Related*, Campaign for Press and Broadcasting Freedom.
Williams, J. (1997) 'Support for all?' in *When Saturday Comes*, No. 121 (March), pp 32–3.

Religion

In this chapter, we will explore and attempt to answer the following questions:

1. **How can we define religion?**
2. **What is the role of religion in society?**
   - **Is religion a source of order and stability?**
   - **Is religion a form of social control?**
   - **Can religion be a force for change?**
   - **What is the role of women in religion?**
3. **How can we categorize different religions?**
   - **What are churches, sects and denominations?**
4. **How can we explain the growth of new religious movements?**
   - **Why do people join?**
   - **Who joins?**
   - **What types of new religious movement are there?**
   - **What happens to them?**
5. **Is religion in decline?**

Religion is a topic which can provoke strong reactions in people. Some may see it as a vital and important part of the human experience, providing guidance and answering the 'big' questions of life. Others may see it as a dangerous phenomenon which continues to cause strife and conflict throughout the world. Then there are others for whom religion is irrelevant and outdated.

Some religions (for example Islam) may have many millions of followers in different countries around the globe, whose whole way of life may be shaped by their beliefs. Clearly, a belief system with this level of potential influence needs examining.

The study of religion by sociologists has raised a number of issues, such as:

- What different forms can religious institutions take?
- What kind of alternative religions are there and how influential are these?
- Are religious beliefs still as strong as they used to be?

HOW CAN WE DEFINE RELIGION?

A number of definitions of the term 'religion' exist. Some tend to be narrow definitions; others are wider. For example, religion can be seen as:

- a belief in the existence of supra-human forces (forces beyond the knowledge or understanding of human beings) which have a powerful influence on life;
- a system of beliefs which explain the individual's place in the world, giving order and meaning to life and providing moral guidance.

Glock and Stark (1969) identify five major features of religious belief:

1. *A religious person will accept the major* ***beliefs*** *of his or her religion, e.g. the teachings of a holy book such as the Bible or Koran.*

2. *A religious person will carry out certain* ***practices*** *to show their commitment, e.g. formal worship, prayer, fasting.*

3. *A religious person will have some* ***experience*** *of, or communication with, a god, e.g. through visiting a sacred place.*

4. *A religious person will have some* ***knowledge*** *and understanding of the teachings of their religion, e.g. details from a holy book.*

5. *A religious person will be expected to adopt* ***behaviour*** *appropriate to their religion, e.g. to love their neighbour or to care for the poor.*

IS FOOTBALL A RELIGION?

Can football be seen as a religion?

1. In a small group, consider the five features of a religion according to Glock and Stark.
2. Using these, identify and note down arguments for and against the idea that football can be seen as a religion.

Sociologists argue that it is difficult to agree on a single, simple definition of religion which can include all of the forms of belief systems found around the world. One way to solve this problem is to consider two basic types of definition: exclusive and inclusive.

An **exclusive** definition focuses on those belief systems that were traditionally classed as religions, such as Islam, Christianity and Hinduism, which have a supra-human element to them. An **inclusive** definition also includes belief systems not traditionally classed as religions, such as fascism and communism, which do not have a supra-human element.

CAN THERE BE A RELIGION WITHOUT A GOD?

A belief system has developed which looks at the world and makes sense of life without depending on a supernatural power such as God. This has become known as Humanism.

Just like religions, Humanism helps people search for answers to the great puzzles of life: 'Why am I here?' ... 'What is life all about?' ... 'What is the universe?' For answers, it looks to the facts which people have found out for themselves through experience and by exploring the world with science.

Source: *The Guardian* (1993)

1 Which definition would we need to use to see Humanism as a type of religion?
2 Write down another example of a belief system which could be seen as a religion if you were using the definition you identified in question 1. Explain your answer.

CHECK YOUR UNDERSTANDING

1 Identify and explain one definition of religion as outlined earlier in this section. (2 marks)
2 Identify and explain two features of religious belief. (4 marks)

WHAT IS THE ROLE OF RELIGION IN SOCIETY?

There is much disagreement among sociologists about the role of religion in society. For example, is it beneficial for society and individuals? Does it simply keep us in our place? Does it prevent changes taking place in society, for example in people's attitudes to contraception?

We can examine three general viewpoints: the functionalist viewpoint, the Marxist viewpoint and the Weberian viewpoint.

The functionalist viewpoint

Religion creates order and stability

Here religion is seen as providing certain functions for the benefit of the individual and society.

Religious beliefs give **meaning** to life and make sense of all experiences, for example why a young person should suffer an accidental death. In this way religion helps individuals to adjust to sudden events, especially unhappy ones, and acts as a means of coming to terms with uncertain situations and of reducing stress and anxiety. By doing this it creates a sense of **order and stability** in society.

Religion can also be seen as an **agency of socialization**, providing guidelines for human behaviour, that are expressed in a variety of norms and values, for example that murder is wrong. These shared values and moral beliefs bring people together to create a sense of **social solidarity**.

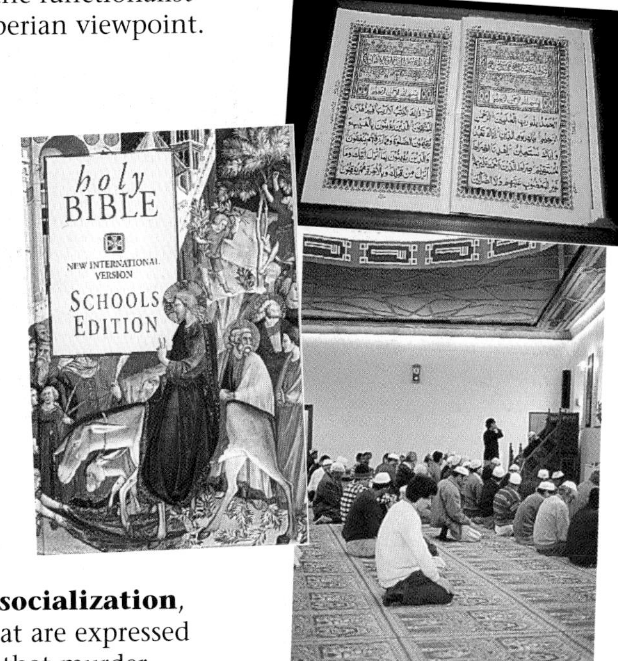

Religion provides guidelines for human behaviour

A COLLAPSE OF MORAL BELIEFS?

Read the extract and discuss the following questions.

Christian Teenagers Show Their Flesh is Rather Weak

Churchgoing teenagers are dishonest, materialistic and have relaxed attitudes towards sex, a survey by the Christian Research Association revealed yesterday. The study found that lying had reached 'epidemic proportions' among young Christians, with more than 90 per cent of churchgoing 14- and 15-year-olds admitting they lied to their parents and teachers and three-quarters to their friends.

Half admitted that they had recently watched an 18-rated film, a third that they had been drunk in the past few weeks, and a quarter confessed that they had already had sex.

Phil Jackman of the Christian charity Agape, which commissioned the study, said: 'What is most alarming is that even those adolescents who do go to church seem to have no moral framework they can rely on. It is the church that is to blame. We must shoulder our responsibility and continue to teach the right path forward.'

Source: *The Guardian*, 26 September 1997

1 In a small group note down three other norms or values that religion may teach us.
2 What norms and values do the teenagers in the study seem to be disregarding?
3 Note down points for and against the idea that, in the 1990s, religion is not effective as an agency of socialization.

The Marxist viewpoint

Karl Marx (1818–83) did not believe that God created the human race. Rather, he believed that people 'invented' God. From the Marxist point of view, religion is used by the powerful groups in society (the ruling classes) to act as a form of **social control** over the rest of society.

Religion is seen as a way in which the ruling classes are able to persuade ordinary people to accept their lot in life rather than seeking to change the way society is organized in order to improve their situation. (For more details on the Marxist viewpoint, see Chapter 3 on Stratification and Differentiation.)

Thus, religion is used to justify the existing inequalities between rich and poor as being God-given, and so leading the poor to accept their position in society. Indeed, poverty is considered by many religions to be a virtue.

Equally, religious beliefs are seen to hold out hope to the hopeless and to ease the pain of oppression by offering the promise of paradise or salvation in the afterlife. By making life more bearable for the poor, religion prevents any thoughts of trying to change society in the here and now, thus allowing the ruling classes to remain at the top of society.

The Weberian viewpoint

Religion as a force for change in society

Max Weber (1864–1920) held a different point of view on the role of religion in society, arguing that in some situations it could be a source of conflict and change rather than a source of stability or social control. For example, the competing religious beliefs of Catholics and Protestants have greatly influenced the conflict in Northern Ireland. The conflict between Muslims and Hindus in India can be seen as partly responsible for the creation of the modern state of Pakistan and thus as an agent of major social change.

Individuals motivated by religious belief can also play a role in bringing about changes in society. For example, Martin Luther King's Christian beliefs influenced his efforts to gain civil rights for black people in America in the 1950s and 1960s.

In some circumstances, one particular religion could be seen as seeking to prevent change, while in other circumstances it could be seen as a force for social change. For example, Catholicism may seek to prevent a change in attitudes to abortion and contraception – seeing them as wrong – but, on the other hand, a form of Catholic teaching, called 'liberation theology', has acted as a revolutionary force for change in fighting against dictatorships in some South American countries.

For Weberian sociologists religion can thus be seen as a strong force for social change as well as providing stability and social control, depending on the circumstances.

PROMOTING OR PREVENTING SOCIAL CHANGE?

Read the following extract.

Archbishop Rejects Gay Reforms

The Archbishop of Canterbury, George Carey, delivered his most uncompromising rejection of gay clergy reform to date at the church's general synod* yesterday, while signalling an international Anglican commission to seek a way forward matching the recent compromise on women priests.

The Church of England committed itself to a wider debate on gay priests, but one with conservative guidelines laid down by senior bishops. Dr. Carey said:

'I know that this statement will distress some, but I don't believe any major change is likely in the foreseeable future, and I do not myself share the assumption that it is only a matter of time before the church will change its mind.'

The Archbishop, however, supported an 'honest, open and tolerant' discussion on the issue. The synod has been dominated by claims from the Lesbian and Gay Christian Movement that many diocesan bishops have already knowingly ordained such clergy in spite of doctrine that active homosexuality is a sin.

* The General Synod is the governing body of the Anglican Church.

Source: *The Guardian*, 15 July 1997

1 What change in church rules is being discussed by the Church of England?
2 According to the article, in which area has a change in the rules already taken place in the Church of England?
3 Write a short paragraph to explain whether the Church of England is acting as a force to promote or prevent change in the context covered by the article.

WHAT ROLES DOES RELIGION PLAY?

In a small group, identify and explain the role that is being played by religion in each of the photos.

Archbishop Desmond Tutu

Christian pro-life campaigners

Floral tributes at Kensington Palace after the death of Diana, Princess of Wales

Taliban forces in Afghanistan

What is the role of women in religion?

An examination of the role and position of women in the many different types of world religion can be seen as part of the wider debate about the role of women in society.

The inequalities faced by women in religious service and practice in some religions are seen by feminist sociologists as reflecting the inequalities faced by women in the wider society.

With the increasing involvement of women at all levels in a range of professions, many now feel that this should also extend to the role of women in religious institutions.

SHOULD WOMEN BE PRIESTS?

In a small group, consider the following arguments used for and against the idea of ordaining women as priests in the Church of England.

Table 11.1 The arguments for and against the ordination of women into the Church of England

FOR	AGAINST
• Women should be equal in the church, which holds that everyone is equal in God's eyes. • Jesus chose only male disciples because, at that time, women could not go about freely or speak in public. • Some passages in the Bible suggest that women should take a leading role or, at least, an equal role. In any case, the Bible approves of slavery, but no one would defend such practices today so why continue to defend discrimination against women? • Churches urgently need women priests as many parishes have no priest at all. • Women are likely to make better priests than men as they may be more compassionate and sympathetic to people's needs	• Jesus was a man and so were his disciples. So priests, who represent Jesus, must also be men. • Some passages in the Bible say that authority must be exercised by men in the Church, as in other areas of life, such as the family. • Women are seen as less pure than men because of menstruation and childbirth, and so are not suitable for the priesthood. • Equality for women does not mean they have to do the same things as men – they can be useful to the church by doing other things,

Source: adapted from *The Guardian* (1993)

1 Discuss and note down the strengths and weaknesses of the arguments given both for and against this issue.
2 To what extent do you think this debate is similar to or different from other debates on equality for women (e.g. on voting rights, equal pay, discrimination in the workplace)?

Should women be ordained?

How do some different religions view women's roles?

- Women cannot become priests in the Roman Catholic or Greek and Russian Orthodox churches.
- In the Jewish faith, the position of women is a key factor in differentiating one branch of tradition from another. Among Orthodox Jews, women cannot become rabbis and must sit apart from men in the synagogue. In Progressive synagogues, women can become rabbis and do not sit apart from men.
- In Islam, as in Christianity, beliefs and practices vary and the position of women varies widely, too. However, only a man can become an imam and lead the congregation in prayer.

- Among Sikhs, both men and women can perform the same tasks in the gurdwara – including reading the scriptures.
- In Protestant churches, such as the Church of Scotland, United Reformed Church, Baptist and Methodist Churches, women can become ministers, although they are outnumbered by men.

Clearly, the position and role of women in religious practices vary. However, the degree of equality that exists does not seem to depend on whether a religion is ancient or more modern, nor on whether it is based in a Western or Eastern country. For example, in the Mormon Church women play a less prominent role than in the First Church of Christ Scientist, even though both are relatively young religions and are based in the West.

CHECK YOUR UNDERSTANDING!

1. Religion can be seen as an agency of socialization. Identify two examples to show how it plays this role. (2 marks)
2. Using examples, explain how religion may be seen as an agent of social control. (4 marks)
3. Identify and describe one example of religion acting as a force for social change. (3 marks)
4. Using examples, explain how religion may sustain inequalities between men and women. (4 marks)

HOW CAN WE CATEGORIZE DIFFERENT RELIGIONS?

There is wide variety among religions and religious organizations in contemporary society, ranging from major world religions with a wide appeal, such as Islam and Christianity, to smaller groups appealing only to particular types of people, such as the Church of Scientology.

Sociologists have attempted to categorize the rich diversity of religions according to differences and similarities based on criteria such as:

- How large is the membership of the particular religious group?
- How well organized is it?
- What is its attitude to other religions?
- What is its relationship with the state?
- What kind of people join?

Three broad models have emerged from this: churches, sects and denominations. You should note, however, that there is not always a clear dividing line between these labels and some religious groups show characteristics of more than one model.

A 'church'

This term refers to large religious organizations that have a complex and formal hierarchy of officials ranked in order of importance. For example, in the Roman Catholic Church the Pope is at the head of the church, followed by the cardinals, archbishops, bishops and priests. The clergy and officials may be professionals and may receive payment.

Churches regard their teachings as offering the only real truth and path to salvation. In this respect, they seek to dominate religious belief and tend to oppose other religious ideas.

CATEGORIZING RELIGIONS

1 In a small group, draw up a list of different religious groups.
2 Try to divide these into different categories using the criteria listed in the text on the opposite page. For example, you might put all of the religions with a large, worldwide membership into one category, and so on.
3 Create a table by writing the names of religious organizations as headings along the top and listing the criteria down the side. Add vertical and horizontal rules to make boxes and then place a tick in the appropriate boxes.

Criteria	Religious organizations		

This should help you to see at a glance the similarities and differences between religious groups.

Churches often have a close relationship with the state and political system. For example, representatives of the Church of England sit in the House of Lords and take part in political decision making. In other countries, such as Pakistan, the link between church and state is much stronger, with Islamic teaching forming the basis of much of the legal system and the rules governing social life. In Eire, which is a predominantly Roman Catholic country, the church has traditionally had close links with the state, but these close ties now appear to be loosening .

Membership of churches is open to all, although, in practice, they tend to recruit more heavily from the higher social classes.

Sects

This is a general term referring to the growing number of smaller religious groups such as 'new religious movements'.

A 'new religious movement'

New religious movements tend not to have a complex structure or paid officials and often rely on a single charismatic leader for guidance and direction. They are usually critical of other religions and see themselves as representing the only real truth. (See pp. 325–33 for more information on new religious movements.)

These groups tend to be critical of the state and often seek to create radical changes in the way society is organized. Some new religious movements reject society completely and members often have no contact with the outside world.

Because of the wide range of types of new religious movements, the characteristics of the membership vary, with some being based mainly among the lower social classes and others mainly among the middle classes. However, members are often expected to be highly committed and to follow strict patterns of behaviour.

Two examples of new religious movements: The Jesus Army and the Hare Krishna movement

Denominations

This term refers to groups that are often seen as intermediate between churches and sects. Indeed, many denominations start life as sects and then go on to become churches as their membership grows and they become less opposed to the state and the way society is organized.

Like churches, denominations have a hierarchy of paid officials and are well organized, but this system is less complex than in churches and there is more emphasis on democratic participation by members. For example, lay preaching (by non-professional clergy) is encouraged.

Denominations tend to be tolerant of the ideas of other religions and are often willing to co-operate with other religious institutions. They are unlikely to reject the wider society but tend not to identify with the state, seeing church and state as separate. Denominations are often more likely than churches to speak out against government policy and political decisions.

The membership of denominations is varied, with lower social classes perhaps attracted by the more radical anti-state aspects, while the middle classes may be attracted by the general spirit of religious tolerance.

WHAT IS THE MOST INFLUENTIAL TYPE OF RELIGIOUS GROUP?

Identify which category of religious group (church, new religious movement or denomination) is likely to be the most influential in society. Explain your answer fully.

CHECK YOUR UNDERSTANDING

1 Identify two criteria for describing a religious group as a church. (2 marks)
2 Identify one difference and one similarity between a church and a denomination. (2 marks)
3 Identify and explain two differences between a church and a new religious movement. (4 marks)

INVESTIGATING RELIGIOUS INSTITUTIONS

1 Using the description of the three broad models of religious institutions on pp. 323–4, identify an example of each one that exists today.

2 For each model you have identified, carry out some research into the following areas:

- size of membership;
- its organization and structure;
- its beliefs;
- its attitudes to the position and role of women.

3 In what ways are your three models similar and in what ways are they different? Do their characteristics overlap?

4 You should present your findings in the form of a short report.

HOW CAN WE EXPLAIN THE GROWTH OF NEW RELIGIOUS MOVEMENTS?

Since the Second World War there has been an increased growth in the numbers and popularity of small religious groups in Western society. According to Eileen Barker (1984), around 2,000 separate groups are currently in existence.

Many of these groups and movements are rooted in traditional religious teachings and practices; for example, the Krishna Consciousness movement is based on Hinduism, and the Healthy-Happy-Holy movement (or 3HO) is a variation on Sikhism. However, other movements are associated with such varied ideas as flying saucers and witchcraft.

For some sociologists, the growth of new religious movements can be seen as evidence of a shift in religious belief away from traditional churches and their teachings to new forms of spirituality and belief systems. Other sociologists argue that the desire to seek new answers and new ways of living highlights a deep dissatisfaction with modern society and a desire to change it.

WHAT IS THE IMPORTANCE OF THE GROWTH IN NEW RELIGIOUS MOVEMENTS?

Make a list of other information we would need to gather before we could say that new religious movements are:

- a sign of a change in religious beliefs;
- an expression of deep dissatisfaction with society.

Why do people join new religious movements?

This question is seen as of particular importance because some – albeit a small minority – of new religious movements have been associated with breaking up families, kidnappings, acts of violence and disorder. For example, members of the Order of the Solar Temple have been associated with mass suicides that took place in Switzerland and Canada in 1994 and 1995.

WHY JOIN A NEW RELIGIOUS MOVEMENT?

1 In a small group, discuss possible reasons why people might join a new religious movement.
2 Produce a list of reasons and try to divide this into reasons that might be 'personal' and those that might be to do with 'society'.

Eileen Barker (1984) has identified a number of general reasons for joining new religious movements:

- **Coercion**, through some form of 'brainwashing', is often cited as a factor in explaining why people join new religious movements. However, it is more likely that an individual seeks out a movement initially, although techniques to encourage them to join may be used later. It is also important to remember that the majority of people are able to resist such techniques and, indeed, that most religions that seek to convert people use persuasive methods – these are not simply confined to new religious movements.
- New religious movements may **answer the needs** of people who are lonely or confused. Joining a group with a clear set of beliefs and direction may provide a sense of stability in an individual's life and bring a sense of purpose. Techniques such as 'love-bombing', where the individual is made to feel the centre of interest, may be used by some groups in order to make lonely individuals feel welcome and so lead to them joining.
- For some, joining a new religious movement may represent a way of **making a contribution** to society or even of changing society.
- New religious movements offer young people an opportunity to show their **independence**, to challenge the views of their parents and to assert their own personalities, values and beliefs.
- For those disillusioned with traditional religions, new religious movements may offer a different kind of **spirituality**.
- Some new religious movements offer opportunities for **self-development** through techniques to improve health, career, relationships, and so on.
- During times of **social upheaval** people may be attracted to new religious movements as they seem to offer stability and a sense of community when all else is changing.

Who joins new religious movements?

As with many other aspects of new religious movements, it is not possible to generalize about what type of people become members of these groups.

The assumption that it is those who are young, deprived or vulnerable in society who are most likely to be drawn to, or recruited by, new religious movements does not reflect reality. Different social classes, genders and age groups are all represented.

SOCIAL UPHEAVAL AND NEW RELIGIOUS MOVEMENTS

Read the following case studies and answer the questions that follow.

The Ghost Dance

The Ghost Dance was a religion which developed among some of the Native American peoples near the end of their struggle with the armed forces of the United States.

Just before dawn on New Year's Day 1889, far out in Western Nevada, a 34-year-old Paiute holy man named Wovoka fell ill with fever. During his delirium, the sky was darkened by an eclipse of the sun, and a great vision came to him. In it, God told him he would rescue all the Indian peoples from the abyss into which they had been cast. An Indian messiah was advancing from the west. If the Indian peoples refrained from all violence, if they were virtuous and honest, and if they danced a sacred dance – the Ghost Dance – they would hasten the coming of the new world. Then all the whites would disappear, all the dead ancestors would come back to life, the buffalo would return, and the prairies would once more abound with game. In the winter of 1890, Kicking Bear, a mystic and former intimate of Crazy Horse, carried the gospel back to Dakota.

Source: Channel 4, *The Wild West – The Way the American West was Lost ad Won*, 1845–93, edited transcript, 1995

The Black Muslims

This was a movement that flourished in America, particularly in the 1960s, as a result of the poverty and deprivation faced by black Americans.

It offers him a REBIRTH. He can shed his old despised identity. It offers him an emotional if not physical OUTLET for his newly articulated hostility toward the white man. It offers him HOPE. Joining the highly moralistic and disciplined Black Muslims gives him the imminent prospect of raising himself from his debilitating condition of poverty and frustration. It also provides him with the GOAL of building for a new glorious future in a united and powerful black society.

Source: Kaplan (1969)

1 Outline what was offered to those who joined:
   - the Ghost Dance;
   - the Black Muslims.

2 What similarities are there in the reasons why people joined these movements?

3 Identify when the Ghost Dance took place and when the Black Muslims were prominent.

A GOOD SOURCE OF MEMBERS?

Read the following article and answer the questions.

Cults 'Target' Vulnerable Students

Student unions around the country fear religious cults are targeting vulnerable new students, many of whom are away from home for the first time.

In Greater Manchester, which has nearly 70,000 students, the union has discovered plans by the Manchester Christian Church, a branch of the International Church of Christ UK (ICC), to rent a room on the campus to hold weekly meetings in October.

The ICC, which has more than 2,000 members in the UK, has already been banned from campuses in London, Birmingham, Edinburgh, Glasgow and Manchester.

The ICC, which claims non-members are damned, has a ministry dedicated to students. Members are recruited on campus and asked to prove their commitment by recruiting more members.

Judith Alexander, aged 20, was recently approached: 'She was incredibly friendly so I gave her my number and address, which she put in a book alongside other numbers. I went to one meeting but decided it wasn't for me. I was then continually rung by her and several members tried to come round to my house to hold prayer meetings and bible readings.'

Michelle Johnson, aged 27, a voluntary worker in Manchester and a former student member of the Manchester Christian Church, said students were expected to give 10 per cent of their income, raise more than £250 a year and give generously to the poor.

Adrian Hill, an elder of the church, said yesterday: 'We encourage students to work hard. Recruitment is too strong a word. These people are just enthusiastically spreading their faith. Their enthusiasm is just thought of as cultish because others do not have the same beliefs.'

Source: *The Guardian*, 1 October 1997

1 Which social group is being targeted by a new religious movement here?

2 From the article, identify possible reasons why this particular social group may be likely to join a new religious movement.

What types of new religious movements are there?

New religious movements take many forms and subscribe to a wide range of beliefs. Some may be based on older religions and some may simply offer guidance and techniques for improving an individual's life.

Roy Wallis (1985) has identified three broad categories to describe the different types of movement:

- world-affirming movements;
- world-accommodating movements; and
- world-rejecting movements.

World-affirming movements

The goals and values of the wider society are accepted and new techniques are offered to followers to enable them to become more successful individuals. For

The Mahareshi Mahesh Yogi

example, improvement in careers, personal relationships or IQ may be offered. There is little or no reference to a 'god'.

For example, Transcendental Meditation (TM), brought to the West by the Hindu Mahareshi Mahesh Yogi in the 1950s and popularized by the Beatles, is a meditation technique in which the follower is given a personal mantra (a word that is repeated over and over like a chant) to focus on during meditation. Through daily practice of meditation, it is believed that the follower can become a more efficient and effective individual. Such ideas have even given rise to a political party – the Natural Law Party.

World-accommodating movements

The goals and values of society are neither fully accepted nor fully rejected by such movements. Followers seek a greater sense of spirituality in life and feel that conventional religion and society in general have lost or neglected this aspect of belief. Believers continue to follow their normal lives (going to work, etc.), but feel that their religious practice and newfound spiritual purity make them better able to deal with the world.

For example, Charismatic Renewal movements believe that individuals can have direct contact with the Holy Spirit. This can be achieved through 'speaking in tongues'. This practice consists of language-like sounds, thought to be the voices of angels, which are uttered by an individual. This may be done as part of a conventionally organized but very lively and enthusiastic style of worship.

World-rejecting movements

The goals and values of society are rejected. These movements seek to change or transform the world, which is seen as entirely corrupt. Followers must cut themselves off from society and either work to create a better society themselves or await the end of the world, which may coincide with the return of a 'messiah'. At this time only the group's own members will be saved.

For example, the Branch-Davidian sect, led by David Koresh, lived apart from the wider society in a large farmhouse in Waco, Texas. The group was awaiting the end of the world. It had armed itself heavily in preparation for this event and this drew the attention of the US police. A siege took place in 1993, which ended in the deaths of most of the members.

The aftermath of the Waco siege

COMPARING NEW RELIGIOUS MOVEMENTS

In a small group, examine the following extracts and answer the question.

1 Identify the differences between the new religious movement each extract is describing.

Scientology

Scientology offered a wide range of practices designed to enable an individual to achieve his full potential as a human being and ultimately as a spiritual entity. It claimed to be able to eliminate psychosomatic and psychological illnesses and their effects, to increase intelligence, and to improve greatly the individual's functioning in inter-personal relations and in his career.

In addition, it promised the committed follower the means to recover extraordinary spiritual powers which it was said that humankind had once possessed but since lost, powers such as the ability to see and hear things at a great distance, to be able to manipulate objects by purely mental means, to gain knowledge of previous lives and to be able to dominate other beings.

Scientology claims to be able to produce these results on the basis of training and 'auditing', a technique of counselling and mental and spiritual exercises. Training and auditing are provided at varying fees, but advancement in Scientology will normally cost several thousand pounds ...

Source: Wallis (1985)

Tom Cruise

John Travolta

Demi Moore

Some famous members of the Church of Scientology

The Damanhurians

The road to the Damanhur community's Temple of Mankind winds up a steep hill behind the village of Vidracco, north of Turin ... It was only in 1992, following instructions given by a disgruntled ex-member of the group, that a state prosecutor accompanied by police discovered that the occultists had created a warren of halls and passages, labyrinths and crypts stretching more than 100 feet down into the hill. Their temple was the size of an 11-storey apartment block....

Damanhur was founded in 1976. Its name is that of a modern-day Egyptian city, which is identified in occult tradition with the ancient settlement of Timinhor, which was called after the Egyptian sun god, Horus.

Almost 20 years on, Damanhur represents an extraordinary achievement, one of the world's biggest alternative colonies. It claims more than 600 members, ranging in age from 86 years down to the newly born. Some who were brought to Damanhur as toddlers are now at university.

Sociologists who have studied the community have stressed its exceptional stability. Members live in some 60 houses scattered over an area of largely unspoilt countryside ... Damanhur has its own schools, which provide an education up to the age of 14, its own fire brigade and civil defence ... About 30 per cent of the group's members work outside. The remainder are employed in its co-operatives, for Damanhur is not merely a remarkable social and political experiment, but also a successful commercial enterprise...

The Damanhurians' own explanations of the community dwell largely on its role as an esoteric research centre. 'We're here because of our common interest in things esoteric,' their founder has said. 'We're researching into mankind's powers and capabilities.'

Source: Hooper (1995)

New age movements

'New age' is a term used to describe a growing area of diverse beliefs and ideas, for example alchemy, creation myths, astrology, herbalism, natural magic, crystal healing, the Grail tradition, Australian Aboriginal tradition, and many others. Indeed, in many bookshops, the 'new age' section is far larger than sections devoted to more 'traditional' religions.

Broadly speaking, new agers reject modern scientific approaches to explaining the world and, instead, focus on the beliefs of ancient and pre-modern cultures. There is also an emphasis on 'green' issues and environmentalism, along with an interest in developing a greater element of spirituality in individuals' lives.

The level of involvement in new age beliefs can vary widely between individuals. For some it may simply reflect an interest in reading books on these subjects; for others, the ideas may lead to a life-changing experience similar to the conversion experiences of those joining churches or new religious movements.

What happens to new religious movements?

Studies have shown that many new religious movements are short-lived and tend to die out relatively quickly, although other new movements are continually appearing. Bryan Wilson (1982) argues that some new religions are more permanent than others and Roy Wallis (1985) suggests that some flourish, grow and develop.

WHAT MAKES A SUCCESSFUL NEW RELIGION?

1 In a small group, discuss why some new religious movements are likely to survive or grow and why some are likely to die out.
2 Note down your arguments and be ready to explain them.

A number of factors have been suggested to try to explain the changing nature of new religious movements.

- Some new religious movements will make such radical demands on members that people will leave altogether and the movement will die out. In some cases, however, the movement may relax its rules in order to attract new members.
- Some researchers see a gradual progression from new religious movement to denomination and, finally, to church. This happens as a result of a movement becoming less radical in outlook and attracting a larger membership. Indeed, it has been suggested that some of today's existing churches may themselves have begun as new religious movements.
- Movements relying on a single charismatic leader to hold the group together may rethink their beliefs or disappear altogether when the leader dies.
- Many new religions appeal to younger people. As members get older they may seek a more 'normal' lifestyle and this may cause the group to alter its beliefs or to die out.
- Perhaps as a result of their beliefs or actions, some movements attract the attention of the police and other law enforcement agencies and may be forced out of existence, for example the Branch Davidians. Other movements may even destroy themselves, perhaps as part of their beliefs.

In general terms, world-affirming movements are thought to have the best chance of survival as they offer members success in modern life and do not demand a withdrawal from society. However, they may face the threat of competition from other movements, offering other techniques for success, in the same way as modern businesses face competition.

THE END OF THE MOVEMENT?

In a small group, read the following extracts and then discuss the following questions, making notes of your responses.

1 Using the extracts, suggest what role the leaders played in the group.
2 In what ways might the deaths of the leader and some of his followers affect the movement?
3 How did the group get its message across?

How the Net Closed on Mass Suicide

John Hochman, a psychiatrist and cult expert, dismissed the idea that the dead had severe mental problems. 'We can see that these folk were motivated, sincere, professional and able to earn a living,' he said.

'They didn't join any religious group to do away with themselves. This came from their leader, and these people are super-conmen who can get money, work, sexual favours from their flock, and even compete with God and have power over life and death.

The belief system is irrelevant – space ships or whatever – that's just to keep the interest going. The creator is the leader and he is the key.'

Source: *The Guardian*, 28 March 1997

Comet Suicide Cult Rises from Dead

Heaven's Gate – the deadly UFO cult whose members committed mass suicide in their San Diego mansion in March – is back in business, recruiting new members on the Internet. Cult members believed they could 'exit' their physical bodies through death to join a spaceship travelling in the wake of the comet Halle-Bopp.

The new version of the cult has been launched by Chuck Humphrey, a former member who survived his own suicide attempt in May. Mr Humphrey (or Rkkody as he was known during his 22 years with Heaven's Gate) has, by his own account, taken over the mantle of former leader Marshall Herff Applewhite (also known as Do). Mr Applewhite died with 38 of his followers after swallowing a cocktail of vodka and Phenobarbital on 23 March.

Mr Humphrey is now marketing the cult's lethal teachings under his own name. He is offering potential members the original Heaven's Gate book, public speaking engagements to evangelise the cult, and, most sinister, copies of the video of 'exit statements' given by cult members before their deaths. The video shows the ecstatic farewell speeches of each cult member as they looked forward to joining the spaceship.

To underline the message that cult members could train themselves to reach a 'level beyond human', Mr Humphrey's website contains an animation of a follower being transformed into an alien.

Source: *The Observer* Review, 3 August 1997

CHECK YOUR UNDERSTANDING

1 Identify and explain two reasons why an individual might join a new religious movement. (4 marks)
2 Identify and explain one difference between a world-affirming movement and a world-rejecting movement. (3 marks)
3 Identify and explain two factors that could cause a new religious movement to undergo changes. (4 marks)

IS RELIGION IN DECLINE?

In order to examine this question we need to use the concept of **secularization**. This term refers to the idea that religion is losing its importance and significance in society. If secularization is taking place, then we can argue that society is becoming increasingly secular (a society where human actions and affairs are not guided by religious teachings and ideas).

The problem of definition

Before we can possibly examine whether secularization is taking place or not, the problem of measuring this process has to be considered. How will we be able to tell if religion is in decline? Will this depend on the definition of 'religion' that is used, the type of religion examined and the country being looked at?

A new style of worship?

PROBLEMS WITH SECULARIZATION

In a small group, discuss the following questions.

1 What evidence can you identify for and against secularization?
2 Identify some possible problems with this evidence.
3 Note down your ideas using a table like the one here.

EVIDENCE FOR	PROBLEM	EVIDENCE AGAINST

Bryan Wilson (1982) defines secularization as 'the process whereby religious thinking, practice and institutions lose social significance'. He also suggests that this process is happening mainly in Western societies such as Britain and the USA. In some countries of the world, such as Saudi Arabia, Pakistan and Afghanistan, Islam is still a very strong force in society, perhaps stronger than ever.

What evidence is there for and against secularization?

Decline in church membership, practice and participation

Statistical evidence, based on church membership, attendance, marriage rates and numbers of clergy, can be used to argue that secularization is occurring.

STATISTICAL EVIDENCE

Examine Table 11.2 and answer the questions that follow.

Table 11.2 Church membership in the UK

	Membership (millions) 1970	1995
Trinitarian churches		
Roman Catholic	2.7	2.0
Anglican	3.0	1.7
Presbyterian	1.8	1.1
Methodist	0.7	0.4
Baptist	0.3	0.2
Other Free Churches	0.5	0.7
Orthodox	0.2	0.3
Total	**9.2**	**6.4**
Non-Trinitarian churches		
Mormons	0.1	0.2
Jehovah's Witnesses	0.1	0.1
Other Non-Trinitarian	0.1	0.3
Total	**0.3**	**0.6**
Other religions		
Muslims	0.1	0.6
Sikhs	0.1	0.4
Hindus	0.1	0.1
Jews	0.1	0.1
Others	0.0	0.1
Total	**0.4**	**1.3**

Source: *Social Trends* (1997)

1 Identify the general trends shown in the table.
2 What conclusions about secularization can you draw from these trends?
3 Identify and explain two reasons why these statistics may not be useful when examining secularization.

Critics of the use of statistics to support the idea of secularization make a number of points:

- Are figures on membership likely to be accurate? For example, can we be sure that each church is collecting its statistics in the same way and with the same regularity?
- Attendance figures and membership figures could differ widely. For example, someone could be a member of a church but might never attend services, while another person might attend the services of a particular church without being an officially confirmed member of that church.
- Can we assume that a decline in church membership does actually show secularization? That is, can we assume that the statistics do reveal a decline in religiosity (the strength of people's belief) and a lack of religious faith? In other words, does membership necessarily indicate religiosity? A number

of surveys have found that significant numbers of people do have some form of religious belief and commitment, although they may not necessarily attend a church or follow religious practices. It is quite possible to believe in a god and be personally quite religious without joining an organized religious group.

- There has been a growth in membership of some new religious movements, such as the Mormons, Krishna Consciousness, and so on, and also a growth of Christian fundamentalist groups. Membership of non-Christian religions is growing in the UK. However, this evidence may indicate a shift in people's belief patterns rather than evidence of secularization.

Table 11.3 Belief in God* (UK 1995)

	(%)
Do not believe in God	11
Do not know if God exists and cannot find evidence for God's existence	15
Believe in a higher power of some kind	12
Believe sometimes	12
Doubt, but believe	23
God exists, with no doubts	21
Can't choose/not answered	7

* Respondents were asked which statement came closest to their belief about God.

Source: *Social Trends* (1997)

Loss of influence in the wider society

Wilson argues that religion is no longer crucial in politics, law or education. Churches have lost their status and role in society.

Critics argue that religious leaders still have a strong influence on politics; for example, bishops sit in the House of Lords and in some countries, such as Iran, religion still has a powerful influence over many aspects of society. Religious institutions do have influence in terms of the religious norms and values followed by people. Christian ethics, for example, underlie the social values and laws of Western societies. Equally, legislation on education in the UK has set down the need for a daily act of worship in schools, which should be broadly Christian in nature.

THE IMPORTANCE OF RELIGIOUS EDUCATION

1. In a small group, discuss the influence of religion in schools. To what extent does it form part of the curriculum and values of a school?
2. What conclusions can you draw about this aspect of secularization?

The increased number of existing religions has reduced the power of religion in society

It is argued that, in the past, only one church had a monopoly over belief in a society and so the church was powerful. Today society is characterized by a plurality (or wide range) of different religions and religious views. The increased numbers of denominations and new religious movements have widened individuals' choice and so reduced the power and influence of any one single religion.

Wilson sees the growth of new religious movements as evidence of secularization because it marks the decline of traditional religion. Critics have argued that, rather than being seen as evidence of secularization, the growth of a plurality of different religions and new religious movements points to the continued vitality of religion and a basic human need for it.

Religions have been forced to modernize and change

In order to survive in a modern, increasingly secular society, and to retain their congregations in the face of competition, churches have had to make changes. We can examine three types of change:

- Churches have had to simplify and modernize their services and organization. For example, religious television in America and the use of the Internet can be seen as an attempt by churches to get their message across where traditional methods have failed.
- Changes in the role of women in some religious institutions have also been seen as an attempt to attract more followers.
- Some churches have considered amalgamating into a single church. This ecumenical movement is seen as a sign of secularization, as religious organizations usually only join together when they are weak rather than strong.

Critics of these arguments suggest that religious organizations have merely adapted themselves to the changing needs of their members rather than responding to any crisis. Thus, changes in organization and the growing use of technology simply reflect the face that religion is keeping pace with modern developments and are not indicators of secularization. Equally, many of the most rapidly growing religious movements, such as Christian Evangelism, are firmly rooted in traditional teachings and beliefs.

So far we have examined a number of arguments surrounding secularization which are based on institutional religion, that is, religious organizations. The following ideas are based on wider issues to do with the nature of belief in society.

THE NEED TO MODERNIZE AND CHANGE

Read the following extracts and answer the questions.

And the Church Saw That Business Was Good

A wave of enthusiasm for management training by the Church of England is introducing a new language of line managers, appraisal and performance indicators to theology.

Moses, Jesus Christ and St Paul are now accorded the status of brilliant managers for their skill as administrators and delegators, according to the Rev. John Sentamu, Bishop of Stepney.

Bishop Sentamu believes the Church must learn business techniques if it is going to be effective in the communication age.

'We've got a product to sell which is the love of God. If you are in the business of communicating a product, you've got to do it well,' he said.

Source: *The Guardian*, 18 October 1997

C of E in Secret Merger Talks with Methodists

Fifty Church of England and Methodist leaders have held an unprecedented private meeting to discuss merging the two Churches.

The Anglican General Synod will vote next month on opening formal talks, while the Methodists will vote in the spring on entering talks.

Participants are publicly playing down talk of a 'merger', but admit privately that declining membership in both Churches is driving a need to 'rationalize resources'.

Some are already predicting a new Church – the Church in England. 'It would basically be Anglican but incorporate a range of Non-Conformist Christian traditions.'

Source: *The Observer*, 19 October 1997

1. Identify the changes being discussed in the extracts.
2. What are the reasons behind these changes?
3. Suggest arguments for and against the two churches going ahead with these changes.

Have scientific explanations replaced religious ones?

Charles Darwin published a theory of evolution which had nothing to do with creation as described in the Bible.

Science has replaced religion in society

Here, secularization is examined in terms both of society and, in particular, of the growth of scientific and rational thought that has led to a decline in religious explanations of the world and religious belief.

SCIENCE V. RELIGION

1 In a small group, discuss religious and scientific explanations for the following events:
- natural disasters;
- disease;
- the origins of humanity.

2 Make a note of your responses.

Max Weber (see pp. 318–19) identified a progressive 'disenchantment' with religion in society, so that the supra-human is no longer significant. Phenomena that were once explained in terms of miracles and the supernatural are now open to scientific explanation based on reason and logic.

Critics of this viewpoint argue that science has not replaced religious beliefs – a high percentage of the population in modern industrial society claim to believe in God. The number of people believing in superstition, fortune telling and astrology also shows that the scientific and rational realm does not reign supreme. Indeed, the increasing interest in 'new age' movements can be seen as further evidence of this.

For others, science and religion are compatible and the existence of scientific explanations does not mean the end of religious ones. For example, medicine may explain death in terms of biological factors, while religion may explain the ultimate meaning of death.

Religion is changing rather than declining

It is argued by some that religion has undergone a process of change rather than a process of secularization. Institutional religion is only one form of religion and although this may be on the decline, religion is not. On an **individual** level, secularization has not occurred.

Berger and Luckman (1963) define religion as any way in which people make sense of the world (an inclusive definition). Religion is thus a basic human activity because we all attempt to make sense of our lives and surroundings. Looked at in this way, religion can be seen as remaining strong in the personal lives of individuals.

RESEARCHING SECULARIZATION

As we have seen, secularization can be examined using a range of indicators such as attendance statistics, loss of influence in politics, and so on. For this piece of research, you need to examine individuals' beliefs in and about religion.

1 Design and carry out questionnaires and unstructured interviews in order to find out :
   - How religious people are (here you will need to decide on a definition of religion and indicators of being religious, e.g. using Glock and Stark's ideas, outlined on p. 316.
   - Whether or not people see religion as of importance.
2 Your sample should allow you to compare the views of older and younger people who follow the same religion in order to see if there has been any decline in religious belief and practice.
3 You should produce a report outlining your approach and findings and evaluating the success of your research.

CHECK YOUR UNDERSTANDING

1 Identify and evaluate two arguments that suggest secularization has taken place. (6 marks)

2 Identify and explain one problem associated with reaching any conclusions about secularization. (3 marks)

SUMMARY

In this chapter, we have covered the following points:

- **Sociologists have put forward two broad definitions of religion. Exclusive definitions relate to religions which have a supra-human element to them, e.g. Christianity. Inclusive religions do not have a supra-human element to them, for example humanism or communism.**
- **Different sociologists have different viewpoints about the role religion plays within society.**
  - **Functionalists argue that religion creates order and stability by giving meaning to life and by providing society with a sense of shared norms and values.**
  - **Marxists argue that God is a `man-made' phenomenon and that religion operates as a form of social control, allowing more powerful groups in society to suppress the less powerful.**
  - **Weberians argue that religion can be the source of social conflict and a force for change within society.**
- **In many world religions, women do not enjoy the same rights as men. Feminists have argued that religion perpetuates many of the inequalities faced by women in society as a whole.**
- **Sociologists have attempted to categorize religions according to various criteria such as membership size, structure and hierarchy, and their relationship with the state. They have identified three main types of religious institution, these are churches, sects and denominations.**
- **The growth of new religious movements is seen by many sociologists as evidence of a growing dissatisfaction with traditional churches and a desire to find new forms of spirituality.**

- **All sorts of people join NRMs for a variety of different reasons including, coercion, and disillusionment with mainstream religions.**
- **NRMs can be broken down into three broad categories: world-affirming movements, world-accommodating movements, and world-rejecting movements.**
- **Many NRMs are shortlived but new NRMs are appearing all the time.**
- **Sociologists disagree about whether or not religion is in decline (a process known as secularization). It is true that regular church attendance is declining but this does not mean that fewer people hold religious beliefs. The decline in membership of traditional churches has, to some extent, been offset by the growth in NRMs and other forms of spirituality.**

EXAMINATION QUESTION 1

Study **Items A** and **B**. Then answer the questions that follow.

Item A

On an average Sunday, 10 per cent of England's adult population choose to be in church, rather than in bed, in the garden or at the DIY shop. One in seven of those go to church twice on Sunday. The English Church Census reveals that 3.7 million adults in England are churchgoers. Also, 1.2 million children under fifteen years of age attend church services or Sunday School, around 14 per cent of the child population. This means that over eight times as many people go to church each week as go to Football League matches.

Source: Parish magazine, Romsey Abbey

Item B **Membership in thousands of selected Christian groups and non-Christian religious groups in the United Kingdom**

	1970	1975	1980	1985
Christian groups				
Mormons	88	80	91	81
Jehovah's Witnesses	62	80	84	101
Spiritualists	45	57	52	49
Non-Christian religious groups				
Muslims	250	400	600	853
Sikhs	75	115	150	80
Hindus	50	100	120	130
Jews	113	111	111	109

Source: adapted from N. Abercrombie and A. Warde, *Contemporary British Society*,

(a) Read **Item A**.

(i) According to the information given, how many adults in England are churchgoers? (1 mark)

(ii) What is the source of the information used by the magazine? (1 mark)

(b) Study **Item B**.

(i) What is the largest non-Christian religious group in the United Kingdom? (1 mark)

(ii) Which Christian group has declined in number in the period covered by the table? (1 mark)

(c) Identify and explain **two** reasons why statistics concerning church membership may be misleading. (4 marks)

(d) Identify and fully explain **two** ways in which the established church affects people's lives in England and Wales today. (4 marks)

(e) Identify and fully explain **one** function that religion performs in a society. (4 marks)

(f) Identify and fully explain **one** way in which people's religious beliefs affect their behaviour. (4 marks)

Source: SEG Summer 1993, Paper 1, Question 2

EXAMINATION QUESTION 2

How far can it be argued that a process of secularization is taking place in Britain today?

(10 marks)

BIBLIOGRAPHY

Beaumont, P. (1997) 'Comet suicide cult rises from dead', *Observer Review*, 3 August.

Bruce, S. (1995) *Religion in Modern Britain*, Oxford University Press.

Bunting, M. (1997) 'And the church saw that business was good', *The Guardian*, 18 October.

Gentleman, A. (1997) 'Christian teenagers show their flesh is rather weak', *The Guardian*, 26 September.

Hooper, J. (1995) 'A temple of doom', *The Weekend Guardian*, 5 August.

Kaplan, H.M. (1969) 'The Black Muslims and the Negro Americans' quest for communion', *British Journal of Sociology*, 20 June .

Reed, C. (1997) 'How the Net closed on mass suicide', *The Guardian*, 28 March.

Sheffield, E. (1997) 'Cults target vulnerable students', *The Guardian*, 1 October.

Social Trends 27 (1997) Office for National Statistics and HMSO.

Wainwright, M. (1997) 'Archbishop rejects gay reforms', *The Guardian*, 15 July.

Wallis, R. 'The sociology of new religions', *Social Studies Review*, Volume 1, No. 1, (September), Philip Allan.

Wroe, M.(1997) 'Church of England in secret merger talks with methodists', *The Observer*, 19 October.

12 CHAPTER

Demography, Population and Urbanization

In this chapter, we will explore and attempt to answer the following questions:

1. **Demography**
   - **What is demography?**
   - **How is demographic data collected?**
   - **Why is demographic data collected?**
2. **Population change**
   - **What are the trends in the size of the population since 1750?**
   - **What factors affect the size of the population?**
   - **What are the trends in the birth rate and the death rate and how do we explain them?**
   - **How has the age structure of the population changed?**
   - **What is the occupational structure of the population?**
   - **How is the population distributed regionally?**
3. **Urbanization**
   - **What is urbanization?**
   - **What is gentrification?**
   - **What is deurbanization?**
   - **What is the impact of urbanization on patterns of social relations?**
   - **What are the differences and similarities between urban and rural social life?**

WHAT IS DEMOGRAPHY?

Demography is the statistical study of the population. This involves examining its size, growth, age and sex distribution, birth rates, death rates, life expectancy, and so on.

Table 12.1 Important terms used in population studies

The crude birth rate	the number of live births per 1,000 of the population (men and women) per year;
The age-specific birth rate	the number of live births per 1,000 women in a particular age group;
The fertility rate	the number of live births per 1,000 women of child-bearing age (usually aged 15–44);
The crude death rate	the number of deaths per 1,000 of the population per year;
The infant mortality rate	the number of deaths of infants under the age of one per 1,000 live births per year;
Life expectancy (at birth)	the average number of years a new-born baby may be expected to live.

We study the population by examining and analysing secondary sources of date, in particular official statistics. Demography is an important topic for sociological investigation because it reveals differences and inequalities in the life chances (see p. 40) of different social groups. For example, by examining demographic data we can learn that life expectancy in Britain varies according to gender and social class. Demography is also an important topic because population statistics and predictions about likely future population can be used practically by policy makers to plan the provision of resources and services, for example in public transport and health care.

Table 12.2 Questions asked by the 1991 census

The census questions ask for specific information on the household, such as:

- the type of tenure (e.g. rented or owned)
- the number of rooms
- whether amenities such as a bath, WC or central heating are available

There are also questions on each person in the household regarding their:

- sex
- date of birth
- marital status
- country of birth
- ethnic group
- whether they have had any long-term illness

There are also work-related questions for household members over the age of 16 on their:

- work status
- occupation
- means of daily journey to work
- place of work
- the number of hours worked per week

People over the age of 18 are questioned on their professional vocational and higher education qualifications.

HOW IS DEMOGRAPHIC DATA COLLECTED?

An important source of data about the whole population is the census, which is carried out by the government every ten years. The population census is based on a questionnaire survey, which is sent by the Registrar General's department to every household in Britain during census year. Although we are legally required to complete the questionnaire, not everyone does. Estimates suggest that over two million people were missed by the 1991 census, including homeless people, people living in temporary accommodation and those who did not complete the forms to avoid paying council tax (the poll tax, as it was then). The level of response to the 1991 census was 97.8 per cent.

For the first time in official statistics, the 1991 census asked a direct question on ethnic-group origin, so providing detailed information on the ethnic composition of the population.

Inevitably, given the massive scale of the census, errors do occur, as the following extract illustrates.

> *Some people are missed entirely, some double-counted; some characteristics such as age and gender are wrongly recorded, wrongly coded or wrongly key punched. In the processing of the 1981 census there were 100,000 keying errors according to the Registrar General's Review. Certain social groups are especially vulnerable to 'getting lost' – the old, adolescents and infants (as all their ages are likely to get distorted), and immigrants. Such omissions may well affect the overall picture of these particular groups.*
>
> Source: Slattery (1986)

A second source of demographic information is the registration of births, marriages and deaths. All births, marriages and deaths must be registered with the registrar at the local council offices. Your birth will be documented on your birth certificate and officially recorded as a statistic. In this sense, each of us is recorded as an official statistic!

Other important sources of demographic data used by sociologists are nationwide surveys, such as the Family Expenditure Survey, the General Household Survey and the Labour Force Survey.

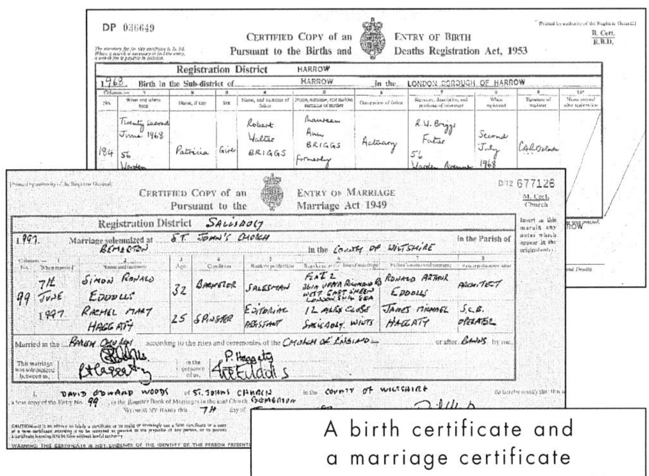

CERTIFIED COPY of an ENTRY OF BIRTH
Pursuant to the Births and Deaths Registration Act, 1953
Registration District HARROW

CERTIFIED COPY of an ENTRY OF MARRIAGE
Pursuant to the Marriage Act 1949

A birth certificate and a marriage certificate

Table 12.3: Sources of demographic information

Survey:	Census of Population	Family Expenditure Survey	General Household Survey	Labour Force Survey
Frequency:	every ten years	continuous	continuous	continuous
Type of respondent:	Household head	Household	All adults in household	All adults in household
Location:	UK	UK	GB	UK
Sample size:	Full count	10,150 addresses	11,914 households	63,000 addresses
Response rate:	98%	66%	80%	82%

Source: adapted from *Social Trends* (1997) p. 230

RESEARCHING DEMOGRAPHY

The following activities require you to undertake research in your school, college or local library.

1. *Social Trends* is published annually by the Office for National Statistics. Identify three different examples of demographic information that are recorded in *Social Trends*.
2. Choose one from the Family Expenditure Survey, the General Household Survey or the Labour Force Survey. After undertaking research, write a paragraph to explain the topics covered by the survey and the information provided by it.

POPULATION STATISTICS

'Birth rates and death rates are more valid than official statistics on crime.' Do you agree with this statement? Give two reasons why you either agree or disagree.

WHY IS DEMOGRAPHIC DATA COLLECTED?

Demographic information is collected by official bodies for a number of reasons.

- It provides a wealth of statistical information on the population in Britain at any one point in time and allows officials to make comparisons over time. Sociologists can also use this information to compare, for example, the birth rates in 1908, 1958 and 1998 in order to understand changing patterns.
- Statisticians are able to make estimates or projections about future likely population trends. They can estimate, for example, the future size of the population, its age structure, and the number of households. Such predictions help central and local government and health authorities to estimate future demand for services, to plan policies and allocate human and financial resources to meet likely needs.

It is important to bear in mind, however, that projections are statistical estimates of how things are likely to turn out. The way things actually turn out in the future will almost certainly be different. Here are some examples.

Education

Projections of educational participation help the government to plan spending on education. The government knows how many babies were born in 1997, so it can predict how many children will require primary school places in 2002–3. The government should also be able to work out how many school teachers will be required, enabling it to provide the necessary teacher training places.

Health

Population projections help the government to provide the type and quality of health services and care that are required. It will be able to train and supply the appropriate number of health workers such as nurses, midwives, paediatricians and general practitioners (GPs). If a dramatic increase in the number of births is predicted, for example, then priority can be given to maternity provision. District health authorities will be better informed in planning services and facilities.

Housing

Local authorities will be able to plan and make provision for rented housing. Provision of specialized dwellings for single people, people with disabilities or for those who are elderly can be prioritized. In the 1990s, the major use of these statistics is to make planning provision for private housing.

CHECK YOUR UNDERSTANDING

1 Explain two reasons why governments try to predict the future size of the population. (4 marks)

2 Explain one problem that governments may face in collecting population statistics. (2 marks)

POPULATION CHANGE

What are the trends in the population since 1750?

Since the beginning of the Industrial Revolution in the mid-eighteenth century, the population of the UK has been growing.

Between the middle of the nineteenth century and the middle of the twentieth, the population more than doubled in size, as shown in Table 12.4. This growth is predicted to continue into the 2020s.

Table 12.4 Estimated populations, 1750–1850 (millions)

	1750	1800	1850
Scotland	1.3	1.6	2.9
Wales	0.3*	0.6	1.2
England	5.8	8.7	16.7
Ireland	2.4	5.2*	6.7

** very approximate figures*

Source: Anderson (1996) p. 211

OVER ONE HUNDRED YEARS OF GROWTH

Table 12.5 UK population summary: census figures, 1851–1951 (thousands)

Year	Population
1851	22,259
1901	38,237
1911	42,082
1921	44,027
1931	46,038
1951	50,225

(There was no census in 1941.)

Source: adapted from *Annual Abstract of Statistics* (1996) p. 16

Table 12.5 summarizes the UK population between 1851 and 1961. Examine this information and then answer the following questions.

1 According to this information, what was the size of the population in **(a)** 1851, and **(b)** 1951?

2 How much larger was the population in 1951 than in 1851?

POPULATION PROJECTIONS INTO THE MILLENNIUM

The UK population is expected to continue to grow, peaking in 2023 at 61.2 million. Look at the figures in Table 12.6. According to this information:

1 Which country had the largest population in 1991?

2 Which country's population is expected to peak in 2011?

3 Which country's population is expected to decline between 1961 and 2031?

4 Which country has the smallest population?

5 What is the expected growth in the total UK population between 1991 and 2031?

Table 12.6 Population of the UK, 1961–2031 (thousands)

	1961	1971	1981	1991	2011	2031
England	43,561	46,412	46,821	48,208	50,757	51,150
Wales	2,635	2,740	2,813	2,891	2,955	2,886
Scotland	5,184	5,236	5,180	5,107	5,083	4,934
Northern Ireland	1,427	1,540	1,538	1,601	1,699	1,750
Total	52,807	55,928	56,352	57,808	60,493	60,720

Source: *Social Trends* (1997) p. 28

WHAT FACTORS AFFECT THE SIZE OF THE POPULATION?

The size of the population is affected by the number of people joining and leaving it. People join the population by being born into it or by migrating from another country. People leave by dying or by emigrating. This means that four factors affect population size: immigration, emigration, the birth rate and the death rate. Let's examine these in more detail.

International migration

Migration refers to the movement of population either nationally, from one region of a country to another, or internationally from one country to another. In addition to births and deaths, international migration will cause a change in the UK population as a whole.

Figures on immigration provide information on the number of people who come to live permanently in Britain from other countries. Figures on emigration show the number of people who leave Britain to settle permanently in another country. Statistics on net migration provide us with information on the number of people leaving the country (outflow) in proportion to the number arriving (inflow).

NET INTERNATIONAL MIGRATION

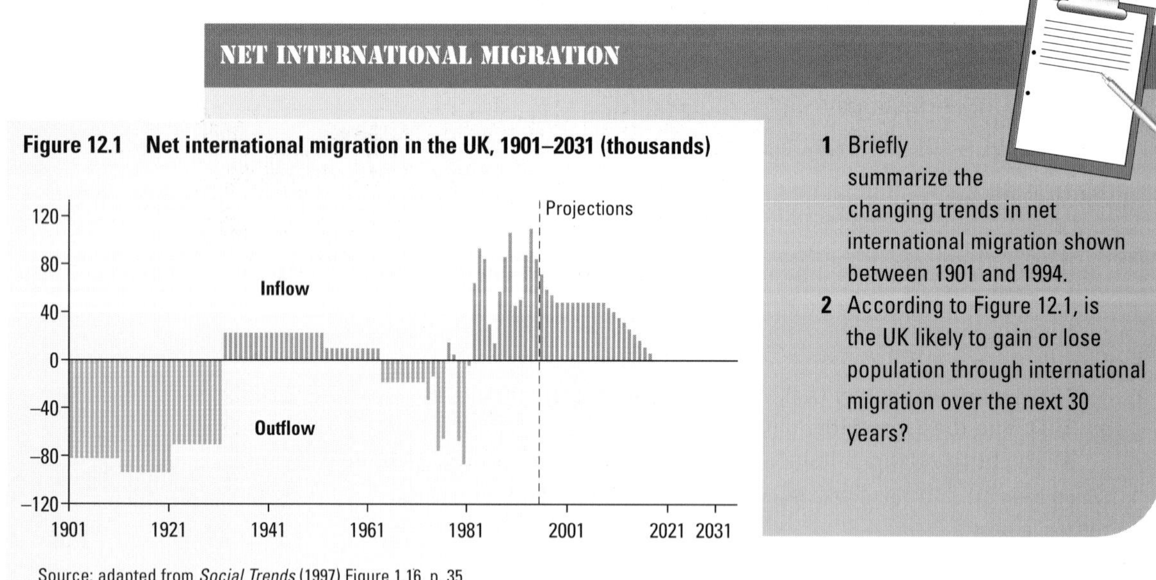

Figure 12.1 Net international migration in the UK, 1901–2031 (thousands)

Source: adapted from *Social Trends* (1997) Figure 1.16, p. 35

1 Briefly summarize the changing trends in net international migration shown between 1901 and 1994.
2 According to Figure 12.1, is the UK likely to gain or lose population through international migration over the next 30 years?

Birth rate

What are the trends in the birth rate over the last hundred years?

The crude birth rate is the number of live births per year per 1,000 of the population. Since the 1900s, the overall trend is of a decline in the birth rate, despite the dramatic increases in the number of births following the two world wars (1914–18, 1939–45) and in the 1960s.

Women born in the 1930s had an average of 2.4 children. Women born in the 1960s are expected to have an average of 1.9 children, while those born after 1980 are expected to have an average of 1.8 children. In general, women are having children later in life, so the average age of a woman having her first baby is expected to rise from 26 for women born in 1945 to over 28 for those born after 1965.

How do we explain the declining birth rate?

A number of factors have been identified in explaining the declining birth rate.

- During the nineteenth century, childrearing among poor families was motivated partly by economic factors. Many parents relied on their children's income and so tended to have bigger families. By the 1920s, factory legislation and the raising of the school leaving age to 14 made it more difficult for children to contribute to the family income through paid employment. Today, there is little financial incentive in having children. On the contrary, bringing up children is expensive!
- The increasing availability of reliable birth control methods has had an impact on the birth rate. The introduction of the contraceptive pill in the 1960s has meant that women now have much greater control over their fertility. The availability of safe and legal abortion (see p. 141) is also significant in explaining the declining birth rate.
- One impact of the feminist movement is that many women have rejected the idea that an adult female's main social role should centre on child care and housework. Greater opportunities in education and employment over the last 25 years have given women a wider range of options. Current predictions suggest that an increasing number of women will choose not to have any children.

THE DECLINING BIRTH RATE

Discuss the possible social and economic problems that may occur with a decline in the birth rate. Make a note of two social and two economic problems.

CHECK YOUR UNDERSTANDING

1 Identify two factors that affect population size. (2 marks)
2 Define the term 'birth rate'. (2 marks)
3 The birth rate in Britain has fallen over the last hundred years. Identify and explain two reasons why it has fallen. (4 marks)

Death rate

The death rate, or mortality rate, is the number of deaths per year per thousand of the population. The death rate in the UK has fallen since the end of the nineteenth century. The declining death rate can be linked to increased life expectancy and declining infant mortality (deaths in the first year of life). Statistics on life expectancy and infant mortality are important because they give us an idea of how healthy the population is. Let's look at each of these in more detail.

Life expectancy

Life expectancy at birth is the average number of years a newly born baby may be expected to live. People are, on average, living longer. Denscombe (1997) states that the UK life expectancy in the fifth century AD stood at around 33 years for men and 27 years for women. By 1901 this had increased to 45.5 for men and 49 for women. Between 1996 and 2031, life expectancy at birth is expected to increase from 79 to 83 years for women and from 74 to 78 years for men.

How do we explain the increase in life expectancy?

Increased life expectancy is linked to a number of factors, including welfare state provisions, developments in public health and medicine, and improvements in diet and nutrition.

The provisions of the welfare state

With the establishment of the welfare state after the Second World War, living standards improved considerably. Today, the state, along with the voluntary and private sectors, provides help to those in need. For example, people have access to damp-free housing through local authority provisions, free health care through the National Health Service (NHS) and social security benefit payments.

Developments in public health and medicine

During the nineteenth and early twentieth centuries, life expectancy rose as a result of government improvements in public health services. Services such as clean water supplies, sewerage and drainage systems, and refuse disposal meant that fewer people died from contagious, waterborne diseases.

Most of the increase in life expectancy, especially among children, results from improvements in preventive measures. Since 1945, much progress has been made in controlling major infectious diseases by taking preventive steps. The development of immunization programmes is an important factor. Between 1994 and 1995, 95 per cent of children in the UK were immunized against diphtheria, whooping cough and polio. Over 90 per cent were immunized against tetanus, measles, mumps and rubella. For women, there are national screening programmes for breast and cervical cancer.

Throughout the twentieth century, increased life expectancy can also be linked to important advances in medicine and surgery as well as to improvements in preventive care. Advanced medical developments such as open heart surgery, kidney dialysis and chemotherapy in the treatment of cancer, help people to live longer.

The Thames Water Tower, London

Improvements in water supplies, sewerage and drainage systems have led to improvements in public health

Improvements in diet and nutrition

Over the last 25 years, there have been changes in our diet which suggest that people are taking more notice of healthy eating messages from health organizations and the media. For example, the consumption of poultry has risen, while the consumption of red meats has fallen since the early 1970s.

A school innoculation

CHILDREN, DIET AND SOCIAL CLASS

There are differences in dietary patterns related to social class. Examine the information in Table 12.7 and then complete the following tasks.

1 Divide the eight items of food into two lists: **(a)** healthy items and **(b)** less healthy items.
2 Examine your list of healthy items. Who eats more of these – children from manual households or children from non-manual households?
3 Examine your list of less healthy food items. Who eats more of these – children from manual households or children from non-manual households?
4 Based on this information, write a short paragraph to summarize the links between children's eating habits and their social class background.

Table 12.7 Eating habits of children aged between one and a half and four and a half years in the UK: by social class of household head

Item of food (measured in grams per week)	Social class of household head	
	Manual	Non-manual
White bread	245	199
Chips	217	176
Meat pies and pastries	162	127
Chocolate sweets	109	91
Sugar	40	24
Bananas	228	239
Apples and pears	207	229
Wholegrain and high-fibre breakfast cereal	121	127

Source: adapted from *Social Trends* (1997) p. 130

SOCIAL CLASS DIFFERENCES IN DIET

In a small group, discuss the possible reasons why there are social class differences in diet. Make a note of the three most significant reasons.

CHECK YOUR UNDERSTANDING

1 What is meant by the term 'death rate'? (2 marks)
2 Identify and explain one reason for the fall in the death rate since 1750. (3 marks)

What is the relationship between life expectancy and social class?

As we have seen, life expectancy has increased since the nineteenth century. However, this fact alone does not give us the full picture. Life expectancy is linked to social class. On average, men in social class I (professionals) can expect to live around seven years longer than men in social class V (manual workers).

Access to health services and social class

The Black Report (1981) highlighted divisions in the quality of health and access to health provision for different social classes. The report identified links between social class and both life expectancy and infant mortality. It concluded that, generally, health inequalities between the social classes had widened since the 1950s. A more recent report, *The Health Divide* (1987), confirmed that such inequalities in health had persisted into the 1980s. Hilary Graham (1997) states that the most recent national evidence confirms that the health divide between social classes is widening.

THE HEALTH GAP

'A child born to parents living on the bottom rung of Britain's class ladder has less chance of reaching adulthood than a child in the highest social class. And a woman in an unskilled manual household is twice as likely to die before the age of 60 as a woman in a professional household.

Between the 1970s and 1990s, death rates among men in higher social classes fell more rapidly than among men lower down the class ladder. Men in professional and managerial groups (social classes I and II) have broadly similar death rates, and the gap between them and men in lower occupational groups (social classes III, IV and V) is growing larger. Among men in social class V, death rates are now higher than they were 20 years ago.'

Source: adapted from Graham (1997)

Read through the extract on the left and then identify three pieces of evidence that suggest that there is a health gap between the social classes.

How do we explain social class differences in life expectancy?

- Social class differences in life expectancy and health have been explained by some in terms of lifestyle and diet. According to this view, members of social class V eat too many chips, smoke too many cigarettes and take insufficient exercise. Cigarette smoking is more common among the manual social groups than the non-manual groups. According to data from *Social Trends* (1997), in 1994–5 men in the unskilled manual group were two and a half times more likely to smoke than those in professional groups. According to evidence in a Department of Health report (1995), however, lifestyle and diet are important factors but they provide only a partial explanation for the social class differences in health and life expectancy. For example, social class differences in health exist even among those who have never smoked. We need to look at other factors.
- The pay and holiday entitlement of manual workers is generally less generous than that of professionals. Similarly, conditions of work differ. Manual workers are more at risk of hazards and accidents at work. Dangerous manual jobs can be found in construction, demolition, chemicals and mining.

- The standard of living of manual workers is likely to be lower than that of professional workers. Manual workers are more likely to live in poor housing and are less likely to be able to afford a well-balanced diet. Hunt (1996) points out that surveys have shown that the middle classes are more aware than others of the importance of a good diet and other aspects of health.
- Professional workers are more likely to be able to afford to pay for private health care. They are more likely to belong to a private health care scheme at work.
- Members of the middle class are more likely to know how the NHS works and may be more confident and assertive in dealing with health care workers.

WOMEN LIVE LONGER THAN MEN

Read through the following extract and then answer these questions:

1 How does Graham explain women's increased life expectancy during the twentieth century?
2 Identify four causes of death that account for much of the higher male death rates, according to Graham.

In Britain in the nineteenth century, women's life expectancy was shorter than men's. Through the twentieth century in Britain, maternal mortality (death of the mother in childbirth) has declined and, with it, women's life expectancy has increased. In the 1980s, it is men whose lives are more at risk: their death rates from causes linked to diet, stress, smoking, vehicle and industrial accidents and drinking are all higher. Deaths from lung cancer, bronchial disease, heart disease, accidents and suicide account for the major part of the higher mortality rates among men. Recently, however, these sex differences in mortality appear to be narrowing.

Source: adapted from Graham (1987)

How do we explain the gender difference in life expectancy?

A number of reasons have been put forward to explain why women tend to live longer than men.

- Men tend to drink and smoke more heavily than women.
- Women are less likely than men to be involved in dangerous jobs; work involving health hazards or the risk of industrial accidents.
- Women are less likely to be involved in vehicle accidents than men.

IS THE GENDER GAP NARROWING?

Graham (1987) suggests that recently the differences in mortality between men and women seem to be narrowing. In a small group, discuss the possible reasons for this. Now make a note of three likely reasons.

CHECK YOUR UNDERSTANDING

1 What is meant by life expectancy? (1 mark)
2 Men and women tend to live longer today than 100 years ago. Identify and explain two reasons for this. (4 marks)
3 State two reasons why women tend to live longer than men. (2 marks)

Infant mortality

Increased life expectancy can be explained in part by reductions in infant and child mortality since the beginning of the twentieth century. The infant mortality rate refers to the number of infant deaths (under one year) per 1,000 live births per year. It is seen as a good indicator of the population's health. In 1981 the rate of infant mortality in the UK was 10.4 deaths per 1,000 live births inside marriage, but by 1994 this figure had fallen to 5.4.

How do we explain the declining infant mortality rate?

Many of the factors that have contributed to the increase in life expectancy also explain the decline in infant mortality rates. In addition, the introduction of a midwifery service in the early part of the twentieth century meant that good practice could now reach a wider audience.

INFANT MORTALITY AND SOCIAL CLASS

Table 12.8 Infant mortality in the UK, by social class based on father's occupation

Social class	Rates per 1,000 live births inside marriage	
	1981	1994
Professional	7.8	4.5
Managerial and technical	8.2	4.5
Skilled non-manual	9.0	5.1
Skilled manual	10.5	5.5
Semi-skilled	12.7	6.4
Unskilled	15.7	6.8
All social classes	10.4	5.4

Source: adapted from Social Trends (1997) p. 122

In the late 1990s, around 4,000 babies under the age of one year died every year, but this does not give us the complete picture. There are differences in infant mortality between different social classes, as Table 12.8 illustrates.

According to this information:

1 In which two groups were deaths within one year of birth least common in both 1981 and 1994?
2 In which two groups were deaths within one year of birth most common in both 1981 and 1994?
3 Which group had an infant mortality rate of 5.5 in 1994?
4 What is the overall trend in infant mortality rates between 1981 and 1994?

How do we explain the social class difference in infant mortality?

- One explanation focuses on the different levels of income and standards of living between professional and unskilled manual workers. Members of social class V are more vulnerable to poverty than those of social class I. Manual workers are more likely than professionals to live in damp or cold housing and this may affect the health of a young baby. People in social class I are able to afford to eat healthily and to take up advice on healthy eating.
- A second explanation is that the different social classes use the medical services to a greater or lesser extent. For example, mothers in social class I may make greater use of pre- and post-natal services.

CHECK YOUR UNDERSTANDING

1 What is meant by the term 'infant mortality rate'? (2 marks)
2 Identify and describe two reasons for the lower infant mortality rate amongst children of professional workers. (4 marks)

What is the link between ethnicity and health?

We have examined health inequalities based on gender and social class. There is also evidence of health inequalities based on ethnicity. Members of some minority ethnic groups experience worse health than other groups. Culley and Dyson (1993) summarize the main features of ethnicity and health differences:

> *There are inequalities between different ethnic groups in terms of patterns of illness and premature death. From the limited data available, we can summarize some of the main features of differences in health and ethnicity. Both the African-Caribbean population and those born in the Indian subcontinent have a higher than average mortality from liver cancer, TB and diabetes. The African-Caribbean population has a significantly higher mortality from strokes and high blood pressure than the average for the country as a whole. The Asian population also has a higher than average mortality from heart disease, but fewer than expected deaths from several cancers that are common in the UK, for example lung cancer. Children from Asian families appear to have a higher than average risk of developing rickets, while the adult population is at increased risk from osteomalacia, or softening of the bones. All black communities appear to suffer disproportionately from deaths due to accidents, poisonings and violence.*
>
> Source: Culley and Dyson (1993)

Hilary Graham (1997) makes the point that the richer minority ethnic groups, including Indians and African Asians, have better health than poorer minority ethnic groups, including Pakistani, Bangladeshi and Caribbean communities.

How do we explain these inequalities in health?

One explanation for these inequalities in health is that they reflect social class differences. Culley and Dyson (1993) point out that the most recent migrants – such as those of Bangladeshi and Pakistani descent – are more likely than migrants of African-Caribbean and Indian descent to be concentrated in the lowest occupational groups and in the poorest housing. Culley and Dyson suggest that people of African-Caribbean and Asian descent are concentrated in:

- low-paid manual occupations;
- jobs in industries that are most hazardous to health, such as laundry, textiles and clothing industries;
- occupations that have been especially affected by successive economic recessions, such as in textiles and footwear.

They argue that shift work, poor job security and fringe benefits, low pay and the high risk of unemployment are all likely to lead to poorer health among black and minority ethnic communities.

A second explanation of health inequalities focuses on racism. Culley and Dyson (1993) suggest that as a result of racism, black and ethnic minority people have poorer access to health resources such as education, employment, good housing and transport facilities than other groups.

How has the age and gender structure of the population changed?

In 1995, the UK had a population of 58.6 million people. Sociologists are interested in examining the structure of the population according to age and gender.

THE AGE AND GENDER STRUCTURE OF THE POPULATION

Figure 12.2 UK population 1995, by gender and age (thousands)

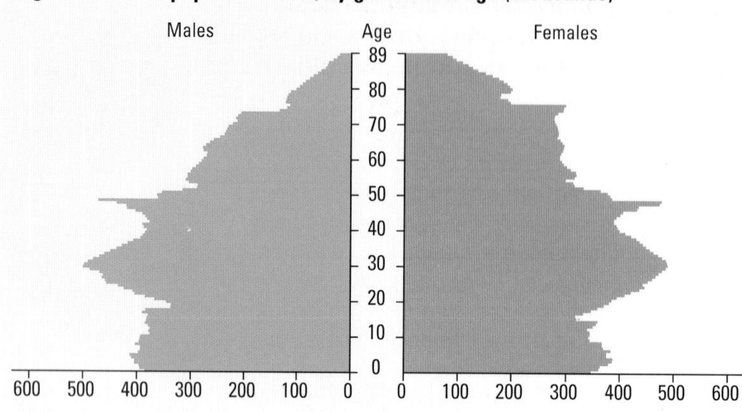

Source: adapted from *Social Trends* (1997) table 1.4, p. 29

1 According to this information:
(a) which gender outnumbers the other until the age of 40?
(b) are there more men or women aged over 80?

2 Using the information, try to work out when two 'baby booms' (dramatic increases in the number of births) occurred during the twentieth century.

Declining birth rates combined with longer life expectancy mean that there are fewer children and young people in the population and an increasing number of people who are in later life.

PROJECTED DEPENDENCY RATIOS

The dependency ratio represents the number of people aged under 16, or over state retirement age, to every 100 people of working age. For example, it is predicted that in 2051 there will be 28 people under 16 and 43 people aged over state retirement age to every 100 people of working age, giving an overall dependency ratio of 71 (28 + 43) per 100.

Table 12.9 UK projected dependency ratios, 1994–2061

Year	Child dependency ratio		Elderly dependency ratio		Overall dependency ratio
1994	34	+	30	=	64
2001	33	+	29	=	62
2011	30	+	31	=	61
2021	28	+	30	=	58
2031	29	+	39	=	68
2041	28	+	43	=	71
2051	28	+	43	=	71
2061	29	+	44	=	73

Source: adapted from *Social Trends* (1997) p. 17

According to the information in Table 12.9:

1 What is the child dependency ratio expected to be in 2021?
2 What is the elderly dependency ratio expected to be in 2041?
3 What is the projected overall dependency ratio in 2031?
4 In general, is the child dependency ratio expected to rise or fall between 2001 and 2061?
5 In general, is the elderly dependency ratio expected to rise or fall between 2011 and 2061?

What are the social consequences of an ageing population?

The UK has an ageing population profile as a result of longer life expectancy and declining birth rates. We have seen that the elderly dependency ratio is expected to increase over the next 50 or so years. One rather negative response to this projection is to focus on the increase in the burden of dependency.

The negative response – the increasing burden of dependency

According to this view, there will be an increasing financial burden on the working population to meet the demand from older members of society for facilities such as personal social services, medical services, hospitals and pensions. Women, as wives and daughters, are likely to be under the most pressure to care for elderly relatives.

One problem with the idea of the increasing burden of dependency, however, is that it tends to lump together all people over the age of 65. Harper (1997) points out that the experience of a healthy, 65-year-old, recently retired married man is very different to that of a frail, widowed woman in her 90s.

The positive response – older people as an asset

A second, more positive approach emphasizes the fact that today, elderly people are generally fitter and more healthy than ever before. People in later life are not only on the receiving end of services – they also provide services. Much of the work within Age Concern, for example, is done by volunteers, the majority of whom are retired. Some commentators suggest that we should aim to encourage more part-time paid work beyond current retirement ages.

> *Elderly people are providers as well as consumers of informal family care and form the backbone of many voluntary organizations. They now comprise an electorally significant proportion of the population, and in the US have organized as an effective political lobby.*
>
> Source: Ginn and Arber (1992)

Living independently in later life

Social and medical advances mean that the quality of later life is improving. Most people are able to maintain reasonably healthy and independent lives into their 70s and 80s. Ginn and Arber (1992) suggest that elderly people are concerned to maintain independence for as long as possible. They do not wish to depend on others because, in so doing, they may lose their self-respect. Ginn and Arber identify three key resources that influence whether an elderly person can live independently in the community: material, health and caring resources. The three kinds of resources interlock to form a resource triangle.

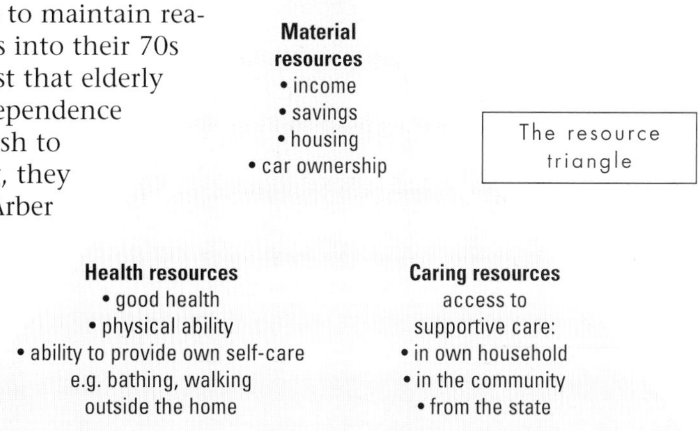

The resource triangle

Material resources
- income
- savings
- housing
- car ownership

Health resources
- good health
- physical ability
- ability to provide own self-care e.g. bathing, walking outside the home

Caring resources
access to supportive care:
- in own household
- in the community
- from the state

Source: adapted from Ginn and Arber (1992)

Ginn and Arber make the important point that an individual's social class, gender and ethnicity influence his or her chance of possessing each type of resource. As a result, class, gender and ethnicity affect an individual's independence, well-being and opportunities for full participation in social life. In their research, Ginn and Arber found gender differences, with older women disadvantaged in each of the three areas. In this way, some people are worse placed than others in later life depending on their gender, ethnicity and social class.

MEETING PEOPLE'S NEEDS IN LATER LIFE

Discuss the likely social and economic effects of increasing numbers of elderly people in the UK. What social changes might be required in order for society to meet the needs of older people?

Now make a note of three significant points raised during your discussion.

CHECK YOUR UNDERSTANDING

1 Explain what is meant by the term 'the burden of dependency'. (2 marks)
2 Explain briefly why this term is not necessarily useful to sociologists. (2 marks)
3 State two positive consequences of the increase in the numbers of people in later life in the UK over the next 20 years. (2 marks)

The occupational structure of the population

Figure 12.3 shows the social class of men and women in the UK based on their occupational status. There are significant differences in the social class structure of men and women.

GENDER AND SOCIAL CLASS

Figure 12.3 The social class of men and women in Great Britain based on occupational status, 1996 (percentages)

Males

Females

Professional

Intermediate

Skilled non-manual

Skilled manual

Partly skilled

Unskilled manual

40 30 20 10 0

0 10 20 30 40

Source: adapted from *Social Trends* (1997) table 1.9, p. 31

1 Using the information in Figure 12.3, draw up two lists, one for the occupational groups that men are more likely to be in and one for the occupational groups women are more likely to be in.
2 Which two occupational groups showed the biggest difference in the percentage of women and men in them?

The regional distribution of the population

The population of the UK is not distributed evenly throughout its member countries, as Table 12.6 shows (see. p. 345). Nor is it distributed evenly around the regions. There has been a population shift from the north to the south, related to changing employment opportunities. Official statistics on regional trends published in 1995 show that East Anglia and the south-west of England have had the fastest-growing populations since 1981, while the populations in Scotland, the north and north-west have all fallen slightly.

Table 12.10 illustrates the changes in the population of Great Britain between 1971 and 1995. Just under one-fifth of the population of Great Britain lived in rural areas in 1995. Overall, the population of these areas grew by 17 per cent between 1971 and 1995, which was faster than that of urban centres.

Table 12.10 Population of Great Britain by type of area, 1971 and 1995 (millions)

Type of area	1971	1995
Prospering areas	11.0	12.6
Mining and industrial areas	13.0	12.1
Urban centres	11.2	11.6
Rural areas	8.9	10.4
Maturer areas*	6.3	6.6
Inner London	4.1	3.6
All areas	54.4	57.0

** Maturer areas include resort and retirement areas*

Source: *Social Trends* (1997) p. 30

CHECK YOUR UNDERSTANDING

Identify and explain fully one reason for the shift in population from the north to the south. (4 marks)

WHAT IS URBANIZATION?

Urbanization refers to the growth in the proportion of the population living in towns and cities. The process of urbanization involves the majority of the population migrating from rural to urban areas, that is, from the countryside to towns and cities. In Britain, this process started at the beginning of the nineteenth century and has continued up to the 1970s. In 1801, only 17 per cent of the population in England and Wales were living in urban areas of over 20,000 people. By 1951, this figure stood at 81 per cent, but by 1981 it had fallen to 76 per cent of the population.

In 1801, 9.73 per cent of the population of England and Wales lived in London and only a further 7.21 per cent lived in towns of 20,000 people or more. But by the middle of the century the urban population of Britain was greater than the rural, and indeed, since 1911 four-fifths of the population have lived in areas defined as urban. The period from the 1840s to the 1870s showed the most rapid rates of urbanization, although places such as Manchester, which doubled its size in the first 30 years of the nineteenth century, were ahead of the national pattern.

Source: Pahl (1970) p. 19

The reason for urbanization

Urbanization in Britain was closely linked to the process of industrialization that involved the mass production of goods by machines in factories. Jewson (1991) points out that in the nineteenth century, factory-based production required a large workforce. As a result, there were high rates of urbanization during the nineteenth century. Masses of people flooded into hastily constructed or expanded industrial towns to take up jobs in factories.

Gentrification

During the early stages of urbanization, the rich lived in the city centres but, later on, those who could afford to do so moved to the suburbs. Today, urban areas are divided broadly along social class lines.

Industrial growth in Staffordshire at the turn of the twentieth century

London Docklands today

A relatively recent development is gentrification, which refers to the migration of the middle classes to the city centres. In London during the 1980s, increasingly affluent middle-class professionals began to buy and renovate run-down Victorian and Georgian housing in relatively poor parts of London. As a result, house prices rose and many local people were unable to purchase houses in these areas. The development of new wealthy areas in places like Islington, for example, is often accompanied by the displacement of the poorer local population.

Abercrombie et al. (1994) suggest that the collapse of employment in British docks and ports has made a large amount of land and property available. Some of this has resulted in relatively expensive housing in dockland areas in cities such as Liverpool, London and Cardiff.

What is meant by the 'inner city'?

The term 'inner city' is usually used to refer to the older, geographically central area of a city, as opposed to its outer area.

What are the characteristics of the inner city?

Many sociologists and journalists characterize inner cities in terms of their social problems. For example, Harrison (1983) documented the problems affecting inner-city areas, in particular those of Hackney in London in the early 1980s. He painted a picture of poverty and disadvantage, crime and heavy policing, substandard health care and poor housing.

Harrison concluded that a radical change in government policy was necessary in order for these problems to be addressed. (See the extract on the right.)

> *The inner city is now, and is likely to remain, Britain's most dramatic and intractable social problem. For here are concentrated the worst housing, the highest unemployment, the greatest density of poor people, the highest crime rates and, more recently, the most serious threat posed to established law and order since the Second World War.*
>
> Source: Harrison (1983) p. 21

Unemployment rates

Inner-city areas have relatively high rates of long-term and youth unemployment among the local population. In July 1995, for example, inner-city Hackney and Haringey had the highest unemployment rates in London. Consequently, some inner-city residents are vulnerable to poverty and deprivation.

Housing problems

Raynsford (1990) identifies three key inner-city housing problems:

- The shortage of housing as a result of the reduction of council housing stock.
- The poor condition of the remaining housing stock. Slum clearance after the Second World War, and later remodernization programmes in the 1960s, succeeded in removing much of the worst housing from the Victorian era. Today, most houses have indoor toilets and baths. However, there is a growing problem of disrepair in privately rented and owner-occupied housing. On many council estates, housing has deteriorated.
- The concentration of poorer, disadvantaged households in certain areas of the city, often in the worst housing conditions.

Other social problems

- **Demand on health and social services**: in view of their poor-quality housing and relative poverty, inner-city areas place a greater demand on health and social services in comparison with other areas.
- **Crime rate**: inner-city areas appear to have higher crime rates than the suburbs and rural areas. This may reflect different policing methods, however. MacGregor (1990) notes that drug use affects all social groups, but that young drug users in inner cities are more visible than wealthy socialites.
- **Pollution problems**: noise and air pollution, for example lead pollution from motor vehicles, are more likely to occur in inner-city areas compared to suburbs and rural areas.
- **Social unrest**: during the summer of 1981, inner-city areas of Manchester, Bristol, London and elsewhere experienced riots. Such riots recurred periodically during the 1980s and can be seen as symptoms of social distress. The causes are, in part, linked to inner-city social problems of poverty, deprivation and unemployment. Some sociologists have explained the causes in terms of policing methods in the inner city, for example the harassment of young black men. MacGregor and Pimlott (1990) note tension between cultural groups, between earlier immigrants and newer ones, and between large sections of urban youth and the police.

Belgravia

Whose problem?

Townsend (1990) makes the point that social problems affecting inner-city areas should be seen in context; they are national rather than local or area problems. He argues that we should avoid stereotyping whole communities and instead focus attention on questioning government policies that create social ills.

Is 'inner city' a useful term?

Raynsford (1990) rejects the definition of 'inner cities' purely in geographical terms. Belgravia and Kensington, for example, are areas of inner London, but they do not exhibit the characteristics normally associated with the term 'inner cities'. He believes that the use of such a term can be misleading because it prompts stereotyped images of dereliction and decaying housing estates. In reality, urban housing problems are much more varied and complex. He suggests that the worst housing problems in urban areas today are found in big Victorian mansions that have been converted into 'bed and breakfast' hotels to accommodate homeless families.

CHECK YOUR UNDERSTANDING

1 Identify two major social problems that exist in Britain's inner cities today. (2 marks)

2 Identify and explain two reasons why 'inner-city' is not necessarily a useful term. (2 marks)

WHAT IS DEURBANIZATION?

Deurbanization or counter-urbanization involves migration from large towns and cities to the countryside, new towns and the suburbs. Deurbanization has occurred in Britain particularly since the late 1960s and early 1970s. As a result, large cities are losing population and smaller areas are gaining population.

Reasons for deurbanization

- As we saw on p. 357, urbanization was linked to industrialization. Deurbanization is closely linked to more recent changes in industry since the 1960s. Many companies and businesses moved to specially created new towns such as Milton Keynes and Runcorn, where land costs were lower. As a result, new employment opportunities are available outside urban areas.
- Developments in transport meant that commuting to the cities on a daily basis became a possibility and so 'commuter belts' developed. Car ownership has increased and a network of motorways has been built. More recent developments in communications technology have meant that people in some occupations can work from home and so are not tied to living in cities.
- People migrate from urban to rural areas because the idea of living in the countryside has appeal. (See pp. 224–5 for more on 'downshifting'.)
- The association of inner cities with social problems has been a factor in deurbanization. Harrison (1983) notes that people with skills or qualifications to offer employers or with enough money to buy houses outside urban areas are more likely to move.

Consequences of deurbanization

The process of deurbanization has had both positive and negative impacts on the countryside and on local communities outside urban areas.

- Employment opportunities have increased as businesses have relocated to rural and other areas outside towns and cities.
- Housing, industrial and motorway developments around new towns have resulted in threats to some areas of outstanding natural beauty or sites of special scientific interest (SSSIs), as environmental campaigners point out.
- Deurbanization has led to social tension between newcomers and local people in some areas, as research by Newby reveals.

Newby's case study of life in the East Anglian countryside in the mid-1980s examines the impact of counter-urbanization.

The influx of urban newcomers to the countryside has generated the feeling that the quality of rural life is being threatened by their arrival. It is believed that the newcomers do not appreciate the value of agricultural work. And at the same time it is thought that such newcomers also seek to preserve the quaint and inappropriate aspects of rural charm. This has led to considerable social tension, since newcomers will often oppose new shopping developments or council houses which would be of particular benefit to farm-workers.

Source: adapted from Abercrombie (1994) p. 321

- The purchase by commuters of homes or second homes in small villages has affected local house prices. In some areas, house prices may be too high for local people.

CHECK YOUR UNDERSTANDING

1. Define the following terms:
   - **(a)** urbanization (2 marks)
   - **(b)** deurbanization (2 marks)
2. Explain briefly why urbanization occurred in the UK in the nineteenth century. (2 marks)
3. Suggest two reasons why deurbanization has occurred in the UK over the last 20 years. (2 marks)
4. State two possible effects of an increase in population size on rural communities. (2 marks)

What impact does urbanization have on patterns of social relations?

Tonnies (1957) tried to make sense of the massive changes brought about by industrialization and urbanization. He suggested that the crucial difference between traditional and new urban industrial societies lay in their social relations. Relationships in pre-industrial society were based on 'community' life, while the urban industrial way of life was based on 'association'.

Community	Association
There is close contact between people who are involved in a close-knit network. People's friends, for example, will all know one another. They will all be familiar with the details of one another's family backgrounds.	People will know little or nothing about the majority of other people they come across on a day-to-day basis. In this sense, most relationships are superficial, anonymous and fleeting.
People feel a sense of belonging and identify with their village and local community. They all share a sense of group solidarity and identity based on shared values and interests.	People do not feel any great sense of community or belonging. They are likely to move from one area to another, for example as a result of promotion at work. A sense of group solidarity does not exist as people tend not to share many interests.
People will come across other members of the community in all of their roles, for example as mother, doctor, neighbour or member of a social club.	People have knowledge of others and relate to them in specific social roles rather than in multiple roles. For example, a person may know their GP as a doctor but not as a neighbour or mother.
A person's status is ascribed or fixed on the basis of his or her family background.	A person's status is achieved. If you know nothing about your neighbour's background you are likely to treat her according to her achieved rather than ascribed status.
There will be a high level of informal social control from within the community, because everyone knows everyone else.	Social relationships tend to be anonymous, so there is less informal social control. If you get into trouble at school, for example, it is unlikely that your teacher will discuss this with your parents informally during a chance meeting at the local social club.

Differences between rural and urban social life today

There has been a long-standing debate among sociologists about whether the patterns of social life in rural areas are very different to those found in large cities. One view stresses the differences between rural and urban social life. Louis Wirth (1938) suggested that there was a distinctive **urban way of life** in cities. He identified three key influences on urban life: size, dense concentration of people, and the social differences between them.

- Cities, he suggested, are huge places that contain thousands of people. As a result, social relationships in cities tend to be superficial, casual and anonymous.
- Cities are compact places where the population is densely concentrated. People tend to live very close to each other, often in overcrowded conditions.
- In cities, people come from a wide variety of backgrounds. There are social differences between people, for example in terms of social class, level of income, ethnicity and cultural background. As a result, there is more potential for conflict and social tension than in rural areas, where people come from more similar backgrounds to one another.

Critics, however, suggest that sociologists such as Tonnies and Wirth present a very rosy and romanticized picture of rural life and a rather negative view of cities. In reality, cities are creative and exciting places, with many employment, leisure and recreational opportunities.

CITY LIFE

Cities are lively and fascinating places. In a small group, discuss the advantages of living in a city. Make a list of at least five advantages.

Similarities between rural and urban social life

Some sociologists argue that rural and urban social life are becoming increasingly similar and that differences are often exaggerated. They point out that social conflict and divisions based, for example, on class and status, exist in rural areas and are not confined to the cities.

People in both rural and urban areas may face similar problems. For many people, the reality of living in the countryside involves social isolation, poor public services and severe poverty. Oppenheim and Harker (1996) point out that rural poverty certainly exists but it is more dispersed or spread out than urban poverty. As a result, poverty is more hidden and less obvious in rural areas than in cities.

A GREEN AND NOT-SO-PLEASANT LAND?

1 With reference to the extract, identify three problems that are faced by some people living in the countryside.
2 Why do you think rural problems often receive less attention than those in inner cities?

In pictures and photographs, rural life can still look idyllic: peace, calm, natural beauty, breathtaking landscapes. But behind the pictures life is different – not just for the poor, but for the middle-income too. The latest national count shows 2 in 5 villages in Britain have no shop, 1 in 3 has no post office, 3 in 5 no school, 3 in 4 no GP. More than half the workers in farming, forestry or fishing earn less than £200 per week. A car is often indispensable for mobility, but a quarter of rural households don't have one. Suicide rates are particularly high in the countryside.

Poverty affects between 20 and 30 per cent of people living in the British countryside. It is usually hidden from view, but it is real, with low pay, isolation and an increasing lack of public services among its starkest characteristics.

Source: *The Guardian*, 28 February 1996

Deurbanization has meant that many urban workers now live in rural areas and commute to work on a daily basis. Newby's study (see p. 361) of life in the East Anglian countryside found that incomers were seen as outsiders rather than as locals, so people in villages were divided into 'them and us'. This suggests that a spirit of community among all villagers based on their shared place of residence is unlikely to exist.

Communities may exist in cities, based on neighbourhood, lifestyle or cultural background, for example. A number of community studies have identified the existence of the **urban village**. In *Family and Kinship in East London*, for example, Young and Willmott (1957) identified the importance of community relationships in their study of urban Bethnal Green. They argued that long residence contributed to the creation of a sense of community with others living there. They highlighted the importance of the family and kinship network that underlay the working-class community in Bethnal Green.

LIFESTYLE CHANGES AND COMMUNITY RELATIONSHIPS

Young and Willmott's research was carried out between 1953 and 1955. Television was hardly part of the culture then; few working-class people had cars, and consumer goods such as washing machines and fridges were much rarer in working-class homes than they are now.

Source: adapted from Pahl (1970) p. 69

In a small group, discuss how the absence of television, washing machines and cars might affect lifestyle.

COMMUNITY, ASSOCIATION AND YOU

We live in an urban industrial society, and so, according to sociologists such as Tonnies, our social relationships will fit in with the association patterns.

1 Do your social relationships fit in with the association pattern? If so, in what ways?
2 Are there any community features in your social relationships? If so, what are they?

Now write a paragraph to explain how useful you find the community/association distinction.

CHECK YOUR UNDERSTANDING

Identify and explain two similarities between urban and rural social life. (4 marks)

SUMMARY

In this chapter, we have covered the following points:

- **Demography is the systematic study of population, including its size, age and gender structure, birth and death rates and life expectancy.**
- **Demographic data is collected because it allows policy makers to plan the allocation of services and resources, such as health, education and housing. Population data also reveals inequalities in life chances between different social groups.**
- **Demographic data is collected in a number of ways: through the**

government census conducted every ten years; though the compulsory registration of births, deaths and marriages; through other nationwide surveys such as the General Household Survey.

- **Since 1750 the population of the UK has grown. This growth is predicted to continue until the 2020s.**
- **The size of the population is affected by international migration (inflow and outflow), the birth rate and the death rate.**
- **The UK's birth rate is declining. Women born since 1960 are tending to have children later in life and to have fewer children than women born before 1960.**
- **The UK's death rate is also declining as life expectancy increases and infant mortality decreases. More people are living longer.**
- **Life expectancy is linked to social class, ethnicity and gender. Socially disadvantaged groups have a lower life expectancy than more privileged groups.**
- **The population of the UK is ageing. The declining birth rate combined with longer life expectancy means that there are fewer young people and more elderly people in the population today.**
- **Urbanization is the growth in the proportion of the population living in towns and cities. Urbanization reached a peak in the 1950s and was linked to the nation's industrialization. Since the late 1960s, the proportion of the population living in urban areas has declined slightly. This phenomenon is known as deurbanization.**
- **Sociologists such at Tonnies have studied the impact of urbanization on patterns of social relations. Tonnies has argued that the 'spirit of community' is weaker in towns and cities than in rural societies. Other sociologists, such as Young and Willmott, have argued that strong social networks may also exist within urban areas, particularly in working-class communities. Many sociologists claim that there are more similarities than differences between urban and rural life in the late twentieth century.**

EXAMINATION QUESTION 1

In what ways might sociologists see life on a housing estate in a large city as similar to, and different from, life in a rural village?

(10 marks)

Source: SEG GCSE Sociology, Summer 1996, Higher Tier, Section C, Question 8, p. 14

EXAMINATION QUESTION 2

In which social class would you expect to find the most disability and illness? Explain the reasons for your answer.

(7 marks)

Source: NEAB GCSE Sociology, June 1996, Tier P, A2 part (d), p. 5

BIBLIOGRAPHY

Abercrombie, N. et al. (1994) *Contemporary British Society*, Polity Press.

Anderson, M. (1996) 'Population change in north-western Europe', in M. Anderson (ed) *British Population History*, Cambridge University Press.

Culley, L. and Dyson, S. (1993) '"Race", inequality and health', in *Sociology Review*, Volume 3, No. 1 (September).

Denscombe, M. (1997) *Sociology Update*, Olympus Books.

DHSS (1981) *Inequalities in Health: Report of a Research Working Group*.

Frankenberg, R. (1969) *Communities in Britain*, Penguin.

Ginn, J. and Arber, S. (1992) 'Gender and resources in later life', in *Sociology Review*, Volume 2, No. 2.

Graham, H. (1987) 'Women, health and illness', *Social Studies Review*, Volume 3, No. 1.

Graham, H. (1997) 'Health: Poverty is a deadly disease', *The Guardian*, 25 June.

Harper, S. (1997) 'Contesting later life', in P. Cloke and J. Little (eds), *Contested Countryside Culture*, Routledge.

Harrison, P. (1983) *Inside the Inner City: Life under the Cutting Edge*, Penguin.

Hunt, S. (1996) 'Diet and inequality: food for thought', *Sociology Review*, Volume 6, No. 1 (September).

Jackson, B. (1968) *Working-Class Community*, Routledge and Kegan Paul.

Jewson, N. (1991) 'The development of cities in capitalist societies', *Sociology Review*, Volume 1, No. 2 (November).

Lee, D. and Newby, H. (1983) *The Problem of Sociology*, Unwin Hyman.

MacGregor, S. (1990) 'The inner-city battlefield', in S. MacGregor and B. Pimlott (eds), *Tackling the Inner Cities*, Clarendon Press.

Newby, H. (1985) *Green and Pleasant Land? Social Change in Rural England*, Wildwood House.

Oppenheim, C. and Harker, L. (1996) *Poverty: The Facts*, 3rd edition, Child Poverty Action Group.

Pahl, R.E. (1970) *Patterns of Urban Life*, Longman.

Raynsford, N. (1990) 'Housing conditions, problems and policies', in S. MacGregor and B. Pimlott (eds), *Tackling the Inner Cities*, Clarendon Press.

Simmons, M. (1996) 'Social change: a terrible kind of beauty' *The Guardian*, 28 February.

Slattery, M. (1986) *Official Statistics*, Tavistock Publications.

Slattery, M. (1991) *Key Ideas in Sociology*, Macmillan Education.

Tonnies, F. (1957) *Community and Society*, Harper and Row.

Townsend, P. (1990) 'Living standards and health in the inner cities', in S. MacGregor and B. Pimlott (eds), *Tackling the Inner Cities*, Clarendon Press.

Urray, J. (1990) 'Urban sociology', in M. Haralambos (ed.), *Developments in Sociology*, Volume 6, Causeway Press.

Wirth, L (1938) 'Urbanism as a way of life', *American Journal of Sociology*, Volume 44, pp. 1–24.

Young, M. and Willmott, P. (1957) *Family and Kinship in East London*, Routledge and Kegan Paul.

Doing Coursework

The following guidance and advice for doing coursework are suggestions only and are not intended to be a definitive statement. You should always seek further advice from your tutor.

Most examination boards require you to complete a piece of coursework as part of your assessment. This is an opportunity for you to 'become a sociologist' and to carry out your own research into an area of social life. In this respect, doing coursework can be both interesting and motivating.

It will also allow you to deepen your understanding of a particular aspect of sociology as well as giving you the chance to put your knowledge of research methods into practice. This aspect of doing coursework will prove beneficial when you answer questions on these areas in the final written exam.

General points to note

While each syllabus has its own requirements, a number of general introductory points should be noted:

- the research project must relate to the syllabus;
- primary and secondary materials should be used;
- keeping to the suggested word length will help you to produce clear and concise work;
- present the project clearly; for example, have a front cover; a table of contents; numbered pages; a clear separation of each section; a bibliography;
- avoid a 'scrapbook' approach. Any photographs, articles, newspaper cuttings and so on must be clearly linked to your work.

THE RESEARCH PROCESS

Although each exam board has its own guidelines for the presentation and content of coursework, we can outline some general areas that are common to most research.

1 Introduction and aims (hypothesis)

- Provide your title and state which area of social life and/or social issue you are investigating.
- State your aims and hypothesis clearly and explicitly; number each aim so that you can refer back to it later in the project.
- State what you hope to discover/test/show/support/refute.
- Identify the area of the syllabus from which your study is taken.
- Explain why you chose this particular topic to study and why you think it is worthy of study.
- Link your topic choice to modern Britain (i.e. state the sociological significance of your topic).

2 Methodology

- Demonstrate that you can use appropriate sociological methods of research successfully.
- State which methods you used and why you selected them in relation to your aims.

3 Background sources

- Provide evidence to show that you have read round your topic. What have other sociologists discovered regarding this topic?
- Use a range of sources, for example questionnaires, books, newspapers, statistics, leaflets, etc. Ensure that you link each source clearly to your aims.

4 Findings

- Provide a clear, detailed and critical discussion of your findings. Your results should be made relevant to your aims by dealing with each of your aims in turn.
- Ensure your approach is clear and analytical. Use the following checklist:
  - state your aim;
  - state your findings; show the raw data;
  - explain your findings. What do they mean? What is the link between the finding and the aim? What are the possible implications of your findings?

  In this way, you can analyse your findings more fully.
- Comment on how accurate and relevant you think your findings are.

5 Evaluation and conclusions

- Make sure you reach relevant conclusions that refer to your aims, findings and methods.
- Summarize your findings and draw relevant conclusions for each aim.
- Reflect on the accuracy of your findings – be critical of yourself!
- Have you supported or rejected your aims and hypothesis? Explain why or why not.
- Evaluate and criticize your use of research methods. Would other methods have been better or more appropriate? Why did you reject other methods?
- Having completed your project, what advice would you give to other people who want to research this topic? What further research might you choose to do in this area?
- Finally, summarize the strengths and weaknesses of your project as a whole.

These guidelines should give you some idea of the types of skills you will need to demonstrate in order to produce a good piece of coursework in sociology. Clearly, the ability to be self-critical in terms of aims, methods, findings, and so on is an important skill to develop.

How to make a start on coursework

Choosing a topic

This can often be the most difficult and frustrating part of doing coursework. If you don't have any clear ideas, you should initially refer to the syllabus or the relevant section of this textbook in order to get a picture of all the possible topic areas you could choose from. Try to select some general areas of interest first, for example:

- Religion
- The Media
- Gender
- Education

Once you have identified some general topics, you will need to break these down into specific issues. It is often a good idea to do this with other people in order to generate a range of ideas.

GENERATING COURSEWORK IDEAS

In a small group, use the general areas identified on p. 368 to generate some specific topic areas.

You should do this by using a spider diagram and brainstorming your ideas. The following example is for education:

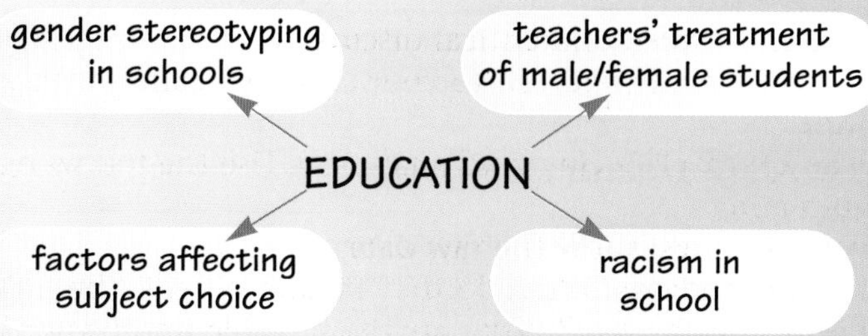

Background reading

Once you have selected a specific topic to research, you should then read around the topic in order to develop your understanding of it, and to help produce some aims for your research.

Producing aims and hypotheses

As a result of your background reading, you should be able to produce some clear aims/hypotheses to investigate. These are essentially precise statements about what you intend to do. The clearer they are, the better. They may, indeed, be based on the aims of previous research in your chosen area.

Carrying out the research

First, you will need to select suitable research methods for the aims you have chosen.

An example of aims for a topic area

General area: Education

Specific area: Gender and subject choice

Aims:

1 to examine trends in subject choice at A level nationally between male and female students;
2 to examine trends in subject choice for A level among male and female Year 11 students at Sunnyview High School;
3 to compare trends at Sunnyview High School with national trends;
4 to discover what factors might affect subject choice for A level among male and female Year 11 students at Sunnyview High School.

CHOOSING METHODS

In a small group, consider the aims outlined in the example for a project on education and subject choice. Note down your ideas for suitable research methods for each aim and be prepared to explain your choices.

Once you have selected your methods, plan the research. This could involve devising a questionnaire or an interview schedule, and selecting areas to cover in an informal interview, etc.

You will then need to carry out a pilot study and make any changes necessary as a result of this. A sample will need to be selected, and arrangements made to contact your respondents, conduct interviews, collect questionnaires, and so on.

Once the research is complete, you will need to analyse the results and write up your project as a whole.

In other words, it is important to be as well organized as possible when you begin your research to ensure you give yourself enough time to meet the deadline for handing it in. Your planning should also, therefore, take into consideration possible problems that you may encounter, such as difficulties in getting questionnaires back from respondents. In this way, careful time management is important here (see Chapter 1, pp. 3–4).

Proposal form
It is often a good idea to get your tutor to look at your initial ideas before proceeding any further with your project. This can be done using a proposal form, which should contain the information shown in the example on the right.

A proposal form

PROPOSAL

1 TITLE ...

2 INITIAL AIMS/HYPOTHESIS ...

3 PROPOSED RESEARCH METHODS ...

This could include your ideas about the sample you will be using.

4 LIST OF SOURCES OF BACKGROUND INFORMATION ...

5 POTENTIAL PROBLEMS YOU MIGHT ENCOUNTER ...

What are the likely problems you might face and how do you propose to deal with them? Is your research likely to be legal, moral and ethical?

6 ANY OTHER THOUGHTS ...

Note down any reservations you may have, or any problem areas at this stage that you wish to discuss with your tutor.

Some ideas for projects

While it is always good for you to select a topic that you want to research, sometimes it helps to have a range of ideas to get you thinking, or to modify to suit your own ideas. Indeed, many exam boards publish their own lists of titles.

The following list gives suggestions for each of the syllabus areas covered in this book.

Stratification and Differentiation

1 Social class and educational attainment.
2 A study on social mobility in a family.

Poverty and the Welfare State

1 A study based on a local health clinic and the use made of it by different social groups.
2 A survey of poverty in a local area, using statistics and interviews.

Families and Households

1 The domestic division of labour linked to ethnicity.
2 A survey of family structures in modern Britain.

Education

1 A study into factors affecting achievement of Bengali students.
2 An investigation into differences in time and attention given to male and female students in school.

Work, Unemployment and Leisure

1 An investigation into women's experiences of work in restaurants.
2 Family leisure patterns and social class.

Crime, Deviance and Social Control

1 A survey of social problems affecting the 16–19 age group.
2 Are women becoming more criminal and, if so, why?

Political Sociology

1 Is there a link between voting patterns and social class?
2 An investigation into a pressure group.

The Mass Media

1 An investigation into the media and political opinion.
2 How are women portrayed in TV advertising?

Religion

1 Are teenagers religious?
2 Does religion still provide social control?

Population and Demography

1 Population trends in Greater Manchester.
2 An investigation into the implications of an ageing population.

Revision Strategies

Before beginning your revision, it is important to do some preparation work.

1 Think about what topic areas you are going to revise.
This may seem fairly obvious, but it is important to be clear on what areas you need to look at. For example, on some courses you may have covered exactly the number of topic areas needed to answer the examination questions, in which case you would need to revise everything. In other cases, you may have covered more topics than you need to – this may lead you to ignore some topics in favour of others in your revision. However, it is better if you can revise as many topics as possible in order to give yourself a wide choice of questions. It is important to get your tutor's advice on this.

2 Identify the different areas and ideas to be covered in each topic.
You will need to identify the main themes or issues, terms, concepts, theories and research findings in each topic. You might consider this to be your 'tool kit' for the topic. By using this tool kit, you should be able to deal with any questions the examiners may ask you.

A REVISION 'TOOL KIT'

Select a topic area you would like to revise. Now identify the contents of the 'tool kit' for this topic using the following headings:

- main themes/issues;
- terms/concepts;
- theories (including any criticisms);
- research findings (including any criticisms).

You could produce this as a table on one side of A4 paper in order to make it as concise, and thus easy to revise from, as possible.

It is also a good idea to develop a **revision checklist** for each topic area. This will involve listing each area covered within a topic, checking whether or not you have all the notes and checking whether you understand them all. If you identify areas you are not sure of, then you need to see your tutor about this. Once you have revised an area, you should then tick it off your list. This will help you to keep track of where you are up to in your revision.

3 Ensure you understand the skills you will be assessed on
It is important that you recognize that the examination is not simply a test of knowledge. You should be familiar with the skills being assessed – for example, your critical and evaluative skills. If you do not feel confident with these, then you should check with your tutor.

4 Gather together the materials you will be using
You should have your notes in order for each topic and have a textbook handy as well.

If you can get hold of past examination papers or questions, these are useful as a check to see how your revision is progressing. You can also use the sample examination questions included in this book at the end of each chapter, as well as questions in the 'Check your Understanding' feature throughout the text.

Another useful source of help might be the examiners' reports published each year. These include the examiners' advice about how to tackle questions, as well as hints about the kinds of answers they are looking for. Check with your teacher about getting copies of these.

Finally, it is sometimes useful to revise with other people as this can help to solve problems you've encountered, as well as keeping you motivated!

Once you have done the preparation, you are ready to start revising.

Revising by doing

It is important to be active in your revision – do something with your notes, handouts, textbook, etc. Take control of them and turn them into something you can usefully revise from. Thus, while everyone has his or her own style of revision, active revision invariably seems the most effective method.

Learning notes

It is a good idea to try to reduce your notes to a more manageable length. 'Making notes on your notes' is a phrase that is often used. Refer to the section on note-taking technique in Chapter 1 (p. 4) for guidance on this.

Next, try to memorize the notes; turn them into a 'tool kit', if appropriate, and tick them off your revision checklist.

Practising skills

You should also try to make time in your revision to practise your sociological skills. For example, you might identify a piece of research from your notes or textbook and try to identify its strengths and weaknesses. Or you might take a major issue and list arguments for and against it.

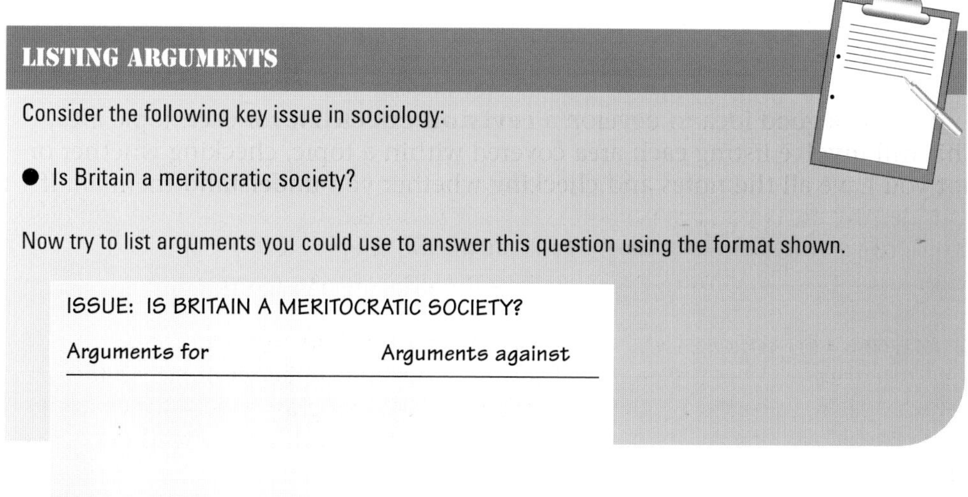

LISTING ARGUMENTS

Consider the following key issue in sociology:

- Is Britain a meritocratic society?

Now try to list arguments you could use to answer this question using the format shown.

ISSUE: IS BRITAIN A MERITOCRATIC SOCIETY?

Arguments for	Arguments against

Another useful way of developing your skills is to flick through a textbook or statistical source, such as *Social Trends*, and try to interpret any tables, graphs or charts you come across.

Practising exams

Before an examination, you may get nervous, particularly if you are unsure of what to expect. It is important, therefore, to try to get as much practice as possible at answering examination questions. This book contains a range of past examination questions for you to practise and it is a good idea to try these under timed conditions.

Revision timetables

Clearly, the revision process is not one you can embark on just before the exam. It is important, therefore, to develop a timetable for your revision.

You could initially use a calendar or wall planner to see how many weeks you have left before the exam begins. You can then make an assessment of how long you could spend on each topic you have to revise.

A format similar to the time management plan described in Chapter 1 (pp. 3–4) could then be used to plan your weekly revision targets.

Examination techniques

It is important to get as much practice with examination questions as possible. However, it is also important to identify good examination practice. What follows is a range of tips based on good practice which should improve your examination technique.

1 *The examination instructions*

Read the instructions on the paper carefully – this will help you to avoid answering too few, or, indeed, too many questions from the paper.

2 *Read the questions carefully*

Taking time to read a question carefully can prevent you from misinterpreting it and so losing marks.

3 *Look for key words*

Questions will include cue words that act as a prompt or instruction to tell you what to do. You might find it helpful to underline these. Some examples are:

- explain ...
- state ...
- define ...
- according to Item ...
- what advantages ...
- explain the extent to which ...
- describe ...
- name ...
- identify ...
- what is meant by ...
- to what extent do you agree that ...

Such words refer to the sociological skills you are being assessed on, for example:

- 'To what extent do you agree that ...' is asking you to assess or evaluate an idea in terms of its strengths and weaknesses.
- 'According to Item ...' is prompting you to examine an item of information and then to interpret what it is saying.
- Words such as 'state' or 'define' are asking you to show some knowledge of the subject matter.

4 *Question instructions*

Follow these carefully – if a question asks for two reasons then you must give two reasons.

5 *Time frame*

If the question refers to a particular time period, for example 'in the last 50 years' or 'in the 1990s', then your answer must include details within this time frame.

6 *Terminology*

Make sure you understand what is meant by terms such as 'trend', 'rate', 'causes', 'consequences', 'effects', etc.

7 *Stimulus material*

(a) As mentioned in Chapter 1 (p. 5), be careful to check what units any statistics are presented in – for example, they may be percentages, in thousands, etc.

(b) Refer to the items when you are instructed to do so, but do not simply copy out large chunks of stimulus material.

(c) Where one mark is on offer by picking out information from an Item, a brief but accurate response is sufficient.

8 Allocation of time

Be careful to give yourself enough time to answer all of the questions adequately. Do not spend too much time on questions only worth one mark. Try to allocate your time in relation to the worth of the question (look at the mark allocation).

9 Re-read your answer

It is easy to make a simple mistake that could be picked up by simply reading through your answer in the last few minutes of an examination.

Index

Note: Page numbers in bold indicate key term definitions in the text.